W9-AAG-898

An Introduction to Management Science
Quantitative Approaches to Decision Making
ELEVENTH EDITION

David R. Anderson

University of Cincinnati

Dennis J. Sweeney

University of Cincinnati

Thomas A. Williams

Rochester Institute of Technology

Prepared by

John S. Loucks

St. Edward's University

THOMSON

SOUTH-WESTERN

Australia · Canada · Mexico · Singapore · Spain · United Kingdom · United States

THOMSON

SOUTH-WESTERN

Study Guide for An Introduction to Management Science:

Quantitative Methods to Decision Making, 11e

David R. Anderson, Dennis J. Sweeney, Thomas A. Williams

Publisher: George Werthman	**Sr. Marketing Manager:** Larry Qualls	**Technology Project Editor:** Chris Wittmer
Sr. Acquisitions Editor: Charles E. McCormick, Jr.	**Sr. Production Editor:** Deanna Quinn	**Sr. Media Editor:** Amy Wilson
Sr. Developmental Editor: Alice C. Denny	**Manufacturing Coordinator:** Diane Lohman	**Printer:** Globus Printing

Contents

Preface

The Study Guide to Accompany An Introduction to Management Science, 11th ed. has been written with several goals in mind. Its objectives are:

1. To provide an outline of the material in the parent text via an opening key concepts section from which the student may design a course of study of the individual techniques and concepts of each chapter.

2. To organize and summarize the material in the parent text in a structured review section.

3. To illustrate the basic concepts of the parent text in detail through the presentation of 115 illustrated problems.

4. To reinforce the basic concepts by providing 175 additional problems and 270 true/false questions whose answers are in the back of the book.

5. To challenge the student by giving several problems requiring more than simple, straightforward application of the techniques of the chapter.

6. To expand the coverage of certain areas beyond the parent text by offering additional insights and algorithms to assist in the solution strategy.

7. To illustrate business applications areas in which management science may be applied.

To accomplish these goals, each chapter has been divided into five basic parts:

1. Key Concepts:
   This section notes the main topic areas of each chapter and denotes which problems illustrate the concept, and which answered problems require the use of the concept in its solution.

   Every major concept of the text is illustrated in at least one problem worked out in detail and, with few exceptions, in at least one answered problem with its answer provided in the back of the book.

2. Review:
   This section summarizes point by point the theoretical foundations, the definitions, and the approaches of every topic area of the chapter. This provides an excellent check-list for understanding the essential points of the chapters.

   A categorical list of important formulas is included in this section where applicable. Major algorithms are described in sentence form and with flow charts at the end of this section where applicable.

3. Illustrated Problems:
   These are problems worked out in full, giving the cumbersome step-by-step details as the problem is worked through to completion. Where applicable, a spreadsheet approach to solving a problem is demonstrated.

4. Answered Problems:
   These problems are for the student to do on his/her own with the answers provided in the back of the book. This enables the student to test him/herself on the individual concepts with brief answers to validate his results.

5. True/False:
   Each chapter contains fifteen true/false questions designed to reinforce the theoretical concepts of the chapter. The answers are provided in the back of the book.

We hope you find this study guide instructive and a useful supplement in your study of management science.

John S. Loucks
St. Edward's University
3001 S. Congress Ave.
Austin, TX 78704
johnsl@admin.stedwards.edu

CHAPTER 1

Introduction

KEY CONCEPTS

CONCEPT	ILLUSTRATED PROBLEMS	ANSWERED PROBLEMS
Management Science Approach	1,2	6,7
Mathematical Models Development	3,4	8,9,10,11,12
Cost, Volume, Profit Analysis	5	13
Marginal Analysis	5	13
Breakeven Analysis	5	13

REVIEW

1. <u>Management science</u> is a <u>quantitative approach to decision making</u> based on the <u>scientific method</u> of problem solving. Synonymous terms are <u>operations research</u> and <u>decision science</u>. It had its early roots in World War II and is flourishing in business and industry with the aid of computers in general and the microcomputer in particular.

2. <u>Problem solving</u> is a process designed to better a current state of affairs, It consists of two phases: (1) decision making; and (2) implementation and evaluation.

3. The <u>decision making process</u> involves: (1) structuring the problem; and (2) analyzing the problem.

4. <u>Structuring the problem</u> includes: (1) defining the problem; (2) identifying the alternatives; and (3) choosing the criteria (single or multiple) to be used to evaluate the alternatives.

5. <u>Analyzing the problem</u> consists of: (1) qualitatively and quantitatively evaluating the alternatives; and (2) making a decision recommendation (choosing an alternative).

6. Evaluating alternatives is often accomplished by experimenting with a <u>model</u>. A model is a representation of a real object or situation. Generally, experimenting with a model is <u>less costly</u>, requires <u>less time</u>, and involves <u>less risk</u>.

7. Three forms of models are iconic, analog, and mathematical. <u>Iconic models</u> are physical replicas (scalar representations) of real objects. <u>Analog models</u> are physical in form, but do not physically resemble the object being modeled.

8. <u>Mathematical models</u> (also called symbolic models), represent real world problems through a system of mathematical formulas and expressions. They are idealizations of real-life problems based on key assumptions, estimates, "guesstimates", and/or statistical analyses.

9. After the problem has been structured, the steps in the <u>quantitative analysis</u> are: (1) mathematical modeling; (2) data preparation; (3) model solution (and refinement); and (4) report generation.

10. Mathematical models relate <u>decision variables</u> (or <u>controllable inputs</u>) with fixed or variable parameters (or <u>uncontrollable inputs</u>). Frequently mathematical models seek to maximize or minimize some <u>objective function</u> subject to <u>constraints</u>.

11. If any of the uncontrollable inputs is subject to variation the model is said to be <u>stochastic</u>. Otherwise the model is said to be <u>deterministic</u>. Generally, stochastic models are more realistic than deterministic models, but they are more difficult to analyze.

12. The values of the decision variables that provide the mathematically-best output are referred to as the <u>optimal solution</u> for the model.

13. If a particular decision alternative does not satisfy one or more of the model constraints, the decision alternative is rejected as being <u>infeasible</u>. If all constraints are satisfied, the decision alternative is <u>feasible</u> and a candidate for the "best" solution or recommended decision.

14. <u>Cost/benefit considerations</u> must be made in selecting an appropriate mathematical model. Frequently a less complicated (and perhaps less precise) model is more appropriate than a more complex and accurate one due to cost and ease of solution considerations.

15. Quantitative analysis should be used as <u>one of many input factors</u> for managerial decision making. It is not a replacement for human decision making.

16. Primary reasons for the use of quantitative analysis are: (1) the <u>problem is complex</u>; (2) the <u>problem is important</u> and/or the decision must be thoroughly justified; (3) the <u>problem is new</u> and there is little or no previous experience to rely on; (4) the <u>problem is repetitive and time-consuming</u> (with varying uncontrollable input values); and (5) <u>what-if questions</u> need to be answered in an efficient manner.

17. <u>Break-even analysis</u> uses a basic mathematical model of the relationship between a volume variable and cost, revenue, or profit. The <u>break-even point</u> is the volume that results in total revenue equaling total cost.

18. <u>Fixed cost</u> is the portion of the total cost that does not depend on the volume variable; this cost remains regardless of the value of the volume variable. <u>Variable cost</u> is the portion of the total cost that is dependent on and varies with the volume variable.

19. <u>Marginal cost</u> is the rate of change of the total cost with respect to the volume variable. <u>Marginal revenue</u> is the rate of change of the total reveune with respect to the volume variable.

20. Linear programming, integer programming, network models, and simulation are among the <u>most frequently used quantitative techniques</u> in business.

ILLUSTRATED PROBLEMS

PROBLEM 1

Consider a construction company building a 250-unit apartment complex. The project consists of hundreds of activities involving excavating, framing, wiring, plastering, painting, landscaping, and more. Some of the activities must be done sequentially and others can be done simultaneously. Also, some of the activities can be completed faster than normal by purchasing additional resources (workers, equipment, etc.).

a) How could a quantitative approach to decision making be used to solve this problem?

b) What would be the uncontrollable inputs?

c) What would be the decision variables of the mathematical model? the objective function? the constraints?

d) Is the model deterministic or stochastic?

e) Suggest assumptions that could be made to simplify the model.

SOLUTION 1

a) A quantitative approach to decision making can provide a structured way to determine the minimum project completion time based on the activities' normal times and then based on the activities' expedited (reduced) times.

b) Normal and expedited activity completion times; activity expediting costs; funds available for expediting; precedence relationships of the activities.

c) Decision variables--which activities to expedite and by how much, and when to start each activity; objective function--minimize project completion time; constraints--do not violate any activity precedence relationships and do not expedite in excess of the funds available.

d) Stochastic--activity completion times, both normal and expedited, are uncertain and subject to variation; activity expediting costs are uncertain; the number of activities and their precedence relationships might change before the project is completed due to a project design change.

e) Make the model deterministic by assuming normal and expedited activity times are known with certainty and are constant. The same assumption might be made about the other stochastic, uncontrollable inputs.

PROBLEM 2

Consider a department store that must make weekly shipments of a certain product from two different warehouses to four different stores.

a) How could a quantitative approach to decision making be used to solve this problem?

b) What would be the uncontrollable inputs for which data must be gathered?

c) What would be the decision variables of the mathematical model? the objective function? the constraints?

d) Is the model deterministic or stochastic?

e) Suggest assumptions that could be made to simplify the model.

SOLUTION 2

a) A quantitative approach to decision making can provide a systematic way to determine a minimum shipping cost from the warehouses to the stores.

b) Fixed costs and variable shipping costs; the demand each week at each store; the supplies each week at each warehouse.

c) Decision variables--how much to ship from each warehouse to each store; objective function--minimize total shipping costs; constraints--meet the demand at the stores without exceeding the supplies at the warehouses.

d) Stochastic--weekly demands fluctuate as do weekly supplies; transportation costs could vary depending upon the amount shipped, other goods sent with a shipment, etc.

e) Make the model deterministic by assuming fixed shipping costs per item, demand is constant at each store each week, and weekly supplies in the warehouses are constant.

PROBLEM 3

An auctioneer has developed a simple mathematical model for deciding the starting bid he will require when auctioning a used automobile. Essentially, he sets the starting bid at seventy percent of what he predicts the final winning bid will (or should) be. He predicts the winning bid by starting with the car's original selling price and making two deductions, one based on the car's age and the other based on the car's mileage. The age deduction is $800 per year and the mileage deduction is $.025 per mile.

a) Develop the mathematical model that will give the starting bid (B) for a car in terms of the car's original price (P), current age (A) and mileage (M).

b) Suppose a four-year old car with 60,000 miles on the odometer is up for auction. If its original price was $12,500, what starting bid should the auctioneer require?

c) The model is based on what assumptions?

SOLUTION 3

a) The expected winning bid can be expressed as:
$$P - 800(A) - .025(M)$$

The entire model is:
$$B = .7(\text{expected winning bid}) \text{ or}$$
$$B = .7(P - 800(A) - .025(M)) \text{ or}$$
$$B = .7(P) - 560(A) - .0175(M)$$

b) $B = .7(12,500) - 560(4) - .0175(60,000) = \$5460.$

c) The model assumes that the only factors influencing the value of a used car are the original price, age, and mileage (not condition, rarity, or other factors). Also, it is assumed that age and mileage devalue a car in a linear manner and without limit. (Note, the starting bid for a very old car might be negative.)

PROBLEM 4

A firm manufactures two products made from steel and has just received this month's allocation of b pounds of steel. It takes a_1 pounds of steel to make a unit of product 1 and it takes a_2 pounds of steel to make a unit of product 2. Let x_1 and x_2 denote this month's production level of product 1 and product 2 respectively.

Denote by p_1 and p_2 the unit profits for products 1 and 2, respectively. The manufacturer has a contract calling for at least m units of product 1 this month. The firm's facilities are such that at most u units of product 2 may be produced monthly.

a) Write a mathematical model for this problem.

b) Suppose $b = 2000$, $a_1 = 2$, $a_2 = 3$, $m = 60$, $u = 720$, $p_1 = 100$, $p_2 = 200$. Rewrite the model with these specific values for the uncontrollable inputs.

c) The optimal solution to (b) is $x_1 = 60$ and $x_2 = 626\ 2/3$. If the product were engines, explain why this is not a true optimal solution for the "real-life" problem.

SOLUTION 4

a) The total monthly profit
$$= \text{(profit per unit of product 1)} \times \text{(monthly production of product 1)}$$
$$+ \text{(profit per unit of product 2)} \times \text{(monthly production of product 2)}$$
$$= p_1x_1 + p_2x_2.$$

The total amount of steel used during monthly production
$$= \text{(steel per unit of product 1)} \times \text{(monthly production of product 1)}$$
$$+ \text{(steel per unit of product 2)} \times \text{(monthly production of product 2)}$$
$$= a_1x_1 + a_2x_2.$$

This quantity must be less than or equal to the allocated b pounds of steel:
$$a_1x_1 + a_2x_2 \le b.$$

The monthly production level of product 1 must be greater than or equal to m:
$$x_1 \ge m.$$

The monthly production level of product 2 must be less than or equal to u:
$$x_2 \le u.$$

The production level for product 2 cannot be negative:
$$x_2 \ge 0.$$

Thus, the model is:

$$\text{MAXIMIZE } p_1x_1 + p_2x_2$$

$$\text{s.t.} \qquad a_1x_1 + a_2x_2 \le b$$

$$x_1 \qquad \ge m$$

$$x_2 \le u$$

$$x_2 \ge 0$$

b) Substituting, the model is:

$$\text{MAXIMIZE } 100x_1 + 200x_2$$

$$\text{s.t.} \qquad 2x_1 + \quad 3x_2 \le 2000$$

$$x_1 \qquad \ge \quad 60$$

$$x_2 \le \quad 720$$

$$x_2 \ge \quad 0$$

c) One cannot produce and sell 2/3 of an engine. Thus the problem is further restricted by the fact that both x_1 and x_2 must be integers. They could remain fractions if it is assumed these fractions are work in progress to be completed the next month.

PROBLEM 5

Ponderosa Development Corporation (PDC) is a small real estate developer operating in the Rivertree Valley. It has seven permanent employees whose monthly salaries are given in the table below:

Employee	Monthly Salary
President	$10,000
VP, Development	6,000
VP, Marketing	4,500
Project Manager	5,500
Controller	4,000
Office Manager	3,000
Receptionist	2,000

PDC leases a building for $2,000 per month. The cost of supplies, utilities, and leased equipment runs another $3,000 per month. PDC builds only one style house in the valley. Land for each house costs $55,000 and lumber, supplies, etc. run another $28,000 per house. Total labor costs are figured at $20,000 per house. The one sales representative of PDC is paid a commission of $2,000 on the sale of each house. The selling price of the house is $115,000.

a) Identify all costs and denote the marginal cost and marginal revenue for each house.

b) Write the monthly cost function $c(x)$, revenue function $r(x)$, and profit function $p(x)$.

c) What is the monthly profit if 12 houses per month are built and sold? Solve algebraically and using a spreadsheet.

d) What is the breakeven point for monthly sales of the houses? Solve algebraically and using a spreadsheet.

SOLUTION 5

a) The monthly salaries total $35,000 and monthly office lease and supply costs total another $5,000. This $40,000 is a monthly fixed cost. The total cost of land, material, labor, and sales commission per house, $105,000, is the marginal cost for a house. The selling price of $115,000 is the marginal revenue per house.

b) $c(x)$ = variable cost + fixed cost = $105,000x + 40,000$
   $r(x) = 115,000x$
   $p(x) = r(x) - c(x) = 10,000x - 40,000$

c) $p(12) = 10,000(12) - 40,000 = $80,000$ monthly profit.

Spreadsheet with formulas

	A	B
1	PROBLEM DATA	
2	Fixed Cost	$40,000
3	Variable Cost Per Unit	$105,000
4	Selling Price Per Unit	$115,000
5	MODEL	
6	Sales Volume	
7	Total Revenue	=B4*B6
8	Total Cost	=B2+B3*B6
9	Total Profit (Loss)	=B7-B8

Spreadsheet with solution

	A	B
1	PROBLEM DATA	
2	Fixed Cost	$40,000
3	Variable Cost Per Unit	$105,000
4	Selling Price Per Unit	$115,000
5	MODEL	
6	Sales Volume	12
7	Total Revenue	$1,380,000
8	Total Cost	$1,300,000
9	Total Profit (Loss)	$80,000

d) $r(x) = c(x)$ or $115,000x = 105,000x + 40,000$. Solving, $x = 4$.

<u>Determining the break-even point using Excel's Goal Seek tool</u>
Step 1: Select the **Tools** pull-down menu
Step 2: Choose the **Goal Seek** option
Step 3: When the **Goal Seek** dialog box appears:
          Enter B9 in the **Set cell** box
          Enter 0 in the **To value** box
          Enter B6 in the **By changing cell** box
          Click **OK**

	A	B
1	PROBLEM DATA	
2	Fixed Cost	$40,000
3	Variable Cost Per Unit	$105,000
4	Selling Price Per Unit	$115,000
5	MODEL	
6	Sales Volume	4
7	Total Revenue	$460,000
8	Total Cost	$460,000
9	Total Profit (Loss)	$0

ANSWERED PROBLEMS

PROBLEM 6

Zipco Printing operates a shop that has five printing machines. The machines differ in their capacities to perform various printing operations due to differences in the machines' designs and operator skill levels. At the start of the workday there are five printing jobs to schedule. The manager must decide what the job-machine assignments should be.

a) How could a quantitative approach to decision making be used to solve this problem?

b) What would be the uncontrollable inputs for which data must be collected?

c) Define the decision variables, objective function, and constraints to appear in the mathematical model.

d) Is the model deterministic or stochastic?

e) Suggest some simplifying assumptions for this problem.

PROBLEM 7

Zizzle Company is a new small local company that is about to manufacture Zizzle briefcases in three styles. The company wants to determine how to use its resources most efficiently to get the product mix that will maximize its profits.

One manager has advocated hiring an outside consulting firm to analyze sales potentials and customer preferences. He suggests doing a complete time and motion study of the production process and analyzing the potential for acquiring additional manpower and material resources. In short, he is advocating an extremely accurate but complex study.

A second manager suggests a simplified model using "best guess", rough approximations and simplifying assumptions as a starting point. The data for this model can be obtained in a short period of time, and the model can be solved in-house at a fraction of the cost of the more complex model.

a) Which manager's advice would you follow? Explain.

b) Would your answer change if Zizzle Company were a large national conglomerate which plans to market tens of thousands of briefcases?

PROBLEM 8

A client of an investment firm has $10,000 available for investment. He has instructed that his money be invested in three stocks so that no more than $5,000 is invested in any one stock but at least $1,000 is invested in each stock. He has further instructed the firm to use its current data and invest in a manner that maximizes his expected overall gain during a one-year period. The stocks, the current price per share, and the firm's projected stock price a year from now are summarized in the following table.

Stock	Current Price	Projected Price 1 Year Hence
James Industries	$25	$35
QM Inc.	$50	$60
Delicious Candy Co.	$100	$125

a) Let s_j = the number of shares of stock j purchased for j = 1 (James), 2 (QM), 3 (Delicious). Formulate a mathematical model for this problem using these decision variables.

b) Let x_j = the number of dollars invested in stock j. Reformulate this mathematical model in terms of these decision variables instead of those used in part (a).

c) If both models were solved using a quantitative approach to decision making, how would you expect the results of the models to compare?

PROBLEM 9

Bank Guard Company provides security service for banks and savings and loan companies during business hours. The number of guards supplied is a function of the average number of people in the facility. One guard is provided for an average of 25 customers.

Let L = the average number of customers in the facility, C_g = the hourly cost per guard, N = the number of guards required, and C = the daily cost for guard service (based on an 8-hour day).

a) Develop a mathematical model for N in terms of L. Then develop a mathematical model for C in terms of N and C_g. Finally, express C in terms of L and C_g.

b) If night guard service costs a flat $$C_n$, develop a mathematical model for 24 hour guard service. Discuss the results with C_g = $10 per hour, C_n = $100 per night and L = 50. Discuss the results with L = 65.

PROBLEM 10

Comfort Plus Inc. (CPI) manufactures a standard dining chair used in restaurants. The demand forecasts for quarter 1 (January-March) and quarter 2 (April-June) are 3700 chairs and 4200 chairs, respectively. CPI has a policy of satisfying all demand in the quarter in which it occurs.

The chair contains an upholstered seat that can be produced by CPI or a subcontractor. The subcontractor currently charges $12.50 per seat, but has announced a new price of $13.75 effective April 1. CPI can produce the seat at a cost of $10.25.

Seats that are produced or purchased in quarter 1 and used to satisfy demand in quarter 2 cost CPI $1.50 each to hold in inventory.

a) What are the controllable inputs?

b) Develop a mathematical model for the total cost (objective) function.

PROBLEM 11

Continuing with problem 10, consider the following additional information. CPI's seat-producing capacity is 3800 seats per quarter. CPI cannot hold more than 300 seats in inventory from quarter to quarter.

a) Complete the mathematical model started in problem 10 by modeling the constraints.

b) Is the model stochastic or deterministic?

c) How would adding a third quarter to the problem change the model?

PROBLEM 12

A retail furniture store has set aside 800 square feet to display its new 18th Century Collection of sofas and chairs. Considering aisle space, it is estimated that each sofa utilizes 50 sq. ft. and each chair utilizes 30 sq. ft. At least five sofas and at least five chairs are to be displayed.

a) Write a mathematical model representing the store's constraints.

b) Suppose the profit on sofas is $200 and on chairs is $100. On a given day, the probability that a displayed sofa will be sold is .03 and that a displayed chair will be sold is .05. Mathematically model each of the following objectives:

1) Maximize the total pieces of furniture displayed.
2) Maximize the total expected number of daily sales.
3) Maximize the total expected daily profit.

PROBLEM 13

Universal Computer is considering producing the new UC15 computer. Its components cost $630 and it will take 1/2 hour to assemble and 1/4 hour to pack. Skilled workers assemble the computer and make $16 per hour. Unskilled laborers pack the computers and make $4 per hour. Packaging material cost $11 per computer.

The computer will be produced in a plant located on Harbor Blvd. and leased for $3,100 per month. Utilities, supplies, insurance, etc. are expected to run another $1,900 per month regardless of the quantity of computers produced. Based on current market conditions, Universal assumes it can sell at $700 each all units it produces.

a) Identify the variable and fixed costs for Universal. Let x = the monthly production quantity of UC15s. Express the monthly cost function in terms of x.

b) Express the revenue function in terms of x.

c) What is the breakeven point?

d) What is the marginal cost of a computer?

e) What will be the monthly profit with a production schedule for UC15 computers of 500 per month?

TRUE/FALSE

___ 14. The optimal solution to a mathematical model is always the policy that should be implemented by the company.

___ 15. A problem to decide monthly shipping patterns is dependent on the amount of product available at the factory. This amount can be modeled by a normal distribution. Thus, this is a stochastic mathematical model.

___ 16. Microcomputers have made most quantitative approaches to decision making more accessible to even moderate size firms.

___ 17. The three most commonly used quantitative approaches to decision making are statistical analyses, simulation, and linear programming.

___ 18. A company seeks to maximize profit subject to limited availability of man-hours. Man-hours is a controllable input.

___ 19. Past data might be used to test the validity of a mathematical model.

___ 20. A toy train layout designed to represent an actual railyard is an example of an analog model.

___ 21. A feasible solution is one that satisfies at least one of the constraints in the problem.

___ 22. The terms stochastic and deterministic have the same meaning in quantitative approaches to decision making.

___ 23. If you are deciding to buy either machine A, B, or C with the objective of minimizing the sum of labor, material and utility costs, you are dealing with a multicriteria decision.

___ 24. If your decision alternatives for dealing with increased product inventory are: (1) build another warehouse, (2) reduce the production rate, and (3) increase the sales rate, you are dealing with a multicriteria decision.

___ 25. Model development should be left to quantitative analysts; the model user's involvement should begin at the implementation stage.

___ 26. The volume that results in marginal revenue equaling marginal cost is called the break-even point.

___ 27. In quantitative analysis, the optimal solution is the mathematically-best solution.

___ 28. Problem solving is narrower in scope than decision making.

CHAPTER 2

Introduction to
Linear Programming

KEY CONCEPTS

CONCEPT	ILLUSTRATED PROBLEMS	ANSWERED PROBLEMS
Formulation	7,8	15,16
Minimization	2,5	9,10,15
Standard Form	1	14
Slack/Surplus Variables	1	16
Equal-to Constraints	3,5	14
Redundant Constraints	5,7	12,13
Extreme Points	2,5	11,16
Alternative Optimal Solutions	7	10,11,15
Infeasibility	4	14
Unbounded	4	11
Spreadsheet Example	2	

REVIEW

1. A <u>mathematical programming</u> problem is one that seeks to maximize an objective function subject to constraints. If both the objective function and the constraints are linear, the problem is referred to as a <u>linear programming</u> problem.

2. <u>Linear functions</u> are functions in which each variable appears in a separate term raised to the first power and is multiplied by a constant (which could be 0).

3. <u>Linear constraints</u> are linear functions that are restricted to be "less than or equal to", "equal to", or "greater than or equal to" a constant.

4. The <u>maximization</u> or <u>minimization</u> of some quantity is the objective in all linear programming problems.

5. A <u>feasible solution</u> satisfies all the problem's constraints.

6. A linear program which is overconstrained so that no point satisfies all the constraints is said to be <u>infeasible</u>. Changes to the objective function coefficients do not affect the feasibility of the problem.

7. An <u>optimal solution</u> is a feasible solution that results in the largest possible objective function value, z, when maximizing or smallest possible z when minimizing.

8. A <u>graphical solution method</u> can be used to solve a linear program with two variables.

9. If a linear program possesses an optimal solution, then an <u>extreme point</u> will be optimal.

10. If a constraint can be removed without affecting the shape of the feasible region, the constraint is said to be <u>redundant</u>. If changes are anticipated to the linear programming model, constraints which were redundant in the original formulation may not be redundant in the revised formulation.

11. In the graphical method, if the objective function line is parallel to a boundary constraint in the direction of optimization, there are <u>alternative optimal solutions</u>, with all points on this line segment being optimal.

12. A feasible region may be <u>unbounded</u> and yet there may be optimal solutions. This is common in minimization problems and is possible in maximization problems.

13. The <u>feasible region</u> for a two-variable linear programming problem can be: a) nonexistent, b) a single point, c) a line, d) a polygon, or e) an unbounded area.

14. <u>Any linear program</u> either (a) is infeasible, (b) has a unique optimal solution or alternate optimal solutions, or (c) has an objective function that can be increased without bound.

15. A linear program in which all the variables are non-negative and all the constraints are equalities is said to be in <u>standard form</u>. Standard form is attained by adding <u>slack variables</u> to "less than or equal to" constraints, and by subtracting <u>surplus variables</u> from "greater than or equal to" constraints. They represent the difference between the left and right sides of the constraints.

16. A <u>nonbinding constraint</u> is one in which there is <u>positive slack or surplus</u> when evaluated at the optimal solution.

17. <u>Slack and surplus variables</u> have objective function coefficients equal to 0. If, however, extra resources could be sold at a profit, or if there were a penalty for surplus resources, the objective function coefficients would not be 0 and these variables would, in effect, become new decision variables.

GRAPHICAL SOLUTION PROCEDURE

1. Graph the constraints and shade in the feasible region, considering the feasible side of each constraint line.

2. Set the objective function equal to any arbitrary constant and graph it. If the line does not lie in the feasible region, move it (maintaining its slope) into the feasible region.

3. Move the objective function line parallel to itself in the direction that increases its value when maximizing (decreases its value when minimizing) until it touches the last point(s) of the feasible region.

4. If the optimal extreme point falls on an axis (say, x_2 axis), use the binding constraint equation to solve for the unknown x^* (in this case x_2^*, since x_1^* is zero). Otherwise, solve the two equations (binding constraints) in two unknowns (x_1^* and x_2^*) that determine the optimal extreme point.

5. Find z by substituting x_1^* and x_2^* in the objective function.

FLOW CHART OF
GRAPHICAL L.P. SOLUTION PROCEDURE

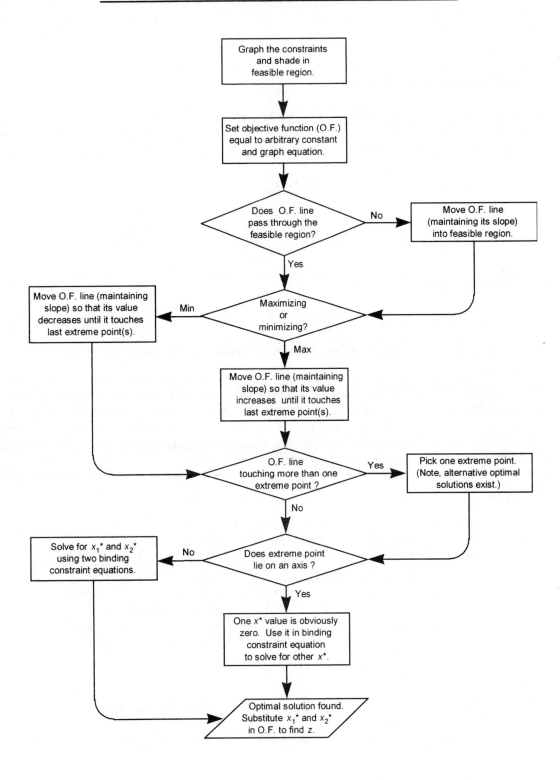

ILLUSTRATED PROBLEMS

PROBLEM 1

Given the following linear program:

$$\text{MAX} \quad 3x_1 + 4x_2$$

$$\text{s.t.} \quad 2x_1 + 3x_2 \leq 24$$

$$3x_1 + x_2 \leq 21$$

$$x_1 + x_2 \leq 9$$

$$x_1, x_2 \geq 0$$

a) Solve the problem graphically.

b) Write the problem in standard form.

c) Given your answer to (a), what are the optimal values of the slack variables.

NOTE: Plotting an initial objective function line involves little more than reversing the objective coefficients for x_1 and x_2. Consider Problem 1 below. The objective line will cross the x_1 axis at 4 (x_2's coefficient) and the x_2 axis at 3 (x_1's coefficient). If the coefficients are too large (or small) for convenient graphing, scale them down (or up) in a consistent manner by dividing (or multiplying) both by, say, 10.

SOLUTION 1

a) (1) <u>Graph the constraints</u>. (See graph on next page.)
Constraint 1: When $x_1 = 0$, then $x_2 = 8$; when $x_2 = 0$, then $x_1 = 12$.
Connect (12,0) and (0,8). The "<" side is below the line.
Constraint 2: When $x_1 = 0$, then $x_2 = 21$; when $x_2 = 0$, then $x_1 = 7$.
Connect (7,0) and (0,21). The "<" side is below the line.
Constraint 3: When $x_1 = 0$, then $x_2 = 9$; when $x_2 = 0$, then $x_1 = 9$.
Connect (9,0) and (0,9). The "<" side is below the line.

<u>Shade in the feasible region</u>.

(2) <u>Graph the objective function</u> by setting the objective function equal to any arbitrary value (say 12) and graphing it. For $3x_1 + 4x_2 = 12$, when $x_2 = 0$, $x_1 = 4$; when $x_1 = 0$, $x_2 = 3$. Connect (4,0) and (0,3), the thick graphed line.

(3) <u>Move the objective function line parallel to itself</u> in the direction that increases its value (upward) until it touches the last point of the feasible region. It is at the intersection of the first and third constraint lines.

(4) <u>Solve these two equations in two unknowns</u>:

$$2x_1 + 3x_2 = 24 \longrightarrow 2x_1 + 3x_2 = 24$$
$$x_1 + x_2 = 9 \longrightarrow 2x_1 + 2x_2 = 18$$
$$x_2 = 6$$

Substituting into $x_1 + x_2 = 9$, then $x_1 = 3$.

(5) <u>Solve for z</u>: $z = 3x_1 + 4x_2 = 3(3) + 4(6) = 33$. Thus the optimal solution is $x_1 = 3$, $x_2 = 6$, $z = 33$.

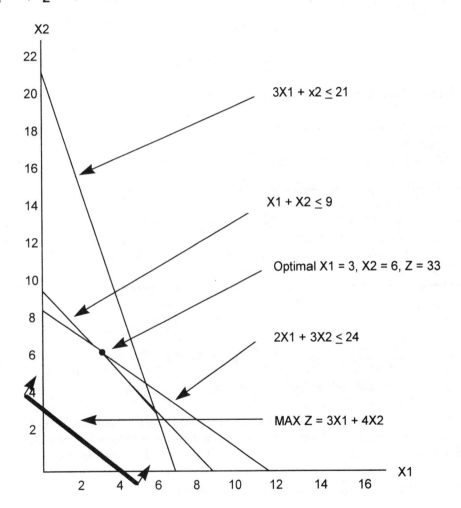

b) To write the problem in standard form, since each constraint is a "$\leq$" constraint, add a slack variable to each constraint.

$$\text{MAX} \quad 3x_1 + 4x_2 + 0s_1 + 0s_2 + 0s_3$$

$$\text{s.t.} \quad 2x_1 + 3x_2 + s_1 \qquad\qquad = 24$$

$$3x_1 + x_2 \qquad + s_2 \qquad = 21$$

$$x_1 + x_2 \qquad\qquad + s_3 = 9$$

$$x_1, x_2, s_1, s_2 \geq 0$$

c) Since the optimal solution was $x_1 = 3$, $x_2 = 6$, then substituting these values into the above equations gives:

$$s_1 = 24 - 2(3) - 3(6) = 0$$

$$s_2 = 21 - 3(3) - 1(6) = 6$$

$$s_3 = \ 9 - 1(3) - 1(6) = 0$$

PROBLEM 2

Given the following linear program:

$$\text{MIN} \quad 5x_1 + 2x_2$$

$$\text{s.t.} \quad 2x_1 + 5x_2 \geq 10$$

$$4x_1 - x_2 \geq 12$$

$$x_1 + x_2 \geq 4$$

$$x_1, x_2 \geq 0$$

a) Solve graphically for the optimal solution.

b) How does one know that although $x_1 = 5$, $x_2 = 3$ is a feasible solution for the constraints, it will never be the optimal solution no matter what objective function is imposed?

c) Solve for the optimal solution using a spreadsheet.

SOLUTION 2

a) (1) <u>Graph the constraints</u>.
Constraint 1: When $x_1 = 0$, then $x_2 = 2$; when $x_2 = 0$, then $x_1 = 5$. Connect (5,0) and (0,2). The ">" side is above this line.

Constraint 2: When $x_2 = 0$, then $x_1 = 3$. But setting x_1 to 0 will yield $x_2 = -12$, which is not the graph. Thus, to get a second point on this line, set x_1 to any number larger than 3 and solve for x_2: when $x_1 = 5$, then $x_2 = 8$. Connect (3,0) and (5,8). The ">" side is to the right.

Constraint 3: When $x_1 = 0$, then $x_2 = 4$; when $x_2 = 0$, then $x_1 = 4$. Connect (4,0) and (0,4). The ">" side is above this line.

<u>Shade in the feasible region</u>.

(2) <u>Graph the objective function</u> by setting the objective function equal to an arbitrary constant (say 20) and graphing it. For $5x_1 + 2x_2 = 20$, when $x_1 = 0$, then $x_2 = 10$; when $x_2 = 0$, then $x_1 = 4$. Connect (4,0) and (0,10).

(3) <u>Move the objective function line</u> in the direction which lowers its value until it touches the last point of the feasible region, determined by the last two constraints.

(4) <u>Solve these two equations in two unknowns</u>. $4x_1 - x_2 = 12$ and $x_1 + x_2 = 4$ Adding these two equations gives: $5x_1 = 16$ or $x_1 = 16/5$. Substituting this into $x_1 + x_2 = 4$ gives: $x_2 = 4/5$.

(5) <u>Solve for $z = 5x_1 + 2x_2$</u> $= 5(16/5) + 2(4/5) = 88/5$. Thus the optimal solution is $x_1 = 16/5$; $x_2 = 4/5$; $z = 88/5$.

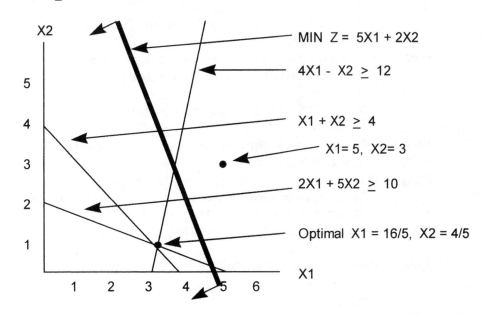

b) (5,3) lies in the feasible region, but it is not an extreme point and can never be optimal.

c) Spreadsheet showing data and formulas

	A	B	C	D
1		LHS Coefficients		
2	**Constraints**	**X1**	**X2**	**RHS**
3	#1	2	5	10
4	#2	4	-1	12
5	#3	1	1	4
6	**Obj.Func.Coeff.**	5	2	
7				
8		Decision Variables		
9		**X1**	**X2**	
10	**Dec.Var.Values**			
11				
12	**Minimized Objective Function**		=B6*B10+C6*C10	
13				
14	**Constraints**	**Amount Used**		**Amount Avail.**
15	#1	=B3*$B$10+C3*$C$10	>=	=D3
16	#2	=B4*$B$10+C4*$C$10	>=	=D4
17	#3	=B5*$B$10+C5*$C$10	>=	=D5

Steps in Using Excel Solver:

Step 1: Select the **Tools** pull-down menu.

Step 2: Select the **Solver** option.

Step 3: When the **Solver Parameters** dialog box appears:
Enter C12 in the **Set Target Cell** box.
Select the **Equal To: Min** option.
Enter B10:C10 in the **By Changing Cells** box.
Select **Add**.

Step 4: When the **Add Constraint** dialog box appears:
Enter B15:B17 in the **Cell Reference** box.
Select >=.
Enter D15:D17 in the **Constraint** box.
Click **OK**.

Step 5: When the **Solver Parameters** dialog box appears:
Choose **Options**.

Step 6: When the **Solver Options** dialog box appears:
Select **Assume Non-Negative**.
Click **OK**.

Step 7: When the **Solver Parameters** dialog box appears:
Choose **Solve**.

Step 8: When the **Solver Results** dialog box appears:
Select **Keep Solver Solution**.
Click **OK**.

	A	B	C	D
8		Decision Variables		
9		X1	X2	
10	Dec.Var.Values	3.20	0.800	
11				
12	Minimized Objective Function		17.600	
13				
14	Constraints	Amount Used		Amount Avail.
15	#1	10.4	>=	10
16	#2	12	>=	12
17	#3	4	>=	4

PROBLEM 3

Given the following linear program:

$$\text{MAX} \quad 4x_1 + 5x_2$$

$$\text{s.t.} \quad x_1 + 3x_2 \le 22$$

$$-x_1 + x_2 \le 4$$

$$x_2 \le 6$$

$$2x_1 - 5x_2 \le 0$$

$$x_1, x_2 \ge 0$$

NOTE: If a constraint's righthand-side value is 0, the constraint line will pass through the origin ($x_1 = 0$, $x_2 = 0$). This is the case with the fourth constraint above.

a) Solve the problem by the graphical method.

b) What would be the optimal solution if the second constraint were $-x_1 + x_2 = 4$?

c) What would be the optimal solution if the first constraint were $x_1 + 3x_2 \ge 22$?

SOLUTION 3

a) (1) <u>Graph the constraints</u>.

Constraint 1: When $x_1 = 0$, $x_2 = 22/3$; when $x_2 = 0$, then $x_1 = 22$. Connect (22,0) and (0,22/3). The "<" side is below this line.

Constraint 2: When $x_1 = 0$, then $x_2 = 4$. Setting x_2 to 0 would give $x_1 = -4$, which is outside the graph. Set x_2 to a number greater than 4 and solve for x_1. When $x_2 = 6$, then $x_1 = 2$. Connect (0,4) and (2,6). (0,0) is on the "<" side.

Constraint 3: This is a horizontal line through $x_2 = 6$.

Constraint 4: When $x_2 = 0$, then $x_1 = 0$; Set x_1 to any positive constant and solve for x_2. When $x_1 = 5$, then $x_2 = 2$. Connect the points (0,0) and (5,2). To determine the "<" side select any arbitrary point on one side of the line and substitute into the inequality. Arbitrarily choosing (0,5), this gives $2(0) - 5(5) = -25$. Thus the side containing (0,5) is the "<" side.

<u>Shade in the feasible region</u>.

(2) <u>Graph the objective function</u> by setting it to an arbitrary value, say 20. For $4x_1 + 5x_2 = 20$, when $x_1 = 0$, then $x_2 = 4$; when $x_2 = 0$, then $x_1 = 5$. Connect with a broken line the points (5,0) and (0,4).

(3) <u>Move the objective function line parallel to itself</u> in the direction which increases its value until it touches the last point of the feasible region. This is at the intersection of the first and fourth constraints.

(4) <u>Solve these two equations in two unknowns</u>:

$$x_1 + 3x_2 = 22 \longrightarrow 2x_1 + 6x_2 = 44$$
$$2x_1 - 5x_2 = 0 \longrightarrow 2x_1 - 5x_2 = 0$$

Subtracting the second equation from the first yields: $11x_2 = 44$ or $x_2 = 4$. Substituting $x_2 = 4$ into the first equation gives $x_1 = 10$.

(5) <u>Substitute for z</u> $= 4x_1 + 5x_2 = 4(10) + 5(4) = 60$. Thus the optimal solution is $x_1 = 10$; $x_2 = 4$; $z = 60$.

b) The feasible region is now the line segment of $-x_1 + x_2 = 4$ between (0,4) and (2,6). (2,6) now gives the optimal solution.

c) The feasible region is now the triangular section between (4,6), (15,6), and (10,4). (15,6) is now the optimal solution.

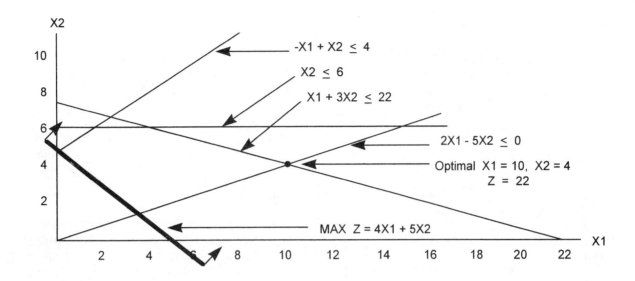

PROBLEM 4

Show graphically why the following two linear programs do not have optimal solutions and explain the difference between the two.

(a) MAX $2x_1 + 6x_2$

    s.t. $4x_1 + 3x_2 \leq 12$

             $2x_1 + x_2 \geq 8$

               $x_1, x_2 \geq 0$

(b) MAX $3x_1 + 4x_2$

    s.t. $x_1 + x_2 \geq 5$

             $3x_1 + x_2 \geq 8$

               $x_1, x_2 \geq 0$

SOLUTION 4

Refer to the graphs on the next page. Note that (a) has no points that satisfy both constraints, hence has no feasible region, and no optimal solution. (a) is infeasible.

Note that in (b) the feasible region is unbounded and the objective function line can be moved parallel to itself without bound so that z can be increased infinitely. (b) is unbounded.

(a)   (b)

PROBLEM 5

Given the following linear program:

$$\text{MIN} \quad 150x_1 + 210x_2$$

$$\text{s.t.} \quad 3.8x_1 + 1.2x_2 \geq 22.8$$

$$x_2 \geq 6$$

$$x_2 \leq 15$$

$$45x_1 + 30x_2 = 630$$

$$x_1, x_2 \geq 0$$

a) Solve the problem graphically. How many extreme points exist for this problem?

b) What would be the optimal solution if the "=" in the fourth constraint was changed to "$\leq$"?

c) If the "=" in the fourth constraint was changed to "$\geq$", how would the problem be affected?

SOLUTION 5

a) (1) Graph the constraints.

Constraint 1: When $x_1 = 0$, $x_2 = 19$; when $x_2 = 0$, then $x_1 = 6$. Connect (6,0) and (0,9). The ">" side is to the right of this line.

Constraint 2: This is a horizontal line through $x_2 = 6$. The ">" side is above this line.

Constraint 3: This is a horizontal line through $x_2 = 15$. The "<" side is above this line.

Constraint 4: When $x_1 = 0$, $x_2 = 21$; when $x_2 = 0$, then $x_1 = 14$. Connect (14,0) and (0,21).

Shade in the feasible region.

> NOTE: The feasible region in this problem is limited to a segment of the line representing the "equal to" constraint. Only two extreme points exist.

(2) Graph the objective function by setting the objective function equal to an arbitrary constant as previously demonstrated or by using the following approach. Scale down the objective coefficients c_1 and c_2 (say, by dividing both by 10 to get 8 and 13, respectively). Now, use x_1's coefficient as a value to plot on the x_2 axis and use x_2's coefficient as a value to plot on the x_1 axis. Connect points (0,15) and (21,0).

(3) Move the objective function line in the direction that lowers its value until it touches the last point of the feasible region. The point is determined by the second and fourth constraints.

(4) Solve for the unknown x by substituting $x_2 = 6$ into $45x_1 + 30x_2 = 630$, yielding $x_1 = 10$.

(5) Solve for z = $150x_1 + 210x_2 = 150(10) + 210(6) = 2760$. Thus the optimal solution is $x_1 = 10$, $x_2 = 6$, and $z = 2760$. [See the graph on the next page.]

b) The feasible region is now shaped by all four constraints. The optimal extreme point is determined by the first and second constraints. Solving these two equations in two unknowns, the optimal solution is (4.105,6), point C on the graph.

c) The optimal solution is now (10,6), point B on the graph, and the first constraint is now redundant.

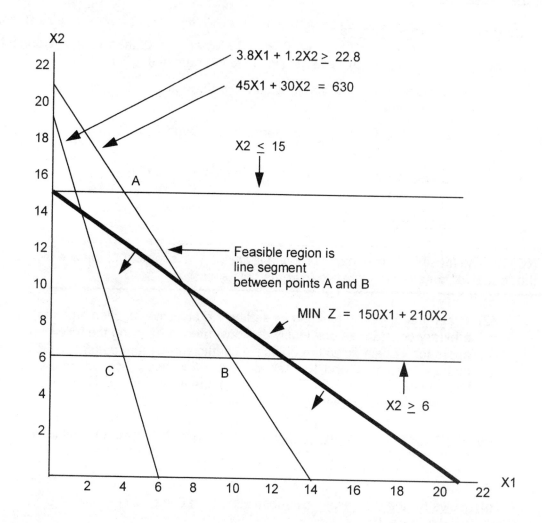

PROBLEM 6

Solve the following linear program graphically.

$$\text{MAX} \quad 5x_1 + 7x_2$$

$$\text{s.t.} \quad x_1 \quad\quad \leq 6$$

$$2x_1 + 3x_2 \leq 19$$

$$x_1 + x_2 \leq 8$$

$$x_1, x_2 \geq 0$$

SOLUTION 6

From the graph below we see that the optimal solution occurs at $x_1 = 5$, $x_2 = 3$, and $z = 46$.

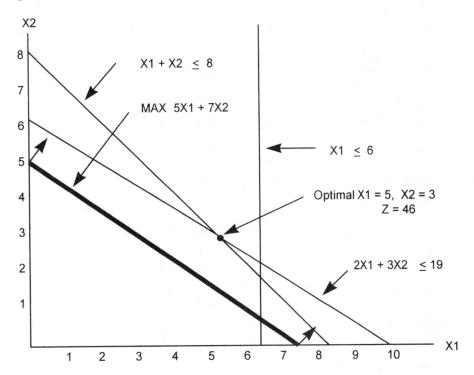

PROBLEM 7

A manager of a small fabrication plant must decide on a production schedule of two new products for the automobile industry. The profit on product 1 is $1(thousand) and on product 2 is $3(thousand).

The manufacture of these products depends largely on the availability of certain subassemblies the plant receives daily from a local distributor. It takes three of these subassemblies for each unit of product 1 and two for each unit of product 2. Twelve such subassemblies are delivered daily.

Further, it takes two hours to make a unit of product 1 and six hours to make a unit of product 2. The plant has assigned only three workers working 8-hour shifts for these new products. Due to limited demand, the manager does not want more than seven units of product 2 produced daily.

a) Formulate this problem as a linear program.

b) Solve graphically for the optimal solution. Describe the set of all optimal solutions. Identify any redundant constraints.

c) Give an optimal daily production schedule that manufactures exactly one unit of product 1.

d) Discuss the applicability of linear programming for this problem.

SOLUTION 7

a) (1) <u>Define variables</u>: x_1 and x_2 = the amount of product 1 and 2 produced daily.

(2) <u>Define objective</u>:
Maximize total daily profits: MAX $1x_1 + 3x_2$ (in thousands of dollars).

(3) <u>Define constraints</u>:
Subassemblies: Number used daily $\leq$ number available: $3x_1 + 2x_2 \leq 12$

Labor: Number of hours used daily $\leq$ (3 men) x (8 hrs./day): $2x_1 + 6x_2 \leq 24$

Product 2: Quantity produced daily $\leq$ specified limit: $x_2 \leq 7$

Non-negativity of variables: $x_1, x_2 \geq 0$

Summarizing,   MAX $1x_1 + 3x_2$

s.t. $3x_1 + 2x_2 \leq 12$

$2x_1 + 6x_2 \leq 24$

$x_2 \leq 7$

$x_1, x_2 \geq 0$

b) Graphically,

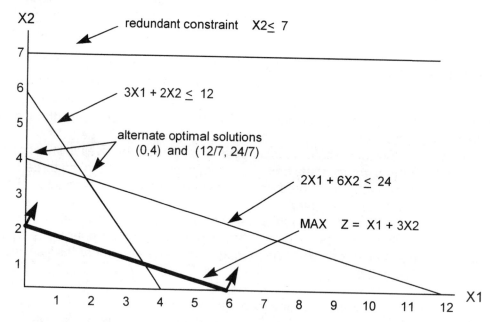

The optimal solution occurs at $x_1 = 0$, $x_2 = 4$ and at $x_1 = 12/7$, $x_2 = 24/7$, and at all points in between on the line $2x_1 + 6x_2 = 24$. At any point on this line, $z = 12$. The $x_2 \leq 7$ constraint does not help shape the feasible region and thus is redundant.

c) On the optimal solution line, $2x_1 + 6x_2 = 24$, when $x_1 = 1$, then $x_2 = 11/3$. Still, $z = 1(1) + 3(11/3) = 12$ (thousand).

d) One must consider whether these variables can be allowed to assume values that are not integers. For continuous production, frequently a fractional value can be considered as "work in progress"; products not finished on one day are simply completed the next day. Thus, LP appears to be appropriate for this problem.

PROBLEM 8

A small company will be introducing a new line of lightweight bicycle frames to be made from special aluminum and steel alloys. The frames will be produced in two models, deluxe and professional, with anticipated unit profits of $10 and $15, respectively.

The number of pounds of aluminum alloy and steel alloy needed per deluxe frame is 2 and 3, respectively. The number of pounds of aluminum alloy and steel alloy needed per professional frame is 4 and 2. A supplier delivers 100 pounds of the aluminum alloy and 80 pounds of the steel alloy weekly. What is the optimal weekly production schedule?

SOLUTION 8

Let x_1 and x_2 equal the number of deluxe and professional frames produced weekly.

$$\text{MAX} \quad 10x_1 + 15x_2$$
$$\text{s.t.} \quad 2x_1 + 4x_2 \leq 100$$
$$3x_1 + 2x_2 \leq 80$$
$$x_1, x_2 \geq 0$$

Solving graphically, the optimal production schedule is to produce $x_1 = 15$ deluxe frames weekly and $x_2 = 17.5$ professional frames weekly for an optimal weekly profit of $412.50.

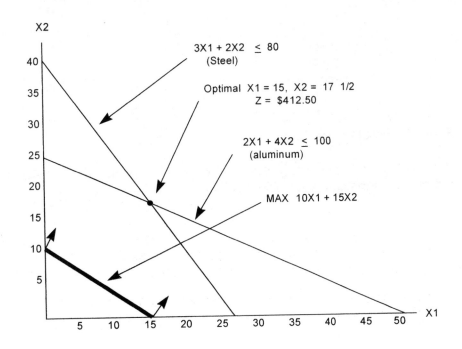

ANSWERED PROBLEMS

PROBLEM 9

Solve graphically for the optimal solution to the following linear program:

$$\text{MIN} \quad 16x_1 + 12x_2$$

$$\text{s.t.} \quad 8x_1 + 4x_2 \leq 36$$

$$x_1 + x_2 \leq 7$$

$$3x_1 + 12x_2 \geq 24$$

$$x_1 + 5x_2 \geq 20$$

$$x_1, x_2 \geq 0$$

PROBLEM 10

Given the following linear program:

$$\text{MAX} \quad 4x_1 + 2x_2$$

$$\text{s.t.} \quad x_1 \leq 4$$

$$3x_1 + 8x_2 \leq 24$$

$$2x_1 + x_2 \geq 6$$

$$x_1, x_2 \geq 0$$

a) Solve the problem graphically.

b) What would be the optimal solution(s) if the objective function were a minimization rather than a maximization objective?

PROBLEM 11

Consider a linear programming problem with the following constraint set:

$$2x_1 + x_2 \geq 4$$

$$x_1 + 2x_2 \geq 5$$

$$x_1 - 2x_2 \leq 1$$

a) Graph the feasible region and note it is unbounded.

NOTE: One might think an unbounded maximization problem would always have an unbounded objective function value. This problem proves the contrary.

---

b) Identify all extreme points.

c) Solve the problem with each of these objective functions: (1) MAX $z = 2x_1 - 5x_2$; (2) MAX $z = 2x_1 - 4x_2$; and (3) MAX $z = 2x_1 - 3x_2$ and discuss the results.

PROBLEM 12

Given the following linear programming problem:

$$\text{MAX} \quad 3x_1 + 5x_2$$

$$\text{s.t.} \quad 4x_1 + 3x_2 \geq 24$$

$$2x_1 + 3x_2 \leq 18$$

$$x_2 \geq 3$$

$$x_1, x_2 \geq 0$$

a) Solve the problem graphically.

NOTE: The feasible region in this problem is limited to a single point. A common error is to mistake this situation for infeasibility.

---

b) What effect would changing the objective function to MAX $5x_1 + 4x_2$ have?

PROBLEM 13

Given the following linear programming problem:

$$MAX \quad 8x_1 + 10x_2$$

$$
\begin{aligned}
s.t. \quad x_1 + \quad x_2 &\leq 35 \\
3x_1 + 2x_2 &\leq 60 \\
x_2 &\leq 15 \\
x_1, x_2 &\geq 0
\end{aligned}
$$

a) Solve for the optimal solution.

b) State why the first constraint is redundant.

c) Suppose the second constraint's right hand side is changed from 60 to 100. Solve for the new optimal solution and show that the first constraint is now binding and NOT redundant.

PROBLEM 14

Consider the following linear program:

$$MAX \quad 60x_1 + 43x_2$$

$$
\begin{aligned}
s.t. \quad x_1 + 3x_2 &\geq 9 \\
6x_1 - 2x_2 &= 12 \\
x_1 + 2x_2 &\leq 10 \\
x_1, x_2 &\geq 0
\end{aligned}
$$

a) Write the problem in standard form.

b) What is the feasible region for the problem?

c) Show that regardless of the values of the actual objective function coefficients, the optimal solution will occur at one of two points. Solve for these points and then determine which one maximizes the current objective function.

PROBLEM 15

A businessman is considering opening a small specialized trucking firm. To make the firm profitable, it is estimated that it must have a daily trucking capacity of at least 84,000 cu. ft. Two types of trucks are appropriate for the specialized operation. Their characteristics and costs are summarized in the table below. Note that truck 2 requires 3 drivers for long haul trips. There are 41 potential drivers available and there are facilities for at most 40 trucks.

The businessman's objective is to minimize the total cost outlay for trucks.

Truck	Cost	Capacity (Cu. ft.)	Drivers Needed
x_1	$18,000	2,400	1
x_2	$45,000	6,000	3

Solve the problem graphically and note there are alternate optimal solutions. Which optimal solution:

a) uses only one type of truck?

b) utilizes the minimum total number of trucks?

c) uses the same number of truck x_1 as truck x_2?

PROBLEM 16

A baseball glove manufacturer has 1200 linear feet of cowhide and 800 linear feet of synthetic material. It makes two styles of baseball gloves: child's and adult's. Requirements and profit PER DOZEN are summarized below:

	Cowhide	Synthetic	Profit
Child's	4	4	$60
Adult's	12	6	$95

a) Solve for the optimal number of dozen of each model to manufacture. What are the values of the slack variables?

b) Suppose the company could make $1 on each unused linear foot of cowhide and $.25 on each unused linear foot of synthetic material. Reformulate the linear programming model. The new optimal solution is to make 200 dozen child models and no adult models and sell 400 linear feet of cowhide. Locate this new point on your graph and show it is not the optimal extreme point of part (a).

TRUE/FALSE

____ 17. A problem formulation that includes a term that is the product of two variables would not be a linear program.

____ 18. A nonbinding constraint, like a binding constraint, helps form the shape (boundaries) of the feasible region.

____ 19. If a linear program has an optimal solution, then an extreme point must be optimal.

____ 20. All optimal solutions are extreme points.

____ 21. A redundant constraint lies entirely within the feasible region.

____ 22. It is possible to have exactly two optimal solutions to a linear programming problem.

____ 23. A linear programming problem can be both unbounded and infeasible.

____ 24. If a problem has a constraint which is parallel to the objective function, then there must be alternative optimal solutions.

____ 25. An infeasible problem is one in which the objective function can be increased to infinity.

____ 26. A slack variable is a variable that represents the difference between the amount of a resource that was available and the actual amount used by the solution.

____ 27. In a feasible problem, an equal-to constraint cannot be redundant.

____ 28. A variable in a linear programming problem must be allowed to assume fractional values.

____ 29. Any change to an objective function coefficient of a variable that is positive in the optimal solution will change the optimal solution.

____ 30. An unbounded feasible region might not result in an unbounded solution for a minimization or maximization problem.

____ 31. Increasing the right-hand side of a nonbinding constraint will not cause a change in the optimal solution.

CHAPTER 3

Linear Programming: Sensitivity Analysis and Interpretation of Solution

KEY CONCEPTS

CONCEPT	ILLUSTRATED PROBLEMS	ANSWERED PROBLEMS
Sensitivity Analysis: Graphical Solution	1,2	12-14
Sensitivity Analysis: Computer Solution	3-6	7-11,15
Changes to Objective Function Coefficients		
Reduced Cost	6	
Range of Optimality	3-6	7-11
Changes to Right Hand Side Values		
Dual Price	3-6	8-11
Range of Feasibility	3-5	8-11
Sunk/Relevant Costs	5	8
100% Rule	3-6	8-11

REVIEW

1. Sensitivity analysis is used to determine how the optimal solution is affected by changes, within specified ranges, in the objective function coefficients and the right-hand side (RHS) values.

2. Sensitivity analysis is important to the manager who must operate in a dynamic environment with imprecise estimates of the coefficients. Sensitivity analysis allows him to ask certain what-if questions about the problem.

3. A reduced cost for a decision variable whose value is 0 in the optimal solution is the amount the variable's objective coefficient would have to improve (increase for maximization problems, decrease for minimization problems) before this variable could assume a positive value. Thus, the reduced cost for a decision variable with a positive value is 0.

4. A range of optimality of an objective function coefficient is found by determining an interval for the objective function coefficient in which the original solution remains optimal while keeping all other data of the problem constant. The value of z might change in this range.

5. Graphically, the limits of a <u>range of optimality</u> are found by changing the slope of the objective function line within the limits of the slopes of the binding constraint lines. This would also apply to simultaneous changes in the objective coefficients. The slope of an objective function line, MAX $c_1x_1 + c_2x_2$, is $-c_1/c_2$, and the slope of a constraint i, $a_{i1}x_1 + a_{i2}x_2 = b_i$, is $-a_{i1}/a_{i2}$.

6. The <u>100% rule</u> states that <u>simultaneous changes in objective function coefficients</u> will not change the optimal solution as long as the sum of the percentages of the change divided by the corresponding maximum allowable change in the range of optimality for each coefficient does not exceed 100%.

7. A <u>dual price</u> for a <u>right-hand side</u> (or resource limit) is the amount the objective function will improve per unit increase in the right-hand side value of a constraint.

8. A <u>dual price</u> reflects the value of an additional unit of the resource if the <u>resource cost</u> is <u>sunk</u>. It represents the extra value over the normal cost of the resource when the resource cost is <u>relevant</u>.

9. A <u>resource cost</u> is <u>relevant</u> if the amount paid for it is dependent upon the amount of the resource used by the decision variables. Relevant costs are reflected in the objective function coefficients.

10. A <u>resource cost</u> is <u>sunk</u> if it must be paid regardless of the amount of the resource actually used by the decision variables. Sunk resource costs are not reflected in the objective function coefficients.

11. Graphically, a <u>dual price</u> is determined by adding +1 to the right hand side value in question and then resolving for the optimal solution in terms of the same two binding constraints. The dual price is equal to the difference in the values of the objective functions between the new and original problems.

12. A <u>nonbinding constraint</u> is one in which there is <u>positive slack or surplus</u> when evaluated at the optimal solution. The dual price for a nonbinding constraint is zero.

13. The <u>range of feasibility</u> for a change in a right-hand side value is the range of values for this parameter in which the original <u>dual price</u> remains constant.

14. Graphically, the <u>range of feasibility</u> is determined by finding the values of a right hand side coefficient such that the same two lines that determined the original optimal solution continue to determine the optimal solution for the problem.

15. The <u>100% rule</u> also states that <u>simultaneous changes in right hand sides</u> will not change the dual prices as long as the sum of the percentages of the changes divided by the corresponding maximum allowable change in the range of feasibility for each right-hand side does not exceed 100%.

16. <u>Computer software packages</u> (such as *The Management Scientist* or *Microsoft Excel*) that solve linear programming problems all give five elements of relevant information about the optimal solution:
    1. The optimal value of the objective function;
    2. Information about the decision variables: (a) their values, (b) their reduced costs;
    3. Information about the constraints: (a) amount of slack or surplus, (b) dual prices;
    4. Ranges of optimality for objective function coefficients: (a) lower limit, (b) upper limit;
    5. Ranges of feasibility for righthand-side values: (a) lower limit, (b) upper limit.

ILLUSTRATED PROBLEMS

PROBLEM 1

Given the following linear program:

$$\text{MAX} \quad 5x_1 + 7x_2$$
$$\text{s.t.} \quad x_1 \quad\quad \leq 6$$
$$2x_1 + 3x_2 \leq 19$$
$$x_1 + x_2 \leq 8$$
$$x_1, x_2 \geq 0$$

The graphical solution to the problem is shown below. From the graph we see that the optimal solution occurs at $x_1 = 5$, $x_2 = 3$, and $z = 46$.

a) Calculate the range of optimality for each objective function coefficient.

b) Calculate the dual price for each resource.

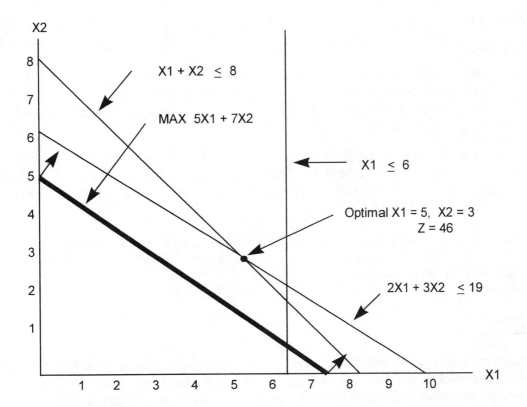

SOLUTION 1

a) The slope of the objective function line is $-c_1/c_2$. The slope of the first binding constraint, $x_1 + x_2 = 8$, is -1 and the slope of the second binding constraint, $2x_1 + 3x_2 = 19$ is -2/3.

Range of optimality for c_1:
Find the range of values for c_1 (with c_2 staying 7) such that the objective function line slope lies between that of the two binding constraints:

$$-1 \leq -c_1/7 \leq -2/3.$$

Multiplying through by -7 (and reversing the inequalities):

$$14/3 \leq c_1 \leq 7.$$

Range of optimality for c_2:
Find the range of values for c_2 (with c_1 staying 5) such that the objective function line slope lies between that of the two binding constraints:

$$-1 \leq -5/c_2 \leq -2/3.$$

Multiplying by -1: $1 \geq 5/c_2 \geq 2/3.$

Inverting, $1 \leq c_2/5 \leq 3/2.$

Multiplying by 5: $5 \leq c_2 \leq 15/2.$

b) Dual prices:

Constraint 1: Since $x_1 \leq 6$ is not a binding constraint, its dual price is 0.

Constraint 2: Change the right hand side of the second constraint to 20 and resolve for the optimal point determined by the last two constraints: $2x_1 + 3x_2 = 20$ and $x_1 + x_2 = 8$. The solution is $x_1 = 4$, $x_2 = 4$, $z = 48$. Hence, the dual price = $z_{new} - z_{old} = 48 - 46 = 2$.

Constraint 3: Change the right hand side value of the third constraint to 9 and resolve for the optimal point determined by the last two constraints: $2x_1 + 3x_2 = 19$ and $x_1 + x_2 = 9$. The solution is: $x_1 = 8$, $x_2 = 1$, $z = 47$. Hence, the dual price is $z_{new} - z_{old} = 47 - 46 = 1$.

Summarizing, the dual price for the first resource is 0, for the second resource is 2, and for the third is 1. Note that these dual prices are only valid in the range of feasibility for each resource.

PROBLEM 2

A small company will be introducing a new line of lightweight bicycle frames to be made from special aluminum and steel alloys. The frames will be produced in two models, deluxe and professional, with anticipated unit profits of $10 and $15, respectively.

The number of pounds of aluminum alloy and steel alloy needed per deluxe frame is 2 and 3, respectively. The number of pounds of aluminum alloy and steel alloy needed per professional frame is 4 and 2, respectively. A supplier delivers 100 pounds of the aluminum alloy and 80 pounds of the steel alloy weekly.

The problem of determining the optimal weekly production schedule can be formulated as follows.

Let: x_1 = the number of deluxe frames produced weekly
       x_2 = the number of professional frames produced weekly

$$\text{MAX} \quad 10x_1 + 15x_2$$
$$\text{s.t.} \quad 2x_1 + 4x_2 \leq 100$$
$$3x_1 + 2x_2 \leq 80$$
$$x_1, x_2 \geq 0$$

Solving graphically, the optimal production schedule is to produce $x_1 = 15$ deluxe frames weekly and $x_2 = 17.5$ professional frames weekly for an optimal weekly profit of $412.50.

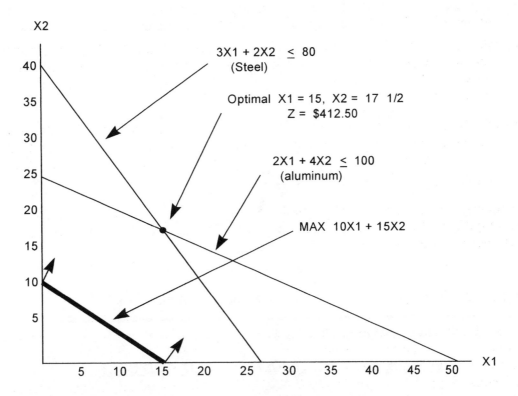

a) Within what limits must the unit profits lie for each of the frames for this solution to remain optimal?

b) Suppose the unit profits assumed all aluminum purchased would be used and hence the profit figures did not include a unit cost for the aluminum. Now extra aluminum can be purchased at $2.50 per pound. Should the company purchase additional pounds of aluminum at that price?

SOLUTION 2

a) Note that the binding constraints are the aluminum and the steel constraints, with slopes -1/2 and -3/2 respectively.
Range of optimality for deluxe profits (c_1):

$$-3/2 \leq -c_1/15 \leq -1/2 \quad \text{or} \quad 15/2 \leq c_1 \leq 45/2.$$

Range of optimality for professional profits (c_2):

$$-3/2 \leq -10/c_2 \leq -1/2 \quad \text{or} \quad 20/3 \leq c_2 \leq 20.$$

b) The aluminum costs are then considered <u>sunk</u> costs and the dual price for aluminum would yield the maximum worth for additional aluminum. Resolve the two equations and two unknown with the right hand side of the aluminum constraint changed to 101.

This results in x_1 = 59/4, x_2 = 143/8, z = $415.625. Hence the dual price for aluminum is $415.625 - $412.50 = $3.125. Since this is greater than the selling price of $2.50 per pound of aluminum, additional aluminum should be purchased at this price.

PROBLEM 3

Consider the following linear program:

$$\text{MAX} \quad 3x_1 + 4x_2 \quad (\$ \text{ Profit})$$

$$\text{s.t.} \quad x_1 + 3x_2 \leq 12$$

$$2x_1 + x_2 \leq 8$$

$$x_1 \leq 3$$

$$x_1, x_2 \geq 0$$

The Management Scientist provided the following solution output:

OBJECTIVE FUNCTION VALUE = 20.000

VARIABLE	VALUE	REDUCED COST
X1	2.400	0.000
X2	3.200	0.000

CONSTRAINT	SLACK/SURPLUS	DUAL PRICES
1	0.000	1.000
2	0.000	1.000
3	0.600	0.000

OBJECTIVE COEFFICIENT RANGES

VARIABLE	LOWER LIMIT	CURRENT VALUE	UPPER LIMIT
X1	1.333	3.000	8.000
X2	1.500	4.000	9.000

RIGHT HAND SIDE RANGES

CONSTRAINT	LOWER LIMIT	CURRENT VALUE	UPPER LIMIT
1	9.000	12.000	24.000
2	4.000	8.000	9.000
3	2.400	3.000	NO UPPER LIMIT

a) What is the optimal solution including the optimal value of the objective function?

b) Suppose the profit on x_1 is increased to $7. Is the above solution still optimal? What is the value of the objective function when this unit profit is increased to $7?

c) If the unit profit on x_2 was $10 instead of $4, would the optimal solution change?

> NOTE: A "change in the optimal solution" refers to a change in the optimal values of the decision variables, not a change in the optimal value of the objective function alone.

d) If simultaneously the profit on x_1 was raised to $5.5 and the profit on x_2 was reduced to $3, would the current solution still remain optimal?

SOLUTION 3

a) According to the output $x_1 = 2.4$ and $x_2 = 3.2$, and $z = \$20.00$.

b) The output states that the solution remains optimal as long as the objective function coefficient of x_1 is between 1.333 and 8.0. Since 7 is within this range, the optimal solution will not change. However, the optimal profit will be affected: $z = 7x_1 + 4x_2 = 7(2.4) + 4(3.2) = \$29.60$.

c) The output states that the solution remains optimal as long as the objective function coefficient of x_2 is between 1.5 and 9.0. Since 10 is outside this range, the optimal solution would change.

d) Use the 100% rule for simultaneous changes. If $c_1 = 5.5$, the amount c_1 changed is 5.5 - 3 = 2.5. The maximum allowable increase is 8 - 3 = 5, so this is a 2.5/5 = a 50% change. If $c_2 = 3$, the amount that c_2 changed is 4 - 3 = 1. The maximum allowable decrease is 4 - 1.5 = 2.5, so this is a 1/2.5 = a 40% change. The sum of the change percentages is 50% + 40% = 90%. Since this does not exceed 100% the optimal solution would not change.

> NOTE: For the 100% rule, a reduction does not offset an increase. For example, increasing c_1 by 70% of its allowed maximum increase and <u>decreasing</u> c_2 by 50% of its allowed maximum decrease does <u>not</u> result in a combined change of 20%. The combined change is 120%, which means the problem should be solved again because the simultaneous changes to c_1 and c_2 might have (probably) changed the optimal solution (x_1 and x_2's values).

PROBLEM 4

Consider the following linear program:

$$\text{MIN} \quad 6x_1 + 9x_2 \ (\$ \text{ cost})$$

$$\text{s.t.} \quad x_1 + 2x_2 \leq 8$$

$$10x_1 + 7.5x_2 \geq 30$$

$$x_2 \geq 2$$

$$x_1, x_2 \geq 0$$

The Management Scientist provided the following solution output:

OBJECTIVE FUNCTION VALUE = 27.000

VARIABLE	VALUE	REDUCED COST
X1	1.500	0.000
X2	2.000	0.000

CONSTRAINT	SLACK/SURPLUS	DUAL PRICES
1	2.500	0.000
2	0.000	-0.600
3	0.000	-4.500

OBJECTIVE COEFFICIENT RANGES

VARIABLE	LOWER LIMIT	CURRENT VALUE	UPPER LIMIT
X1	0.000	6.000	12.000
X2	4.500	9.000	NO UPPER LIMIT

RIGHT HAND SIDE RANGES

CONSTRAINT	LOWER LIMIT	CURRENT VALUE	UPPER LIMIT
1	5.500	8.000	NO UPPER LIMIT
2	15.000	30.000	55.000
3	0.000	2.000	4.000

a) What is the optimal solution including the optimal value of the objective function?

b) Suppose the unit cost of x_1 is decreased to $4. Is the above solution still optimal? What is the value of the objective function when this unit cost is decreased to $4?

c) How much can the unit cost of x_2 be decreased without concern for the optimal solution changing?

d) If simultaneously the cost of x_1 was raised to $7.5 and the cost of x_2 was reduced to $6, would the current solution still remain optimal?

e) If the right-hand side of constraint 3 is increased by 1, what will be the effect on the optimal solution?

SOLUTION 4

a) According to the output x_1 = 1.5 and x_2 = 2.0, and the objective function value = 27.00.

b) The output states that the solution remains optimal as long as the objective function coefficient of x_1 is between 0 and 12. Since 4 is within this range, the optimal solution will not change. However, the optimal total cost will be affected: $z = 6x_1 + 9x_2 =$ 4(1.5) + 9(2.0) = $24.00.

c) The output states that the solution remains optimal as long as the objective function coefficient of x_2 does not fall below 4.5.

d) Use the 100% rule for simultaneous changes. If c_1 = 7.5, the amount c_1 changed is 7.5 - 6 = 1.5. The maximum allowable increase is 12 - 6 = 6, so this is a 1.5/6 = 25% change. If c_2 = 6, the amount that c_2 changed is 9 - 6 = 3. The maximum allowable decrease is 9 - 4.5 = 4.5, so this is a 3/4.5 = 66.7% change. The sum of the change percentages is 25% + 66.7% = 91.7%. Since this does not exceed 100% the optimal solution would not change.

e) A dual price represents the improvement in the objective function value per unit increase in the right-hand side. A negative dual price indicates a deterioration (negative improvement) in the objective, which in this problem means an increase in total cost because we're minimizing. Since the right-hand side remains within the range of feasibility, there is no change in the optimal solution. However, the objective function value increases by $4.50.

PROBLEM 5

A small company will be introducing a new line of lightweight bicycle frames to be made from special aluminum and steel alloys. The frames will be produced in two models, deluxe and professional. The anticipated unit profits are currently $10 for a deluxe frame and $15 for a professional frame.

The number of pounds of each alloy needed per frame is summarized in the table below. A supplier delivers 100 pounds of the aluminum alloy and 80 pounds of the steel alloy weekly.

	Aluminum Alloy	Steel Alloy
Deluxe	2	3
Professional	4	2

Use a spreadsheet to determine how many frames of each type should be produced?

a) What is the optimal solution including the optimal value of the objective function?

b) Suppose the profit on deluxe frames is increased to $20. Is the above solution still optimal? What is the value of the objective function when this unit profit is increased to $20?

c) If the unit profit on deluxe frames were $6 instead of $10 would the optimal solution change?

d) If simultaneously the profit on deluxe frames were raised to $16 and the profit on professional frames were raised to $17, would the current solution still remain optimal?

e) Given that aluminum is a sunk cost, what is the maximum amount the company should pay for 50 extra pounds of aluminum? (Constraint 1 pertains to aluminum availability.)

f) How would your answer to (e) change if aluminum were a relevant cost?

SOLUTION 5

The steps to follow in setting up and using a spreadsheet are outlined on the next page.

Spreadsheet showing data and formulas

	A	B	C	D
1		Material Requirements		Amount
2	Material	Deluxe	Profess.	Available
3	Aluminum	2	4	100
4	Steel	3	2	80
5	Profit/Bike	10	15	
6		Decision Variables		
7		Deluxe	Professional	
8	Bikes Made			
9				
10	Maximized Total Profit		=B5*B8+C5*C8	
11				
12	Constraints	Amount Used		Amount Avail.
13	Aluminum	=B3*B8+C3*C8	<=	=D3
14	Steel	=B4*B8+C4*C8	<=	=D4

Steps in Using Excel Solver:

Step 1: Select the **Tools** pull-down Menu.
Step 2: Select the **Solver** option.
Step 3: When the **Solver Parameters** dialog box appears:
   Enter C10 in the **Set Target Cell** box.
   Select the **Equal To: Max** option.
   Enter B8:C8 in the **By Changing Cells** box.
   Select **Add**.
Step 4: When the **Add Constraint** dialog box appears:
   Enter B13:B14 in the **Cell Reference** box.
   Select <=.
   Enter D13:D14 in the **Constraint** box.
   Click **OK**.
Step 5: When the **Solver Parameters** dialog box appears:
   Choose **Options**.
Step 6: When the **Solver Options** dialog box appears:
   Select **Assume Non-Negative**.
   Click **OK**.
Step 7: When the **Solver Parameters** dialog box appears:
   Choose **Solve**.
Step 8: When the **Solver Results** dialog box appears:
   Select **Keep Solver Solution**.
   Select **Sensitivity** in the Reports box.
   Click **OK**.

Sensitivity Report

Adjustable Cells

Cell	Name	Final Value	Reduced Cost	Objective Coefficient	Allowable Increase	Allowable Decrease
$B$8	Deluxe	15	0	10	12.5	2.5
$C$8	Profess.	17.500	0.000	15	5	8.333333333

Constraints

Cell	Name	Final Value	Shadow Price	Constraint R.H. Side	Allowable Increase	Allowable Decrease
$B$13	Aluminum	100	3.125	100	60	46.66666667
$B$14	Steel	80	1.25	80	70	30

a) According to the output x_1 (deluxe frames) = 15, and x_2 (professional frames) = 17.5, and this yields an objective function value of $412.50.

b) The output states that the solution remains optimal as long as the objective function coefficient of x_1 is between 7.5 and 22.5. Since 20 is within this range, the optimal solution will not change. However the optimal profit will be affected: $z = 20x_1 + 15x_2 = 20(15) + 15(17.5) = 562.50.

c) The output states that the solution remains optimal as long as the objective function coefficient of x_1 is between 7.5 and 22.5. Since 6 is outside this range, the optimal solution would change.

d) Use the 100% rule for simultaneous changes. If $c_1 = 16$, the amount c_1 changed is 16 - 10 = 6 . The maximum allowable increase is 22.5 - 10 = 12.5, so this is a 6/12.5 = 48% change. If $c_2 = 17$, the amount that c_2 changed is 17 - 15 = 2. The maximum allowable increase is 20 - 15 = 5 so this is a 2/5 = 40% change. The sum of the change percentages is 88%. This is less than 100%, so the optimal solution would not change.

e) Since the cost for aluminum is a sunk cost, the dual price provides the value of extra aluminum. The dual price for aluminum is $3.125 per pound. Thus, the value of 50 additional pounds is = $156.25.

   This analysis is valid only if the change is within the range of feasibility for aluminum. From the output we can see that the maximum allowable increase for aluminum is 60. Since 50 is in this range, then the $156.25 is valid.

f) If aluminum were a relevant cost, the dual price would be the amount above the normal price of aluminum the company would be willing to pay. Thus if initially aluminum cost $4 per pound, then additional units in the range of feasibility would be worth $4 + $3.125 = $7.125 per pound.

PROBLEM 6

Comfort Plus Inc. (CPI) manufactures a standard dining chair used in restaurants. The demand forecasts for quarter 1 (January-March) and quarter 2 (April-June) are 3700 chairs and 4200 chairs, respectively. CPI has a policy of satisfying all demand in the quarter in which it occurs.

The chair contains an upholstered seat that can be produced by CPI or purchased from DAP, a subcontractor. DAP currently charges $12.50 per seat, but has announced a new price of $13.75 effective April 1. CPI can produce the seat at a cost of $10.25. CPI can produce up to 3800 seats per quarter.

Seats that are produced or purchased in quarter 1 and used to satisfy demand in quarter 2 cost CPI $1.50 each to hold in inventory, but maximum inventory cannot exceed 300 seats.

The problem was formulated as follows:

x_1 = number of seats produced by CPI in quarter 1,
x_2 = number of seats purchased from DAP in quarter 1,
x_3 = number of seats carried in inventory from quarters 1 to 2,
x_4 = number of seats produced by CPI in quarter 2, and
x_5 = number of seats purchased from DAP in quarter 2.

$$\text{MIN} \quad 10.25x_1 + 12.5x_2 + 1.5x_3 + 10.25x_4 + 13.75x_5 \quad \text{(costs)}$$

$$\text{s.t.} \quad x_1 + x_2 - x_3 \geq 3700 \quad \text{(quarter 1 demand)}$$

$$x_3 + x_4 + x_5 \geq 4200 \quad \text{(quarter 2 demand)}$$

$$x_1 \leq 3800 \quad \text{(CPI's production capacity in quarter 1)}$$

$$x_4 \leq 3800 \quad \text{(CPI's production capacity in quarter 2)}$$

$$x_3 \leq 300 \quad \text{(inventory capacity)}$$

$$x_1, x_2 \ x_3, \ x_4, \ x_5 \geq 0$$

The Management Scientist provided the following solution output:

OBJECTIVE FUNCTION VALUE = 82175.000

VARIABLE	VALUE	REDUCED COST
X1	3800.000	0.000
X2	0.000	0.250
X3	100.000	0.000
X4	3800.000	0.000
X5	300.000	0.000

CONSTRAINT	SLACK/SURPLUS	DUAL PRICES
1	0.000	-12.250
2	0.000	-13.750
3	0.000	2.000
4	0.000	3.500
5	200.000	0.000

OBJECTIVE COEFFICIENT RANGES

VARIABLE	LOWER LIMIT	CURRENT VALUE	UPPER LIMIT
X1	NO LOWER LIMIT	10.250	12.250
X2	12.250	12.500	NO UPPER LIMIT
X3	1.250	1.500	3.500
X4	NO LOWER LIMIT	10.250	13.750
X5	11.750	13.750	14.000

RIGHT HAND SIDE RANGES

CONSTRAINT	LOWER LIMIT	CURRENT VALUE	UPPER LIMIT
1	3500.000	3700.000	3800.000
2	3900.000	4200.000	NO UPPER LIMIT
3	3700.000	3800.000	4000.000
4	0.000	3800.000	4100.000
5	100.000	300.000	NO UPPER LIMIT

a) What is the optimal solution including the optimal value of the objective function?

b) If the per-unit inventory cost increased from $1.50 to $2.50, would the optimal solution change? Would the optimal value of the objective function change?

c) If in quarter 2 CPI's per-seat production cost increased by $1.25 and DAP changed its mind about the announced price increase (thus leaving it at $12.50 per seat), would the optimal solution change?

d) If DAP reduced its per-seat selling price in quarter 1 from $12.50 to $12.25, should CPI purchase any seats in quarter 1?

e) How much is it worth to CPI to increase its inventory capacity from 300 seats to 400?

f) If CPI increased its production capacity by 100 seats in both quarters 1 and 2, what would be the savings for CPI (ignoring the capacity-expansion expense)?

SOLUTION 6

a) CPI will produce 3800 seats in quarter 1 and another 3800 in quarter 2. 100 seats will be carried in inventory from quarter 1 to quarter 2. 300 seats will be purchased from DAP in quarter 2. Total cost for this plan is $82,175.

b) The optimal solution will not change as a result of a change in the per-unit inventory cost as long as the cost remains in the range of $1.25 to $3.50. The objective function value <u>will</u> change; it will increase by $100 to $82,275.

c) Use the 100% rule for simultaneous changes. The amount c_4 changed is 1.25. The maximum allowable increase is 13.75 - 10.25 = 3.50, so this is a 1.25/3.50 = 35.7% change. If c_5 = 12.50, the amount that c_5 changed is 13.75 - 12.50 = 1.25. The maximum allowable decrease is 13.75 - 11.75 = 2.00, so this is a 1.25/2.00 = 62.5% change. The sum of the percentages is 98.2%; the optimal solution would not change.

d) x_2 is the number of seats purchased from DAP in quarter 1 and its current value is 0. Its reduced cost value is 0.25, indicating that if c_2 improved (decreased in this case) by 0.25 or more, x_2 would have a positive value in the new optimal solution. c_2 = $12.25 represents an improvement of exactly 0.25, so the answer is yes.

e) Increasing the inventory capacity (without other changes) will not benefit CPI. Actually, a <u>decrease</u> as great as 200 seats will not change the optimal solution. This is indicated by the slack value of 200 for constraint 5.

f) Based on the dual prices for constraints 3 and 4, the objective function value (total cost) will decrease (remember, we're minimizing) by $5.50 (2.00 + 3.50) for each unit increase in CPI's production capacity in quarters 1 and 2. We can conclude that a 100-unit capacity increase will reduce the total cost by $550 <u>if</u> the 100% rule has not been violated. It has not. (For constraint 3 the percent of allowed increase is 50% (100/200) and for constraint 4 the percent of allowed increase is 33%, for a total of 83%.)

ANSWERED PROBLEMS

PROBLEM 7

Regal Investments has just received instructions from a client to invest in two stocks, one an airline stock, the other an insurance stock. The total maximum appreciation in stock value over the next year is to be maximized subject to the following restrictions: (1) the total investment shall not exceed $100,000., (2) at most $40,000 is to be invested in the insurance stock, and (3) quarterly dividends must total at least $2,600.

The airline stock is currently selling for $40 per share and its quarterly dividend is $1 per share. The insurance stock is currently selling for $50 per share and the quarterly dividend is $1.50 per share. Regal's analysts predict that over the next year the airline stock will increase $2 per share and the insurance stock will increase $3 per share.

The Management Scientist provided the following solution output:

OBJECTIVE FUNCTION VALUE = 5400.000

VARIABLE	VALUE	REDUCED COST
X1	1500.000	0.000
X2	800.000	0.000

CONSTRAINT	SLACK/SURPLUS	DUAL PRICES
1	0.000	0.050
2	0.000	0.010
3	100.000	0.000

OBJECTIVE COEFFICIENT RANGES

VARIABLE	LOWER LIMIT	CURRENT VALUE	UPPER LIMIT
X1	0.000	2.000	2.400
X2	2.500	3.000	NO UPPER LIMIT

RIGHT HAND SIDE RANGES

CONSTRAINT	LOWER LIMIT	CURRENT VALUE	UPPER LIMIT
1	96000.000	100000.000	NO UPPER LIMIT
2	20000.000	40000.000	100000.000
3	NO LOWER LIMIT	2600.000	2700.000

a) How should the client's money be invested to satisfy his restrictions?

b) Suppose Regal's estimate of the airline stock's appreciation is in error. Within what limits must the actual appreciation lie for the answer in (a) to remain optimal?

PROBLEM 8

A company produces two products made from aluminum and copper. The table below gives the unit requirements, the unit production man-hours required, the unit profit and the availability of the resources (in tons).

	Aluminum	Copper	Man-hours	Unit Profit
Product 1	1	0	2	50
Product 2	1	1	3	60
Available	10	6	24	

The Management Scientist provided the following solution output:

OBJECTIVE FUNCTION VALUE = 540.000

VARIABLE	VALUE	REDUCED COST
X1	6.000	0.000
X2	4.000	0.000

CONSTRAINT	SLACK/SURPLUS	DUAL PRICES
1	0.000	30.000
2	2.000	0.000
3	0.000	10.000

OBJECTIVE COEFFICIENT RANGES

VARIABLE	LOWER LIMIT	CURRENT VALUE	UPPER LIMIT
X1	40.000	50.000	60.000
X2	50.000	60.000	75.000

RIGHT HAND SIDE RANGES

CONSTRAINT	LOWER LIMIT	CURRENT VALUE	UPPER LIMIT
1	9.000	10.000	12.000
2	4.000	6.000	NO UPPER LIMIT
3	20.000	24.000	26.000

a) What is the optimal production schedule?

b) Within what range for the profit on product 2 will the solution in (a) remain optimal? What is the optimal profit when $c_2 = 70$?

c) Suppose that simultaneously the unit profits on x_1 and x_2 changed from 50 to 55 and 60 to 65 respectively. Would the optimal solution change?

d) Explain the meaning of the "DUAL PRICES" column. Given the optimal solution, why should the dual price for copper be 0?

e) What is the increase in the value of the objective function for an extra unit of aluminum?

f) Man-hours were not figured into the unit profit as it must pay three workers for eight hours of work regardless of the number of man-hours used. What is the dual price for man-hours? Interpret.

g) On the other hand, aluminum and copper are resources that are ordered as needed. The unit profit coefficients were determined by: (selling price per unit) - (cost of the resources per unit). The 10 units of aluminum cost the company $100. What is the most the company should be willing to pay for extra aluminum?

PROBLEM 9

A small company produces only two sizes of frames for stereo receivers: standard size and slim-line. The accounting department has provided the following analysis of the unit profit:

	Standard	Slim-Line
Selling Price	$6.00	$4.25
Raw Materials	$0.75	$0.50
	(1.5 units @ .50/unit)	(1 unit @ .50/unit)
Packaging	$0.25	$0.25
Labor*	0.40 hours	0.25 hours
Profit (excluding labor costs)	$5.00	$3.50

• Labor is considered a fixed cost as it is performed by salaried workers at the plant.

There are 350 units of the raw material and 300 packing boxes available daily. (Both products utilize the same packing boxes.) At most 10 workers (at 8 hrs./day) will be assigned to this project.

The Management Scientist provided the following output:

OBJECTIVE FUNCTION VALUE = 1100.000

VARIABLE	VALUE	REDUCED COST
X1	33.333	0.000
X2	266.667	0.000

CONSTRAINT	SLACK/SURPLUS	DUAL PRICES
1	33.333	0.000
2	0.000	1.000
3	0.000	10.000

OBJECTIVE COEFFICIENT RANGES

VARIABLE	LOWER LIMIT	CURRENT VALUE	UPPER LIMIT
X1	3.500	5.000	5.600
X2	3.125	3.500	5.000

RIGHT HAND SIDE RANGES

CONSTRAINT	LOWER LIMIT	CURRENT VALUE	UPPER LIMIT
1	316.667	350.000	NO UPPER LIMIT
2	200.000	300.000	320.000
3	75.000	80.000	90.000

a) What is the optimal daily production plan?

b) What is the maximum profit for standard models that will keep the same optimal solution as (a)?

c) What is the new optimal solution and optimal profit if an additional worker (8 additional hours) is assigned to the project? (Hint: The output states the current values for the right-hand sides of the constraints. Compare them with the resource data provided in the problem description to determine the constraint that corresponds with each resource.)

PROBLEM 10

Consider Problem 9 further.

a) Suppose c_1 was changed from 5 to 5.5. Would the optimal solution change?

b) Suppose c_2 was changed from 3.5 to 4. Would the optimal solution change?

c) Suppose simultaneously c_1 changed to 5.5 and c_2 changed to 4. Would the optimal solution change?

d) What is the dual price for man-hours? Interpret.

e) What is the dual price for the packaging? Interpret.

f) Suppose simultaneously the amount of material available increased from 350 to 500, the number of boxes available increased from 300 to 310 and the number of man-hours increased from 80 to 84. What conclusion can be drawn regarding the dual prices?

Note: If the range of optimality for an objective function coefficient (or the range of feasibility for a right-hand side) involved in a simultaneous change is unlimited in the direction of the change, the change to this coefficient (or constant) is of no concern.

PROBLEM 11

A client of an investment firm has $10,000 available for investment. He has instructed that his money be invested in three stocks so that no more than $5,000 is invested in any one stock but at least $1,000 is invested in each stock. He has further instructed the firm to use its current data and invest in a manner that maximizes his expected overall gain during a one-year period.

The stocks, the current price per share, and the firm's projected stock price a year from now are summarized in the following table.

Stock	Current Price	Projected Price 1 Year Hence
James Industries	$25	$35
QM Inc.	$50	$60
Delicious Candy Co.	$100	$125

This problem was formulated as follows:

x_1 = number of shares of James Industries to purchase,
x_2 = number of shares of QM Inc. to purchase, and
x_3 = number of shares of Delicious Candy Co. to purchase.

$$\text{MAX} \quad 10x_1 + 10x_2 + 25x_3$$

$$
\begin{array}{llll}
\text{s.t.} & 25x_1 + 50x_2 + 100x_3 \leq 10000 & (\$ \text{ available}) \\
& 25x_1 \leq 5000 & (\text{max. } \$ \text{ stock 1}) \\
& 50x_2 \leq 5000 & (\text{max. } \$ \text{ stock 2}) \\
& 100x_3 \leq 5000 & (\text{max. } \$ \text{ stock 3}) \\
& 25x_1 \geq 1000 & (\text{min. } \$ \text{ stock 1}) \\
& 50x_2 \geq 1000 & (\text{min. } \$ \text{ stock 2}) \\
& 100x_3 \geq 1000 & (\text{min. } \$ \text{ stock 3}) \\
& x_1, x_2, x_3 \geq 0
\end{array}
$$

*** Use the computer output on the next page to help answer the following questions. ***

a) What is the optimal solution including the optimal value of the objective function?

b) How should the dual price for constraint 6 be interpreted?

c) If the client had an additional $1000 available for investing how much would the expected overall one-year gain increase?

d) If the client increased the allowed maximum investment amount to $6000 for just one stock, should it be Delicious Candy (the stock with the greatest gain)? Why?

e) Based on your stock choice in (d) above, how much would the objective function increase?

f) For your stock choice in (d) above, how much could the allowed maximum investment amount be raised before the optimal investment mix might change?

g) If the expected one-year gains on James Industries and QM Inc. each increased by $1.00, would the optimal investment mix change?

The Management Scientist provided the following solution output:

OBJECTIVE FUNCTION VALUE = 3200.000

VARIABLE	VALUE	REDUCED COST
X1	200.000	0.000
X2	20.000	0.000
X3	40.000	0.000

CONSTRAINT	SLACK/SURPLUS	DUAL PRICES
1	0.000	0.250
2	0.000	0.150
3	4000.000	0.000
4	1000.000	0.000
5	4000.000	0.000
6	0.000	-0.050
7	3000.000	0.000

OBJECTIVE COEFFICIENT RANGES

VARIABLE	LOWER LIMIT	CURRENT VALUE	UPPER LIMIT
X1	6.250	10.000	NO UPPER LIMIT
X2	NO LOWER LIMIT	10.000	12.500
X3	20.000	25.000	40.000

RIGHT HAND SIDE RANGES

CONSTRAINT	LOWER LIMIT	CURRENT VALUE	UPPER LIMIT
1	7000.000	10000.000	11000.000
2	4000.000	5000.000	8000.000
3	1000.000	5000.000	NO UPPER LIMIT
4	4000.000	5000.000	NO UPPER LIMIT
5	NO LOWER LIMIT	1000.000	5000.000
6	0.000	1000.000	4000.000
7	NO LOWER LIMIT	1000.000	4000.000

PROBLEM 12

Given the following linear program:

$$\text{MAX} \quad 6x_1 + 5x_2$$

$$\text{s.t.} \quad x_1 + x_2 \leq 6$$

$$2x_1 + x_2 \leq 8$$

$$x_1 \quad\quad \leq 3$$

$$x_1, x_2 \geq 0$$

a) Solve graphically for the optimal solution.

b) Calculate the range of optimality for both c_1 and c_2.

c) What is the new optimal point when c_2 exceeds the upper limit determined in (a)?

d) Determine and interpret the dual price for iron (resource of second constraint).

e) For what values of zinc, the third resource, will its dual price be 0?

PROBLEM 13

The Asia Import Company (AIC) has 600 cu. ft. of excess cargo space on its ships and has decided to import two new items: jade figurines and linen placemats. Each container of jade figurines is 4 cu. ft. and will net a profit of $80 per container. Each container of linen placemats is 2 cu. ft. and will realize a profit of $60 per container. AIC expects no more than 140 containers of jade figurines available on any trip.

Additionally, AIC wishes to use no more than 480 man-hours for loading, storing, and processing the items through customs. The normal estimate is that a container requires 2 man-hours. However, because of special agricultural restrictions, an extra 2 man-hours can be expected for the linen products.

a) Using the graphical method, determine the number of containers of each item that should be shipped.

b) What is the range of profit on jade containers for which the solution in (a) remains optimal?

c) Determine the value of: (1) an extra man-hour; (2) an extra cubic foot of cargo space; and, (3) the availability of an extra jade container.

PROBLEM 14

Tom manages Leisure Time Motors, a dealership selling minivans and large travel trailers. He is trying to decide how to allocate 90,000 square feet of outside display space to his two products. The products differ in terms of required display space, monthly upkeep, and generated monthly profit as summarized below on a per-unit basis:

	Space Requirement	Monthly Upkeep	Monthly Profit
Minivan	300 sq. ft.	2.0 man-hours	$3200
Trailer	500	3.2	4500

Leisure Motors has three yard men, each working a 150-hour month, keeping the minivans and trailers clean. Tom feels he needs a minimum of 50 minivans on display. The manufacturer of his trailers requires that he display at least 75 trailers.

a) Graphically solve for the numbers of minivans and trailers on display that will maximize Leisure Time's profit.

b) Calculate the range of optimality for both c_1 and c_2.

c) Determine the dual price for yard men, the resource of the second constraint. Interpret.

PROBLEM 15

Harvey owns a Harley motorcycle and a Hauler pickup. The Harley gets an average of 45 miles per gallon (mpg) using 93 octane gasoline that sells for $1.35 per gallon. The Hauler averages 26 mpg using 89 octane that sells for $1.17 per gallon.

The Harley requires 15 hours of maintenance work per 5000 miles ridden. The Hauler requires 10 hours of maintenance per 5000 miles. Harvey does his own maintenance work, but he cannot devote more than 100 hours annually to the task.

Harvey predicts he will have to travel 45,000 miles in the upcoming year. He would like to ride his Harley a minimum of 5,000 miles annually in order to stay in practice.

a) How should Harvey divide his mileage among his Harley and Hauler so that his annual fuel expense is minimized.

b) What is the value of an additional hour of Harvey's time per year for maintenance?

c) By how much will Harvey's annual fuel expense increase for each mile that he travels in excess of 45,000?

TRUE/FALSE

____ 16. Any change to an objective function coefficient of a variable which is positive in the optimal solution will change the optimal value of the objective function.

____ 17. The dual price for labor hours is $25. The profit coefficients c_1 and c_2 take into account a $10 per hour labor cost. Then the maximum value of an overtime hour is $35.

____ 18. Ranges of optimality or feasibility are calculated for a single change only, and they assume no other coefficients in the problem have been changed.

____ 19. Regarding the 100 percent rule, it is possible for the optimal solution to <u>not</u> change even though changes in the objective function coefficients exceed 100 percent.

____ 20. If the range of feasibility for b_1 is between 16 and 37, then if $b_1 = 22$, the optimal solution will not change from the original optimal solution.

____ 21. The 100 percent rule can be applied to changes in both objective function coefficients and right-hand sides at the same time.

____ 22. Relevant costs should be reflected in the objective function, but sunk costs should not.

____ 23. Degeneracy occurs when the dual price equal zero for one of the binding constraints.

____ 24. For any constraint, either its slack/surplus value must be zero or its dual price must be zero.

____ 25. For any decision variable, either its value must be zero or its reduced cost must be zero.

____ 26. If the dual price for the right-hand side of a ≤ constraint is zero, there is no upper limit on its range of feasibility.

____ 27. A ≤ constraint cannot have a negative dual price, regardless of whether it is a maximization or minimization problem.

____ 28. Slack corresponds to ≤ constraints.

____ 29. The Management Scientist can only be used to solve linear programs in two variables.

____ 30. Dual prices are only valid within the range of feasibility.

CHAPTER 4

Linear Programming Applications

KEY CONCEPTS

CONCEPT	ILLUSTRATED PROBLEMS	ANSWERED PROBLEMS
Programming Applications:		
Blending	1,4	15
Equipment Acquisition	2	11,16
Multiperiod Planning	3	12
Product Mix	4	13,14,15
Staff Scheduling	5	21
Portfolio Selection	6	17
Data Envelopment Analysis	7	20
Media Selection	8	18
Transportation	9	19
Revenue Management	10	

┌──────────────┐
│   **REVIEW**   │
└──────────────┘

1. <u>Linear programming applications</u> include problems in production, marketing, finance, and numerous other business-related areas.

2. To develop a <u>good formulation</u>, one should strive to understand the problem thoroughly. Then one should: (1) define the decision variables (the inputs over which you have direct control); (2) define the objective (the goal that you wish to maximize or minimize); and, (3) define the constraints (the restrictions that deter you from even better values for the objective function.) Frequently it is advisable to write the objective function and constraints in English first before translating them into mathematical notation.

3. <u>Computer packages</u>, such as *The Management Scientist* or *Microsoft Excel* may be used to solve linear programming problems giving the optimal solution and appropriate sensitivity analyses.

4. <u>Data Envelopment Analysis (DEA)</u> is an application of linear programming used to determine the relative operating efficiency of units with the same goals and objectives (e.g. banks, schools, company divisions, etc.)

5. DEA creates a fictitious composite unit made up of an optimal weighted average (W_1, W_2, etc.) of existing units. Then an individual unit, k, can be compared by determining E, the fraction of this unit's input resources required by the "optimal" composite unit.

6. The DEA model is given by:

   MIN E

   S.T. Weighted outputs $\geq$ Unit k's output . . . for each measured output

   Weighted inputs $\leq E$ (Unit k's input) . . . for each measured input

   The sum of the weights = 1

   E, weights ≥ 0

7. In DEA, if the optimal value of E is less than 1, unit k is less efficient than the composite unit and can be judged relatively inefficient. If $E = 1$, there is no evidence that unit k is inefficient, but one cannot conclude that unit k is absolutely efficient.

8. <u>Revenue management</u> involves the managing of short-term demand for a fixed perishable inventory in order to maximixe the revenue potential for an organization.

ILLUSTRATED PROBLEMS

NOTE: Students often confuse a constraint for the objective in a problem. If there is a limit imposed on an entity, it probably represents a constraint. (We are solving for the objective function's limit.)

NOTE: A common dilemma is whether to use "=" or an inequality sign ($\leq$ or $\geq$) in a constraint. The use of "=" when not necessary might result in an infeasible problem. Quite often, if you are choosing between "$\leq$" and "=", "$\leq$" will do no harm if you are maximizing ("$\geq$" if you are minimizing); equality is likely to be achieved if it is possible. Of course, using "$\leq$" when you should be using "$\geq$" is very harmful!

PROBLEM 1

Frederick's Feed Company receives four raw grains from which it blends its dry pet food. The pet food advertises that each 8-ounce can meets the minimum daily requirements for vitamin C, protein and iron. The cost of each raw grain as well as the vitamin C, protein, and iron units per pound of each grain are summarized below.

Grain	Vitamin C Units/lb	Protein Units/lb	Iron Units/lb	Cost/lb
1	9	12	0	.75
2	16	10	14	.90
3	8	10	15	.80
4	10	8	7	.70

Frederick's is interested in producing the 8-ounce mixture at minimum cost while meeting the minimum daily requirements of 6 units of vitamin C, 5 units of protein, and 5 units of iron.

a) Formulate this problem as a linear program.

b) Solve for the optimal solution using a program such as *The Management Scientist*.

c) If the mixture costs 5.4 cents to can and Frederick's puts a 50% markup on the package to its retailers, how much will it charge its retailers for an 8-ounce can?

SOLUTION 1

a) Define the decision variables

x_j = the pounds of grain j (j = 1,2,3,4) used in the 8-ounce mixture

Define the objective function

Minimize the total cost for an 8-ounce mixture:
Min $.75x_1 + .90x_2 + .80x_3 + .70x_4$

Define the constraints

The total weight of the mixture ($x_1 + x_2 + x_3 + x_4$) is 8-ounces (.5 pounds):
(1) $x_1 + x_2 + x_3 + x_4 = .5$

Total amount of Vitamin C in the mixture is at least 6 units:
(2) $9x_1 + 16x_2 + 8x_3 + 10x_4 \geq 6$

Total amount of protein in the mixture is at least 5 units:
(3) $12x_1 + 10x_2 + 10x_3 + 8x_4 \geq 5$

Total amount of iron in the mixture is at least 5 units:
(4) $14x_2 + 15x_3 + 7x_4 \geq 5$

Nonnegativity of variables: $x_j \geq 0$ for all j

b) When solved by *The Management Scientist* the following output was generated:

OBJECTIVE FUNCTION VALUE = 0.406

VARIABLE	VALUE	REDUCED COSTS
X1	0.099	0.000
X2	0.213	0.000
X3	0.088	0.000
X4	0.099	0.000

Thus, the optimal blend is about .10 lb. of grain 1, .21 lb. of grain 2, .09 lb. of grain 3, and .10 lb. of grain 4.

c) The mixture costs Frederick's 40.6 cents. With 5.4 cents for packaging, this brings their costs to 46 cents. A 50% markup would mean it would charge retailers 1.5(46) = 69 cents per can.

PROBLEM 2

Floataway Tours has $400,000 that may be used to purchase new rental boats for hire during the summer. The boats can be purchased from two different manufacturers. Pertinent data concerning the boats are summarized below:

Boat	Manufacturer	Cost	Maximum Seating	Expected Daily Profit
Speedhawk	Sleekboat	$6000	3	$ 70
Silverbird	Sleekboat	$7000	5	$ 80
Catman	Racer	$5000	2	$ 50
Classy	Racer	$9000	6	$110

Floataway Tours would like to purchase at least 50 boats and would like to purchase the same number from Sleekboat as from Racer to maintain goodwill. Also, Floataway Tours wishes to have a total seating capacity of at least 200.

a) Formulate this as an LP.

b) Solve the problem using a spreadsheet.

SOLUTION 2

a) The problem can be formulated as follows:

Define the decision variables

x_1 = number of Speedhawks ordered
x_2 = number of Silverbirds ordered
x_3 = number of Catmans ordered
x_4 = number of Classys ordered

Define the objective function

Maximize total expected daily profit:

Maximize (Expected daily profit per unit)(Number of units)
MAX $70x_1 + 80x_2 + 50x_3 + 110x_4$

Define the constraints

Spend no more than $400,000:

(1) $6000x_1 + 7000x_2 + 5000x_3 + 9000x_4 \leq 400,000$

Purchase at least 50 boats:

(2) $x_1 + x_2 + x_3 + x_4 \geq 50$

Number of boats from Sleekboat equals number of boats from Racer:

(3) $x_1 + x_2 = x_3 + x_4$ or $x_1 + x_2 - x_3 - x_4 = 0$

Capacity at least 200:

(4) $3x_1 + 5x_2 + 2x_3 + 6x_4 \geq 200$

Nonnegativity of variables:

$x_j \geq 0$, for $j = 1,2,3,4$

b) Refer to Chapters 2 and 3 of this study guide for coverage of the steps to follow in setting up and using a spreadsheet to solve an LP.

Spreadsheet showing the optimal solution

	A	B	C	D	E	F
1			LHS Coefficients			
2	Constraints	X1	X2	X3	X4	RHS
3	#1	6	7	5	9	420
4	#2	1	1	1	1	50
5	#3	1	1	-1	-1	0
6	#4	3	5	2	6	200
7	Obj.Func.	70	80	50	110	
8						
9			Decision Variable Values			
10			X1	X2	X3	X4
11	No. of Boats		28	0	0	28
12						
13	Maximum Total Profit		5040			
14						
15	Constraints		LHS		RHS	
16	Spending Max.		420.0	<=	420	
17	Min. # Boats		56.0	>=	50	
18	Equal Sourcing		0.0	=	0	
19	Min. Seating		252.0	>=	200	

Sensitivity Report

Adjustable Cells						
Cell	Name	Final Value	Reduced Cost	Objective Coefficient	Allowable Increase	Allowable Decrease
$D$12	X1	28	0	70	45	1.875
$E$12	X2	0	-2	80	2	1E+30
$F$12	X3	0	-12	50	12	1E+30
$G$12	X4	28	0	110	1E+30	16.36363636

Constraints						
Cell	Name	Final Value	Shadow Price	Constraint R.H. Side	Allowable Increase	Allowable Decrease
$E$17	#1	420.0	12.0	420	1E+30	45
$E$18	#2	56.0	0.0	50	6	1E+30
$E$19	#3	0.0	-2.0	0	70	30
$E$20	#4	252.0	0.0	200	52	1E+30

PROBLEM 3

Burt Wheeler is the production manager of Wheeler Wheels, Inc. Burt has just received orders for 1,000 standard wheels and 1,250 deluxe wheels next month and for 800 standard and 1,500 deluxe wheels the following month. All orders are to be filled.

The cost of producing standard wheels is $10 and deluxe wheels is $16. Overtime rates are 50% higher. There are 1,000 hours of regular time and 500 hours of overtime available each month. The cost of storing one wheel from one month to the next is $2.

Develop a two-month production schedule for Burt of standard and deluxe wheel production if it takes .5 hour to make a standard wheel and .6 hour to make a deluxe wheel and solve using a program such as *The Management Scientist*.

SOLUTION 3

Define the decision variables

We must determine how many of each type of wheel to make each month during regular time and overtime; also we must determine the number of each wheel stored from one month to the next. Thus we want to determine the production levels, x_j, as follows:

	Month 1		Month 2	
	Reg. Time	Overtime	Reg. Time	Overtime
Standard	x_1	x_2	x_5	x_6
Deluxe	x_3	x_4	x_7	x_8

Also let,

y_1 = number of standard wheels stored from month 1 to month 2.
y_2 = number of deluxe wheels stored from month 1 to month 2.

Define the objective function

Minimize total production and storage costs:
Min (cost per wheel)(number of wheels produced) + $2y_1$ + $2y_2$
Min $10x_1 + 15x_2 + 16x_3 + 24x_4 + 10x_5 + 15x_6 + 16x_7 + 24x_8 + 2y_1 + 2y_2$

Define the constraints

Standard Wheel Production Month 1 = (Requirements) + (Amount Stored)

(1) $x_1 + x_2 = 1,000 + y_1$ $\longrightarrow$ $x_1 + x_2 - y_1 = 1,000$

Deluxe Wheel Production Month 1 = (Requirements) + (Amount Stored)

(2) $x_3 + x_4 = 1,250 + y_2$ $\longrightarrow$ $x_3 + x_4 - y_2 = 1,250$

Standard Wheel Production Month 2 = (Requirements) - (Amount Stored)

(3) $x_5 + x_6 = 800 - y_1$ $\longrightarrow$ $x_5 + x_6 + y_1 = 800$

Deluxe Wheel Production Month 2 = (Requirements) - (Amount Stored)

(4) $x_7 + x_8 = 1,500 - y_2$ $\longrightarrow$ $x_7 + x_8 + y_2 = 1,500$

Regular Hours Used Month 1 $\leq$ Regular Hours Available Month 1:

(5) $.5x_1 + .6x_3 \leq 1000$

Overtime Hours Used Month 1 $\leq$ Overtime Hours Available Month 1:

(6) $.5x_2 + .6x_4 \leq 500$

Regular Hours Used Month 2 $\leq$ Regular Hours Available Month 2:

(7) $.5x_5 + .6x_7 \leq 1000$

Overtime Hours Used Month 2 $\leq$ Overtime Hours Available Month 2:

(8) $.5x_6 + .6x_8 \leq 500$

Nonnegativity of variables:

$x_j \geq 0, j = 1,,8$ and $y_j \geq 0 \ j = 1,2$

The Management Scientist provided the following solution:

OBJECTIVE FUNCTION VALUE = 67500.000

VARIABLE	VALUE	REDUCED COSTS
X1	500.000	0.000
X2	500.000	0.000
X3	1250.000	0.000
X4	0.000	2.000
X5	200.000	0.000
X6	600.000	0.000
X7	1500.000	0.000
X8	0.000	2.000
Y1	0.000	2.000
Y2	0.000	2.000

Thus, the recommended production schedule is:

	Month 1		Month 2	
	Reg. Time	Overtime	Reg. Time	Overtime
Standard	500	500	200	600
Deluxe	1250	0	1500	0

No wheels are stored and the minimum total cost is $67,500.

PROBLEM 4

Target Shirt Company makes three varieties of shirts: Collegiate, Traditional and European. These shirts are made from different combinations of cotton and polyester.

The cost per yard of unblended cotton is $5 and for unblended polyester is $4. Target can receive up to 4,000 yards of raw cotton and 3,000 yards of raw polyester fabric weekly. The table below pertinent data concerning the manufacture of the shirts.

Shirt	Total Yards	Fabric Requirements	Weekly Contracts	Weekly Demand	Selling Price
Collegiate	1.00	At least 50% cotton	500	600	$14.00
Traditional	1.20	No more than 20% polyester	650	850	$15.00
European	.90	As much as 80% polyester	280	675	$18.00

Formulate and solve a linear program that would give a manufacturing policy for Target Shirt Company.

SOLUTION 4

Define the decision variables

Not only must we decide how many shirts to make and how much fabric to purchase, we also need to decide how much of each fabric is blended into each shirt.

Let, s_j = the total number of shirt style j produced
         f_i = the number of yards of material i purchased
       x_{ij} = yards of fabric i blended into shirt style j

where i = 1 (cotton) or 2 (polyester) and
          j = 1 (collegiate), 2(traditional), or 3 (European)

Define the objective function

Maximize the overall profit.
To determine the profit function, subtract the cost of purchasing the fabric from the shirt sales revenue. Thus the objective function is:

MAX $14s_1 + 15s_2 + 18s_3 - 5f_1 - 4f_2$

Define the constraints

Definition of Total Number of Shirts of Each Style

Total Number of each style =
(Total Yardage used in making the style) / (Yardage/Shirt)

(1) Collegiate: $s_1 = (x_{11} + x_{21}) / 1 \longrightarrow s_1 - x_{11} - x_{21} = 0$

(2) Traditional: $s_2 = (x_{12} + x_{22}) / 1.2 \longrightarrow 1.2s_2 - x_{12} - x_{22} = 0$

(3) European: $s_3 = (x_{13} + x_{23}) / .9 \longrightarrow .95s_3 - x_{13} - x_{23} = 0$

Definition of Total Yardage of Materials

(4) Cotton: $f_1 = x_{11} + x_{12} + x_{13} \longrightarrow f_1 - x_{11} - x_{12} - x_{13} = 0$

(5) Polyester: $f_2 = x_{21} + x_{22} + x_{23} \longrightarrow f_2 - x_{21} - x_{22} - x_{23} = 0$

Weekly Availability of the Resources

(6) Cotton: $f_1 \leq 4000$

(7) Polyester: $f_2 \leq 3000$

Meet Weekly Contracts

(8) Collegiate: $s_1 \geq 500$

(9) Traditional: $s_2 \geq 650$

(10) European: $s_3 \geq 280$

Do Not Exceed Weekly Demand

(11) Collegiate: $s_1 \leq 600$

(12) Traditional: $s_2 \leq 850$

(13) European: $s_3 \leq 675$

Fabric Requirements

Collegiate At Least 50% Cotton:
(Total yds. of Cotton in Colleg. Shirts) $\geq$ [(.5(1.00) yds./shirt)(number of colleg. shirts)]

(14) $x_{11} \geq .5s_1 \longrightarrow x_{11} - .5s_1 \geq 0$

Traditional At Most 20% Polyester:
(Total yds. Polyester in Tradit. Shirts) $\leq$ [.2(1.20) yds./shirt)(number of tradit. shirts)]

(15) $x_{22} \leq .24s_2 \longrightarrow x_{22} - .24s_2 \leq 0$

European At Most 80% Polyester:
(Total yds. Polyester in Europ. Shirts) $\leq$ [.8(.90) yds./shirt)(number of Europ. shirts)]

(16) $x_{23} \leq .72s_3 \longrightarrow x_{23} - .72s_3 \leq 0$

Nonnegativity of variables

$s_j, f_i, x_{ij} \geq 0$ for $i = 1,2$ and $j = 1,2,3$.

The *Management Scientist* provided the following solution:

OBJECTIVE FUNCTION VALUE =   23152.500

VARIABLE	VALUE	REDUCED COSTS
X11	300.000	0.000
X12	816.000	0.000
X13	121.500	0.000
X21	300.000	0.000
X22	204.000	0.000
X23	486.000	0.000
S1	600.000	0.000
S2	850.000	0.000
S3	675.000	0.000
F1	1237.500	0.000
F2	990.000	0.000

PROBLEM 5

The Accounting Department at Lenny's Restaurant requires information on the total number of employees it will be hiring for its new restaurant located across the street from a major university. Lenny's has broken down its requirements into 4-hour periods.

Time Period	Employees Required
7am-11am	12
11am- 3pm	20
3pm- 7pm	18
7pm-11pm	22
11pm- 7am	Closed

Staffing is done by hiring personnel for eight-hour shifts commencing at 7am, 11am, and 3pm. Also, there are enough students willing to work the before and after school eight-hour shift covering 7am-11am and 7pm-11pm.

a) Formulate and solve for the minimum number of personnel the Accounting Department at Lenny's should expect for this new restaurant.

b) Based on the solution in part (a), determine the timing and amount of overstaffing that will occur.

SOLUTION 5

a) Define the decision variables

x_1 = number of workers hired for 7am-3pm shift
x_2 = number of workers hired for 11am-7pm shift
x_3 = number of workers hired for 3pm-11pm shift
x_4 = number of workers hired for 7am-11am and 7pm-11pm shift

<u>Define the objective function</u>

Minimize the total number of personnel hired:

Min $x_1 + x_2 + x_3 + x_4$

<u>Define the constraints</u>

Total personnel working during each 4-hour period must be greater than or equal to the number of employees required:

(1) $x_1 + x_4 \geq 12$
(2) $x_1 + x_2 \geq 20$
(3) $x_2 + x_3 \geq 18$
(4) $x_3 + x_4 \geq 22$

Nonnegativity of variables:

$x_j \geq 0$ for $j = 1,2,3,4$

The Management Scientist provided the following solution:

OBJECTIVE FUNCTION VALUE = 42.000

VARIABLE	VALUE	REDUCED COSTS
X1	20.000	0.000
X2	0.000	0.000
X3	18.000	0.000
X4	4.000	0.000

CONSTRAINT	SLACK/SURPLUS	DUAL PRICES
1	12.000	0.000
2	0.000	-1.000
3	0.000	0.000
4	0.000	-1.000

There are alternate optimal solutions, one of which is: $x_1 = 12$, $x_2 = 8$, $x_3 = 22$, $x_4 = 0$.

b) The timing and amount of overstaffing corresponds to the constraint surplus values shown in the computer output. The only four-hour period that is overstaffed is 7am-11am. It is overstaffed by 12 workers. Thus, the total man-hours of overstaffing is 4(12) = 48.

PROBLEM 6

Winslow Savings has $20 million available for investment. It wishes to invest over the next four months in such a way that it will maximize the total interest earned over the four month period as well as have at least $10 million available at the start of the fifth month for a high rise building venture in which it will be participating.

For the time being, Winslow wishes to invest only in 2-month government bonds (earning 2% over the 2-month period) and 3-month construction loans (earning 6% over the 3-month period). Each of these is available each month for investment. Funds not invested in these two investments are liquid and earn 3/4 of 1% per month when invested locally.

Formulate and solve a linear program that will help Winslow Savings determine how to invest over the next four months if at no time does it wish to have more than $8 million in either government bonds or construction loans.

SOLUTION 6

<u>Define the decision variables</u>

g_j = amount of <u>new</u> investment in government bonds in month j
c_j = amount of <u>new</u> investment in construction loans in month j
l_j = amount invested locally in month j, where j = 1,2,3,4

<u>Define the objective function</u>

Maximize the total interest earned over the four-month period:

MAX (interest rate on investment)(amount invested)
MAX $.02g_1 + .02g_2 + .02g_3 + .02g_4 + .06c_1 + .06c_2 + .06c_3 + .06c_4$
$+ .0075l_1 + .0075l_2 + .0075l_3 + .0075l_4$

<u>Define the constraints</u>

Month 1's total investment amount limited to $20 million:

(1) $g_1 + c_1 + l_1 = 20,000,000$

Month 2's total investment amount limited to principle and interest invested locally in Month 1:

(2) $g_2 + c_2 + l_2 = 1.0075l_1$ or $g_2 + c_2 - 1.0075l_1 + l_2 = 0$

Month 3's total investment amount limited to principle and interest invested in government bonds in Month 1 and locally invested in Month 2:

(3) $g_3 + c_3 + l_3 = 1.02g_1 + 1.0075l_2$ or $- 1.02g_1 + g_3 + c_3 - 1.0075l_2 + l_3 = 0$

Month 4's total investment amount limited to principle and interest invested in construction loans in Month 1, goverment bonds in Month 2, and locally invested in Month 3:

(4) $g_4 + c_4 + l_4 = 1.06c_1 + 1.02g_2 + 1.0075l_3$
$or - 1.02g_2 + g_4 - 1.06c_1 + c_4 - 1.0075l_3 + l_4 = 0$

$10 million must be available at start of Month 5:

(5) $1.06c_2 + 1.02g_3 + 1.0075l_4 \geq 10,000,000$

No more than $8 million in government bonds at any time:

(6) $g_1 \leq 8,000,000$
(7) $g_1 + g_2 \leq 8,000,000$
(8) $g_2 + g_3 \leq 8,000,000$
(9) $g_3 + g_4 \leq 8,000,000$

No more than $8 million in construction loans at any time:

(10) $c_1 \leq 8,000,000$
(11) $c_1 + c_2 \leq 8,000,000$
(12) $c_1 + c_2 + c_3 \leq 8,000,000$
(13) $c_2 + c_3 + c_4 \leq 8,000,000$

Nonnegativity:

$g_j, c_j, l_j \geq 0$ for $j = 1,2,3,4$

The Management Scientist provided the following solution:

OBJECTIVE FUNCTION VALUE =   1429213.7987

VARIABLE	VALUE	REDUCED COSTS
G1	8000000.0000	0.0000
G2	0.0000	0.0000
G3	5108613.9228	0.0000
G4	2891386.0772	0.0000
C1	8000000.0000	0.0000
C2	0.0000	0.0453
C3	0.0000	0.0076
C4	8000000.0000	0.0000
I1	4000000.0000	0.0000
I2	4030000.0000	0.0000
I3	7111611.0772	0.0000
I4	4753562.0831	0.0000

PROBLEM 7

The Langley County School District is trying to determine the relative efficiency of its three high schools. In particular, it wants to evaluate Roosevelt High School.

The district is evaluating performances on SAT scores, the number of seniors finishing high school, and the number of students who enter college as a function of the number of teachers teaching senior classes, the prorated budget for senior instruction, and the number of students in the senior class.

Input	Roosevelt	Lincoln	Washington
Senior Faculty	37	25	23
Budget ($100,000's)	6.4	5.0	4.7
Senior Enrollments	850	700	600

Output	Roosevelt	Lincoln	Washington
Average SAT Score	800	830	900
High School Graduates	450	500	400
College Admissions	140	250	370

Solve the linear program using *The Management Scientist*. Comment on the relative efficiency of Roosevelt High School for each of the output measures.

SOLUTION 7

a) The goal of data envelopment analysis is to compare Roosevelt High School to a fictitious <u>composite</u> high school developed by determining an optimal set of weights of all high schools in the Langley School District.

This set of weights minimizes the fraction, E, of Roosevelt High School's input resources required by the composite school.

If $E = 1$, the composite high school requires the same input resources as Roosevelt's and there would be no evidence that Roosevelt High School is inefficient. If $E < 1$, Roosevelt High School is operating inefficiently with its given inputs and further study of Roosevelt should be made to determine the reasons for this inefficiency.

<u>Define the decision variables</u>

> E = Fraction of Roosevelt High School's input resources required by the composite high school
> w_1 = Weight applied to Roosevelt High School's input/output resources by the composite high school
> w_2 = Weight applied to Lincoln High School's input/output resources by the composite high school
> w_3 = Weight applied to Washington High School's input/output resources by the composite high school

<u>Define the objective</u>

> Minimize the fraction of Roosevelt High School's input resources required by the composite high school:
>
> Min E

<u>Define the constraints</u>

> Sum of the Weights is 1:
>
> (1) $w_1 + w_2 + w_3 = 1$

Output Constraints:

Since $w_1 = 1$ is possible, each output of the composite school must be at least as great as that of Roosevelt:

(2) $800w_1 + 830w_2 + 900w_3 \geq 800$ (SAT Scores)
(3) $450w_1 + 500w_2 + 400w_3 \geq 450$ (Graduates)
(4) $140w_1 + 250w_2 + 370w_3 \geq 140$ (College Admissions)

Input Constraints:

The input resources available to the composite school is a fractional multiple, E, of the resources available to Roosevelt. Since the composite high school cannot use more input than that available to it, the input constraints are:

(5) $37w_1 + 25w_2 + 23w_3 \leq 37E$ (Faculty)
(6) $6.4w_1 + 5.0w_2 + 4.7w_3 \leq 6.4E$ (Budget)
(7) $850w_1 + 700w_2 + 600w_3 \leq 850E$ (Seniors)

Nonnegativity of variables:

$E, w_1, w_2, w_3 \geq 0$

b) The problem was solved by *The Management Scientist* and the output is below.

OBJECTIVE FUNCTION VALUE =   0.765

VARIABLE	VALUE	REDUCED COSTS
E	0.765	0.000
W1	0.000	0.235
W2	0.500	0.000
W3	0.500	0.000

CONSTRAINT	SLACK/SURPLUS	DUAL PRICES
1	0.000	-0.235
2	65.000	0.000
3	0.000	-0.001
4	170.000	0.000
5	4.294	0.000
6	0.044	0.000
7	0.000	0.001

    The output shows that the composite high school is made up of equal weights of Lincoln High School and Washington High School. Roosevelt High School is 76.5% efficient compared to this composite high school when measured by college admissions (because of the 0 slack on this constraint (#4)). It is less than 76.5% efficient when using measures of SAT scores and high school graduates (there is positive slack in constraints 2 and 3.)

PROBLEM 8

The SMM Company, which is manufacturing a new instant salad machine, has $280,000 to spend on advertising. The product is only to be test marketed initially in the Dallas area. The money is to be spent on an advertising blitz during one weekend (Friday, Saturday, and Sunday) in January, and SMM is limited to television advertising.

The company has three options available: day time advertising, evening news advertising and the Super Bowl. Even though the Super Bowl is a national telecast, the Dallas Cowboys will be playing in it, and hence, the viewing audience will be especially large in the Dallas area. A mixture of one-minute TV spots is desired. The table below gives pertinent data:

	Cost Per Ad	Estimated New Audience Reached With Each Ad
Day Time	$5,000	3000
Evening News	$7,000	4000
Super Bowl	$100,000	75,000

SMM has decided to take out at least one ad in each option. Further, there are only two Super Bowl ad spots available. There are 10 day time spots and 6 evening news spots available daily. SMM wants to have at least 5 ads per day, but spend no more than $50,000 on Friday and no more than $75,000 on Saturday. Formulate and solve a linear program to help SMM decide how the company should advertise over the weekend.

SOLUTION 8

Define the decision variables

x_1 = the number of day ads on Friday
x_2 = the number of day ads on Saturday
x_3 = the number of day ads on Sunday
x_4 = the number of evening ads on Friday
x_5 = the number of evening ads on Saturday
x_6 = the number of evening ads on Sunday
x_7 = the number of Super Bowl ads

Define the objective function

Maximize the estimated total new audience reached:

MAX (new audience reached per ad of each type)(number of ads of each type)
MAX $3000x_1 + 3000x_2 + 3000x_3 + 4000x_4 + 4000x_5 + 4000x_6 + 75000x_7$

Define the constraints

Take out at least one ad of each type:

(1) $x_1 + x_2 + x_3 \geq 1$
(2) $x_4 + x_5 + x_6 \geq 1$
(3) $x_7 \geq 1$

10 daytime spots available:

(4) $x_1 \leq 10$
(5) $x_2 \leq 10$
(6) $x_3 \leq 10$

6 evening news spots available:

(7) $x_4 \leq 6$
(8) $x_5 \leq 6$
(9) $x_6 \leq 6$

Only two Super Bowl ad spots available:

(10) $x_7 \leq 2$

At least 5 ads per day:

(11) $x_1 + x_4 \geq 5$
(12) $x_2 + x_5 \geq 5$
(13) $x_3 + x_6 + x_7 \geq 5$

Spend no more than $50,000 on Friday:

(14) $5000x_1 + 7000x_4 \leq 50000$

Spend no more than $75,000 on Saturday:

(15) $5000x_2 + 7000x_5 \leq 75000$

Spend no more than $350,000 in total:

(16) $5000x_1 + 5000x_2 + 5000x_3 + 7000x_4 + 7000x_5 + 7000x_6 + 100000x_7 \leq 280000$

Nonnegativity:

$x_j \geq 0 \quad j = 1,...,7$

The Management Scientist provided the following solution:

OBJECTIVE FUNCTION VALUE =   197800.000

VARIABLE	VALUE	REDUCED COSTS
X1	7.600	0.000
X2	5.000	0.000
X3	2.000	0.000
X4	0.000	0.000
X5	0.000	0.000
X6	1.000	0.000
X7	2.000	0.000

PROBLEM 9

The Navy has 9,000 pounds of material in Albany, Georgia which it wishes to ship to three installations: San Diego, Norfolk, and Pensacola. They require 4,000, 2,500, and 2,500 pounds respectively. The following gives the shipping costs per pound for truck, railroad, and airplane transit.

	Destination		
Mode	San Diego	Norfolk	Pensacola
Truck	$12	$ 6	$ 5
Railroad	20	11	9
Airplane	30	26	28

Government regulations require equal distribution of shipping among the three carriers. Formulate and solve a linear program to determine the shipping arrangements (mode, destination, and quantity) that will minimize the total shipping cost.

SOLUTION 9

Define the decision variables

We want to determine the pounds of material, x_{ij}, to be shipped by mode i to destination j. The following table summarizes the decision variables:

	Destination		
Mode	San Diego	Norfolk	Pensacola
Truck	x_{11}	x_{12}	x_{13}
Railroad	x_{21}	x_{22}	x_{23}
Airplane	x_{31}	x_{32}	x_{33}

Define the objective function

Minimize the total shipping cost:

MIN (shipping cost per pound for each mode/destination pairing)
      X (number of pounds shipped by mode/destination pairing):
MIN $12x_{11} + 6x_{12} + 5x_{13} + 20x_{21} + 11x_{22} + 9x_{23} + 30x_{31} + 26x_{32} + 28x_{33}$

Define the constraints

Equal use of transportation modes:

(1) $x_{11} + x_{12} + x_{13} = 3000$
(2) $x_{21} + x_{22} + x_{23} = 3000$
(3) $x_{31} + x_{32} + x_{33} = 3000$

Destination material requirements:

(4) $x_{11} + x_{21} + x_{31} = 4000$
(5) $x_{12} + x_{22} + x_{32} = 2500$
(6) $x_{13} + x_{23} + x_{33} = 2500$

Nonnegativity of variables:

$x_{ij} \geq 0$, $i = 1,2,3$ and $j = 1,2,3$

The Management Scientist provided the following solution:

OBJECTIVE FUNCTION VALUE = 142000.000

VARIABLE	VALUE	REDUCED COSTS
X11	1000.000	0.000
X12	2000.000	0.000
X13	0.000	1.000
X21	0.000	3.000
X22	500.000	0.000
X23	2500.000	0.000
X31	3000.000	0.000
X32	0.000	2.000
X33	0.000	6.000

To summarize: San Diego will receive 1000 lbs. by truck and 3000 lbs. by airplane; Norfolk will receive 2000 lbs. by truck and 500 lbs. by railroad; Pensacola will receive 2500 lbs. by railroad. The total shipping cost will be $142,000.

> NOTE: This problem is referred to as a transportation problem. Transportation problems have a mathematical structure that has enabled management scientists to develop efficient, specialized procedures for solving them. These procedures are covered in Chapter 7.

PROBLEM 10

LeapFrog Airways provides passenger service for Indianapolis, Baltimore, Memphis, Austin, and Tampa. LeapFrog has two WB828 airplanes, one based in Indianapolis and the other in Baltimore. Each morning the Indianapolis based plane flies to Austin with a stopover in Memphis, and the Baltimore based plane flies to Tampa with a stopover in Memphis. Both planes have a coach section with a 120-seat capacity.

LeapFrog uses two fare classes: a discount fare D class and a full fare F class. Leapfrog's products, each referred to as an origin destination itinerary fare (ODIF), are listed below with their fares and forecasted demand.

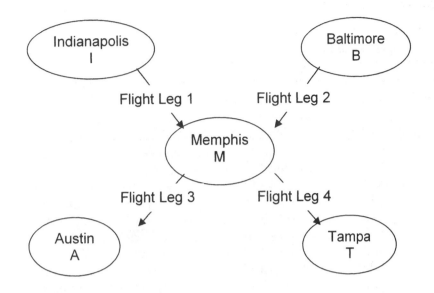

ODIF	Origin	Destination	Fare Class	ODIF Code	Fare	Demand
1	Indianapolis	Memphis	D	IMD	175	44
2	Indianapolis	Austin	D	IAD	275	25
3	Indianapolis	Tampa	D	ITD	285	40
4	Indianapolis	Memphis	F	IMF	395	15
5	Indianapolis	Austin	F	IAF	425	10
6	Indianapolis	Tampa	F	ITF	475	8
7	Baltimore	Memphis	D	BMD	185	26
8	Baltimore	Austin	D	BAD	315	50
9	Baltimore	Tampa	D	BTD	290	42
10	Baltimore	Memphis	F	BMF	385	12
11	Baltimore	Austin	F	BAF	525	16
12	Baltimore	Tampa	F	BTF	490	9
13	Memphis	Austin	D	MAD	190	58
14	Memphis	Tampa	D	MTD	180	48
15	Memphis	Austin	F	MAF	310	14
16	Memphis	Tampa	F	MTF	295	11

Develop a linear programming model for LeapFrog's problem situation and determine how many seats LeapFrog should allocate to each ODIF.

SOLUTION 9

Define the decision variables

There are 16 variables, one for each ODIF.

IMD = number of seats allocated to Indianapolis-Memphis-Discount class
IAD = number of seats allocated to Indianapolis-Austin-Discount class
ITD = number of seats allocated to Indianapolis-Tampa-Discount class
IMF = number of seats allocated to Indianapolis-Memphis-Full Fare class
IAF = number of seats allocated to Indianapolis-Austin-Full Fare class
ITF = number of seats allocated to Indianapolis-Tampa-Full Fare class
BMD = number of seats allocated to Baltimore-Memphis-Discount class
BAD = number of seats allocated to Baltimore-Austin-Discount class
BTD = number of seats allocated to Baltimore-Tampa-Discount class
BMF = number of seats allocated to Baltimore-Memphis-Full Fare class
BAF = number of seats allocated to Baltimore-Austin-Full Fare class
BTF = number of seats allocated to Baltimore-Tampa-Full Fare class
MAD = number of seats allocated to Memphis-Austin-Discount class
MTD = number of seats allocated to Memphis-Tampa-Discount class
MAF = number of seats allocated to Memphis-Austin-Full Fare class
MTF = number of seats allocated to Memphis-Tampa-Full Fare class

Define the objective function

Maximize total revenue:

Max (fare per seat for each ODIF) x (number of seats allocated to the ODIF).
Max 175IMD + 275IAD + 285ITD + 395IMF + 425IAF + 475ITF
　　　+ 185BMD + 315BAD + 290BTD + 385BMF + 525BAF
　　　　+ 490BTF + 190MAD + 180MTD + 310MAF + 295MTF

Define the constraints

There are 4 capacity constraints, one for each flight leg:

(1) IMD + IAD + ITD + IMF + IAF + ITF ≤ 120 (Indianapolis-Memphis leg)
(2) BMD + BAD + BTD + BMF + BAF + BTF ≤ 120 (Baltimore-Memphis leg)
(3) IAD + IAF + BAD + BAF + MAD + MAF ≤ 120 (Memphis-Austin leg)
(4) ITD + ITF + BTD + BTF + MTD + MTF ≤ 120 (Memphis-Tampa leg)

There are 16 demand constraints, one for each ODIF:

(5)	IMD ≤ 44	(11)	BMD ≤ 26	(17)	MAD ≤ 58
(6)	IAD ≤ 25	(12)	BAD ≤ 50	(18)	MTD ≤ 48
(7)	ITD ≤ 40	(13)	BTD ≤ 42	(19)	MAF ≤ 14
(8)	IMF ≤ 15	(14)	BMF ≤ 12	(20)	MTF ≤ 11
(9)	IAF ≤ 10	(15)	BAF ≤ 16		
(10)	ITF ≤ 8	(16)	BTF ≤ 9		

Nonnegativity constraints:　　IMD, IAD, ITD, ..., MTF ≥ 0

The problem was solved by *The Management Scientist* and the output is below.

OBJECTIVE FUNCTION VALUE =　94735.000

VARIABLE	VALUE	REDUCED COSTS
IMD	44.000	0.000
IAD	3.000	0.000
ITD	40.000	0.000
IMF	15.000	0.000
IAF	10.000	0.000
ITF	8.000	0.000
BMD	26.000	0.000
BAD	50.000	0.000
BTD	7.000	0.000
BMF	12.000	0.000
BAF	16.000	0.000
BTF	9.000	0.000
MAD	27.000	0.000
MTD	45.000	0.000
MAF	14.000	0.000
MTF	11.000	0.000

CONSTRAINT	SLACK/SURPLUS	DUAL PRICES
1	0.000	85.000
2	0.000	110.000
3	0.000	190.000
4	0.000	180.000
5	0.000	90.000
6	22.000	0.000
7	0.000	20.000
8	0.000	310.000
9	0.000	150.000
10	0.000	210.000
11	0.000	75.000
12	0.000	15.000
13	35.000	0.000
14	0.000	275.000
15	0.000	225.000
16	0.000	200.000
17	31.000	0.000
18	3.000	0.000
19	0.000	120.000
20	0.000	115.000

PROBLEM 11

Fullerton Trucking has $550,000 allocated to purchase at least 40 trucks. It will buy both Japanese and American-built trucks, but keeping with its "BUY-AMERICAN" image, it wishes to purchase at least twice as many American as Japanese-built trucks. Fullerton has narrowed its choices to three American and three Japanese models. It wishes to purchase at least 20 two-seat models. The following table summarizes the data for each model:

Truck	Country	Cost	Capacity	Seats
Hauler	U.S.	$20,000	2.00 tons	2
Mauler	U.S.	$16,000	1.00	2
Bruiser	U.S.	$13,000	.75	1
Econotruck	Japan	$ 9,000	.50	1
T-150	Japan	$12,000	.75	2
Maxitruck	Japan	$17,000	1.50	2

a) Formulate and solve this problem as a linear program with the objective of maximizing the overall trucking capacity.

b) Why is linear programming not the technically correct procedure to use to solve this problem?

PROBLEM 12

National Wing Company (NWC) is gearing up for the new B-48 contract. Currently NWC has 100 equally qualified workers. Over the next three months NWC has made the following commitments for wing production:

Month	Contract
May	20
June	24
July	30

Each worker can either be placed in production or can train new recruits. A new recruit can be trained to be an apprentice in one month. The next month, he, himself, becomes a qualified worker (after two months from the start of training). Each trainer can train two recruits. The production rate and salary per employee is estimated below.

Employee	Production Rate (Wings/Month)	Salary Per Month
Production	.6	$3,000
Trainer	.3	$3,300
Apprentice	.4	$2,600
Recruit	.05	$2,200

At the end of July, NWC wishes to have no recruits or apprentices but have at least 140 full-time workers. Formulate and solve a linear program for NWC to accomplish this at minimum total cost.

PROBLEM 13

Triumph Trumpet Company makes two styles each of both trumpets and cornets: deluxe and professional models. Its unit profit on deluxe trumpets is $80 and on deluxe cornets is $60. The professional models realize twice the profit of the deluxe models.

Trumpets and cornets are made basically from two mixtures of two different brass alloys. The amount of each alloy (in pounds) required to produce each type of horn is summarized in the following table along with the monthly availability to Triumph of the alloys.

	Trumpets		Cornets		Monthly
	Deluxe	Pro.	Deluxe	Pro.	Availability
Alloy 1	2	1.5	1.5	1	2000
Alloy 2	1	1.5	1	1.5	1800

Triumph must fulfill contracts calling for at least 500 deluxe trumpets and 300 deluxe cornets monthly. Monthly demand for professional trumpets is not expected to exceed 150 and for professional cornets is not expected to exceed 100. Production set-ups are such that the company will produce exactly twice as many trumpets as cornets.

Formulate and solve this problem as a linear program.

PROBLEM 14

Millard Construction is contemplating building a planned community with the help of federal funds. These funds are to be distributed only if Millard meets federal standards for low cost housing. There are three types of units -- houses, town-houses, and high rise condominiums. There are three styles each of the houses and town-houses -- low cost, standard, and deluxe. The high rise condominiums will have standard and deluxe models.

The amount of total ground space (including allowances for parking and green belts) is given in the following table:

	Ground Area (Sq. Ft.)		
	Low Cost	Standard	Deluxe
Houses	1800	2200	3000
Town-Houses	740	1600	2230
Condominiums	X	1000	1500

The profit to Millard per unit is summarized in the following table:

	Profit ($1000's)		
	Low Cost	Standard	Deluxe
Houses	5	12	25
Town-Houses	4	10	18
Condominiums	X	9	16

Millard has 300,000 square feet for construction. To make the project "work", Millard wants houses and town-houses each to occupy between 25% and 40% of the total area while condominiums only need to occupy 10% to 25% of the total area.

The federal government requires that at least 25% of the total units built in the complex be low cost units.

a) Formulate this problem as a linear program.

b) Solve for the optimal solution using a computer package such as *The Management Scientist.*

c) Why is linear programming not the technically correct formulation procedure for this problem?

PROBLEM 15

Delicious Candy Company manufactures three types of candy bars-- Chompers, Smerks, and Delicious Chocolate. All three candies come in a one-ounce size while Delicious Chocolate also comes in a one-pound mini-bar bag.

The basic ingredients used are chocolate, peanuts, and caramel. Delicious Chocolate is all chocolate, while Chompers consists of chocolate and caramel, and Smerks consists of chocolate, caramel and peanuts. Chompers' recipe allows for the amount of caramel to be anywhere between 18% and 28% of the candy bar's weight with chocolate making up the rest. Smerks' recipe calls for an equal amount of caramel and peanuts, with chocolate making up between 20% and 40% of the bar's weight.

For each one-ounce bar, labor and packaging costs $.012, while labor and packaging for the one-pound bag costs $.039. The company has production facilities for making up to 20,000 one-ounce bars and up to 1000 one-pound bags daily.

Delicious has contracts to produce at least 3000 one-ounce bars of each type of candy daily. Also, the difference between the number of Chompers and the number of Smerks produced must be less than 10% of the total number of Chompers and Smerks made. The present prices for chocolate, caramel, and peanuts are $1.60, $.95, and $1.40 per pound respectively. The company has contracts which will supply it with at least 1,000 pounds of chocolate, exactly 350 pounds of caramel, and at most 500 pounds of peanuts daily.

The company currently sells Chompers one-ounce bars for $.14, Smerks one-ounce bars for $.16, Delicious Chocolate one- ounce bars for $.15, and Delicious Chocolate one-pound bags for $2.30. Formulate and solve a linear program that would determine the optimal daily production schedule and ingredients required. (HINT: Variables must be established for each product type and the amount of each ingredient in each product.)

PROBLEM 16

WeBuild Construction must decide how many small bulldozers to purchase or lease for the coming year. Bulldozers may be purchased for $40,000 each and their salvage value at the end of a year is $20,000. WeBuild can also lease bulldozers for $8,000 per year payable in advance.

WeBuild has $1,000,000 available in its budget for purchase and/or lease of bulldozers. Any monies not invested in purchasing or leasing bulldozers will be invested at 8%.

There are 60 projects each requiring four bulldozers throughout the year. Because of timing and reliability, each new bulldozer will be available for eight projects, whereas each leased bulldozer will be available for five projects.

Formulate and solve for the number of bulldozers WeBuild should purchase and lease to minimize its total annual cost.

PROBLEM 17

John Sweeney is an investment advisor who is attempting to construct an "optimal portfolio" for a client who has $400,000 cash to invest. There are ten different investments, falling into four broad categories that John and his client have identified as potential candidates for this portfolio.

The following table lists the investments and their important characteristics. Note that Unidyde Equities (stocks) and Unidyde Debt (bonds) are two separate investments, whereas First General REIT is a single investment that is considered both an equities and a real estate investment.

Category	Investment	Exp. Annual After Tax Return	Liquidity Factor	Risk Factor
Equities	Unidyde Corporation	15.0%	100	60
	Col. Must. Restaurants	17.0%	100	70
	First General REIT	17.5%	100	75
Debt	Metropolitan Electric	11.8%	95	20
	Unidyde Corporation	12.2%	92	30
	Lemonville Transit	12.0%	79	22
Real Estate	Fairview Apartment Partn.	22.0%	0	50
	First General REIT		(See above)	
Money	T-Bill Account	9.6%	80	0
	Money Market Fund	10.5%	100	10
	All Saver's Certificate	12.6%	0	0

Formulate and solve a linear program to accomplish John's objective as an investment advisor which is to construct a portfolio that maximizes his client's total expected after-tax return over the next year, subject to a number of constraints placed upon him by the client for the portfolio:

1. Its (weighted) average liquidity factor must be at least 65.
2. The (weighted) average risk factor must be no greater than 55.
3. At most, $60,000 is to be invested in Unidyde stocks or bonds.
4. No more than 40% of the investment can be in any one category except the money category.
5. No more than 20% of the investment can be in any one investment except the money market fund.
6. At least $1,000 must be invested in the money market fund.
7. The maximum investment in All Saver's Certificates is $15,000.
8. The minimum investment desired for debt is $90,000.
9. At least $10,000 must be placed in a T-Bill account.

PROBLEM 18

BP Cola must decide how much money to allocate for new soda and traditional soda advertising over the coming year. The advertising budget is $10,000,000.

Because BP wants to push its new sodas, at least one-half of the advertising budget is to be devoted to new soda advertising. However, at least $2,000,000 is to be spent on its traditional sodas. BP estimates that each dollar spent on traditional sodas will translate into 100 cans sold, whereas, because of the harder sell needed for new products, each dollar spent on new sodas will translate into 50 cans sold. To attract new customers BP has lowered its profit margin on new sodas to 2 cents per can as compared to 4 cents per can for traditional sodas.

How should BP allocate its advertising budget if it wants to maximize its profits while selling at least 750 million cans?

PROBLEM 19

Maybury Public School System has three high schools to serve a territory divided into five districts. The capacity of each high school, the student population in each district, and the distance (in miles) between each school and the center of each district are listed in the table below:

| District | High School | | | Student |
	McHale	McCallum	McBride	Population
Northeast	1.5	2.5	0.5	700
Southeast	4	1.5	3	1100
Southwest	2.5	3	3.5	900
Northwest	0.5	4	1.5	600
Central	1	2	1	800
Capacity	1500	1800	1100	

Formulate and solve a linear program to determine the school-student assignment that minimizes the total student-miles traveled per day.

PROBLEM 20

The June Company is a department store chain serving three states in the South: Georgia, Alabama, and Mississippi. Recently management has been concerned about the relative efficiency of its Alabama store.

The June Company tabulates the monthly gross sales of home appliances, clothing, home entertainment, and all other divisions and measures these outputs against inputs of store size, number of sales personnel for the store, and the population service area for each store (defined as the number of adults over 16 living within a 35 mile radius of the store.)

The tables below give the average monthly values for each of the inputs and outputs based on last year's data. Based on last year's data, use data envelopment analysis to formulate and solve a linear program to help June Company determine the relative efficiency of its Alabama store.

	Georgia	Alabama	Mississippi
Inputs			
Store Size (1000's sq. ft.)	25	24	18
Sales Personnel	250	210	180
Service Area Population (1000's)	600	750	375
Outputs: Average Monthly Sales ($mil.)			
Appliances	1.2	0.8	0.6
Clothing	2.2	1.4	1.5
Home Entertainment	1.6	1.5	1.6
All Others	2.7	2.0	2.1

PROBLEM 21

Niteton Power and Light Company (NPLC) wants to develop an efficient work schedule for its full- and part-time customer service clerks. The number of clerks needed to provide adequate service during each hour the office is open on a weekday is given below:

Hour	8-9am	9-10	10-11	11-12pm	12-1	1-2	2-3	3-4	4-5	5-6
Clerks	5	4	6	8	10	9	7	4	7	5

A full-time clerk works 3 hours, has a 1-hour break, and then works another 3 hours. Part-time clerks work 4 consecutive hours. Full-timers get paid for their break. All clerks start work on the hour.

NPLC's office manager insists that at least one full-time clerk be on duty during all open hours and that a minimum of four full-time clerks are on the payroll. A full-time clerk costs NPLC $9.00 per hour, and a part-timer costs $6.50 per hour.

Formulate and solve a linear program that will provide a schedule that will meet NPLC's customer service needs at a minimum labor cost. (Hint: there are 4 different full-time shifts and 7 different part-time shifts.)

TRUE/FALSE

____ 22. Sunk costs should be viewed as relevant costs when developing the objective function for a linear programming model.

____ 23. Double-subscript notation for decision variables should be avoided unless the number of decision variables exceeds nine.

____ 24. Generating the data for large-scale LP models can be more time consuming than either the formulation of the model or the development of the computer solution.

____ 25. Using minutes as the unit of measurement on the left-hand side of a constraint and using hours on the right-hand side is acceptable since both are a measure of time.

____ 26. No real-world problem, when correctly formulated, has an unbounded solution.

____ 27. A company makes two products from steel; one requires 2 tons of steel and the other requires 3 tons. There are 100 tons of steel available daily. A constraint on daily production could be written as: $2x_1 + 3x_2 \leq 100$.

____ 28. Compared to the problems in the textbook, real-world problems generally require more variables and constraints.

____ 29. For the multiperiod production scheduling problem in the textbook, period n - 1's ending inventory variable was also used as period n's beginning inventory variable.

____ 30. To reliably answer "what-if" questions about the effects of changes in the parameters used in an LP formulation, one should always resolve the problem.

____ 31. If a real-world problem is correctly formulated, it is impossible to have alternative optimal solutions.

____ 32. A company makes two products, A and B. A sells for $100 and B sells for $90. The variable production costs are $30 per unit for A and $25 for B. The company's objective could be written as: MAX $190x_1 - 55x_2$.

____ 33. The primary limitation of linear programming's applicability is the requirement that all decision variables be nonnegative.

____ 34. If an LP problem is not correctly formulated, the computer will indicate it is infeasible when trying to solve it.

____ 35. The wide-spread use of linear programming is due largely to the fact that the nature of most business functions is linear.

____ 36. A decision maker would be wise to not deviate from the optimal solution found by an LP model because it is the best solution.

CHAPTER 5

Linear Programming: The Simplex Method

KEY CONCEPTS

CONCEPT	ILLUSTRATED PROBLEMS	ANSWERED PROBLEMS
Problem Formulation	7	14
Standard Form	1,2,4,5,7	8,9,10,14,15
Tableau Form	1,2,3,4,5,6,7	8,9,10,12,13,14,15
Artificial Variables	2,4,5,7	9,10,11,15
Minimization Problems	2,4	8,10
Infeasibility	5	11
Unboundedness	5	11
Alternate Optimal Solutions	6,7	14
Degeneracy		13

REVIEW

1. The <u>simplex method</u> is an algebraic method for solving linear programs. (See description of algorithm on the next page.) The more recently developed Karmarkar method holds promise of solving large linear programs even more quickly than the simplex method.

2. The steps leading to the simplex method are as follows:

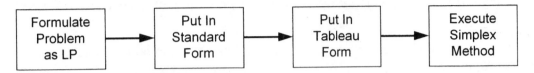

3. Putting an LP formulation into <u>standard form</u> involves adding slack and/or subtracting surplus variables, as discussed in Chapter 2.

4. The <u>simplex tableau</u> is a convenient means for performing the calculations required by the simplex method.

5. A set of equations is in <u>tableau form</u> if for each equation: (1) its right hand side (RHS) is non-negative, and (2) there is a <u>basic variable</u>. A basic variable for an equation is a variable whose coefficient in the equation is +1 and whose coefficient in all other equations of the problem is 0.

6. If a constraint is formulated with a <u>negative right-hand side</u>, multiply it by -1 before adding slack, surplus, or artificial variables.

7. To generate an initial tableau form, <u>artificial variables</u> must be added to all constraints which do not have a basic variable. These normally include "greater than or equal to" constraints and "equal to" constraints.

8. <u>Artificial variables</u> are given an objective function coefficient of $-M$ in maximization problems ($+M$ in minimization problems), where M is an extremely large number. Once an artificial variable becomes non-basic, it may be eliminated from further consideration by dropping its column.

9. If the problem has a <u>minimization objective</u>, multiply the objective function by -1 before using the simplex method.

10. A <u>basic feasible solution</u> for a problem in tableau form is found by setting the basic variables equal to the right hand side values of the equations and the other variables (the <u>non-basic variables</u>) to 0.

11. Basic feasible solutions are equivalent to <u>extreme points</u>, and for a linear program with an optimal solution, a basic feasible solution must be optimal.

12. The $c_j - z_j$ row of a simplex tableau represents the amount the objective function will increase per unit increase in the corresponding column variable. For a maximization problem, the most positive entry in this row determines the <u>entering variable</u>.

13. A <u>tableau's right-hand side</u> gives the values of the current basic variables.

14. The minimizing ratio between the right hand side values and positive numbers in the column of the entering variable determines which current basic variable will reach zero first as the entering variable is increased. This variable is called the <u>leaving variable</u>.

15. <u>Infeasibility</u> is detected in the simplex method when an artificial variable remains positive in the final tableau.

16. A linear program has an <u>unbounded solution</u> if all entries in an entering column are non-positive.

17. A linear program has <u>alternate optimal solutions</u> if the final tableau has a $c_j - z_j$ value equal to 0 for a non-basic variable.

18. A <u>degenerate solution</u> to a linear program is one in which at least one of the basic variables equals 0. This can occur at formulation or if there is a tie for the minimizing value in the ratio test to determine the leaving variable.

SETTING UP INITIAL SIMPLEX TABLEAU

Step 1: If the problem is a minimization problem, multiply the objective function by -1.

Step 2: If the problem formulation contains any constraints with negative right-hand sides, multiply each constraint by -1.

Step 3: Add a slack variable to each $\leq$ constraint.

Step 4: Subtract a surplus variable and add an artificial variable to each $\geq$ constraint.

Step 5: Add an artificial variable to each = constraint.

Step 6: Set each slack and surplus variable's coefficient in the objective function equal to zero.

Step 7: Set each artificial variable's coefficient in the objective function equal to -*M*, where *M* is a very large number.

Step 8: Each slack and artificial variable becomes one of the basic variables in the initial basic feasible solution.

FLOW CHART FOR
SETTING UP INITIAL SIMPLEX TABLEAU

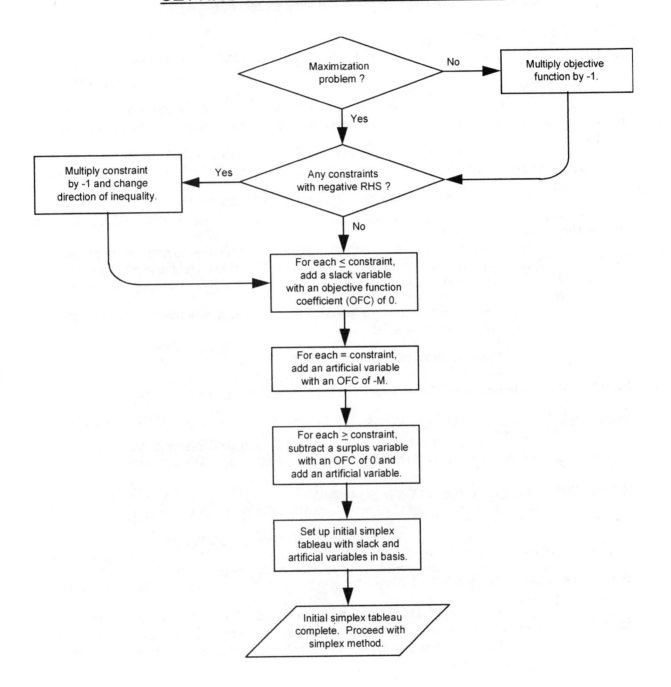

SIMPLEX METHOD

Starting with the initial simplex tableau:

Step 1: Determine the entering variable.
Identify the variable with the most positive value in the $c_j - z_j$ row.

Step 2: Determine the leaving variable.
For each positive number in the entering column, compute the ratio of the right-hand side values divided by these entering column values.

If there are no positive values in the entering column, STOP; the problem is unbounded.

Otherwise, select the variable with the minimal ratio.

Step 3: Generate the next tableau.
(The entering column is called the pivot column and the leaving row is called the pivot row. The entry which is at the intersection of the pivot row and the pivot column is called the pivot element.)

(a) Divide the pivot row by the pivot element to get a new row. We designate this new row as (row *).

(b) Replace each non-pivot row i with:
[new row i] = [current row i] - [(a_{ij}) x (row *)],
where a_{ij} is the value in entering column j of row i

Step 4: Calculate the z_j row for the new tableau.
For each column j, multiply the objective function coefficients of the basic variables by the corresponding numbers in column j and sum them.

Step 5: Calculate the $c_j - z_j$ row for the new tableau.
For each column j, subtract the z_j row from the c_j row in the tableau.

If none of the values in the $c_j - z_j$ row are positive, GO TO STEP 1.

If there is an artificial variable in the basis with a positive value, the problem is infeasible. STOP.

Otherwise, an optimal solution has been found. The current values of the basic variables are optimal. The optimal values of the non-basic variables are all zero. If any non-basic variable's $c_j - z_j$ value is 0, alternate optimal solutions might exist. STOP.

FLOW CHART OF SIMPLEX METHOD

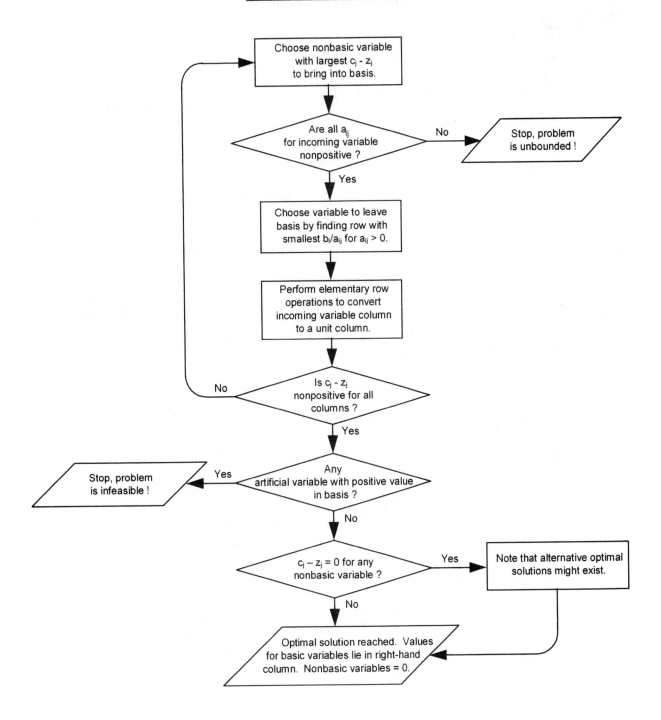

ILLUSTRATED PROBLEMS

PROBLEM 1

Solve the following problem by the simplex method:

$$\text{MAX} \quad 12x_1 + 18x_2 + 10x_3$$

$$\text{s.t.} \quad 2x_1 + 3x_2 + 4x_3 \leq 50$$

$$x_1 - x_2 - x_3 \geq 0$$

$$x_2 - 1.5x_3 \geq 0$$

$$x_1, x_2, x_3 \geq 0$$

SOLUTION 1

The first step is to write the problem in standard form. We can avoid introducing artificial variables to the second and third constraints by multiplying each by -1 (making them $\leq$ constraints). Thus, slack variables s_1, s_2, and s_3 are added to the three constraints, respectively.

$$\text{MAX} \quad 12x_1 + 18x_2 + 10x_3$$

$$\text{s.t.} \quad 2x_1 + 3x_2 + 4x_3 + s_1 \qquad = 50$$

$$-x_1 + x_2 + x_3 \quad + s_2 \quad = 0$$

$$-x_2 + 1.5x_3 \qquad + s_3 = 0$$

$$x_1, x_2, x_3, s_1, s_2, s_3 \geq 0$$

This gives the following first tableau: (on next page)

		x_1	x_2	x_3	s_1	s_2	s_3		
Basis	c_B	12	18	10	0	0	0		
s_1	0	2	3	4	1	0	0	50	
s_2	0	-1	1	1	0	1	0	0	(* row)
s_3	0	0	-1	1.5	0	0	1	0	
z_j		0	0	0	0	0	0	0	
$c_j - z_j$		12	18	10	0	0	0		

Iteration 1

(Step 1) The most positive $c_j - z_j = 18$. Thus x_2 is the entering variable.

(Step 2) Take the ratio between the right hand side and positive numbers in the x_2 column:

$$50/3 \ = 16 \ 2/3$$
$$0/1 \ = 0 \ \longleftarrow \quad \text{minimum}$$

s_2 is the leaving variable and the 1 is the pivot element.

(Step 3) Divide the second row by 1, the pivot element. Call the "new" (in this case, unchanged) row the "* row".
Subtract 3 x (* row) from row 1.
Subtract -1 x (* row) from row 3.
New rows 1, 2, and 3 are shown in the tableau below.

(Step 4) The new z_j row values are obtained by multiplying the c_B column by each column, element by element and summing.
For example, $z_1 = 5(0) + -1(18) + -1(0) = -18$.

(Step 5) The new $c_j\text{-}z_j$ row values are obtained by subtracting z_j value in a column from the c_j value in the same column.
For example, $c_1\text{-}z_1 = 12 - (-18) = 30$.

Thus, the tableau on the next page is derived with x_2 replacing s_2 as a basic variable.

Basis	c_B	x_1 12	x_2 18	x_3 10	s_1 0	s_2 0	s_3 0		
s_1	0	5	0	1	1	-3	0	50	(* row)
x_2	18	-1	1	1	0	1	0	0	
s_3	0	-1	0	2.5	0	1	1	0	
z_j		-18	18	18	0	18	0	0	
$c_j - z_j$		30	0	-8	0	-18	0		

Iteration 2

(Step 1) The most positive $c_j - z_j = 30$. x_1 is the entering variable.

(Step 2) Take the ratio between the right hand side and positive numbers in the x_1 column:

$$10/5 = 2 \longleftarrow \text{minimum}$$

There are no ratios for the second and third rows because their column elements (-1) are negative. Thus, s_1 (corresponding to row 1) is the leaving variable and 5 is the pivot element.

(Step 3) Divide row 1 by 5, the pivot element. (Call this new row 1 the "* row").
Subtract (-1) x (* row) from the second row.
Subtract (-1) x (* row) from the third row.
New rows 1, 2, and 3 are shown in the tableau below.

(Step 4) The new z_j row values are obtained by multiplying the c_B column by each column, element by element and summing.
For example, $z_3 = .2(12) + 1.2(18) + .2(0) = 24$.

(Step 5) The new c_j-z_j row values are obtained by subtracting z_j value in a column from the c_j value in the same column.
For example, c_3-$z_3 = 10 - (24) = -14$.

Thus, the following tableau is derived with x_1 replacing s_1 as a basic variable.

Basis	C_B	x_1 12	x_2 18	x_3 10	s_1 0	s_2 0	s_3 0		
x_1	12	1	0	.2	.2	-.6	0	10	(* row)
x_2	18	0	1	1.2	.2	.4	0	10	
s_3	0	0	0	2.7	.2	.4	1	10	
z_j		12	18	24	6	0	0	300	
$c_j - z_j$		0	0	-14	-6	0	0		

Since there are no positive numbers in the $c_j - z_j$ row, this tableau is optimal. The optimal solution is: $x_1 = 10$; $x_2 = 10$; $x_3 = 0$; $s_1 = 0$; $s_2 = 0$ $s_3 = 10$, and the optimal value of the objective function, $z = 300$.

PROBLEM 2

Solve the following problem by the simplex method:

$$\text{MIN} \quad 8x_1 + 5x_2 + 4x_3$$

$$\text{s. t.} \quad x_1 + x_2 + \qquad \geq 10$$

$$x_2 + x_3 \geq 15$$

$$x_1 + \qquad x_3 \geq 12$$

$$20x_1 + 10x_2 + 15x_3 \leq 300$$

$$x_1, x_2, x_3 \geq 0$$

SOLUTION 2

First, write the problem in standard form. Constraints 1, 2, and 3 each require a surplus variable. Constraint 4 requires a slack variable.

$$\text{MIN} \quad 8x_1 + 5x_2 + 4x_3$$

$$\text{s. t.} \quad x_1 + x_2 - \qquad s_1 \qquad \geq 10$$

$$x_2 + x_3 - s_2 \qquad \geq 15$$

$$x_1 + \qquad x_3 - \qquad s_3 \qquad \geq 12$$

$$20x_1 + 10x_2 + 15x_3 + \qquad s_4 \leq 300$$

$$x_1, x_2, x_3, s_1, s_2, s_3, s_4 \geq 0$$

To put in tableau form, add artificial variables a_1, a_2, and a_3 to the constraints 1, 2, and 3, respectively. Since this is a minimization problem, the a's have objective coefficients of $+M$.

$$\text{MIN} \quad 8x_1 + 5x_2 + 4x_3 \qquad\qquad + Ma_1 + Ma_2 + Ma_3$$

$$
\begin{aligned}
\text{s. t.} \quad x_1 + \; x_2 - \quad\;\; s_1 \qquad\qquad\qquad\qquad &\geq 10 \\
x_2 + \; x_3 - \; s_2 \qquad\qquad\qquad &\geq 15 \\
x_1 + \qquad\; x_3 - \quad\; s_3 \qquad\qquad &\geq 12 \\
20x_1 + 10x_2 + 15x_3 + \qquad\quad s_4 \qquad &\leq 300
\end{aligned}
$$

$$x_1, x_2, x_3, s_1, s_2, s_3, s_4, a_1, a_2, a_3 \geq 0$$

Before beginning the simplex method, the objective function is converted to maximization by multiplying it by -1.

Iteration 1

Basis	c_B	x_1 -8	x_2 -5	x_3 -4	s_1 0	s_2 0	s_3 0	s_4 0	a_1 -M	a_2 -M	a_3 -M	
a_1	-M	1	1	0	-1	0	0	0	1	0	0	10
a_2	-M	0	1	1	0	-1	0	0	0	1	0	15
a_3	-M	1	0	1	0	0	-1	0	0	0	1	12
s_4	0	20	10	15	0	0	0	1	0	0	0	300
z_j		-2M	-2M	-2M	M	M	M	0	-M	-M	-M	-37M
$c_j - z_j$		2M-8	2M-5	2M-4	-M	-M	-M	0	0	0	0	

Iteration 2 (Drop the a_3 column)

Basis	c_B	x_1 -8	x_2 -5	x_3 -4	s_1 0	s_2 0	s_3 0	s_4 0	a_1 -M	a_2 -M	
a_1	-M	1	1	0	-1	0	0	0	1	0	10
a_2	-M	-1	1	0	0	-1	1	0	0	1	3
x_3	-4	1	0	1	0	0	-1	0	0	0	12
s_4	0	5	10	0	0	0	15	1	0	0	120
z_j		-4	-2M	-4	M	M	-M+4	0	-M	-M	-13M -48
$c_j - z_j$		-4	2M-5	0	-M	-M	M-4	0	0	0	

Iteration 3 (Drop the a_2 column)

Basis	c_B	x_1	x_2	x_3	s_1	s_2	s_3	s_4	a_1	
		-8	-5	-4	0	0	0	0	-M	
a_1	-M	2	0	0	-1	1	-1	0	1	7
x_2	-5	-1	1	0	0	-1	1	0	0	3
x_3	-4	1	0	1	0	0	-1	0	0	12
s_4	0	15	0	0	0	10	5	1	0	90
	z_j	-2M+1	-5	-4	M	-M+5	M-1	0	-M	-7M-63
	$c_j - z_j$	2M-9	0	0	-M	M-5	-M+1	0	0	

Iteration 4 (Drop the a_1 column)

Basis	c_B	x_1	x_2	x_3	s_1	s_2	s_3	s_4	
		-8	-5	-4	0	0	0	0	
x_1	-8	1	0	0	-1/2	1/2	-1/2	0	7/2
x_2	-5	0	1	0	-1/2	-1/2	1/2	0	13/2
x_3	-4	0	0	1	1/2	-1/2	-1/2	0	17/2
s_4	0	0	0	0	15/2	5/2	25/2	1	75/2
	z_j	-8	-5	-4	9/2	1/2	7/2	0	-189/2
	$c_j - z_j$	0	0	0	-9/2	-1/2	-7/2	0	

This is the optimal tableau. Thus the optimal solution is: $x_1 = 7/2$; $x_2 = 13/2$; $x_3 = 17/2$; $s_1 = 0$; $s_2 = 0$; $s_3 = 0$; $s_4 = 75/2$. Because we multiplied the objective function by -1, the optimal maximization value of z is 189/2 or 94.5.

PROBLEM 3

At some iteration of the simplex method, the tableau is the following:

Basis	c_B	x_1 10	x_2 6	s_1 0	s_2 0	s_3 0	s_4 0	
x_2	6	0	1	3	0	-2	0	7
s_2	0	0	0	4	1	3	0	8
x_1	10	1	0	-2	0	2	0	16
s_4	0	0	0	0	0	4	1	10
z_j		10	6	-2	0	8	0	202
$c_j - z_j$		0	0	2	0	-8	0	

a) Explain the meaning of each number in the tableau.

b) Note s_1 will be the entering variable. Explain why the ratio test is performed only on positive numbers in the s_1 column.

c) Use the simplex method to solve for the optimal solution.

SOLUTION 3

a) The c_j row gives the gross increase in z per unit increase in the corresponding variable. The z_j row gives the gross decrease in z per unit increase in the corresponding variable. Thus, the $c_j - z_j$ row gives the "net increase" in z per unit increase in the corresponding variable.

The large matrix (the a_{ij}'s) give the amount the basic variable associated with row i will decrease per unit increase in the corresponding variable of column j.

The c_B column gives the objective function coefficients for the basic variables. The numbers on the right hand side give the current values of the basic variables, i.e. $x_2 = 7$, $s_2 = 8$, $x_1 = 16$, $s_4 = 10$. The bottom right number gives the value of $z = 202$.

b) As noted in (a), the a_{ij}'s are the amount of decrease in the basic variable of row i per unit increase in the corresponding variable of column j. Hence, as for every unit s_1 is increased, x_2 decreases by 3, s_2 decreases by 4, and x_1 increases by 2. s_4 will not change as s_1 is increased. From one iteration to the next the variables must stay non-negative. Thus s_1 can increase to 7/3 before x_2 goes to 0 and to 2 (=8/4) before s_2 goes to 0. These are the only limiting factors.

c) (Step 1) The most positive $c_j - z_j$ is 2. s_1 enters.

(Step 2) The ratio test on positive numbers in the s_1 column gives:

$$7/3 = 7/3$$
$$8/4 = 2 \quad \longleftarrow \quad \text{minimum}$$

s_2 leaves.

(Step 3) Divide row 2 by 4 to give a new (* row).
   Subtract 3 x (* row) from row 1.
   Subtract -2 x (* row) from row 3.
   Leave row 4 as it is.

(Steps 4 and 5 are reflected in the tableau below.)

Basis	c_B	x_1 10	x_2 6	s_1 0	s_2 0	s_3 0	s_4 0		
x_2	6	0	1	0	-3/4	-17/4	0	1	
s_1	0	0	0	1	1/4	3/4	0	2	(* row)
x_1	10	1	0	0	1/2	7/2	0	20	
s_4	0	0	0	0	0	4	1	10	
z_j		10	6	0	1/2	19/2	0	206	
$c_j - z_j$		0	0	0	-1/2	-19/2	0		

Since the $c_j - z_j$ row has no positive numbers, this is the optimal tableau and the optimal solution: $x_1 = 20$, $x_2 = 1$, $s_1 = 2$, $s_2 = 0$, $s_3 = 0$, $s_4 = 10$, and $z = 206$.

PROBLEM 4

Given the following minimization problem:

$$\text{MIN} \quad 2x_1 - 3x_2 - 4x_3$$

$$\text{s. t.} \quad x_1 + x_2 + x_3 \le 30$$

$$2x_1 + x_2 + 3x_3 \ge 60$$

$$x_1 - x_2 + 2x_3 = 20$$

$$x_j \ge 0 \quad j = 1,2,3$$

a) Write the problem in standard form. Explain why this is not tableau form.

b) Add artificial variables and amend the objective function appropriately to obtain the first tableau form.

c) Solve the problem by the simplex method.

SOLUTION 4

a)

$$\text{MIN} \quad 2x_1 - 3x_2 - 4x_3$$

$$\text{s. t.} \quad x_1 + x_2 + x_3 + s_1 = 30$$

$$2x_1 + x_2 + 3x_3 \quad -s_2 = 60$$

$$x_1 - x_2 + 2x_3 = 20$$

$$x_j \ge 0 \quad j = 1,2,3; \quad s_j \ge 0 \quad j = 1,2$$

This is not tableau form because the second and third constraints do not have basic variables, i.e. variables whose coefficient in that constraint is +1, and whose coefficient in the other constraints is 0.

b) Add artificial variables a_2 and a_3 to the second and third constraints, respectively. Since this is a minimization problem, the a's objective function coefficients are $+M$.

$$\text{MIN} \quad 2x_1 - 3x_2 - 4x_3 \qquad + Ma_2 + Ma_3$$

$$\text{s. t.} \quad x_1 + x_2 + x_3 + s_1 \qquad = 30$$

$$2x_1 + x_2 + 3x_3 \quad -s_2 + a_2 \qquad = 60$$

$$x_1 - x_2 + 2x_3 \qquad + a_3 = 20$$

$$x_j \ge 0 \quad j = 1,2,3; \quad s_j, a_j \ge 0 \quad j = 1,2$$

c) The objective function is multiplied by -1, so that we can use the maximization algorithm.

<u>Iteration 1</u>

Basis	c_B	x_1 -2	x_2 3	x_3 4	s_1 0	s_2 0	a_2 -M	a_3 -M	
s_1	0	1	1	1	1	0	0	0	30
a_2	-M	2	1	3	0	-1	1	0	60
a_3	-M	1	-1	2	0	0	0	1	20
	z_j	-3M	0	-5M	0	M	-M	-M	-80M
	$c_j - z_j$	3M-2	3	5M+4	0	-M	0	0	

<u>Iteration 2</u> (Drop the a_3 column)

Basis	c_B	x_1 -2	x_2 3	x_3 4	s_1 0	s_2 0	a_2 -M	
s_1	0	1/2	3/2	0	1	0	0	20
a_2	-M	1/2	5/2	0	0	-1	1	30
x_3	4	1/2	-1/2	1	0	0	0	10
	z_j	-(1/2)M + 2	-(5/2)M - 2	4	0	M	-M	-30M + 40
	$c_j - z_j$	(1/2)M - 4	(5/2)M + 5	0	0	-M	0	

<u>Iteration 3</u> (Drop the a_2 column)

Basis	c_B	x_1 -2	x_2 3	x_3 4	s_1 0	s_2 0	
s_1	0	1/5	0	0	1	3/5	2
x_2	3	1/5	1	0	0	-2/5	12
x_3	4	3/5	0	1	0	-1/5	16
	z_j	3	3	4	0	-2	100
	$c_j - z_j$	-5	0	0	0	2	

Iteration 4 (Final tableau)

Basis	c_B	x_1 -2	x_2 3	x_3 4	s_1 0	s_2 0	
s_2	0	1/3	0	0	5/3	1	10/3
x_2	3	1/3	1	0	2/3	0	40/3
x_3	4	2/3	0	1	1/3	0	50/3
	z_j	11/3	3	4	10/3	0	320/3
	$c_j - z_j$	-17/3	0	0	-10/3	0	

The optimal solution is: $x_1 = 0$; $x_2 = 40/3$; $x_3 = 50/3$; $s_1 = 0$; $s_2 = 10/3$. We multiplied the objective function by -1, so the optimal minimization value of $z = -320/3$.

PROBLEM 5

Solve problem #4 (two problems, actually) of Chapter 2 by the simplex method.

SOLUTION 5

First Problem: The standard form is:

MAX $2x_1 + 6x_2$

s. t. $4x_1 + 3x_2 + s_1 \qquad = 12$

$\qquad 2x_1 + x_2 \qquad - s_2 = 8$

$\qquad x_1, x_2, s_1, s_2 \geq 0$

Artificial variable a_2 is added to the second constraint to obtain the first tableau form. (a_2 has an objective function coefficient of $-M$.)

Iteration 1

Basis	c_B	x_1 2	x_2 6	s_1 0	s_2 0	a_2 -M	
s_1	0	4	3	1	0	0	12
a_2	-M	2	1	0	-1	1	8
	z_j	-2M	-M	0	M	-M	-8M
	$c_j - z_j$	2M+2	6+M	0	-M	0	

Iteration 2

Basis	c_B	x_1 2	x_2 6	s_1 0	s_2 0	a_2 -M	
x_1	2	1	3/4	1/4	0	0	3
a_2	-M	0	-1/2	-1/2	-1	1	2
	z_j	2	(1/2)M+3/2	(1/2)M +1/2	M	-M	-2M+6
	$c_j - z_j$	0	-(1/2)M +9/2	-(1/2)M-1/2	-M	0	

This is the last tableau since all $c_j - z_j \leq 0$. But since an artificial variable is still positive, this indicates the problem is <u>infeasible</u>.

<u>Second Problem</u>:   The standard form is:

$$\text{MAX} \quad 3x_1 + 4x_2$$

$$\text{s. t.} \quad x_1 + x_2 - s_1 \quad\quad = 5$$

$$3x_1 + x_2 \quad - s_2 = 8$$

$$x_1, x_2, s_1, s_2 \geq 0$$

Artificial variables are added to both constraints to obtain the initial tableau form.

Iteration 1

Basis	c_B	x_1 3	x_2 4	s_1 0	s_2 0	a_1 -M	a_2 -M	
a_1	-M	1	1	-1	0	1	0	5
a_2	-M	3	1	0	-1	0	1	8
	z_j	-4M	-2M	M	M	-M	-M	-13M
	$c_j - z_j$	4M+3	2M+4	-M	-M	0	0	

Iteration 2 (Drop a_2)

Basis	c_B	x_1 3	x_2 4	s_1 0	s_2 0	a_1 -M	
a_1	-M	0	2/3	-1	1/3	1	7/3
x_1	3	1	1/3	0	-1/3	0	8/3
	z_j	3	-(2/3)M+1	M	-(1/3)M-1	-M	-(7/3)M+8
	$c_j - z_j$	0	(2/3)M+3	-M	(1/3)M+1	0	

Iteration 3 (Drop a_1)

Basis	c_B	x_1 3	x_2 4	s_1 0	s_2 0	
x_2	4	0	1	-3/2	1/2	7/2
x_1	3	1	0	1/2	-1/2	3/2
	z_j	3	4	-9/2	1/2	37/2
	$c_j - z_j$	0	0	9/2	-1/2	

Iteration 4

Basis	c_B	x_1 3	x_2 4	s_1 0	s_2 0	
x_2	4	3	1	0	-1	8
s_1	0	2	0	1	-1	3
	z_j	12	4	0	-4	32
	$c_j - z_j$	-9	0	0	4	

Note that $c_4 - z_4 = 4$ (positive) but its column is all non-positive. This indicates that the problem is <u>unbounded</u>.

PROBLEM 6

Given the following optimal tableau for a linear programming problem:

Basis	c_B	x_1	x_2	x_3	s_1	s_2	s_3	s_4	
		2	4	6	0	0	0	0	
s_3	0	0	0	2	4	-2	1	0	8
x_2	4	0	1	2	2	-1	0	0	6
x_1	2	1	0	-1	1	2	0	0	4
s_4	0	0	0	1	3	2	0	1	12
z_j		2	4	6	10	0	0	0	32
$c_j - z_j$		0	0	0	-10	0	0	0	

a) Give the optimal solution associated with this tableau.

b) Give an optimal solution with x_3 replacing x_2 in the tableau.

c) Give an optimal solution with x_2 replacing x_1 in the tableau in part a).

d) Take an arbitrary weighted average of the extreme points found in (a), (b), and (c), say .5, .3, .2 respectively. Show that this point is feasible by substituting into the equations defined by the above tableau, and demonstrate that it is optimal by showing its objective function value is 32. CONCLUSION: A weighted average of optimal solutions is also optimal.

SOLUTION 6

a) $x_1 = 4$; $x_2 = 6$; $x_3 = 0$; $s_1 = 0$; $s_2 = 0$; $s_3 = 8$; $s_4 = 12$; $z = 32$

b) x_3 is non-basic and its $c_3 - z_3 = 0$. This indicates that there are alternate optimal solutions. This 0 indicates that if x_3 were increased, the value of the objective function would not change.

Thus, another optimal solution may be found by choosing x_3 as the entering variable and performing one iteration of the simplex method. This gives the following tableau:

Basis	c_B	x_1 2	x_2 4	x_3 6	s_1 0	s_2 0	s_3 0	s_4 0	
s_3	0	0	-1	0	2	-1	1	0	2
x_3	6	0	1/2	1	1	-1/2	0	0	3
x_1	2	1	1/2	0	2	3/2	0	0	7
s_4	0	0	-1/2	0	2	5/2	0	1	9
z_j		2	4	6	10	0	0	0	32
$c_j - z_j$		0	0	0	-10	0	0	0	

The solution is $x_1 = 7$; $x_2 = 0$; $x_3 = 3$; $s_1 = 0$; $s_2 = 0$; $s_3 = 2$; $s_4 = 9$; $z = 32$

c) Similarly doing an iteration of the simplex iteration using s_2 as the entering variable in the given tableau yields:

Basis	c_B	x_1 2	x_2 4	x_3 6	s_1 0	s_2 0	s_3 0	s_4 0	
s_3	0	1	0	1	5	0	1	0	12
x_2	4	1/2	1	3/2	5/2	0	0	0	8
s_2	0	1/2	0	-1/2	1/2	1	0	0	2
s_4	0	-1	0	2	2	0	0	1	8
z_j		2	4	6	10	0	0	0	32
$c_j - z_j$		0	0	0	-10	0	0	0	

This gives an optimal solution of: $x_1 = 0$ $s_1 = 0$ $z = 32$
$x_2 = 8$ $s_2 = 2$
$x_3 = 0$ $s_3 = 12$
$s_4 = 8$

d) Take: .5 x (Values in part (a)) + .3 x (Values in part (b)) + .2 x (Values in part (c)).

This gives: $x_1 = .5(4) + .3(7) + .2(0) = 4.1$
$x_2 = .5(6) + .3(0) + .2(8) = 4.6$
$x_3 = .5(0) + .3(3) + .2(0) = .9$
$s_1 = .5(0) + .3(0) + .2(0) = 0$
$s_2 = .5(0) + .3(0) + .2(2) = .4$
$s_3 = .5(8) + .3(2) + .2(12) = 7.0$
$s_4 = .5(12) + .3(9) + .2(8) = 10.3$

Feasibility:

The first equation is: $2x_3 + 4s_1 - 2s_2 + s_3 = 8$
Substituting, $2(.9) + 4(0) - 2(.4) + 7 = 8$

The second equation is: $x_2 + 2x_3 + 2s_1 - s_2 = 6$
Substituting, $4.6 + 2(.9) + 2(0) - .4 = 6$

The third equation is: $x_1 - x_3 + s_1 + 2s_2 = 4$
Substituting, $4.1 - .9 + 0 + 2(.4) = 4$

The fourth equation is: $x_3 + 3s_1 + 2s_2 + s_4 = 12$
Substituting, $.9 + 3(0) + 2(.4) + 10.3 = 12$.

Therefore this solution is feasible.

Optimality:

$z = 2x_1 + 4x_2 + 6x_3 = 2(4.1) + 4(4.6) + 6(.9) = 32$.

Thus, this is also an optimal solution.

PROBLEM 7

The Hondasaki Motorbike Company has the capability of making three kinds of motorbikes -- the C-90, the C-250, and the C-700.

Although this is a small company, only three materials (denoted A, B, C) are in short enough supply to limit production. Daily supplies of materials A, B, and C are 400 lbs., 200 lbs., and 300 lbs., respectively. Whereas Hondasaki may have unused material B and C, all material A must be used daily for safety reasons.

The profit per motorbike and the amount of material needed to make each motorbike are given in the following table.

Motorbike	Profit	Material A	Material B	Material C
C-90	$140	2	1	1
C-250	$300	8	1	0
C-700	$400	2	4	1

a) Solve for the optimal daily production of motorbikes.

b) How much of each of the materials A, B, and C are used daily?

SOLUTION 7

a) This problem can be formulated as follows:

x_1 = number of C-90's produced daily
x_2 = number of C-250's produced daily
x_3 = number of C-700's produced daily

$$\text{MAX} \quad 140x_1 + 300x_2 + 400x_3$$

$$\text{s. t.} \quad 2x_1 + 8x_2 + 2x_3 = 400$$

$$x_1 + x_2 + 4x_3 \leq 200$$

$$x_1 + x_3 \leq 300$$

$$x_1, x_2, x_3 \geq 0$$

First add slack variables, s_2 and s_3, to the second and third constraints, respectively. Then add an artificial variable, a_1, to the first constraint. This gives the initial tableau (on the next page).

Using the simplex method, the optimal solution is to produce 40C-250's and 40 C-700's daily for an optimal daily profit of $28,000. Note that because $c_1 - z_1$ is zero, there are alternate optimal solutions.

b) From the optimal tableau, $s_2 = 0$, $s_3 = 260$. All of material A and B is used and 40 (= 300 - 260) of material C is used.

Iteration 1

Basis	c_B	x_1 140	x_2 300	x_3 400	s_2 0	s_3 0	a_1 -M	
a_1	-M	2	8	2	0	0	1	400
s_2	0	1	1	4	1	0	0	200
s_3	0	1	0	1	0	1	0	300
z_j		-2M	-8M	-2M	0	0	-M	-400M
$c_j - z_j$		2M +140	8M +300	2M +400	0	0	0	

Iteration 2 (Drop a_1)

Basis	c_B	x_1 140	x_2 300	x_3 400	s_2 0	s_3 0	
x_2	300	1/4	1	1/4	0	0	50
s_2	0	3/4	0	15/4	1	0	150
s_3	0	1	0	1	0	1	300
z_j		75	300	75	0	0	15,000
$c_j - z_j$		65	0	325	0	0	

Iteration 3 (This is the optimal tableau)

Basis	c_B	x_1 140	x_2 300	x_3 400	s_2 0	s_3 0	
x_2	300	1/5	1	0	-1/15	0	40
x_3	400	1/5	0	1	4/15	0	40
s_3	0	4/5	0	0	-4/15	1	260
	z_j	140	300	400	260/3	0	28,000
	$c_j - z_j$	0	0	0	-260/3	0	

ANSWERED PROBLEMS

PROBLEM 8

Consider the following linear program:

$$\text{MIN} \quad 2x_1 + 3x_2 + 8x_3$$
$$\text{s. t.} \quad 4x_1 + 2x_2 + \ x_3 \geq 15$$
$$2x_1 + \ x_2 + 6x_3 \geq 30$$
$$x_1, x_2, x_3 \geq 0$$

a) Write the problem in standard form.

b) Why can you not multiply the equations in (a) by -1 to obtain a first tableau to begin the simplex method?

c) Solve the problem by the simplex method.

NOTE: The number of decision variables with optimal values greater than zero cannot exceed the number of constraints. One of the x's in Problem 8 is sure to have an optimal value of zero. (If more than one x equals zero, we have a degenerate solution.)

PROBLEM 9

Solve the following problem by the simplex method:

$$\text{MAX} \quad x_1 + 2x_2 - 3x_3$$

$$\begin{aligned}
\text{s. t.} \quad x_1 \quad & \geq \; 5 \\
2x_1 + 3x_2 + 4x_3 & \leq \; 24 \\
3x_1 + 2x_2 + x_3 & = \; 18 \\
x_1, x_2, x_3 & \geq 0
\end{aligned}$$

PROBLEM 10

Solve the following problem by the simplex method.

$$\text{MIN} \quad 3x_1 + 5x_2 + 1x_3$$

$$\begin{aligned}
\text{s. t.} \quad 2x_1 + 4x_2 + 3x_3 & \geq \; 20 \\
5x_1 + 4x_2 + 6x_3 & \leq \; 45 \\
x_2 - .5x_3 & \leq \; 0 \\
x_1 \quad & \geq \; 3 \\
x_1, x_2, x_3 & \geq \; 0
\end{aligned}$$

PROBLEM 11

Consider the following tableaus which have been generated at various times in different maximization linear programs. Give each tableau one of the following characterizations and perform the indicated operation consistent with the choice you have made.

Characterization	Operation
a) Tableau is optimal.	Give the optimal solution.
b) Tableau is feasible but not yet optimal.	Do one complete iteration of the simplex method.
c) Tableau indicates the entire problem is infeasible.	State why.
d) Tableau is infeasible, but cannot yet state whether or not the problem is feasible.	Do one complete iteration of the simplex method.
e) Tableau indicates the problem is unbounded.	State why.

a)

Basis	c_B	x_1 10	x_2 8	x_3 6	s_1 0	s_2 0	s_3 0	a_2 -M	
s_1	0	2	3	4	1	0	0	0	24
a_2	-M	0	1	2	0	-1	0	1	16
s_3	0	1	1	2	0	0	1	0	10
	z_j	0	-M	-2M	0	M	0	-M	-16M
	$c_j - z_j$	10	M+8	2M+6	0	-M	0	0	

b)

Basis	c_B	x_1 4	x_2 6	x_3 10	s_1 0	s_2 0	
s_1	0	3	0	6	1	-1	18
x_2	6	1	1	2	0	2	14
	z_j	6	6	12	0	12	84
	$c_j - z_j$	-2	0	-2	0	-12	

c)

Basis	c_B	x_1 5	x_2 6	x_3 7	s_1 0	s_2 0	
x_1	5	1	0	0	4	0	6
s_2	0	0	0	-2	-2	1	16
x_2	6	0	1	-1	2	0	26
	z_j	5	6	-6	32	0	186
	$c_j - z_j$	0	0	13	-32	0	

d)

Basis	c_B	x_1 10	x_2 8	x_3 4	s_1 0	s_3 0	a_2 -M	
x_1	10	1	2	0	1	0	0	6
a_2	-M	0	-2	0	-1	-1	1	4
x_3	4	0	6	1	1	2	0	2
	z_j	10	2M+44	4	M+14	M+8	-M	-4M+68
	$c_j - z_j$	0	-2M-36	0	-M-14	-M-8	0	

e)

Basis	c_B	x_1 4	x_2 5	x_3 7	s_1 0	s_2 0	
x_3	7	0	0	1	0	0	12
s_2	0	0	2	0	0	1	14
s_1	0	0	3	0	1	0	18
x_1	4	1	-1	0	0	0	20
	z_j	4	-4	7	0	0	164
	$c_j - z_j$	0	9	0	0	0	

PROBLEM 12

Consider the following tableau at a particular iteration of the simplex method:

Basis	c_B	x_1 4	x_2 2	x_3 -1	s_1 0	s_2 0	s_3 0	
		0	1	-1	6	0	1	10
		0	0	4	2	1	1	20
		1	0	0	-3	0	1	30
	z_j							
	$c_j - z_j$							

a) Complete the tableau above.

b) What is the current basic solution?

c) What would be the change in the objective function for each of the following cases:
   (1) x_3 were increased by 1   (3) s_1 were increased by 1.5
   (2) x_3 were increased by 3   (4) s_3 were increased by 2

d) What is the entering variable? Write the equations corresponding to the above tableau. Now, delete all the non-basic variables (since they are set to 0 anyway) except for the entering variable. Use this remaining set of three equations in four unknowns to justify why the ratio test is only performed on positive numbers in the entering column.

e) Explain why the entering variable could not be increased to 10 at this iteration.

f) To what value will the entering variable increase?

g) Use (d) and (f) to determine by how much the objective function will be increased in the next tableau. Use your equations in (d) to determine the values of the other basic variables in the next tableau.

h) Do one iteration of the simplex method to justify your answer in (g).

PROBLEM 13

Consider the following linear programming tableau:

		x_1	x_2	x_3	s_1	s_2	s_3	
Basis	c_B	5	2	1	0	0	0	
x_3	1	2	0	1	-6	1	0	8
x_2	2	1	1	0	4	0	0	4
s_3	0	4	0	0	3	-3	1	20
z_j		4	2	1	2	1	0	16
$c_j - z_j$		1	0	0	-2	-1	0	

a) Do one iteration of the simplex method by choosing the first row as the leaving row. What is the new basic solution? Based on the new $c_j - z_j$ row, is this solution optimal?

b) Repeat (a), but this time choose the second row as the leaving row. What is the new basic solution? Does the new $c_j - z_j$ row indicate that the solution is optimal?

c) Interpret the results of (a) and (b) by stating a conclusion concerning optimality when degeneracy occurs.

PROBLEM 14

The Doorco Company can produce three kinds of closet doors. Each door must go through two operations: production and finishing. There are 1,000 man-hours available in the production area weekly and 600 man-hours available in the finishing area weekly. Below is a chart which summarizes the number of hours each door must spend in each area as well as the unit profit per door.

Door	Production	Finishing	Profit
Basic	2	2	$3
Standard	3	2	$6
Deluxe	4	2	$8

a) Using the simplex method, show there is an optimal solution in which only one type of door is produced.

b) Using your resulting optimal tableau in (a), give another optimal solution in which two types of doors are produced.

PROBLEM 15

Given the following maximization problem:

$$\text{MAX} \quad 2x_1 + 5x_2 + 5x_3 + 3x_4$$

$$\text{s. t.} \quad 10x_1 + 12x_2 + 10x_3 + 9x_4 \leq 150$$

$$x_1 + x_2 + x_3 \geq 12$$

$$-x_1 + x_2 + x_3 - x_4 \leq 0$$

$$x_j \geq 0 \quad j = 1,2,3,4$$

a) Write the problem in standard form.

b) Set up the initial simplex tableau.

c) Solve the problem by the simplex method.

TRUE/FALSE

16. Once an artificial variable becomes non-basic, it can be dropped from the simplex tableau.

17. If the same slack variable enters the basis more than once, degeneracy exists.

18. Any tableau with a positive value for an artificial variable is infeasible.

19. Suppose x_4 is a non-basic variable in the optimal tableau in which all right-hand values are positive, but $c_4 - z_4 = 0$. Then there exist optimal solutions with x_4 equal to 0 and also optimal solutions with x_4 positive.

20. One optimal solution to a linear program must be a basic feasible solution.

21. If x_4 is the entering variable and its corresponding column contains all non-positive entries, the problem is infeasible.

22. All elements in the $c_j - z_j$ row of a simplex tableau must be ≤ 0 for the current solution to be optimal.

23. A problem with degenerate basic feasible solutions could theoretically cycle between non-optimal solutions without reaching the optimal solution.

24. The ratio test determines which current basic variable reaches zero first as the entering variable is increased from zero.

25. A basic solution can be either feasible or infeasible.

26. Writing an LP problem in standard form sometimes requires the introduction of one or more artificial variables.

27. The c_j row determines the "gross" increase, and the z_j row determines the "gross" decrease, in the objective function per unit increase in the variables. Hence, the $c_j - z_j$ row gives the "net" increase in the objective function per unit increase in the variables.

28. Degeneracy results from there being alternate optimal solutions to a problem.

29. If there are any slack or surplus variables in the basis, the solution is infeasible for the real-world problem.

30. The simplex method is applicable to maximization problems only.

CHAPTER 6

Simplex-Based Sensitivity Analysis and Duality

KEY CONCEPTS

CONCEPT	ILLUSTRATED PROBLEMS	ANSWERED PROBLEMS
Range of Optimality	1-3	7-11
Dual Prices	1-4	7-11
Range of Feasibility	2,4	7,10,11
100% Rule	3	10
Relevant/Sunk Costs	3	8,9,10
Duality	5,6	12,13

REVIEW

1. The <u>range of optimality</u> for an objective function coefficient is the range of that coefficient for which the current <u>optimal solution</u> will remain optimal (keeping all other coefficients constant). The objective function value may change is that range.

2. Given an optimal tableau, the <u>range of optimality</u> for c_k can be calculated as follows:
   (a) Change the objective function coefficient to c_k in the c_j row.
   (b) If x_k is basic, then also change the objective function coefficient to c_k in the c_B column and recalculate the z_j row in terms of c_k.
   (c) Recalculate the $c_j - z_j$ row in terms of c_k. Determine the range of values for c_k that keep all entries in the $c_j - z_j$ row less than or equal to 0.

3. If c_k changes to values outside the <u>range of optimality</u>, a new $c_j - z_j$ row may be generated. The simplex method may then be continued to determine a new optimal solution.

4. A <u>dual price</u> for a constraint is the increase in the objective function value resulting from a one-unit increase in its right-hand side value.

5. Dual prices are found in the optimal tableau as follows:
    (a) "less than or equal to" constraint: z_j value of the corresponding slack variable for the constraint,
    (b) "greater than or equal to" constraint: negative of the z_j value of the corresponding surplus variable for the constraint,
    (c) "equal to" constraint: z_j value of the corresponding artificial variable for the constraint.

6. The range of feasibility for a right hand side coefficient is the range of that coefficient for which the dual price remains unchanged. It is also the range for which the current set of basic variables remains the optimal set of basic variables (although their values change.)

7. The range of feasibility for a right-hand side coefficient of a "less than or equal to" constraint, b_k, is calculated as follows:
    (a) Express the right-hand side in terms of Δb_k by adding Δb_k times the column of the k-th slack variable to the current optimal right hand side.
    (b) Determine the range of Δb_k that keeps the right-hand side greater than or equal to 0.
    (c) Add the original right-hand side value b_k (from the original tableau) to these limits for Δb_k to determine the range of feasibility for b_k.

8. The range of feasibility for "greater than or equal to" constraints is similarly found except one subtracts Δb_k times the current column of the k-th surplus variable from the current right hand side in step (a) above. For equality constraints this range is similarly found by adding Δb_k times the current column of the k-th artificial variable to the current right hand side. Otherwise the procedure is the same.

9. For simultaneous changes of two or more objective function coefficients the 100% rule provides a guide to whether the optimal solution changes. It states that as long as the sum of the percent changes in the coefficients from their current value to their maximum allowable increase or decrease does not exceed 100%, the solution will not change. Similarly, for dual prices, the 100% rule can be applied to changes in the right-hand side coefficients.

10. Every linear program (called the primal) has associated with it another linear program called the dual.

11. A maximization linear program is said to be in canonical form if all constraints are "less than or equal to" constraints and the variables are non-negative. The constraints for a minimization problem in non-negative variables in canonical form are "greater than or equal to" constraints.

12. The dual of a maximization problem in canonical form is a minimization problem in canonical form. The rows and columns of the two programs are interchanged and hence the objective function coefficients of one are the right hand side values of the other and vice versa.

13. The optimal value of the objective function of the <u>primal</u> problem equals the optimal value of the objective function of the <u>dual</u> problem.

14. The <u>dual variables</u> are the "value per unit" of the corresponding primal resource, i.e. the dual prices. Thus, they are found in the z_j row of the optimal simplex tableau according to rule 5 on the previous page.

15. If the <u>dual</u> is solved, the <u>optimal primal solution</u> is found in z_j row of the corresponding surplus variable in the optimal dual tableau. The optimal value of the primal's slack variables are the negative of the $c_j - z_j$ entries in the optimal dual tableau for the dual variables.

16. <u>Convert any linear program</u> to a maximization problem in canonical form as follows:
    (a) minimization objective function: multiply it by -1
    (b) "less than or equal to" constraint: leave alone
    (c) "greater than or equal to" constraint: multiply it by -1
    (d) "equal to" constraints: form two constraints, one "less than or equal to", the other "greater than or equal to"; then multiply this "greater than or equal to" constraint by -1.

17. By employing the rules of (16), the dual can be found to any linear program.

18. Solving the dual might be computationally <u>more efficient</u> when the primal has numerous constraints and few variables.

FLOW CHART FOR
PRIMAL-TO-DUAL CONVERSION

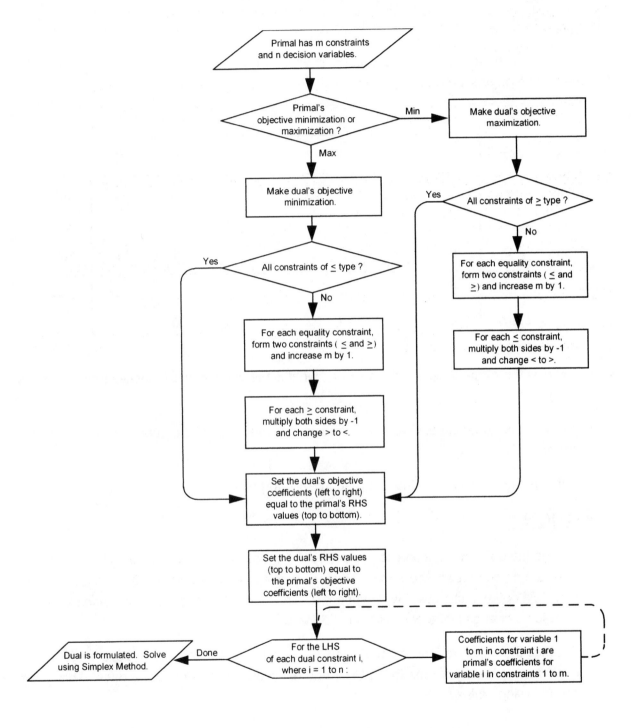

ILLUSTRATED PROBLEMS

PROBLEM 1

Consider the following optimal tableau in which s_1, s_2, and s_3 were the slack variables added to the original problem.

Basis	c_B	x_1 5	x_2 25	x_3 4	x_4 10	s_1 0	s_2 0	s_3 0	
x_4	10	0	2	1	1	1	0	-1	50
x_1	5	1	3	-1	0	-1	0	4	80
s_2	0	0	4	2	0	4	1	1	100
	z_j	5	35	5	10	5	0	10	900
	$c_j - z_j$	0	-10	-1	0	-5	0	-10	

a) What is the range of optimality of c_2 and what is the value of the objective function in this range?

b) What is the range of optimality of c_1 and what is the value of the objective function in this range?

c) What is the dual price for the first resource? Interpret.

SOLUTION 1

a) Change the objective function coefficient c_2 in the coefficient row. Since x_2 is non-basic, there are no changes in the z_j row. Thus, only $c_2 - z_2$ changes to $c_2 - 35$. For the tableau to remain optimal, this quantity must be ≤ 0. Thus, $c_2 - 35 \leq 0$ or $c_2 \leq 35$. Since x_2 is 0, there is no change in the objective function value.

b) Replace the objective function coefficient for x_1 with c_1. Since x_1 is basic, change the coefficient in the c_B column for x_1 to c_1 and recalculate the z_j and $c_j - z_j$ rows. This gives the following tableau:

Basis	c_B	x_1 c_1	x_2 25	x_3 4	x_4 10	s_1 0	s_2 0	s_3 0	
x_4	10	0	2	1	1	1	0	-1	50
x_1	c_1	1	3	-1	0	-1	0	4	80
s_2	0	0	4	2	0	4	1	1	100
z_j		c_1	$20+3c_1$	$10-c_1$	10	$10-c_1$	0	$-10+4c_1$	500
$c_j - z_j$		0	$5-3c_1$	$-6+c_1$	0	$-10+c_1$	0	$10-4c_1$	

All $c_j - z_j$ must remain ≤ 0 for the above tableau to remain optimal.

For $5 - 3c_1 \leq 0$, then $c_1 \geq 5/3$.
For $-6 + c_1 \leq 0$, then $c_1 \leq 6$.
For $-10 + c_1 \leq 0$, then $c_1 \leq 10$.
For $10 - 4c_1 \leq 0$, then $c_1 \geq 5/2$.

Combining all these inequalities, the range of optimality for c_2 is:
$$5/2 \leq c1 \leq 6$$

As seen from above, in this range, the value of the objective function is $500+80c_1$.

c) The dual price for the first resource is the z_j value for s_1. Hence, the dual price for the first resource is 5. It is the amount the objective function will increase per unit increase in the availability of the first resource available.

PROBLEM 2

Given the following linear program:

$$\text{MAX } 2x_1 + x_2 + 3x_3$$

$$\text{s. t.} \quad x_1 + 4x_2 + 4x_3 \leq 20$$

$$4x_1 + 4x_2 + x_3 \leq 20$$

$$x_1, x_2, x_3 \geq 0$$

a) Solve this linear program by the simplex method.

b) Calculate the range of optimality for each of the three decision variables.

c) Suppose a profit could be made on the slack of the first resource. What profit value on this slack would be sufficient to change the optimal solution?

d) By how much would the optimal value of the objective function change for a unit increase of the second resource?

e) Calculate the range of feasibility for b_2. Interpret.

SOLUTION 2

a)

Basis	c_B	x_1 2	x_2 1	x_3 3	s_1 0	s_2 0	
s_1	0	1	4	(4)	1	0	20
s_2	0	4	4	1	0	1	20
z_j		0	0	0	0	0	0
$c_j - z_j$		2	1	3	0	0	

Basis	c_B	x_1 2	x_2 1	x_3 3	s_1 0	s_2 0	
x_3	3	1/4	1	1	1/4	0	5
s_2	0	(15/4)	3	0	-1/4	1	15
z_j		3/4	3	3	3/4	0	15
$c_j - z_j$		5/4	-2	0	-3/4	0	

		x_1	x_2	x_3	s_1	s_2	
Basis	c_B	2	1	3	0	0	
x_3	3	0	4/5	1	4/15	-1/15	4
x_1	2	1	4/5	0	-1/15	4/15	4
z_j		2	4	3	2/3	1/3	20
$c_j - z_j$		0	-3	0	-2/3	-1/3	

Optimal solution: $x_1 = 4$, $x_2 = 0$, $x_3 = 4$, $s_1 = 0$, $s_2 = 0$, $z = 20$

b) For c_1: Since x_1 is basic, change the objective function coefficient in the objective function row and c_B column. The z_j row and $c_j - z_j$ rows must be recalculated in terms of c_1.

z_j	c_1	$(12/5) + (4/5)c_1$	3	$(4/5) - (1/15)c_1$	$(-1/5) + (4/15)c_1$
c_j-z_j	0	$(-7/5) - (4/5)c_1$	0	$(-4/5) + (1/15)c_1$	$(1/5) - (4/15)c_1$

For $(-7/5) - (4/5)c_1 \leq 0$, then $c_1 \geq -7/4$.
For $(-4/5) + (1/15)c_1 \leq 0$, then $c_1 \leq 12$.
For $(1/5) - (4/15)c_1 \leq 0$, then $c_1 \geq 3/4$.
Thus $3/4 \leq c_1 \leq 12$.

For c_2: Since x_2 is a non-basic variable, only change x_2's objective function coefficient value to c_2. The z_j value for x_2 remains 4. Hence its $c_j - z_j$ value is $c_2 - 4$. Since this quantity must be ≤ 0, then $c_2 \leq 4$ is the only restriction.

For c_3: Since x_3 is basic, change the objective function coefficient in the objective function row and c_B column. The z_j row and $c_j - z_j$ rows must be recalculated in terms of c_3.

z_j	2	$(8/5) + (4/5)c_3$	c_3	$(-2/15) + (4/15)c_3$	$(8/15) - (1/15)c_3$
c_j-z_j	0	$(-3/5) - (4/5)c_3$	0	$(2/15) - (4/15)c_3$	$(-8/15) + (1/15)c_3$

For $(-3/5) - (4/5)c_3 \leq 0$, then $c_3 \geq -3/4$.
For $(2/15) - (4/15)c_3 \leq 0$, then $c_3 \geq 1/2$.
For $(-8/15) + (1/15)c_3 \leq 0$, then $c_3 \leq 8$.
Thus $1/2 \leq c_3 \leq 8$.

c) Change s_1's objective function coefficient to c_4. The only other change would be in the $c_j - z_j$ row for s_1 and would be: $c_4 - 2/3$. For optimality this quantity must be ≤ 0. Thus $c_4 \leq 2/3$. If $c_4 \geq 2/3$, then the optimal solution will change.

d) This is the dual price for the second constraint. It is found in the s_2 column in the z_j row of the optimal tableau and is 1/3.

e) The new RHS is altered by Δb_2 x (the current s_2 column). To maintain feasibility, the RHS must stay ≥ 0.

$$\text{Thus, } 4 - (1/15)\, \Delta b_2 \geq 0 \quad \text{or} \quad \Delta b_2 \leq 60.$$
$$\text{and, } 4 + (4/15)\, \Delta b_2 \geq 0 \quad \text{or} \quad \Delta b_2 \geq -15.$$

Thus, $-15 \leq \Delta b_2 \leq 60$, or since b_2 was originally 20, the range of feasibility for b_2 is: $5 \leq b_2 \leq 80$. Within this range the dual prices remain constant.

PROBLEM 3

Jonni's Toy Company produces stuffed toy animals and is gearing up for the Christmas rush by hiring temporary workers giving it a total production crew of 30 workers. Jonni's makes two sizes of stuffed animals. The profit, the production time and the material used per toy animal is summarized in the table below. Workers work 8 hours per day and there are up to 2000 pounds of material available daily.

Size	Profit	Production Time (hrs.)	Material (lbs.)
Small	$3	.10	1
Large	$8	.30	2

a) Find the optimal daily production level by the simplex method.

b) Calculate the range of the profits on each of the animals such that the solution in (a) does not change.

c) Will the solution change if the profit on small animals is increased by $.75? Will the objective function value change?

d) Will the solution change if the profit on large animals is increased by $.75? Will the objective function value change?

e) Will the solution change if the profits on both large and small animals are increased by $.75? Will the value of the objective function change?

f) The unit profits do not include a per unit labor cost. Given this, what is the maximum wage Jonni should pay for overtime?

SOLUTION 3

a) x_1 = number of small stuffed animals produced daily
x_2 = number of large stuffed animals produced daily

$$\text{MAX} \quad 3x_1 + 8x_2$$

$$\text{s. t.} \quad .1x_1 + .3x_2 \leq 240$$

$$x_1 + 2x_2 \leq 2000$$

$$x_1, x_2 \geq 0$$

		x_1	x_2	s_1	s_2	
Basis	c_B	3	8	0	0	
s_1	0	.1	.3	1	0	240
s_2	0	1	2	0	1	2000
z_j		0	0	0	0	0
$c_j - z_j$		3	8	0	0	

		x_1	x_2	s_1	s_2	
Basis	c_B	3	8	0	0	
x_2	8	1/3	1	10/3	0	800
s_2	0	1/3	0	-20/3	1	400
z_j		8/3	8	80/3	0	6400
$c_j - z_j$		1/3	0	-80/3	0	

		x_1	x_2	s_1	s_2	
Basis	c_B	3	8	0	0	
x_2	8	0	1	10	-1	400
x_1	3	1	0	-20	3	1200
z_j		3	8	20	1	6,800
$c_j - z_j$		0	0	-20	-1	

Produce 1200 small and 400 large stuffed animals daily for a daily profit of $6,800.

b) Range of optimality for small stuffed animals (c_1)
Replace 3 by c_1 in the objective function row and c_B column.
Then recalculate z_j and $c_j - z_j$ rows.

z_j	c_1	8	80	$-20c_1$	-8	$+3c_1$	$3200 + 1200c_1$
$c_j - z_j$	0	0	-80	$+20c_1$	8	$-3c_1$	

For the $c_j - z_j$ row to remain non-positive, $8/3 \leq c_1 \leq 4$

Range of optimality for large stuffed animals (c_2)
Replace 8 by c_2 in the objective function row and c_B column.
Then recalculate z_j and $c_j - z_j$ rows.

z_j	3	c_2	-60	$+10c_2$	9	$-c_2$	$3600 + 400c_2$
$c_j - z_j$	0	0	60	$-10c_2$	-9	$+c_2$	

For the $c_j - z_j$ row to remain non-positive, $6 \leq c_2 \leq 9$

c) If the profit on small stuffed animals is changed to $3.75, this is within the range of optimality and the optimal solution will not change. However, since x_1 is a basic variable at positive value, changing its objective function coefficient will change the value of the objective function to $3200 + 1200(3.75) = 7700$.

d) If the profit on large stuffed animals is changed to $8.75, this is within the range of optimality and the optimal solution will not change. However, since x_2 is a basic variable at positive value, changing its objective function coefficient will change the value of the objective function to $3600 + 400(8.75) = 7100$.

e) If both the profits change by $.75, since the maximum increase for c_1 is $1 (from $3 to $4) and the maximum increase in c_2 is $1 (from $8 to $9), the overall sum of the percent changes is $(.75/1) + (.75/1) = 75\% + 75\% = 150\%$. This total is greater than 100%; both the optimal solution and the value of the objective function change.

f) Since the unit profits do not include a per unit labor cost, man-hours is a sunk cost. Thus the dual price for man-hours gives the maximum worth of man-hours (overtime). This is found in the z_j row in the s_1 column (since s_1 is the slack for man-hours) and is $20.

PROBLEM 4

Consider problem 7 of Chapter 5 in which three types of motorcycles were being produced with three constraining materials. Suppose one could purchase either material B or material C for $90 per pound. Which material(s) should be purchased if the per unit profits reflected a $15 per pound cost of material A, a $20 per pound cost of material B and a $25 per pound cost of material C? Within what limits of the material are you sure this would be a correct decision?

The optimal tableau was:

Basis	c_B	x_1 140	x_2 300	x_3 400	s_2 0	s_3 0	
x_2	300	1/5	1	0	-1/15	0	40
x_3	400	1/5	0	1	4/15	0	40
s_3	0	4/5	0	0	-4/15	1	260
z_j		140	300	400	260/3	0	28,000
$c_j - z_j$		0	0	0	-260/3	0	

SOLUTION 4

The dual price for material B is the z_j value of s_2 and is 260/3 = $86.67. In this problem, material costs are <u>relevant</u> costs and hence the dual prices reflect the premium above the normal cost of the resource if it is positive. Thus since material B was figured at $20 per pound, its true value given this solution is $20 + $86.67 = $106.67, and would be worth the $90 per pound purchase. This price is valid within the range of feasibility.

To calculate the range of feasibility for b_2, determine the range of values for Δb_2 that keep: (current RHS) + [Δb_2 x (s_2 column)] $\geq$ 0.

$$40 - 1/15 \ \Delta b_2 \geq 0 \quad \text{or} \quad \Delta b_2 \leq 600$$
$$40 + 4/15 \ \Delta b_2 \geq 0 \quad \text{or} \quad \Delta b_2 \geq -150$$
$$260 - 4/15 \ \Delta b_2 \geq 0 \quad \text{or} \quad \Delta b_2 \leq 975.$$

Thus we are sure this would be a correct decision for another 600 additional units of material B. Since the dual price for material C is 0, one should not purchase additional units of material C.

PROBLEM 5

Given the following linear program:

$$\text{MAX} \quad 4x_1 + 3x_2$$

$$\text{s. t.} \quad x_1 + x_2 \leq 8$$

$$3x_1 + 2x_2 \leq 18$$

$$2x_1 + 5x_2 \leq 15$$

$$5x_1 - x_2 \leq 10$$

$$x_1, x_2 \geq 0$$

a) Write the dual linear program.

b) Solve the dual problem.

c) From the optimal tableau of the dual, determine the optimal solution to the primal problem.

d) Verify the result in (c) by solving the primal graphically.

e) Why would solving the dual problem by the simplex method for this problem be more convenient than solving the primal problem by the simplex method?

NOTE: To write the dual LP, essentially turn the primal LP on its side. That is, turn the primal 90 degrees counter-clockwise, with the exception of its objective coefficients; they are turned 90 degrees clockwise and become the dual's right-hand side.

SOLUTION 5

a) There are four variables and two constraints in the dual. The rows of the dual are formed from the columns of the primal:

$$\text{MIN} \quad z = 8u_1 + 18u_2 + 15u_3 + 10u_4$$

$$\text{s. t.} \quad u_1 + 3u_2 + 2u_3 + 5u_4 \geq 4$$

$$u_1 + 2u_2 + 5u_3 - u_4 \geq 3$$

$$u_1, u_2, u_3, u_4 \geq 0$$

b) Put the problem in tableau form and change the objective function to a maximization by multiplying it by -1. Then solve it by the simplex method.

		u_1	u_2	u_3	u_4	s_1	s_2	a_1	a_2	
Basis	c_B	-8	-18	-15	-10	0	0	-M	-M	
a_1	-M	1	3	2	5	-1	0	1	0	4
a_2	-M	1	2	(5)	-1	0	-1	0	1	3
	z_j	-2M	-5M	-7M	-4M	M	M	-M	-M	-7M
	c_j - z_j	2M+8	5M+18	7M+15	4M+10	-M	-M	0	0	

		u_1	u_2	u_3	u_4	s_1	s_2	a_1	
Basis	c_B	-8	-18	-15	-10	0	0	-M	
a_1	-M	3/5	11/5	0	(27/5)	-1	2/5	1	14/5
u_3	-15	1/5	2/5	1	-1/5	0	-1/5	0	3/5
	z_j	-3/5M -3	-11/5M -6	-15	-27/5M +3	M	-2/5M +3	-M	-14/5M -9
	c_j - z_j	3/5M -5	11/5M -12	0	27/5M -13	-M	2/5M -3	0	

		u_1	u_2	u_3	u_4	s_1	s_2	
Basis	c_B	-8	-18	-15	-10	0	0	
u_4	-10	3/27	11/27	0	1	-5/27	2/27	14/27
u_3	-15	6/27	13/27	1	0	-1/27	-5/27	19/27
	z_j	-120/27	-305/27	-15	-10	65/27	55/27	-425/27
	c_j - z_j	-96/27	-181/27	0	0	-65/27	-55/27	

The optimal dual solution is: $u_1 = 0$; $u_2 = 0$; $u_3 = 19/27$; $u_4 = 14/27$; with $z = 425/27$.

c) x_1 and x_2 are found in the z_j row of the optimal tableau of the surplus variables, s_1 and s_2. Hence the optimal solution to the primal is $x_1 = 65/27$ and $x_2 = 55/27$, giving the same value of $z = 425/27$.

d) The optimal solution is at the intersection of $2x_1 + 5x_2 = 15$ and $5x_1 - x_2 = 10$. Solving these two equations in two unknowns gives $x_1 = 65/27$, $x_2 = 55/27$. The optimal value of the objective function $z = 4(65/27) + 3(55/27) = 425/27$.

e) There are fewer constraints and hence one can expect fewer iterations and fewer computations per iteration.

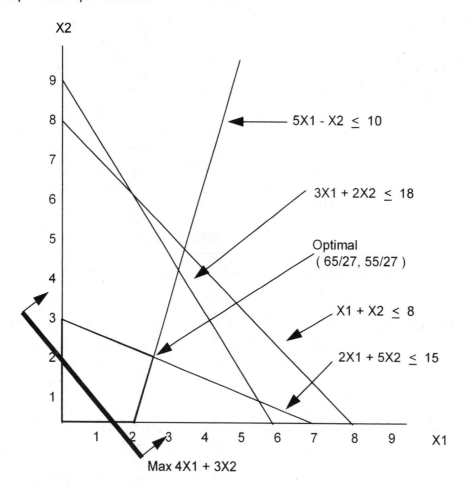

PROBLEM 6

Given the following linear program:

$$\text{MAX} \quad 2x_1 + x_2 + 3x_3$$

$$\text{s. t.} \quad x_1 + 2x_2 + 3x_3 \leq 15$$

$$3x_1 + 4x_2 + 6x_3 \geq 24$$

$$x_1 + x_2 + x_3 = 10$$

$$x_1, x_2, x_3 \geq 0$$

a) Write the primal in canonical form.

b) Write the dual of the canonical primal.

c) Where do you find the optimal value of the dual variables in the optimal primal tableau?

SOLUTION 6

a) Constraint (1) is a "$\leq$" constraint; leave it alone. Constraint (2) is a "$\geq$" constraint; multiply it by -1. Constraint (3) is an "=" constraint; rewrite this as two constraints, one a "$\leq$", the other a "$\geq$" constraint, and then multiply the "$\geq$" constraint by -1.

$$\text{MAX} \quad 2x_1 + x_2 + 3x_3$$

$$\text{s. t.} \quad x_1 + 2x_2 + 3x_3 \leq 15$$

$$-3x_1 - 4x_2 - 6x_3 \leq -24$$

$$x_1 + x_2 + x_3 \leq 10$$

$$-x_1 - x_2 - x_3 \leq -10$$

$$x_1, x_2, x_3 \geq 0$$

b) There are four dual variables, u_1, u_2, u_3', u_3''.   The objective function coefficients of the dual are the RHS of the primal. The RHS of the dual is the objective function coefficients of the primal. The rows of the dual are the columns of the primal.

$$\text{MIN} \quad 15u_1 - 24u_2 + 10u_3' - 10u_3''$$

$$\text{s. t.} \quad u_1 - 3u_2 + u_3' - u_3'' \geq 2$$

$$2u_1 - 4u_2 + u_3' - u_3'' \geq 1$$

$$3u_1 - 6u_2 + u_3' - u_3'' \geq 3$$

$$u_1, u_2, u_3', u_3'' \geq 0$$

c) The optimal solution to the dual is found in the z_j row of the corresponding slack variable of the primal in the optimal tableau.

$$\boxed{\textbf{ANSWERED PROBLEMS}}$$

PROBLEM 7

Given the following LP:

$$\text{MAX}\quad 6x_1 + 5x_2$$

$$\text{s. t.}\quad x_1 + x_2 \le 6$$

$$2x_1 + x_2 \le 8$$

$$x_1 \qquad \le 3$$

$$x_1, x_2 \ge 0$$

The optimal tableau is:

Basis	c_B	x_1	x_2	s_1	s_2	s_3	
		6	5	0	0	0	
s_3	0	0	0	1	-1	1	1
x_2	5	0	1	2	-1	0	4
x_1	6	1	0	-1	1	0	2
z_j		6	5	4	1	0	32
$c_j - z_j$		0	0	-4	-1	0	

a) What is the dual price for the first constraint's resource? For what range of feasibility is this dual price valid?

b) For what values of c_2 would the current solution remain optimal? What is the optimal profit when $c_2 = 4$?

PROBLEM 8

Consider the following LP:

$$\text{MAX} \quad 5x_1 + 2x_2 + 3x_3$$

$$\text{s. t.} \quad x_1 + x_2 + x_3 \le 10$$

$$2x_1 + 3x_2 + 4x_3 \le 24$$

$$x_1, x_2, x_3 \ge 0$$

a) Solve the LP and give the range of optimality for all of the objective function coefficients, including slack variables.

b) If you were offered another unit of the first resource for $4 would you accept the offer, considering the resource is a sunk cost for the problem. Would you pay $20 for five additional units?

PROBLEM 9

A small manufacturing firm makes three products from combinations of aluminum and steel. The manufacturing time as well as the amounts of each of the resources required to make one unit and the unit profits are summarized in the table below. There are 500 production hours, 600 lbs. of aluminum, and 900 lbs. of steel available each week.

Product	Profit	Production Hours	Aluminum	Steel
1	$40	1	2	1
2	$60	1	2	2
3	$80	2	2	3

a) Formulate and solve as a linear program.

b) What is the range of the profit on product 2 for which the solution in (a) remains optimal?

c) What is the profit if $c_2 = 70$?

d) Workers are currently paid $16 per hour. If they demand time and a half for overtime, should the firm schedule overtime? Discuss both in the context of labor being a sunk cost and labor being a relevant cost.

PROBLEM 10

Consider problem 9 above.

a) Management is considering cost cutting measures that would raise the unit profit on each product by an amount, x. What is the maximum value of x for which it is certain that the solution found in part (a) of problem 9 remains optimal?

b) Calculate the range of feasibility for aluminum and steel.

c) Explain in the context of this problem how aluminum and steel could be relevant costs and how they could be sunk costs. In each case, interpret the range of feasibility from part b).

d) A wholesale distribution company is selling packages containing one pound each of both aluminum and steel. What is the maximum number of these packages the manufacturing firm could purchase without affecting the dual prices?

PROBLEM 11

Plant Electronics is considering producing three new computer boards on a daily basis. Each board will be produced from various combinations of plastic, copper, and transistors. The amount of each resource required per unit, the unit profitability, and the availability of the resources are summarized in the following table:

Board	Plastic	Copper	Transistors	Profit
X12	2	1	1	$40
T7	1	2	1	$15
V8	1	1	1	$30
Daily Avail.	80	60	70	

The problem was solved with x_1, x_2, and x_3 representing the number of X12, T7, and V8 boards produced respectively giving the following optimal tableau:

Basis	c_B	x_1 40	x_2 15	x_3 30	s_1 0	s_2 0	s_3 0	
x_1	40	1	-1	0	1	-1	0	20
x_3	30	0	3	1	-1	2	0	40
s_3	0	0	-1	0	0	-1	1	10
z_j		40	50	30	10	20	0	2000
$c_j - z_j$		0	-35	0	-10	-20	0	

a) Give the optimal solution and the optimal daily profit.

b) A supplier is willing to sell Plant additional amounts of the resources. The available packages are listed below. If one of the packages can be purchased, which one should be purchased? Explain. (Assume sunk costs for the resources.)

Resource	Quantity	Package Price
Plastic	30	$240
Copper	10	$150
Transistors	100	$100

c) If management decides to raise the price of the T7 model so that its profit increases from $15 to $55, will the optimal product mix change? If so, what is the new optimal mix?

PROBLEM 12

Given the following linear program:

$$\text{MAX} \quad 10x_1 + 8x_2$$

$$\text{s. t.} \quad x_1 + 3x_2 \leq 15$$

$$4x_1 + x_2 \leq 16$$

$$x_1, x_2 \geq 0$$

a) Formulate the dual linear program.

b) Solve both the primal and dual graphically.

c) Solve the primal by the simplex method. Show that the optimal value of the dual variables are, in fact, those determined in (b).

PROBLEM 13

Given the following linear program:

$$\text{MAX} \quad 3x_1 + 2x_2 - 3x_3$$

$$\text{s. t.} \quad x_1 + 3x_2 + 8x_3 \leq 56$$

$$2x_1 - x_2 - x_3 = 14$$

$$x_2 \geq 5$$

$$x_1, x_2, x_3 \geq 0$$

a) Write the problem in canonical form.

b) Write the dual to the canonical form.

c) Take the dual to this dual problem. Conclusion?

TRUE/FALSE

14. Simplex-based sensitivity analysis is applicable to primal tableaus, but not dual tableaus.

15. The range of optimality for an objective function coefficient, c_k, is determined by finding the range of values of c_k that keep the $c_j - z_j$ row less than or equal to 0.

16. In sensitivity analysis of the objective function coefficient, c_3, *The Management Scientist* states a maximum increase of 75 and an maximum decrease of 25. Currently c_3 is 130. If c_3 is changed to 150, the optimal solution does not change.

17. You cannot mix a right-hand side change and an objective function change when applying the 100 percent rule.

18. In the sensitivity analysis of the right-hand side coefficient, b_4, *The Management Scientist* states a maximum increase of 20 and maximum decrease of 10. Currently b_4 is 15. If b_4 changes to 25, the optimal solution does not change.

19. If the primal has few constraints, but relatively many variables, solving the dual is often faster.

20. Constraint 3 is a $\leq$ constraint and the optimal solution has $s_3 = 6$. Thus the dual price for this constraint must be 0.

21. A dual price for a resource is valid only in the range of feasibility for that resource.

22. Dual prices are found in the z_j row of the optimal tableau in the slack, surplus, or artificial variable columns.

23. The dual linear program for a maximization problem in canonical form seeks to maximize the value of the resources.

24. There is a dual price associated with each decision variable.

25. When the primal is unbounded, the dual is unbounded.

26. If simultaneous changes in the objective function violate the 100% rule (exceed 100%), the optimal solution will change.

27. The optimal values of the primal decision variables are given by the z_j entries for the surplus variables in the dual's optimal simplex tableau.

28. The primal and its dual cannot have the same optimal objective function value because one is a minimization problem and the other is a maximization.

CHAPTER 7

Transportation, Assignment, and Transshipment Problems

KEY CONCEPTS

CONCEPT	ILLUSTRATED PROBLEMS	ANSWERED PROBLEMS
Transportation Problems		
Network Representation	1	8
Dummy Sources	2,3	9,10
Maximization Problems	3	11
Unacceptable Routes	3	11
Spreadsheet Solution	2	
Assignment Problem		
Network Representation	4	13
Maximization Problems	5	12,14
Unacceptable Assignments	5	14
Transshipment Problem		
Network Representation	6,7	15
LP Formulation	6	15
Production and Inventory Application	7	

REVIEW

1. A <u>network model</u> is one which can be represented by a set of nodes, a set of arcs, and functions (e.g. costs, supplies, demands, etc.) associated with the arcs and/or nodes.

2. Transportation, assignment, and transshipment problems of this chapter, and PERT/CPM problems in Chapter 10 are all examples of <u>network problems</u>.

3. Each of the three models of this chapter (transportation, assignment, and transshipment models) can be formulated as <u>linear programs</u> and solved by general purpose linear programming codes. However, there are many computer packages (including The Management Scientist) which contain separate computer codes for these models which take advantage of their network structure. This radically enhances the speed of solving particularly large problems.

4. For each of the three models in this chapter, if the right-hand side of the linear programming formulations are all integers, the optimal solution will be in terms of <u>integer values</u> for the decision variables.

TRANSPORTATION PROBLEM

1. The <u>transportation problem</u> seeks to minimize the total shipping costs of transporting goods from m origins (each with a supply s_i) to n destinations (each with a demand d_j), when the unit shipping cost from an origin, i, to a destination, j, is c_{ij}.

2. The <u>network representation</u> for a transportation problem with two sources and three destinations is given below:

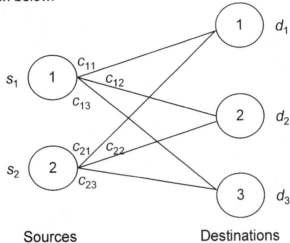

Sources   Destinations

3. Transportation problems are special cases of linear programs. The <u>linear programming formulation</u> in terms of the amounts shipped from the origins to the destinations, x_{ij}, can be written as:

$$\text{MIN } \Sigma_i \Sigma_j c_{ij} x_{ij}$$

$$\text{s. t.} \quad \Sigma_j x_{ij} \le s_i \text{ for each origin } i$$

$$\Sigma_I x_{ij} = d_j \text{ for each destination } j$$

$$x_{ij} \ge 0 \text{ for all } i \text{ and } j.$$

4. The following <u>special-case modifications</u> to the linear programming formulation can be made:
   (a) Minimum shipping guarantees from i to j: $x_{ij} \ge L_{ij}$
   (b) Maximum route capacity from i to j: $x_{ij} \le L_{ij}$
   (c) Unacceptable routes: delete the variable

5. To solve the transportation problem as it is formulated above, it is required that the sum of the supplies at the origins equals or exceeds the sum of the demands at the destinations. If total supply is less than total demand, a <u>dummy origin</u> is added. The objective function coefficient associated with any route stemming from a dummy origin has a value of zero.

ASSIGNMENT PROBLEM

1. An <u>assignment problem</u> seeks to minimize the total cost assignment of m workers to m jobs, given that the cost of worker i performing job j is c_{ij}. It assumes all workers are assigned and each job is performed.

2. The <u>network representation</u> of an assignment problem with three workers and three jobs is:

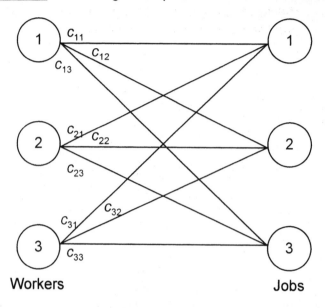

Workers   Jobs

3. The <u>linear programming formulation</u> of the assignment problem using $x_{ij} = 0$ or 1 denoting whether worker i is assigned to job j is:

$$\text{MIN } \Sigma_i \Sigma_j c_{ij} x_{ij}$$

$$\text{s. t.} \quad \Sigma_j x_{ij} = 1 \quad \text{for each worker } i$$

$$\Sigma_I x_{ij} = 1 \quad \text{for each job } j$$

$$x_{ij} = 0 \text{ or } 1 \text{ for all } i \text{ and } j.$$

4. An assignment problem is a <u>special case of a transportation problem</u> in which all supplies and all demands are equal to 1; hence assignment problems may be solved as linear programs.

5. A modification to the <u>right-hand side</u> of the linear program can be made if a worker is permitted to work more than 1 job.

TRANSSHIPMENT PROBLEM

1. <u>Transshipment problems</u> are transportation problems in which a shipment may move through intermediate nodes (transshipment nodes) before reaching a particular destination node.

2. The <u>network representation</u> for a transshipment problem with two sources, three intermediate nodes, and two destinations is given below:

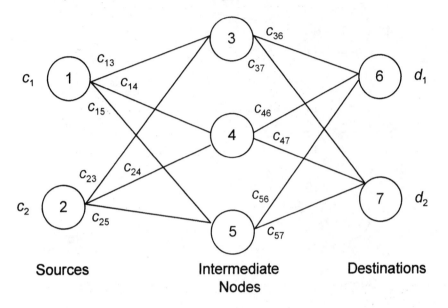

Sources   Intermediate   Destinations
Nodes

3. The <u>linear programming formulation</u> for the transshipment problem with x_{ij} representing the shipment from node i to node j is:

$$\text{MIN } \Sigma_i \Sigma_j c_{ij} x_{ij}$$

$$\text{s. t.} \quad \Sigma_j x_{ij} \le s_i \quad \text{for each origin } i$$

$$\Sigma_l x_{ik} - \Sigma_j x_{kj} = 0 \quad \text{for each intermediate node } k$$

$$\Sigma_l x_{ij} = d_j \quad \text{for each destination } j$$

$$x_{ij} \ge 0 \quad \text{for all } i \text{ and } j.$$

4. A <u>capacitated transshipment problem</u> is a transshipment problem involving one or more routes (arcs) that have a shipping capacity (upper limit).

ILLUSTRATED PROBLEMS

PROBLEM 1

Given the following minimum cost transportation network:

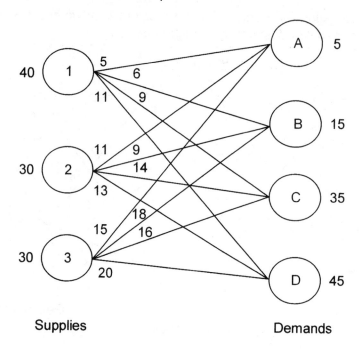

Supplies   Demands

a) Formulate this problem as a linear program.

b) Solve the problem using *The Management Scientist* or similar package.

SOLUTION 1

a) Linear Programming Formulation

Define the decision variables:
Q_{1A} , Q_{1B} , Q_{1C} , Q_{1D} = Quantity shipped from Source 1 to Destinations A, B, C, D
Q_{2A} , Q_{2B} , Q_{2C} , Q_{2D} = Quantity shipped from Source 2 to Destinations A, B, C, D
Q_{3A} , Q_{3B} , Q_{3C} , Q_{3D} = Quantity shipped from Source 3 to Destinations A, B, C, D

Define objective: Minimize overall shipping costs:
$$\text{Min } 5Q_{1A} + 6Q_{1B} + 9Q_{1C} + 11Q_{1D} + 11Q_{2A} + 9Q_{2B} + 14Q_{2C} + 13Q_{2D} + 15Q_{3A} + 18Q_{3B} + 16Q_{3C} + 20Q_{3D}$$

Define the constraints:
Amount out of Origin 1: $Q_{1A} + Q_{1B} + Q_{1C} + Q_{1D} \leq 40$
Amount out of Origin 2: $Q_{2A} + Q_{2B} + Q_{2C} + Q_{2D} \leq 30$
Amount out of Origin 3: $Q_{3A} + Q_{3B} + Q_{3C} + Q_{3D} \leq 30$

Amount into Destination A: $Q_{1A} + Q_{2A} + Q_{3A} \leq 5$
Amount into Destination B: $Q_{1B} + Q_{2B} + Q_{3B} \leq 15$
Amount into Destination C: $Q_{1C} + Q_{2C} + Q_{3C} \leq 35$
Amount into Destination D: $Q_{1D} + Q_{2D} + Q_{3D} \leq 45$
Non-negativity of variables: $Q_{1A} , Q_{1B} , Q_{1C} , Q_{1D} \geq 0$
$Q_{2A} , Q_{2B} , Q_{2C} , Q_{2D} \geq 0$
$Q_{3A} , Q_{3B} , Q_{3C} , Q_{3D} \geq 0$

b) *The Management Scientist* provided the following solution:

OBJECTIVE FUNCTION VALUE = 1195.000

VARIABLE	VALUE	REDUCED COSTS
Q_{1A}	5.000	0.000
Q_{1B}	15.000	0.000
Q_{1C}	5.000	0.000
Q_{1D}	15.000	0.000
Q_{2A}	0.000	4.000
Q_{2B}	0.000	1.000
Q_{2C}	0.000	3.000
Q_{2D}	30.000	0.000
Q_{3A}	0.000	3.000
Q_{3B}	0.000	5.000
Q_{3C}	30.000	0.000
Q_{3D}	0.000	2.000

CONSTRAINT	SLACK/SURPLUS	DUAL PRICES
1	0.000	7.000
2	0.000	5.000
3	0.000	0.000
4	0.000	-12.000
5	0.000	-13.000
6	0.000	-16.000
7	0.000	-18.000

PROBLEM 2

Building Brick Company (BBC) has orders for 80 tons of bricks at three suburban locations as follows: Northwood -- 25 tons, Westwood -- 45 tons, and Eastwood -- 10 tons. BBC has two plants, each of which can produce 50 tons per week. How should end of week shipments be made to fill the above orders given the following delivery cost per ton:

	Northwood	Westwood	Eastwood
Plant 1	24	30	40
Plant 2	30	40	42

a) Formulate this problem as a linear program.

b) Solve the problem using a spreadsheet.

SOLUTION 2

a) Let T_{1N} = Number of tons of brick shipped from Plant 1 to Northwood
T_{1W} = Number of tons of brick shipped from Plant 1 to Westwood
T_{1E} = Number of tons of brick shipped from Plant 1 to Eastwood
T_{2N} = Number of tons of brick shipped from Plant 2 to Northwood
T_{2W} = Number of tons of brick shipped from Plant 2 to Westwood
T_{2E} = Number of tons of brick shipped from Plant 2 to Eastwood

Min $24T_{1N} + 30T_{1W} + 40T_{1E} + 30T_{2N} + 40T_{2W} + 42T_{2E}$

s.t. $T_{1N} + T_{1W} + T_{1E} \leq 50$
$T_{2N} + T_{2W} + T_{2E} \leq 50$
$T_{1N} + T_{2N} = 25$
$T_{1W} + T_{2W} = 45$
$T_{1E} + T_{2E} = 10$
$T_{1N}, T_{1W}, T_{1E}, T_{2N}, T_{2W}, T_{2E} \geq 0$

b) *The Management Scientist* provided the following solution:

OBJECTIVE FUNCTION VALUE = 2490.000

VARIABLE	VALUE	REDUCED COSTS
T_{1N}	5.000	0.000
T_{1W}	45.000	0.000
T_{1E}	0.000	4.000
T_{2N}	20.000	0.000
T_{2W}	0.000	4.000
T_{2E}	10.000	0.000

CONSTRAINT	SLACK/SURPLUS	DUAL PRICES
1	0.000	6.000
2	20.000	0.000
3	0.000	-30.000
4	0.000	-36.000
5	0.000	-42.000

Thus the optimal solution is:

From	To	Amount	Cost
Plant 1	Northwood	5	120
Plant 1	Westwood	45	1,350
Plant 2	Northwood	20	600
Plant 2	Eastwood	10	420
	Total Cost =		$2,490

b) Refer to Chapters 2 and 3 of this study guide for coverage of the steps to follow in setting up and using a spreadsheet to solve an LP.

Spreadsheet showing optimal solution

	A	B	C	D	E	F	G
1		LHS Coefficients					
2	Constraint	X11	X12	X13	X21	X22	X23
3	#1	1	1	1			
4	#2				1	1	1
5	#3	1			1		
6	#4		1			1	
7	#5			1			1
8	Obj.Coefficients	24	30	40	30	40	42
9							
10		X11	X12	X13	X21	X22	X23
11	Dec.Var.Values	5	45	0	20	0	10
12	Minimized Total Shipping Cost				2490		
13							
14	Constraints			LHS		RHS	
15	P1.Cap.			50	<=	50	
16	P2.Cap.			30	<=	50	
17	N.Dem.			25	=	25	
18	W.Dem.			45	=	45	
19	E.Dem.			10	=	10	

Sensitivity Report

Adjustable Cells						
		Final	Reduced	Objective	Allowable	Allowable
Cell	Name	Value	Cost	Coefficient	Increase	Decrease
$B$11	X11	5	0	24	4	4
$C$11	X12	45	0	30	4	1E+30
$D$11	X13	0	4	40	1E+30	4
$E$11	X21	20	0	30	4	4
$F$11	X22	0	4	40	1E+30	4
$GH$1	X23	10.000	0.000	42	4	1E+30

Constraints						
		Final	Shadow	Constraint	Allowable	Allowable
Cell	Name	Value	Price	R.H. Side	Increase	Decrease
$D$16	P2.Cap	30.0	0.0	50	1E+30	20
$D$17	N.Dem	25.0	30.0	25	20	20
$D$18	W.Dem	45.0	36.0	45	5	20
$D$19	E.Dem	10.0	42.0	10	20	10
$D$15	P1.Cap	50.0	-6.0	50	20	5

PROBLEM 3

Telly's Toy Company produces three kinds of dolls called Bertha, Holly, and Terri. Maximum production quantities for the dolls are 1,000, 2,000, and 2,000 per week, respectively. These dolls are purchased by three large department stores: Shears, Nichols and Words. Each department store wishes 1,500 total dolls per week form Telly's. However, Words does not want any Bertha dolls.

Because of past commitments and the sizes of other orders from Telly's, unit profits per doll vary from store to store for each style of doll. These are summarized as follows:

	Shears	Nichols	Words
Bertha	$ 5	$10	X
Holly	$16	$ 8	$ 9
Terri	$12	$ 9	$11

a) Formulate this maximization transportation problem as a linear program.

b) Solve the problem using *The Management Scientist* or similar package.

SOLUTION 3

a) The origins are the dolls, the destinations are the stores.

Let: D_{BS}, D_{BN} = Number of Bertha dolls shipped to Shears, Nichols
D_{HS}, D_{HN}, D_{HW} = Number of Holly dolls shipped to Shears, Nichols, Words
D_{TS}, D_{TN}, D_{TW} = Number of Terri dolls shipped to Shears, Nichols. Words

MAX $5D_{BS} + 10D_{BN} + 16D_{HS} + 8D_{HN} + 9D_{HW} + 12D_{TS} + 9D_{TN} + 11D_{TW}$

s.t.
$$D_{BS} + D_{BN} \leq 1000$$
$$D_{HS} + D_{HN} + D_{HW} \leq 2000$$
$$D_{TS} + D_{TN} + D_{TW} \leq 2000$$
$$D_{BS} + D_{HS} + D_{TS} = 1500$$
$$D_{BN} + D_{HN} + D_{TN} = 1500$$
$$D_{HW} + D_{TW} = 1500$$
$$D_{BS}, D_{BN}, D_{HS}, D_{HN}, D_{HW}, D_{TS}, D_{TN}, D_{TW} \geq 0$$

b) *The Management Scientist* provided the following solution:

OBJECTIVE FUNCTION VALUE = 55000.000

VARIABLE	VALUE	REDUCED COSTS
D_{BS}	0.000	12.000
D_{BN}	1000.000	0.000
D_{HS}	1500.000	0.000
D_{HN}	0.000	1.000
D_{HW}	0.000	2.000
D_{TS}	0.000	4.000
D_{TN}	500.000	0.000
D_{TW}	1500.000	0.000

CONSTRAINT	SLACK/SURPLUS	DUAL PRICES
1	0.000	1.000
2	500.000	0.000
3	0.000	0.000
4	0.000	16.000
5	0.000	9.000
6	0.000	11.000

The optimal solution is:

Dolls	Store	Shipment	Profit
Bertha	Nichols	1000	$10,000
Holly	Shears	1500	$24,000
Shari	Nichols	500	$ 4,500
Shari	Words	1500	$16,500
		Total Profit =	$55,000

PROBLEM 4

A contractor pays his subcontractors a fixed fee plus mileage for work performed. On a given day the contractor is faced with three electrical jobs associated with various projects. He has four electrical subcontractors which are located at various places throughout the area. Given below are the distances between the subcontractors and the projects.

		Project		
		A	B	C
	Westside	50	36	16
Subcontractors	Federated	28	30	18
	Goliath	35	32	20
	Universal	25	25	14

a) Draw a network representation of this problem.

b) Formulate and solve this problem as a linear program.

SOLUTION 4

a) This is an assignment problem.

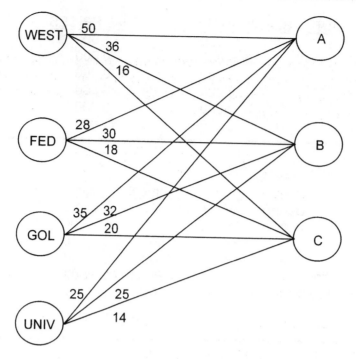

b) Let: $A_{ij} = 1$ if Subcontractor I is assigned to Project j;
   $= 0$ otherwise
   where: i is Westside, Federated, Universal, Goliath
           j is A, B, C

MIN $50A_{WA} + 36A_{WB} + 16A_{WC} + 28A_{FA} + 30A_{FB} + 18A_{FC}$
      $+ 35A_{UA} + 32A_{UB} + 20A_{UC} + 25A_{GA} + 25A_{GB} + 14A_{GC}$

s.t. $A_{WA} + A_{WB} + A_{WC} \leq 1$
       $A_{FA} + A_{FB} + A_{FC} \leq 1$
       $A_{UA} + A_{UB} + A_{UC} \leq 1$
       $A_{GA} + A_{GB} + A_{GC} \leq 1$
       $A_{WA} + A_{FA} + A_{UA} + A_{GA} = 1$
       $A_{WB} + A_{FB} + A_{UB} + A_{GB} = 1$
       $A_{WC} + A_{FC} + A_{UC} + A_{GC} = 1$
       $A_{WA} , A_{WB} , A_{WC} , A_{FA} , A_{FB} , A_{FC} , A_{UA} , A_{UB} , A_{UC} , A_{GA} , A_{GB} , A_{GC} \geq 0$

The optimal assignment is:

Subcontractor	Project	Distance
Westside	C	16
Federated	A	28
Universal	B	25
Goliath	(unassigned)	---

Total distance is 69 miles

PROBLEM 5

A foreman is trying to assign crews to produce the maximum number of parts per hour of a certain product. He has three crews and four possible work centers. The estimated number of parts per hour for each crew at each work center is summarized below. Solve for the optimal assignment of crews to work centers.

	Work Center			
	WC1	WC2	WC3	WC4
Crew A	15	20	18	30
Crew B	20	22	26	30
Crew C	25	26	27	30

SOLUTION 5

This is a maximization assignment problem with fewer crews than work centers. A dummy crew is created to make the problem feasible.

The Management Scientist provided the following solution:

OBJECTIVE FUNCTION VALUE =   55000.000

VARIABLE	VALUE	REDUCED COSTS
A_{A1}	0.000	12.000
A_{A2}	0.000	0.000
A_{A3}	0.000	0.000
A_{A4}	1.000	1.000
A_{B1}	0.000	2.000
A_{B2}	0.000	4.000
A_{B3}	1.000	0.000
A_{B4}	0.000	0.000
A_{C1}	0.000	12.000
A_{C2}	1.000	0.000
A_{C3}	0.000	0.000
A_{C4}	0.000	1.000
A_{D1}	1.000	2.000
A_{D2}	0.000	4.000
A_{D3}	0.000	0.000
A_{D4}	0.000	0.000

CONSTRAINT	SLACK/SURPLUS	DUAL PRICES
1	0.000	18.000
2	0.000	23.000
3	0.000	24.000
4	0.000	-1.000
5	0.000	1.000
6	0.000	2.000
7	0.000	3.000
8	0.000	12.000

An optimal solution is:

Crew	Work Center	Parts/Hour
Crew A	WC4	30
Crew B	WC3	26
Crew C	WC2	26
----------	WC1	---
	Total Parts Per Hour =	82

PROBLEM 6

Thomas Industries and Washburn Corporation supply three firms (Zrox, Hewes, Rockwright) with customized shelving for its offices. They both order shelving from the same two manufacturers, Arnold Manufacturers and Supershelf, Inc. Because of long standing contracts based on past orders, unit costs from the manufacturers to the suppliers are given below:

	Thomas	Washburn
Arnold	5	8
Supershelf	7	4

The chart below gives the cost to install the shelving at the various locations:

	Zrox	Hewes	Rockwright
Thomas	1	5	8
Washburn	3	4	4

Currently weekly demands by the users are 50 for Zrox, 60 for Hewes, and 40 for Rockwright. Both Arnold and Supershelf can supply at most 75 units to its customers.

a) Draw the network representation for this problem.

b) Formulate and solve this problem as a transshipment linear program.

SOLUTION 6

a) Arnold Manufacturers and Supershelf are manufacturers (origins) and Zrox, Hewes, and Rockwright are customers (destinations). Thomas and Washburn represent transshipment points (middlemen) supplying Arnold and Supershelf products to their customers.

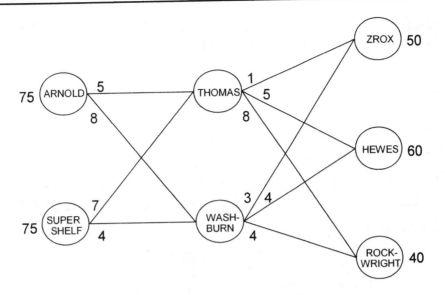

b) Linear Programming Formulation and Solution

Define the decision variables:

x_{ij} = amount shipped from manufacturer i to supplier j
x_{jk} = amount shipped from supplier j to customer k
i = 1 (Arnold), 2 (Supershelf)
j = 3 (Thomas), 4 (Washburn)
k = 5 (Zrox), 6 (Hewes), 7 (Rockwright)

Define objective: Minimize overall shipping costs:

MIN $5x_{13} + 8x_{14} + 7x_{23} + 4x_{24} + 1x_{35} + 5x_{36} + 8x_{37} + 3x_{45} + 4x_{46} + 4x_{47}$

Define the constraints:

Amount out of Arnold:	$x_{13} + x_{14} \leq 75$
Amount out of Supershelf:	$x_{23} + x_{24} \leq 75$

Amount through Thomas:	$x_{13} + x_{23} - x_{35} - x_{36} - x_{37} = 0$
Amount through Washburn:	$x_{14} + x_{24} - x_{45} - x_{46} - x_{47} = 0$

Amount into Zrox:	$x_{35} + x_{45} = 50$
Amount into Hewes:	$x_{36} + x_{46} = 60$
Amount into Rockwright:	$x_{37} + x_{47} = 40$

Non-negativity of variables: $x_{ij} \geq 0$, for all i and j.

The Management Scientist provided the following solution:

OBJECTIVE FUNCTION VALUE =   1150.000

VARIABLE	VALUE	REDUCED COSTS
X13	75.000	0.000
X14	0.000	2.000
X23	0.000	4.000
X24	75.000	0.000
X35	50.000	0.000
X36	25.000	0.000
X37	0.000	3.000
X45	0.000	3.000
X46	35.000	0.000
X47	40.000	0.000

Thus the optimal solution is:

From	To	Amount	Cost
Arnold	Thomas	75	375
Thomas	Zrox	50	50
Thomas	Hewes	25	125
Supershelf	Washburn	75	300
Washburn	Hewes	35	140
Washburn	Rockwright	40	160
		Total Cost =	$1,150

PROBLEM 7

Fodak must schedule its production of camera film for the first four months of the year. Film demand (in 1000s of rolls) in January, February, March and April is expected to be 300, 500, 650 and 400, respectively. Fodak's production capacity is 500 thousand rolls of film per month. The film business is highly competitive, so Fodak cannot afford to lose sales or keep its customers waiting. Meeting month i's demand with month $i+1$'s production is unacceptable.

Film produced in month i can be used to meet demand in month i or can be held in inventory to meet demand in month $i+1$ or month $i+2$ (but not later due to the film's limited shelflife). There is no film in inventory at the start of January.

The film's production and delivery cost per thousand rolls will be $500 in January and February. This cost will increase to $600 in March and April due to a new labor contract. Any film put in inventory requires additional transport costing $100 per thousand rolls. It costs $50 per thousand rolls to hold film in inventory from one month to the next.

a) Modeling this problem as a transshipment problem, draw the network representation.

b) Formulate and solve this problem as a linear program.

c) How might the network in (a) be changed if there was no limit on the length of time film could be held in inventory?

SOLUTION 7

a) The source nodes in this transshipment problem are the four months of production. The destination nodes are the four months of demand. The intermediate nodes are the first three months' ending inventory (there is no reason to be holding any inventory at the end of April).

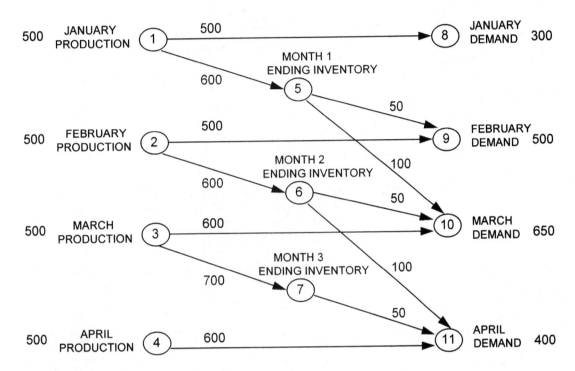

b) Linear Programming Formulation and Solution

Define the decision variables:

x_{ij} = amount of film "moving" between node i and node j

Define objective: Minimize total production, transportation, and inventory holding cost:

$$\text{MIN} \quad 600x_{15} + 500x_{18} + 600x_{26} + 500x_{29} + 700x_{37} + 600x_{310} + 600x_{411} + 50x_{59}$$
$$+ 100x_{510} + 50x_{610} + 100x_{611} + 50x_{711}$$

Define the constraints:

Amount (1000's of rolls) of film produced in January: $\quad x_{15} + x_{18} \leq 500$
Amount (1000's of rolls) of film produced in February: $\quad x_{26} + x_{29} \leq 500$
Amount (1000's of rolls) of film produced in March: $\quad x_{37} + x_{310} \leq 500$
Amount (1000's of rolls) of film produced in April: $\quad x_{411} \quad\quad \leq 500$

Amount (1000's of rolls) of film in/out of January inventory: $x_{15} - x_{59} - x_{510} = 0$
Amount (1000's of rolls) of film in/out of February inventory: $x_{26} - x_{610} - x_{611} = 0$
Amount (1000's of rolls) of film in/out of March inventory: $\quad x_{37} - x_{711} \quad\quad = 0$
Amount (1000's of rolls) of film satisfying January demand: $x_{18} \quad\quad\quad = 300$

Amount (1000's of rolls) of film satisfying February demand $x_{29} + x_{59}$ = 500
Amount (1000's of rolls) of film satisfying March demand: $x_{310} + x_{510} + x_{610}$ = 650
Amount (1000's of rolls) of film satisfying April demand: $x_{411} + x_{611} + x_{711}$ = 400

Non-negativity of variables: $x_{ij} \geq 0$, for all i and j.

The Management Scientist provided the following solution:

OBJECTIVE FUNCTION VALUE = 1045000.000

VARIABLE	VALUE	REDUCED COSTS
X15	150.000	0.000
X18	300.000	0.000
X26	0.000	100.000
X29	500.000	0.000
X37	0.000	250.000
X310	500.000	0.000
X411	400.000	0.000
X59	0.000	0.000
X510	150.000	0.000
X610	0.000	0.000
X611	0.000	150.000
X711	0.000	0.000

c)

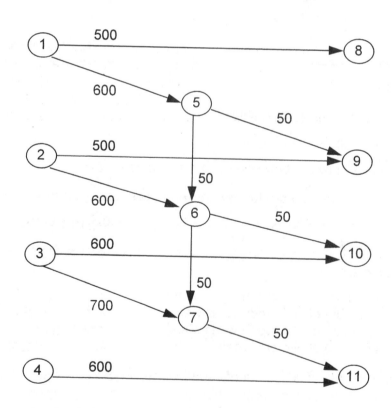

ANSWERED PROBLEMS

PROBLEM 8

The Navy has 9,000 pounds of material in Albany, Georgia which it wishes to ship to three installations: San Diego, Norfolk, and Pensacola. They require 4,000, 2,500, and 2,500 pounds, respectively. Laws require equal allotment of shipping among the 3 carriers. The following gives the shipping costs per pound for truck, railroad, and airplane transit.

	San Diego	Norfolk	Pensacola
Truck	$12	$ 6	$ 5
Railroad	$20	$11	$ 9
Airplane	$30	$26	$28

a) Draw the network representation of this problem.

b) Formulate this problem as a linear program.

c) Solve for the optimal shipping strategy.

PROBLEM 9

There are four marketing research firms (MR1, MR2, MR3, MR4) that Hairways has faith in to advertise its products. Hairways has just come out with a new hairspray and they wish to have 30 newspaper ads, 15 television ads, and 25 radio ads available within three months. Given the size of the firms it is expected that MR1 can produce 15 total ads, MR2 can produce 25 total ads, MR3 can produce 10 total ads, and MR4 can produce 20 total ads. The bids submitted (in thousands of dollars per ad) are:

	MR1	MR2	MR3	MR4
Newspaper	16	10	12	12
Television	26	20	30	21
Radio	22	15	23	14

a) Formulate this problem as a linear program and show that it fits the structure of a transportation problem.

b) Find a solution with six media-firm combinations.

c) Give another solution with five media-firm combinations.

d) Give another solution with seven media-firm combinations.

PROBLEM 10

The city of Francene has 25 contracts up for bids in each of four different departments: Sanitation, Police Services, Parks Department, and Administration.

Three different consulting firms are bidding on the contracts: Ace Consulting, Band Corporation, and QM Associates. Ace has personnel for 40 contracts, Band for 40, and QM for 30. Because contracts are similar within each department, each firm is able to set a fixed bid per contract for each department. The bid price (in $1000s per contract) is summarized below:

	Sanitation	Police	Parks	Administration
Ace	10	15	14	16
Band	15	18	8	10
QM	12	12	12	12

How should the contracts be awarded and how much will the city spend?

PROBLEM 11

Independent Auditors (IA) has committed 100 of its auditors in three locations (35 from its Los Angeles branch, 30 from its Chicago branch, and 35 from its New York branch) to audit firms in three cities: 25 for Denver, 35 for Atlanta, and 40 for New York. Because of possible charges of conflicts of interest, no New York based IA auditor will audit a New York firm. Taking into account all costs and revenues, and the following profit table giving the average profit per auditor (in $1000's), solve for IA's optimal distribution of auditors.

	Denver	Atlanta	New York
Los Angeles	25	18	10
Chicago	30	35	20
New York	14	24	X

PROBLEM 12

Emily Rodd, manager of Camp Pinnacle, must assign her five head counselors to cabins for the summer. The counselors have cabin assignment preferences (based on cabin size, location, condition and other factors). The counselors' cabin preference ratings on a 1-to-9 scale (9 being most favorable) are listed below:

	\multicolumn{5}{c}{Cabin}
	1	2	3	4	5
Abbey	3	9	7	5	5
Babbs	6	8	3	5	7
Carla	2	8	5	2	7
Diane	7	4	2	2	9
Ellsa	6	8	5	2	5

Help Emily make the counselor-cabin assignments that will maximize the sum of the preference ratings achieved.

PROBLEM 13

In addition to Pine City's established microcomputer firm, Local Computer, there are three new microcomputer firms that have opened up in the area. In an effort to establish good relations, Manny's Manufacturing plans on buying one computer system from each of the new firms and two from Local Computer. Manny's has five plants, each with different needs, and hence Manny needs to install five different systems. The bids (in $1,000's) from the firms are:

| | Plant | | | | |
	P1	P2	P3	P4	P5
Computer Town	10	12	14	18	20
Computer World	11	13	15	14	18
Universal Comp	6	14	24	20	19
Local Computer	14	15	16	22	25

a) Give a network representation for this problem.

b) Solve for the optimal assignment strategy.

c) Suppose Computer World did not have the system needed by P5. How would this have affected the optimal solution?

d) Suppose Computer World did not have the systems needed by P4 or P5. How would this have affected the optimal solution?

PROBLEM 14

A plant manager for a sporting goods manufacturer is in charge of assigning the manufacture of four new aluminum products to four different departments. Because of varying expertise and workloads, the different departments can produce the new products at various rates. If only one product is to be produced by each department and the daily output rates are given in the table below, which department should manufacture which product to maximize total daily product output? (Note: Department 1 does not have the facilities to produce golf clubs.)

Department	Bats	Tennis Rackets	Golf Clubs	Racquetball Rackets
1	100	60	X	80
2	100	80	140	100
3	110	75	150	120
4	85	50	100	75

PROBLEM 15

RVW (Restored Volkswagens) buys 15 used VW's at each of two car auctions each week held at different locations. It then transports the cars to repair shops it contracts with. When they are restored to RVW's specifications, RVW sells 10 each to three different used car lots.

There are various costs associated with the average purchase and transportation prices from each auction to each repair shop. Also there are transportation costs from the repair shops to the used car lots. RVW is concerned with minimizing its total cost given the costs in the table below.

a) Given the costs below, draw a network representation for this problem.

	Repair Shops				Used Car Lots		
	S1	S2			L1	L2	L3
Auction 1	550	500		S1	250	300	500
Auction 2	600	450		S2	350	650	450

b) Formulate and solve this problem as a transshipment linear programming model.

TRUE/FALSE

____ 16. Flow in a transportation network is limited to one direction.

____ 17. If a transportation problem has four origins and five destinations, the LP formulation of the problem will have nine constraints.

____ 18. In a transportation problem, if the total supply is less than the total demand, a dummy source is included in the linear programming formulation.

____ 19. The transportation, assignment, and transshipment problems are all special cases of linear programming models known as network models and can be solved by the simplex method.

____ 20. In the general assignment problem, one agent can be assigned to several tasks.

____ 21. In a transportation problem with total supply equal to total demand, if there are four origins and seven destinations, and there is a unique optimal solution, the optimal solution will utilize 11 shipping routes.

____ 22. The assignment problem can be considered to be a transportation problem, but the opposite is not true.

____ 23. In assignment problems, dummy agents or tasks are created when the number of agents and tasks is not equal.

____ 24. A transshipment problem is a generalization of the transportation problem in which certain nodes are neither supply nodes nor destination nodes.

____ 25. The assignment problem is a special case of the transportation problem in which all supply and demand values equal one.

____ 26. To compensate for a transshipment route with limited capacity, add a constraint to the LP.

____ 27. A transportation problem with 3 sources and 4 destinations will have 7 variables in the objective function.

____ 28. All of the transportation costs associated with a dummy origin are zero, regardless of whether you are maximizing or minimizing.

____ 29. The optimal solution to a transportation problem will never include a shipment from a dummy origin.

____ 30. Transshipment problem allows shipments both in and out of some nodes while transportation problems do not.

CHAPTER 8

Integer Linear Programming

KEY CONCEPTS

CONCEPT	ILLUSTRATED PROBLEMS	ANSWERED PROBLEMS
All-Integer Linear Program	1,2	6,7,8,11,12,13
Mixed-Integer Linear Program	2	11,13
ILP: Maximization	1,3	6,7
ILP: Minimization	2	11
Rounding LP Solution	1	6,10,12
Graphical Solution	1,2	6
0-1 Integer Linear Program	3,4,5	9,10
Special 0-1 Constraints	3	8,9
Spreadsheet Example	1,3	

REVIEW

1. A linear program in which all the variables are restricted to be integers is called an <u>integer linear program (ILP)</u>. If only a subset of the variables are restricted to be integers, the problem is called a <u>mixed integer linear program (MILP)</u>.

2. <u>Binary variables</u> are variables whose values are restricted to be 0 or 1. If all variables are restricted to be 0 or 1, the problem is called a <u>0-1 or binary integer program</u>.

3. Many practical applications involve only binary integer variables and hence many computer codes are written only for this case (such as LINDO/PC). <u>Binary expansion</u> is a mathematical technique which may be used to convert any integer variable into the sum of binary variables.

4. <u>Rounding</u> the values of the variables obtained by solving the linear programming problem may yield an infeasible solution or a solution that might be feasible but not optimal for the ILP or MILP.

5. For problems in which x_i and and x_j represent binary variables designating whether projects i and j have been completed, the following <u>special constraints</u> may be formulated:

    (a) At most <u>k out of n</u> projects will be completed: $\Sigma_j x_j \leq k$

    (b) Project j is <u>conditional</u> on project i: $x_j - x_i \leq 0$

    (c) Project i is a <u>corequisite</u> for project j: $x_j - x_i = 0$

    (d) Projects i and j are <u>mutually exclusive</u>: $x_i + x_j \leq 1.$

6. <u>Sensitivity analysis</u> information for integer linear programming does not have the same connotation as that for linear programming and should be either discarded or used with great caution. In fact, small changes in the coefficients of an integer program can cause large changes in its optimal solution or even cause the problem to be infeasible.

ILLUSTRATED PROBLEMS

PROBLEM 1

Given the following all-integer linear program:

$$\text{MAX} \quad 3x_1 + 2x_2$$

$$\text{s. t.} \quad 3x_1 + x_2 \leq 9$$

$$x_1 + 3x_2 \leq 7$$

$$-x_1 + x_2 \leq 1$$

$$x_1, x_2 \geq 0 \text{ and integer}$$

a) Solve the problem as a linear program ignoring the integer constraints. Show that the optimal solution to the linear program gives fractional values for both x_1 and x_2.

b) What is the solution obtained by rounding fractions greater than of equal to 1/2 to the next larger number? Show that this solution is not a feasible solution.

c) What is the solution obtained by rounding down all fractions? Is it feasible?

d) Enumerate all points in the linear programming feasible region in which both x_1 and x_2 are integers, and show that the feasible solution obtained in (c) is not optimal and that in fact the optimal integer is not obtained by any form of rounding.

e) Solve the problem as an integer linear program using a computer spreadsheet.

SOLUTION 1

a) From the graph on the next page, the optimal solution to the linear program is $x_1 = 2.5$, $x_2 = 1.5$, $z = 10.5$.

b) By rounding the optimal solution of $x_1 = 2.5$, $x_2 = 1.5$ to $x_1 = 3$, $x_2 = 2$, this point lies outside the feasible region.

c) By rounding the optimal solution down to $x_1 = 2$, $x_2 = 1$, we see that this solution indeed is an integer solution within the feasible region, and substituting in the objective function, it gives $z = 8$.

d) There are eight feasible integer solutions in the linear programming feasible region with z values as follows:

	x_1	x_2	z	
1.	0	0	0	
2.	1	0	3	
3.	2	0	6	
4.	3	0	9	← optimal
5.	0	1	2	
6.	1	1	5	
7.	2	1	8	← part (c) solution
8.	1	2	7	

$x_1 = 3$, $x_2 = 0$ is the optimal solution. Rounding the LP solution ($x_1 = 2.5$, $x_2 = 1.5$) would not have been optimal.

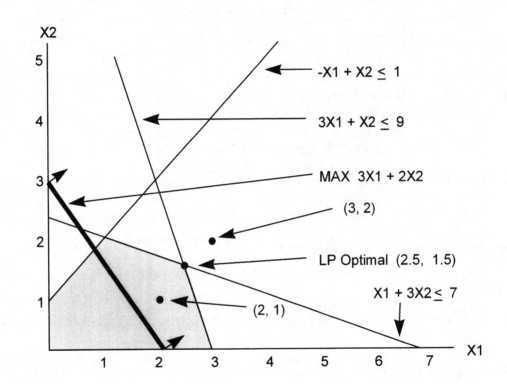

e) Spreadsheet showing data and formulas

	A	B	C	D
1		LHS Coefficients		
2	**Constraint**	**X1**	**X2**	**RHS**
3	#1	3	1	9
4	#2	1	3	7
5	#3	-1	1	1
6	**Obj.Coefficients**	3	2	
7				
8			**X1**	**X2**
9	Optimal Decision Variable Values			
10	Maximized Objective Function		=B6*C9+C6*D9	
11				
12	Constraints	LHS		RHS
13	#1	=B3*$C$9+C3*$D$9	<=	=D3
14	#2	=B4*$C$9+C4*$D$9	<=	=D4
15	#3	=B5*$C$9+C5*$D$9	<=	=D5

The necessary steps in using Excel to solve an integer LP are as follows:

Step 1: Select the **Tools** pull-down menu.

Step 2: Select the **Solver** option.

Step 3: When the **Solver Parameters** dialog box appears:

Enter C10 in the **Set Target Cell** box.

Select the **Equal To: Max** option.

Enter C9:D9 in the **By Changing Cells** box.

Select **Add**.

When the **Add Constraint** dialog box appears:

Enter B13:B15 in the **Cell Reference** box.

Select <=.

Enter D13:D15 in the **Constraint** box.

Click **OK**.

Select **Add**.

When the **Add Constraint** dialog box appears:

Enter C9:D9 in the **Cell Reference** box.

Select **int**.

Click **OK**.

Step 4: When the **Solver Parameters** dialog box appears:

Choose **Options**.

Step 5: When the **Solver Options** dialog box appears:

Select **Assume Non-Negative**.

Click **OK**.

Step 6: When the **Solver Parameters** dialog box appears:

Choose **Solve**.

Step 8: When the **Solver Results** dialog box appears:

Select **Keep Solver Solution**.

Click **OK**.

Spreadsheet showing optimal solution

	A	B	C	D
8			**X1**	**X2**
9	Optimal Dec. Var. Values		3.000	2.942E-12
10	Maximized Obj. Function		9.000	
11				
12	Constraints	LHS		RHS
13	#1	9	<=	9
14	#2	3	<=	7
15	#3	-3	<=	1

PROBLEM 2

Given the following problem:

$$\text{MIN} \quad 2x_1 + x_2$$

$$\text{s. t.} \quad x_1 + 3x_2 \geq 5$$

$$8x_1 + 3x_2 \geq 17$$

$$x_1, x_2 \geq 0$$

a) Solve for the optimal solution to the linear program.

b) Suppose only x_2 were restricted to be an integer. What is the optimal solution to this mixed integer linear program?

c) Suppose both x_1 and x_2 were restricted to be integers. Determine the optimal solution to the all-integer linear program.

d) Make a comment about the relative optimal values of the objective functions for the linear program, mixed integer program, and the all-integer program.

SOLUTION 2

a) The optimal solution is $x_1 = 1\ 5/7$, $x_2 = 1\ 2/21$, $z = 4\ 11/21$.

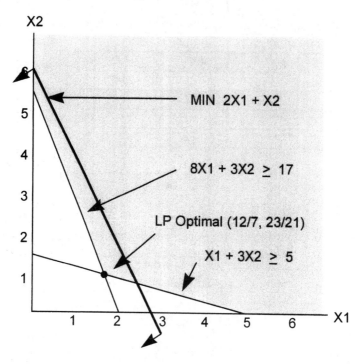

b) Since only x_2 must be integer, the solution must lie on a line of constant integer value of x_2, i.e. $x_2 = 0$, or $x_2 = 1$, etc. The graph below indicates that for each integer value for x_2 the minimum value of z is attained at the minimum value for x_1.

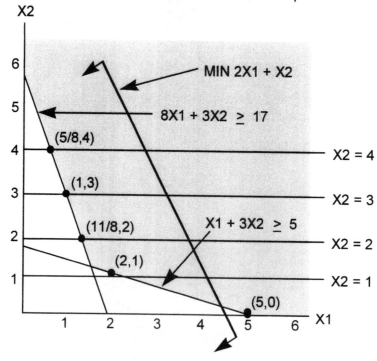

The following table summarizes the corresponding values for x_1 and z for increasing values of x_2.

x_2	Smallest Feasible x_1	z
0	5	10
1	2	5
2	1 3/8	4 3/4
3	1	5
4	5/8	5 1/4

(For higher values of x_2, z continues to increase.)

Hence, the optimal mixed integer solution is x_1 = 1 3/8, x_2 = 2, z = 4 3/4.

c) The graph below indicates feasible integer points that are closest to the constraint boundaries. It can be observed that the otimal solution to the all-integer problem is attained at x_1 = 2, x_2 = 1 and at x_1 = 1, x_2 = 3. Both give z = 5.

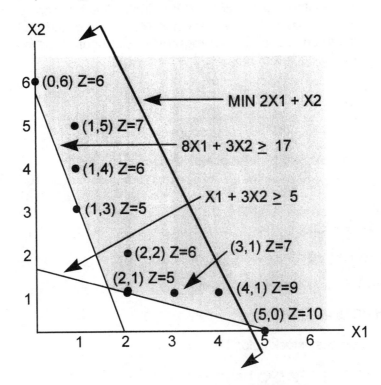

d) The optimal value for the linear program is "better" than for the mixed integer program, which in turn is better than that for the all-integer program.

PROBLEM 3

Metropolitan Microwaves, Inc. is planning to expand its operations into other electronic appliances. The company has identified seven new product lines it can carry. The required initial investment and floor space (sq. ft.) and the expected rate of return on each line.

Product Line	Initial Investment	Floor Space	Expected Rate of Return
1. TV/VCRs	$ 6,000	125	8.1%
2. Color TVs	12,000	150	9.0
3. Projection TVs	20,000	200	11.0
4. VCRs	14,000	40	10.2
5. DVD Players	15,000	40	10.5
6. Video Games	2,000	20	14.1
7. Home Computers	32,000	100	13.2

Metropolitan has decided that they should not stock projection TVs unless they stock either TV/VCRs or color TVs. Also, they will not stock both VCRs and DVD players, and they will stock video games if they stock color TVs. Finally, the company wishes to introduce at least three new product lines. If the company has $45,000 to invest and 420 sq. ft. of floor space available, formulate an integer linear program for Metropolitan to maximize its overall expected return. Use a spreadsheet to solve this binary LP.

SOLUTION 3

Define variables: x_j = 1 if product line j is introduced; = 0 otherwise.

Define objective function: Maximize total overall expected return:
MAX $.081(6000)x_1 + .09(12000)x_2 + .11(20000)x_3 + .102(14000)x_4 + .105(15000)x_5$
$+ .141(2000)x_6 + .132(32000)x_7$

Define constraints:
1) Money: $6x_1 + 12x_2 + 20x_3 + 14x_4 + 15x_5 + 2x_6 + 32x_7 \leq 45$

2) Space: $125x_1 + 150x_2 + 200x_3 + 40x_4 + 40x_5 + 20x_6 + 100x_7 \leq 420$

3) Stock projection TVs only if stock TV/VCRs or color TVs: $x_1 + x_2 \geq x_3$ or $x_1 + x_2 - x_3 \geq 0$

4) Not stock both VCRs and DVD players: $x_4 + x_5 \leq 1$

5) Stock video games if they stock color TV's: $x_2 - x_6 = 0$.

6) At least 3 new lines: $x_1 + x_2 + x_3 + x_4 + x_5 + x_6 + x_7 \geq 3$

7) Variables are 0 or 1: x_j = 0 or 1 for j = 1,,,7.

Spreadsheet showing data and formulas

	A	B	C	D	E	F	G	H	I
1		LHS Coefficients							
2	**Constraints**	**X1**	**X2**	**X3**	**X4**	**X5**	**X6**	**X7**	**RHS**
3	#1	6	12	20	14	15	2	32	45
4	#2	125	150	200	40	40	20	100	420
5	#3	1	1	-1					0
6	#4				1	1			1
7	**#5**		1				-1		0
8	**#6**	1	1	1	1	1	1	1	3
9	Obj.Func.Coeff.	486	1080	2200	1428	1575	282	4224	
10									
11		**X1**	**X2**	**X3**	**X4**	**X5**	**X6**	**X7**	
12	**Dec.Values**								
13	**Maximized Total Expected Return**				#				
14									
15	**Constraints**		**LHS**				**RHS**		
16	Money		##		<=		=I3		
17	Space		etc.		<=		=I4		
18	TVs		etc.		>=		=I5		
19	VCRs/DVDs		etc.		<=		=I6		
20	Video		etc.		=		=I7		
21	Lines		etc.		>=		=I8		

\# = B9*B12+C9*C12+D9*D12+E9*E12+F9*F12+G9*G12+H9*H12

\## = B3*$B$12+C3*$C$12+D3*$D$12+E3*$E$12+F3*$F$12+G3*$G$12+H3*$H$12

Refer to Problem 1 above for coverage of the steps to follow in using a spreadsheet to solve an LP. The additional/exceptional steps necessary to solve a <u>binary</u> LP using *Excel* are as follows:

> In the **Solver Parameters** dialog box:
> > Select **Add**.
> > When the **Add Constraint** dialog box appears:
> > > Enter B12:H12 in the **Cell Reference** box.
> > > Select **binary**.
> > > Click **OK**.
> > Select **Options**.
> > When the **Solver Options** dialog box appears:
> > > Enter 0 in the **Tolerance** box.
> > > Click **OK**.

Optimal Solution:
> Metropolitan should stock TV/VCRs, projection TVs, and DVD players for a total expected return of $4,261.

PROBLEM 4

Tom's Tailoring has five idle tailors and four custom garments to make. The estimated time (in hours) it would take each tailor to make each garment is listed below. (An 'X' in the table indicates an unacceptable tailor-garment assignment.)

			Tailor		
Garment	1	2	3	4	5
Wedding gown	19	23	20	21	18
Clown costume	11	14	X	12	10
Admiral's uniform	12	8	11	X	9
Bullfighter's outfit	X	20	20	18	21

Formulate and solve an integer program for determining the tailor-garment assignments that minimize the total estimated time spent making the four garments. No tailor is to be assigned more than one garment and each garment is to be worked on by only one tailor.

Note: This problem is referred to as an assignment problem. An alternative approach to optimally solving an assignment problem is covered in Chapter 7.

SOLUTION 4

This problem can be formulated as a 0-1 integer program. The LP solution to this problem will automatically be integer (0-1).

Define the decision variables:

x_{ij} = 1 if garment i is assigned to tailor j; = 0 otherwise.
Number of decision variables = [(number of garments)(number of tailors)]
$$- \text{(number of unacceptable assignments)} = [4(5)] - 3 = 17.$$

Define the objective function:

Minimize total time spent making garments:
$$\text{MIN } 19x_{11} + 23x_{12} + 20x_{13} + 21x_{14} + 18x_{15} + 11x_{21} + 14x_{22} + 12x_{24} + 10x_{25}$$
$$+ 12x_{31} + 8x_{32} + 11x_{33} + 9x_{35} + 20x_{42} + 20x_{43} + 18x_{44} + 21x_{45}$$

Define the constraints:

Exactly one tailor per garment:
1) $x_{11} + x_{12} + x_{13} + x_{14} + x_{15} = 1$
2) $x_{21} + x_{22} + x_{24} + x_{25} = 1$
3) $x_{31} + x_{32} + x_{33} + x_{35} = 1$
4) $x_{42} + x_{43} + x_{44} + x_{45} = 1$

No more than one garment per tailor:
5) $x_{11} + x_{21} + x_{31} \leq 1$
6) $x_{12} + x_{22} + x_{32} + x_{42} \leq 1$
7) $x_{13} + x_{33} + x_{43} \leq 1$
8) $x_{14} + x_{24} + x_{44} \leq 1$
9) $x_{15} + x_{25} + x_{35} + x_{45} \leq 1$

Nonnegativity: $x_{ij} \geq 0$ for $i = 1,..,4$ and $j = 1,..,5$

Optimal Solution:
  Assign wedding gown to tailor 5
  Assign clown costume to tailor 1
  Assign admiral uniform to tailor 2
  Assign bullfighter outfit to tailor 4

Total time spent = 55 hours

PROBLEM 5

Market Pulse Research has conducted a study for Lucas Furniture on some designs for a new commercial office desk. Three attributes were found to be most influential in determining which desk is most desirable: number of file drawers, the presence or absence of pullout writing boards, and simulated wood or solid color finish. Listed below are the part-worths for each level of each attribute provided by a sample of 7 potential Lucas customers.

	File Drawers			Pullout Writing Boards		Finish	
Consumer	0	1	2	Present	Absent	Simul. Wood	Solid Color
1	5	26	20	18	11	17	10
2	18	11	5	12	16	15	26
3	4	16	22	7	13	11	19
4	12	8	4	18	9	22	14
5	19	9	3	4	14	30	19
6	6	15	21	8	17	20	11
7	9	6	3	13	5	16	28

Suppose the overall utility (sum of part-worths) of the current favorite commercial office desk is 50 for each customer. What is the product design that will maximize the share of choices for the seven sample participants? Formulate and solve, using Lindo or Excel, this 0 – 1 integer programming problem.

SOLUTION 5

Define the decision variables:

There are 7 I_{ij} decision variables, one for each level of attribute.
I_{ij} = 1 if Lucas chooses level i for attribute j; 0 otherwise.

There are 7 Y_k decision variables, one for each consumer in the sample.
Y_k = 1 if consumer k chooses the Lucas brand, 0 otherwise.

Define the objective function:

Maximize the number of consumers preferring the Lucas brand desk.
MAX $Y_1 + Y_2 + Y_3 + Y_4 + Y_5 + Y_6 + Y_7$

Define the constraints:

There is one constraint for each consumer in the sample.

$5I_{11} + 26I_{21} + 20I_{31} + 18I_{12} + 11I_{22} + 17I_{13} + 10I_{23} - 50Y_1 \geq 1$

$18I_{11} + 11I_{21} + 5I_{31} + 12I_{12} + 16I_{22} + 15I_{13} + 26I_{23} - 50Y_2 \geq 1$

$4I_{11} + 16I_{21} + 22I_{31} + 7I_{12} + 13I_{22} + 11I_{13} + 19I_{23} - 50Y_3 \geq 1$

$12I_{11} + 8I_{21} + 4I_{31} + 18I_{12} + 9I_{22} + 22I_{13} + 14I_{23} - 50Y_4 \geq 1$

$19I_{11} + 9I_{21} + 3I_{31} + 4I_{12} + 14I_{22} + 30I_{13} + 19I_{23} - 50Y_5 \geq 1$

$6I_{11} + 15I_{21} + 21I_{31} + 8I_{12} + 17I_{22} + 20I_{13} + 11I_{23} - 50Y_6 \geq 1$

$9I_{11} + 6I_{21} + 3I_{31} + 13I_{12} + 5I_{22} + 16I_{13} + 28I_{23} - 50Y_7 \geq 1$

There is one constraint for each attribute.

$I_{11} + I_{21} + I_{31} = 1$

$I_{12} + I_{22} = 1$

$I_{13} + I_{23} = 1$

Optimal Solution:

Lucas should choose these product features:

1 file drawer	$(I_{21} = 1)$
No pullout writing boards	$(I_{22} = 1)$
Simulated wood finish	$(I_{13} = 1)$

Three sample participants would choose the Lucas design:

Participant 1	$(Y_1 = 1)$
Participant 5	$(Y_5 = 1)$
Participant 6	$(Y_6 = 1)$

┌─────────────────────────────┐
│ **ANSWERED PROBLEMS** │
└─────────────────────────────┘

PROBLEM 6

Given the following all-integer linear program:

$$\text{MAX} \quad 15x_1 + 2x_2$$
$$\text{s. t.} \quad 7x_1 + x_2 \leq 23$$
$$3x_1 - x_2 \leq 5$$
$$x_1, x_2 \geq 0 \text{ and integer}$$

a) Solve the problem as an LP, ignoring the integer constraints.

b) What solution is obtained by rounding up fractions greater than or equal to 1/2? Is this the optimal integer solution?

c) What solution is obtained by rounding down all fractions? Is this the optimal integer solution? Explain.

d) Show that the optimal z value for the ILP is lower than that for the optimal LP.

e) Why is the optimal z value for the ILP problem always less than or equal to the corresponding LP's optimal z value? When would they be equal? Comment on the MILP's optimal z compared to the corresponding LP & ILP.

PROBLEM 7

Given the following all-integer linear programming problem:

$$\text{MAX} \quad 3x_1 + 10x_2$$
$$\text{s. t.} \quad 2x_1 + x_2 \leq 5$$
$$x_1 + 6x_2 \leq 9$$
$$x_1 - x_2 \geq 2$$
$$x_1, x_2 \geq 0 \text{ and integer}$$

a) Solve the problem graphically as a linear program.

b) Show that there is only one integer point and it is optimal.

c) Suppose the third constraint was changed to $x_1 - x_2 \geq 2.1$. What is the new optimal solution to the LP? ILP?

PROBLEM 8

Given the following all-integer linear programming problem:

$$\text{MAX} \quad 5x_1 + 4x_2$$

$$\text{s. t.} \quad 4x_1 + x_2 \leq 10$$

$$5x_1 + 3x_2 \leq 15$$

$$x_1 + x_2 \leq 4$$

$$x_1, x_2 \geq 0 \text{ and integer}$$

a) Solve the LP relaxation of this problem. Does this provide an upper bound or lower bound for the value of the objective function for the ILP?

b) Solve by inspection for the optimal solution to the ILP.

c) Suppose the objective function was changed to MAX $z = 5x_1 + 3x_2$. What is the new optimal solution to this problem?

PROBLEM 9

Tower Engineering Corporation is considering undertaking several proposed projects for the next fiscal year. The projects, the number of engineers and the number of support personnel required for each project, and the expected profits for each project are summarized in the following table:

	Project					
	1	2	3	4	5	6
Engineers Required	20	55	47	38	90	63
Support Personnel Required	15	45	50	40	70	70
Profit ($1,000,000s)	1.0	1.8	2.0	1.5	3.6	2.2

Formulate and solve an integer program that maximizes Tower's profit subject to the following management constraints:

(1) Use no more than 175 engineers
(2) Use no more than 150 support personnel
(3) If either project 6 or project 4 is done, both must be done
(4) Project 2 can be done only if project 1 is done
(5) If project 5 is done, project 3 must not be done and vice versa
(6) No more than three projects are to be done.

PROBLEM 10

Kloos Industries has projected the availability of capital over each of the next three years to be $850,000, $1,000,000, and $1,200,000, respectively. It is considering four options for the disposition of the capital:

(1) Research and development of a promising new product
(2) Plant expansion
(3) Modernization of its current facilities
(4) Investment in a valuable piece of nearby real estate

Monies not invested in these projects in a given year will NOT be available for following year's investment in the projects. The expected benefits three years hence from each of the four projects and the yearly capital outlays of the four options are summarized in the table below in $1,000,000's.

In addition, Kloos has decided to undertake exactly two of the projects, and if plant expansion is selected, it will also modernize its current facilities.

	Capital Outlays			Projected
Options	Year 1	Year 2	Year 3	Benefits
New Product R&D	.35	.55	.75	5.2
Plant Expansion	.50	.50	0	3.6
Modernization	.35	.40	.45	3.2
Real Estate	.50	0	0	2.8

Formulate and solve this problem as a binary programming problem.

PROBLEM 11

Given the following problem:

$$\text{MIN} \quad 5x_1 + 8x_2$$

$$\text{s. t.} \quad x_1 + x_2 \geq 7.2$$

$$x_1 + 4x_2 \geq 20$$

$$5x_1 + 3x_2 \leq 34$$

$$x_1, x_2 \geq 0$$

a) Solve the mixed-integer problem where x_1 must be integer.

b) Solve the problem where both x_1 and x_2 must be integer.

PROBLEM 12

A business manager for a grain distributor is asked to decide how many containers of each of two grains to purchase to fill its 1,600 pound capacity warehouse. The table below summarizes the container size, availability, and expected profit per container upon distribution.

Grain	Container Size	Containers Available	Container Profit
A	500 lbs.	3	$1,200
B	600 lbs.	2	$1,500

a) Formulate as a linear program with the decision variables representing the number of containers purchased of each grain. Solve for the optimal solution.

b) What would be the optimal solution if you were not allowed to purchase fractional containers?

c) There are three possible results from rounding an LP solution to obtain an integer solution:
   (1) the rounded optimal LP solution will be the optimal IP solution;
   (2) the rounded optimal LP solution gives a feasible, but not optimal IP solution;
   (3) the rounded optimal LP solution is an infeasible IP solution.

For this problem (i) round <u>down</u> all fractions; (ii) round <u>up</u> all fractions; (iii) round <u>off</u> (to the nearest integer) all fractions (NOTE: Two of these are equivalent.) Which result above (1, 2, or 3) occurred under each rounding method?

PROBLEM 13

Given the following problem:

$$\text{MIN} \quad 4x_1 + 7x_2$$

$$\text{s. t.} \quad x_1 + 6x_2 \geq 14$$

$$2x_1 + 5x_2 \geq 22$$

$$3x_1 + x_2 \geq 10$$

$$x_1, x_2 \geq 0$$

a) Solve the mixed integer problem where x_1 is required to be integer.

b) Using (a), solve the all-integer linear program.

TRUE/FALSE

____ 14. The optimal solution to a linear program gave $x_1 = 2.58$ and $x_2 = 1.32$. If x_1 and x_2 were restricted to be integers, then $x_1 = 3$, $x_2 = 1$ will give a feasible solution, but not necessarily an optimal integer solution.

____ 15. The objective function coefficients are all integers for an ILP. The optimal solution to the LP is $x_1 = 2.58$, $x_2 = 1.32$, and $z = 14.28$. The solution was rounded to $x_1 = 3$, $x_2 = 1$ and $z = 14$, and this is a feasible solution. Then this must be the optimal solution to the ILP.

____ 16. Project 5 must be completed before project 6 is started. The constraint would be: $x_5 - x_6 \leq 0$.

____ 17. If the LP relaxation of an integer program has a feasible solution, them the integer program has a feasible solution.

____ 18. A mixed-integer linear program involves both discrete and continuous variables.

____ 19. The optimal solution to an integer linear program still must occur at an extreme point of the feasible region formed by the functional constraints.

____ 20. If at most three of five projects are to be completed, the constraint would be: $x_1 + x_2 + x_3 + x_4 + x_5 \leq 3$.

____ 21. Multiple-choice constraints involve binary variables.

____ 22. The classic assignment problem can be modeled as a 0-1 integer program.

____ 23. An optimal integer solution of $x_1 = 3$, $x_2 = 5$, $z = 150$ has been found for an ILP. For the linear programming formulation, the range of optimality for c_1 was between 15 and 30 with a current $c_1 = 20$. Then if c_1 is increased to 21 in the ILP, the new optimal value of the objective function must be 153.

____ 24. For a minimization ILP, a lower bound is found when any integer solution is determined.

____ 25. For some types of ILP problems their LP relaxation solutions are optimal.

____ 26. The product design and market share optimization problem is sometimes called the share of choices problem.

____ 27. Generally, the optimal solution to an integer linear program is less sensitive to the constraint coefficients than is a linear program.

____ 28. The use of integer variables involves a tradeoff between modeling flexibility and solution difficulty.

CHAPTER 9

Network Models

KEY CONCEPTS

CONCEPT	ILLUSTRATED PROBLEMS	ANSWERED PROBLEMS
Shortest Route Problem	1,2	7,10,12
Minimal Spanning Tree Problem	3	6,9,11
Maximal Flow Problem	4	5,8,13

REVIEW

1. <u>Computer codes</u> for specific network problems (e.g. shortest route, minimal spanning tree, and maximal flow) are extremely efficient and can solve even large problems relatively quickly. The Management Scientist contains computer codes for each of these problems.

SHORTEST ROUTE PROBLEM

1. The <u>shortest-route</u> problem is concerned with finding the shortest path in a network from one node (or set of nodes) to another node (or set of nodes).

2. If all arcs in the network have nonnegative values then a <u>labeling algorithm</u> can be used to find the shortest paths from a particular node to all other nodes in the network.

SHORTEST ROUTE ALGORITHM

Note: We use the notation [ ] to represent a <u>permanent label</u> and ( ) to represent a <u>tentative label</u>.

1. Assign node 1 the permanent label [0,S]. The first number is the distance from node 1; the second number is the preceding node. Since node 1 has no preceding node, it is labeled S for the starting node.

2. Compute tentative labels, (d,n), for the nodes that can be reached directly from node 1. d = the direct distance from node 1 to the node in question -- this is called the <u>distance value</u>. n indicates the preceding node on the route from node 1 -- this is called the <u>preceding node value</u>. (All nodes labeled in this step have $n = 1$.)

3. Identify the tentatively labeled node with the smallest distance value. Suppose it is <u>node k</u>. Node k is now <u>permanently labeled</u> (using [,] brackets). If all nodes are permanently labeled GO TO STEP 5.

4. Consider all nodes (i) <u>without permanent labels</u> that can be reached directly from the node k identified in step 3. For each, calculate the quantity t as follows:
    t = (arc distance from node k to node i) + (distance value at node k).
   If the non-permanently labeled node has a tentative label:
      Compare t with the current distance value at the tentatively labeled node in question.
         If t < distance value of the tentatively labeled node:
            Replace the tentative label in question with (t,k).
         If $t \geq$ distance value of the tentatively labeled node:
            Keep the current tentative label.
   If the non-permanently labeled node does not have a tentative label:
      Create a tentative label of (t,k) for the node in question.
   In either case GO TO STEP 3.

5. The permanent labels identify the shortest distance from node 1 to each node as well as the preceding node on the shortest route. The shortest route to a given node can be found by working backwards by starting at the given node and moving to its preceding node. Continuing this procedure from the preceding node will provide the shortest route from node 1 to the node in question.

NOTE: If you are only interested in the shortest route from node *I* to node *j*, you have your solution in hand when node *j* is permanently labeled - even though some other nodes might not yet be permanently labeled.

FLOW CHART OF
SHORTEST-ROUTE ALGORITHM

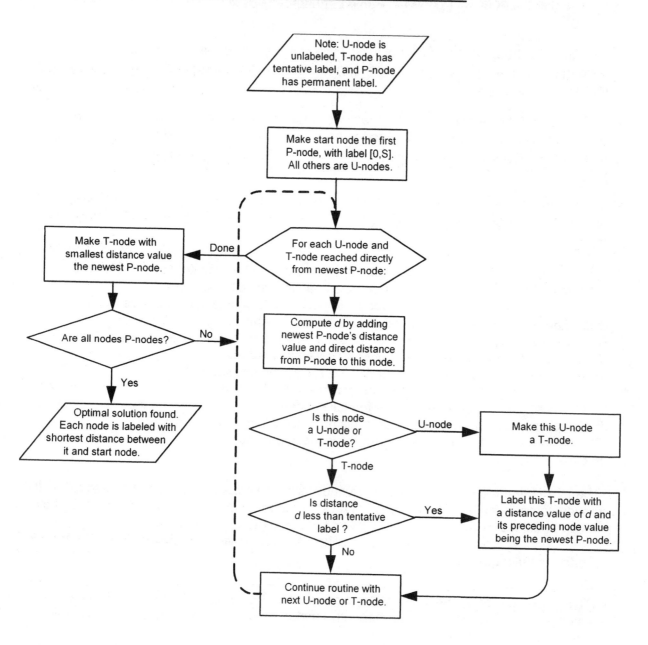

MINIMAL SPANNING TREE PROBLEM

1. A <u>tree</u> is a set of connected arcs that does not form a cycle.

2. A <u>spanning tree</u> is a tree that connects all nodes of a network.

3. The <u>minimal spanning tree</u> problem seeks to determine the minimum sum of arc lengths necessary to connect all nodes in a network. It can be solved by a <u>greedy algorithm</u>. (The algorithm is presented at the end of this section.)

MINIMAL SPANNING TREE ALGORITHM

1. Arbitrarily begin at any node and connect it to the closest node. The two nodes are referred to as <u>connected nodes</u>, and the remaining nodes are referred to as <u>unconnected nodes</u>.

2. Identify the unconnected node that is closest to one of the connected nodes (break ties arbitrarily). Add this new node to the set of connected nodes. Repeat this step until all nodes have been connected.

NOTE: The criterion to be minimized in the minimal spanning tree algorithm and the shortest-route algorithm is not limited to distance even though the terms "closest" and "shortest" are used in describing the procedures. Other criteria include time and cost. (Neither time nor cost is necessarily linearly related to distance.)

MAXIMAL FLOW PROBLEM

1. The <u>maximal flow</u> problem is concerned with determining the maximal volume of flow from one node (called the <u>source</u>) to another node (called the <u>sink</u>) in a given period of time.

2. In the maximal flow problem, each arc has a <u>maximum arc flow capacity</u> which limits the flow through the arc.

3. The maximal flow problem can be modeled as a <u>capacitated transshipment problem</u> and solved as a linear program.

ILLUSTRATED PROBLEMS

PROBLEM 1

Find the shortest route from node 1 to all other nodes in the network below.

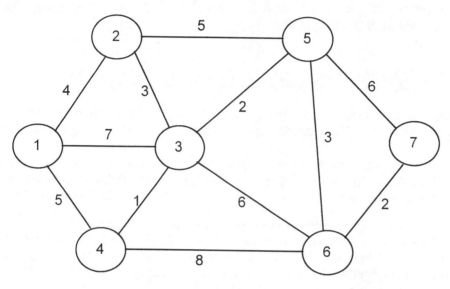

SOLUTION 1

Iteration 1

1. Assign node 1 the permanent label [0,S].

2. Since nodes 2, 3, and 4 are connected to node 1 by only one arc assign the tentative labels of (4,1) to node 2; (7,1) to node 3; (5,1) to node 4. The first part of this tentative label indicates the distance between node 1 and the node in question. The second part of the label indicates that the preceding node was node 1.

3. Node 2 is the tentatively labeled node with the smallest distance (4) , and hence becomes the <u>new permanently labeled node</u>. The network should now appear as follows:

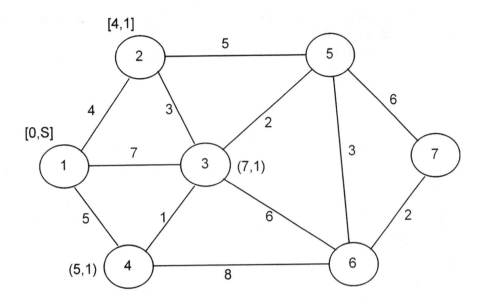

4. For each node with a tentative label which is connected to node 2 by just one arc, compute the sum of its arc length plus the distance value of node 2 (which is 4).

Node 3: 3 + 4 = 7 (not smaller than current label; do not change.)
Node 5: 5 + 4 = 9 (assign tentative label to node 5 of (9,2) since node 5 had no label.)

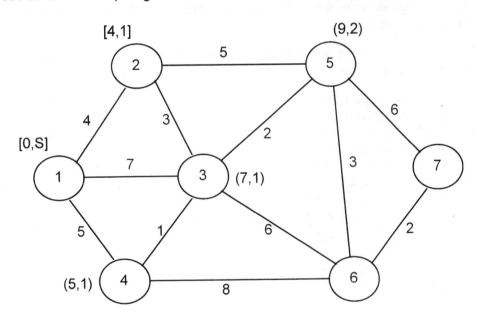

Iteration 2

3. Node 4 has the smallest tentative label distance (5). It now becomes the new permanently labeled node.

4. For each node with a tentative label that is connected to node 4 by just one arc, compute the sum of its arc length plus the distance value of node 4 (which is 5).

Node 3: $1 + 5 = 6$ (replace the tentative label of node 3 by (6,4) because 6 < 7, the current distance.)

Node 6: $8 + 5 = 13$ (assign tentative label to node 6 of (13,4) since node 6 had no label.)

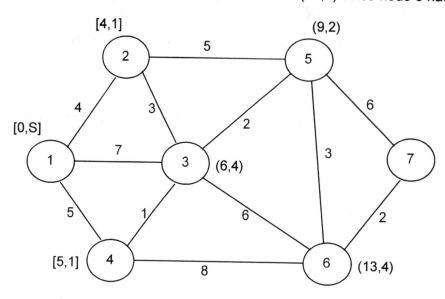

Iteration 3

3. Node 3 has the smallest tentative distance label (6). It now becomes the new permanently labeled node.

4. For each node with a tentative label that is connected to node 3 by just one arc, compute the sum of its arc length plus the distance to node 3 (which is 6).

Node 5: $2 + 6 = 8$ (replace the tentative label of node 5 with (8,3) since 8 < 9, the current distance)

Node 6: $6 + 6 = 12$ (replace the tentative label of node 6 with (12,3) since 12 < 13, the current distance)

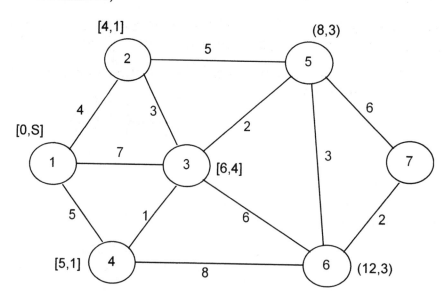

Iteration 4

3. Node 5 has the smallest tentative label distance (8). It now becomes the new permanently labeled node.

4. For each node with a tentative label that is connected to node 5 by just one arc, compute the sum of its arc length plus the distance value of node 5 (which is 8).

    Node 6: 3 + 8 = 11 (replace the tentative label of node 6 with (11,5) since 11 < 12, the current distance)

    Node 7: 6 + 8 = 14 (assign tentative label to node 7 of (14,5) since it had no label.)

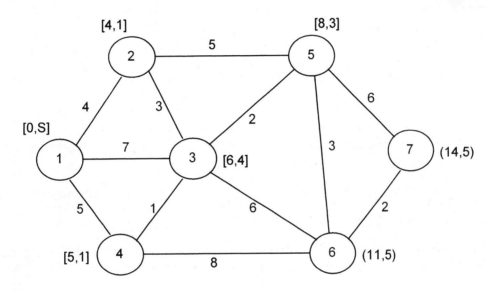

Iteration 5

3. Node 6 has the smallest tentative label distance (11). It now becomes the new permanently labeled node.

4. For each node with a tentative label that is connected to node 6 by just one arc, compute the sum of its arc length plus the distance value of node 6 (which is 11).

    Node 7: 2 + 11 = 13 (replace the tentative label of node 7 with (13,6) since 13 < 14, the current distance)

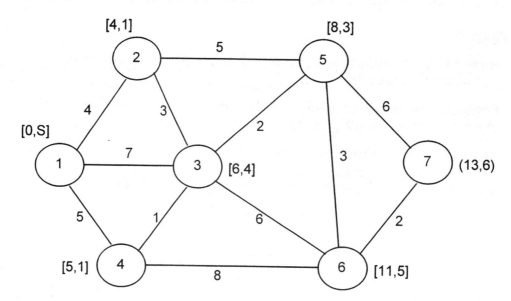

Iteration 6

3. Node 7 becomes permanently labeled, and hence all nodes are now permanently labeled. Thus proceed to summarize in Step 5.

5. Summarizing by tracing the shortest routes backward through the permanent labels:

Node	Minimum Distance	Shortest Route
2	4	1-2
3	6	1-4-3
4	5	1-4
5	8	1-4-3-5
6	11	1-4-3-5-6
7	13	1-4-3-5-6-7

PROBLEM 2

Susan Winslow has an important business meeting in Paducah this evening. She has a number of alternate routes by which she can travel from the company headquarters in Lewisburg (city 1) to Paducah (city 6). The network below summarizes the various routes.

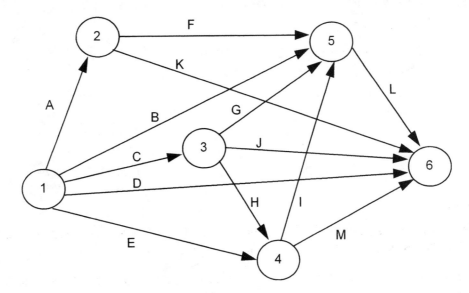

The following table gives the method of travel, travel time, and ticket cost associated with each of the branches of the network.

Route	Method	Time (hours)	Ticket Cost
A	Train	4	$ 20
B	Plane	1	$115
C	Bus	2	$ 10
D	Taxi	6	$ 90
E	Train	3 1/3	$ 30
F	Bus	3	$ 15
G	Bus	4 2/3	$ 20
H	Taxi	1	$ 15
I	Train	2 1/3	$ 15
J	Bus	6 1/3	$ 25
K	Taxi	3 1/3	$ 50
L	Train	1 1/3	$ 10
M	Bus	4 2/3	$ 20

If Susan earns a salary of $15 per hour, what route should she take to minimize the total overall travel costs?

SOLUTION 2

First determine the appropriate values for the arcs. As Susan is interested in minimizing her total travel costs, each arc value would represent the total cost of traveling over that arc. Thus: Arc Cost = $15 x (Travel Time) + (Ticket cost). Now solve this problem by the shortest route algorithm using these costs for the "distances".

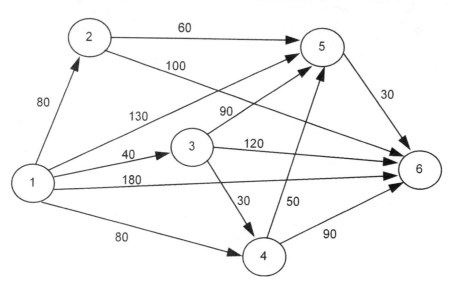

Iteration 1

1. Assign node 1 the permanent label [0,S].

2. Nodes 2, 3, 4, 5, and 6 are connected to node 1 by one arc. Assign a tentative label of (80,1) to node 2; (40,1) to node 3; (80,1) to node 4; (130,1) to node 5; and, (180,1) to node 6.

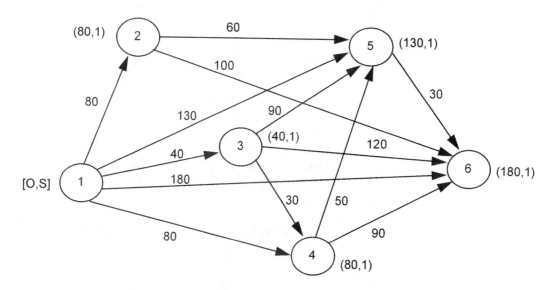

3. Node 3 has the tentatively labeled node with the smallest distance (40), and hence becomes the new permanently labeled node.

4. For each node with a tentative label that is connected to node 3 by just one arc, compute the sum of its arc length plus the distance value of node 3 (which is 40).

Node 4: 30 + 40 = 70 (Replace tentative label with (70,3))
Node 5: 90 + 40 = 130 (Leave the current tentative label)
Node 6: 120 + 40 = 160 (Replace tentative label with (160,3))

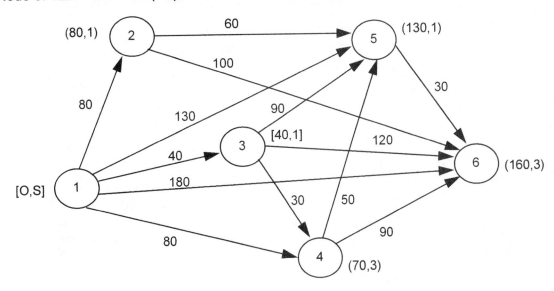

Iteration 2

3. Node 4 has the smallest tentative label distance (70). It now becomes the new permanently labeled node.

4. For each node with a tentative label that is connected to node 4 by just one arc, compute the sum of its arc length plus the distance of node 4 (which is 70).

Node 5: 50 + 70 = 120 (replace tentative label with (120,4))
Node 6: 90 + 70 = 160 (leave the current tentative label)

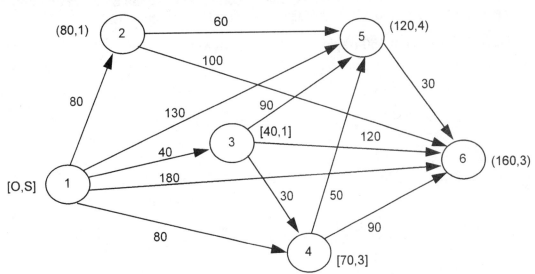

Iteration 3

3. Node 2 has the smallest tentative label distance (80). It now becomes the new permanently labeled node.

4. For each node with a tentative label that is connected to node 2 by just one arc, compute the sum of its arc length plus the distance value of node 2 (which is 80).

Node 5: 60 + 80 = 140 (leave the current tentative label)
Node 6: 100 + 80 = 180 (leave the current tentative label)

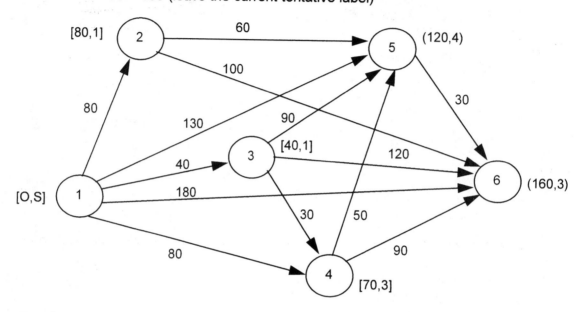

Iteration 4

3. Node 5 has the smallest tentative label distance (120). It now becomes the new permanently labeled node.

4. For each node with a tentative label that is connected to node 5 by just one arc, compute the sum of its arc length plus the distance of node 5 (which is 120).

Node 6: 30 + 120 = 150 (replace tentative label with (150,5))

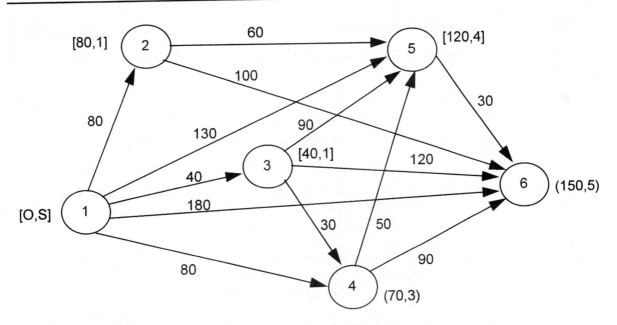

Iteration 5

3. Node 6 is the only tentatively labeled node, and hence it becomes permanently labeled. Since all nodes are labeled, go to STEP 5 -- determining the optimal solution.

5. The minimum cost is $150. Tracing the route backwards, the minimum cost route is:

[1 – 3 – 4 – 5 – 6]   or   [C (bus) – H (taxi) – I (train) – L (train)].

PROBLEM 3

Find the minimal spanning tree in the following network:

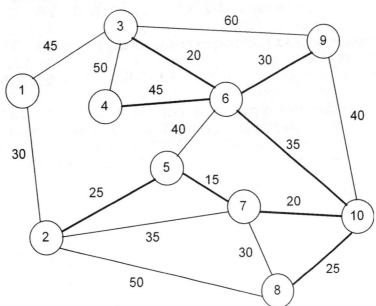

Note: For a minimal spanning tree problem with n nodes, the optimal number of arcs used is always $n - 1$.

SOLUTION 3

Arbitrarily selecting node 1, we see that its closest node is node 2 (distance = 30).
Therefore, initially we have: Connected nodes: 1,2   Unconnected nodes: 3,4,5,6,7,8,9,10
Chosen arcs: 1-2

The closest unconnected node to a connected node is node 5 (distance = 25 to node 2).
Node 5 becomes a connected node. Connected nodes: 1,2,5
Unconnected nodes: 3,4,6,7,8,9,10   Chosen arcs: 1-2, 2-5

The closest unconnected node to a connected node is node 7 (distance = 15 to node 5).
Node 7 becomes a connected node.   Connected nodes: 1,2,5,7
Unconnected nodes: 3,4,6,8,9,10   Chosen arcs: 1-2, 2-5, 5-7

The closest unconnected node to a connected node is node 10 (distance = 20 to node 7).
Node 10 becomes a connected node.   Connected nodes: 1,2,5,7,10
Unconnected nodes: 3,4,6,8,9   Chosen arcs: 1-2, 2-5, 5-7, 7-10
The closest unconnected node to a connected node is node 8 (distance = 25 to node 10).
Node 8 becomes a connected node.   Connected nodes: 1,2,5,7,10,8
Unconnected nodes: 3,4,6,9   Chosen arcs: 1-2, 2-5, 5-7, 7-10, 10-8

Now, the closest unconnected node to a connected node is node 6 (distance = 35 to
node 10). Node 6 becomes a connected node.   Connected nodes: 1,2,5,7,10,8,6
Unconnected nodes: 3,4,9   Chosen arcs: 1-2, 2-5, 5-7, 7-10, 10-8, 10-6

The closest unconnected node to a connected node is node 3 (distance = 20 to node 6).
Node 3 becomes a connected node.   Connected nodes: 1,2,5,7,10,8,6,3
Unconnected nodes: 4,9   Chosen arcs: 1-2, 2-5, 5-7, 7-10, 10-8, 10-6, 6-3

The closest unconnected node to a connected node is node 9 (distance = 30 to node 6).
Node 9 becomes a connected node.   Connected nodes: 1,2,5,7,10,8,6,3,9
Unconnected nodes: 4   Chosen arcs: 1-2, 2-5, 5-7, 7-10, 10-8, 10-6, 6-3, 6-9

The remaining unconnected node is node 4. It is closest to connected node 6
(distance = 45). Thus, the minimal spanning tree (displayed below) consists of:
        Arcs: 1-2, 2-5, 5-7, 7-10, 10-8, 10-6, 6-3, 6-9, 6-4
        Values: 30 + 25 + 15 + 20 + 25 + 35 + 20 + 30 + 45 = 245

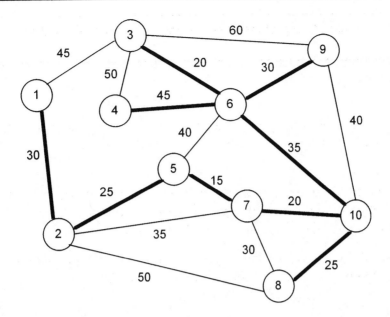

NOTE: The minimal spanning tree algorithm can be executed with minimal writing effort. Assuming you have drawn a network representation of the problem, simply darken the minimum-value arcs you are choosing to connect one node with another. The unconnected nodes will always be evident and the solution, when you reach it, will also be clear.

PROBLEM 4

Find the maximal flow from node 1 to node 7 in the following network.

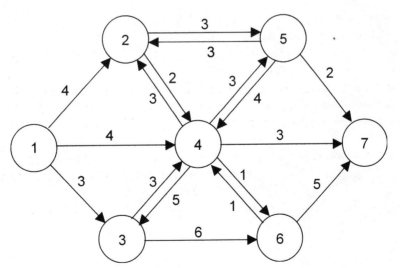

SOLUTION 4

First, add an arc from node 7 back to node 1 to represent the total flow through the network. There is no capacity on the newly added arc.

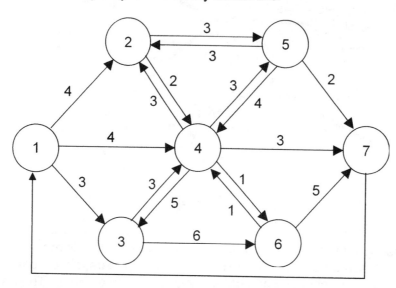

Now we will formulate the problem as a capacitated transshipment problem.

Decision variables:
  x_{ij} = amount of flow from node i to node j

Objective function:
  Maximize the flow through the network: Max x_{71}

Constraints:
  Conservation of flow for each node:
  (1) $x_{12} + x_{13} + x_{14} - x_{71} = 0$ (node 1)
  (2) $x_{24} + x_{25} - x_{12} - x_{42} - x_{52} = 0$ (node 2)
  (3) $x_{34} + x_{36} - x_{13} - x_{43} = 0$ (node 3)
  (4) $x_{42} + x_{43} + x_{45} + x_{46} + x_{47} - x_{14} - x_{24} - x_{34} - x_{54} - x_{64} = 0$ (node 4)
  (5) $x_{52} + x_{54} + x_{57} - x_{25} - x_{45} = 0$ (node 5)
  (6) $x_{64} + x_{67} - x_{36} - x_{46} = 0$ (node 6)
  (7) $x_{71} - x_{47} - x_{57} - x_{67} = 0$ (node 7)

  Capacity for each arc:
  (8) $x_{12} \le 4$ (14) $x_{36} \le 6$ (20) $x_{52} \le 3$
  (9) $x_{13} \le 3$ (15) $x_{42} \le 3$ (21) $x_{54} \le 4$
  (10) $x_{14} \le 4$ (16) $x_{43} \le 5$ (22) $x_{57} \le 2$
  (11) $x_{24} \le 2$ (17) $x_{45} \le 3$ (23) $x_{64} \le 1$
  (12) $x_{25} \le 3$ (18) $x_{46} \le 1$ (24) $x_{67} \le 5$
  (13) $x_{34} \le 3$ (19) $x_{47} \le 3$

  Nonnegativity:
  All $x_{ij} \ge 0$

The LP was solved using *The Management Scientist* . Two solutions are given below.

Objective Function Value =   10.000

Variable	Solution 1	Solution 2
x12	3.000	3.000
x13	3.000	3.000
x14	4.000	4.000
x24	1.000	1.000
x25	2.000	2.000
x36	5.000	4.000
x43	2.000	1.000
x46	0.000	1.000
x47	3.000	3.000
x57	2.000	2.000
x67	5.000	5.000
x71	10.000	10.000

ANSWERED PROBLEMS

PROBLEM 5

Federated Express operates a fleet of cargo planes and is in the package delivery business. FedEx is interested in knowing what is the maximum it could transport in one day indirectly from Los Angeles to Tampa (via Denver, St. Louis, Dallas, and/or Houston) if its direct flight was out of service. FedEx's indirect routes from Los Angeles to Tampa, along with their respective estimated excess shipping capacities (measured in hundreds of cubic feet per day), are shown in the network below.

Is there sufficient excess capacity to indirectly ship 5000 cubic feet of packages in one day? What is the maximum FedEx could ship and how would it be routed?

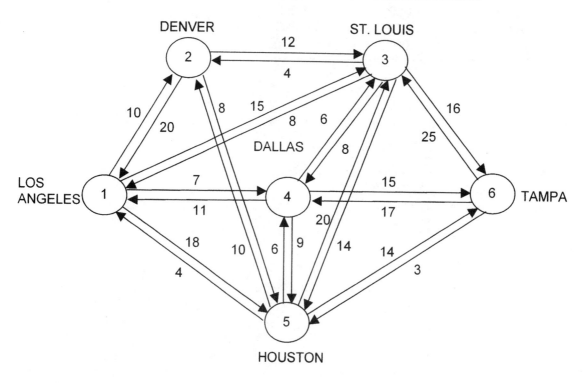

PROBLEM 6

Griffith's Cherry Preserve is a combination wild animal habitat and amusement park. Besides their phenomenally successful wild animal safari tour, there are eight different theme areas in the amusement park.

One problem encountered by management is to develop a method by which people can efficiently travel between each area of the park. Management has learned that a people mover can be constructed at a cost of $50 per foot.

If the following network represents the distances (in feet) between each area of the park for which a people mover is possible, determine the minimum cost for such a system.

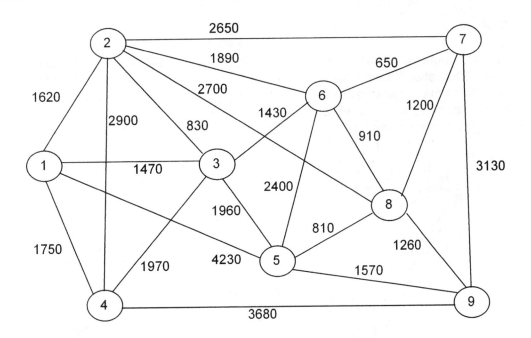

PROBLEM 7

Harvey Hubbell is a graduate student in statistics at a major East Coast university. Harvey believes he has devised a new system for gambling and wishes to spend his summer in Las Vegas testing out his theory.

Harvey has obtained information on one-way discount airfares between relevant pairs of cities. This is given in the network below.

If Harvey's objective is to fly from his home in Philadelphia to Las Vegas for the minimum total cost airfare, what route should he travel?

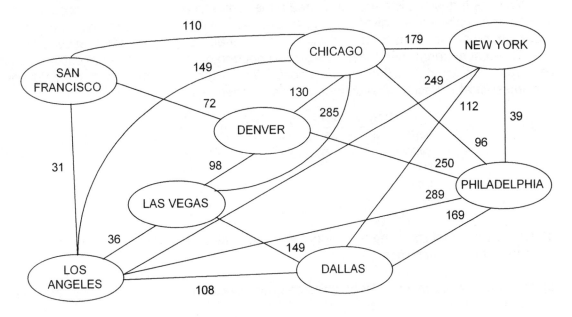

PROBLEM 8

Northeast Energy Consortium is a cooperative venture of eight electrical utility companies. The network below gives a representation of the electrical capacity among these companies over their major transmission lines for a typical day in July.

If the numbers on the arcs represent megawatt capacity over the links between the companies, what is the maximum amount of electricity that can flow from utility A to utility B?

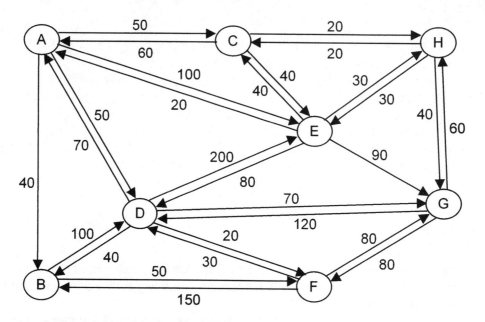

PROBLEM 9

Watkins Industries is planning to create the "office of the future" for its executive branch. The company plans to install two word processors, two printers, a laser copier, and a facsimile transmission machine. All will be interconnected using an ethernet system.

The cost of connecting these devices will depend on how the ethernet cable is routed between the machines. Ethernet cable costs $25 per foot to install. The table below gives the approximate direct routing distance in feet between various pairs of machines.

	WP1	WP2	P1	P2	LC	FT
WP1	0	46	16	23	100	29
WP2		0	81	44	67	98
P1			0	45	57	36
P2				0	38	73
LC					0	52

a) Use the minimal spanning tree algorithm to determine the least cost method of connecting all machines.

b) How much cheaper would it be if the company decided not to hook up the second printer to this system?

PROBLEM 10

Consider problem 2. Which path should Susan Winslow take to travel from Lewisburg to Paducah if she earned only $6 per hour? What would be the answer if she earned $60 per hour?

PROBLEM 11

Wondercamp is planning a new resort for the urban professional who wishes to "get back to nature". For a hefty fee, it plans to transport clients up the Crocodile River by canoe and then have their clients camp at one of eight designated campsites.

They must build a 1000-yard trail from the river to the first campsite as there are no feasible alternatives. It then wishes to build a sequence of trails (of minimum total length) so that every campsite can be reached from any other campsite. A study of the terrain of the area has yielded the following possibilities for trails between campsites. Which trails should be built?

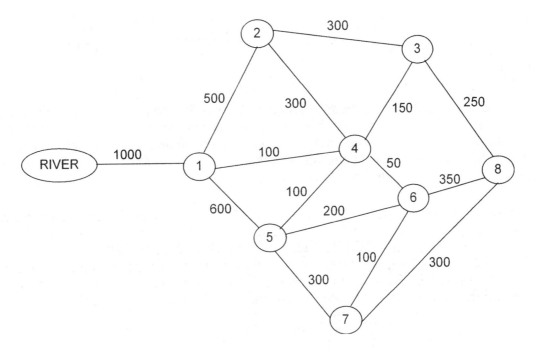

PROBLEM 12

Quicksilver Messenger Service needs to get an important package from Flatsburg (node 1) to Peakston (node 8) as quickly as possible. The network below is a model of the highways that lie between Flatsburg and Peakston. The arc values are travel times in minutes. Which route should Quicksilver take?

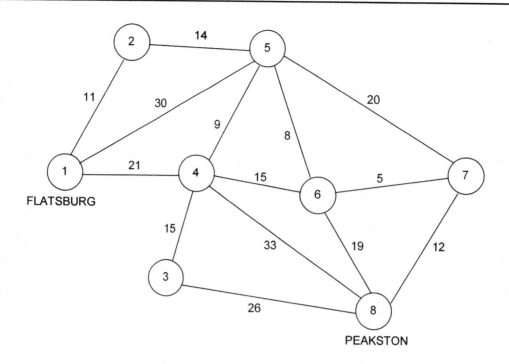

PROBLEM 13

Trans Oceanic Shipping Company has 5 cargo ships that sail between New York and Tel Aviv. Trans Oceanic has been offered a contract to ship up to 120,000 pounds of Jaffa oranges from Tel Aviv to New York in April. After a careful analysis, management has determined the following relevant ship capacities (in 1000's of pounds) during April. How many pounds of oranges can Trans Oceanic ship?

		Athens	Rome	Paris	London	New York
	Tel Aviv	60	20	40	--	--
	Athens	--	15	40	--	20
FROM	Rome	10	--	20	40	--
	Paris	40	30	--	30	40
	London	--	10	25	--	60

TO (heading spanning Athens–New York columns)

TRUE/FALSE

14. If one wishes to find the shortest distance necessary to interconnect all nodes in a network one should use the shortest-route algorithm.

15. If the unique shortest path from node 1 to node 8 goes from node 1 to node 3 to node 5 to node 9 to node 8, then the shortest path from node 1 to node 9 must go through node 3.

16. A maximal flow problem with 8 nodes will require 16 conservation-of-flow constraints.

17. To use the maximal flow algorithm, each arc's capacity must be the same in both directions.

18. It is possible for shortest-route, minimal spanning tree, and maximal flow problems to have alternative optimal solutions.

19. In the shortest-route algorithm, once a node is given a permanent label one can find the shortest route to that node from node 1.

20. The maximal flow problem can be modeled as a capacitated assignment problem.

21. If the shortest route between two nodes in a network passes through every node in the network, then this must also be the minimal spanning tree for the network.

22. Using the shortest-route algorithm, it is possible for a permanently labeled node to have its label values change.

23. In each iteration of the minimal spanning tree algorithm, the number of connected nodes is increased by one.

24. The maximum amount that can flow from source to sink along a path is equal to the total of the arc capacities on that path.

25. The minimal spanning tree algorithm is unusual for a greedy algorithm in that it is optimal.

26. The solution found by the shortest-route algorithm shows the shortest distance between any pair of nodes in the network.

27. The number of iterations required to solve a shortest-route problem depends on the amount of tentative labeling done.

28. The number of arcs in a minimal spanning tree depends only on the number of nodes in the network and not on distances.

CHAPTER 10

Project Scheduling: PERT/CPM

KEY CONCEPTS

CONCEPT	ILLUSTRATED PROBLEMS	ANSWERED PROBLEMS
Construction of PERT Networks	1,2	6,8,12,13
PERT Analysis with Certain Times	1	6,7,9
PERT Analysis with Uncertain Times	2,4	8,10,11
Activity Earliest/Latest Times	1,2,5	7,9,14
Time/Cost Analysis	3,4	9-13
LP Formulation for Crashing	3	12,13

REVIEW

1. <u>PERT</u> (Program Evaluation Review Technique) is used to plan the scheduling of individual activities that make up a project.

2. A <u>PERT network</u> can be constructed to model the <u>precedence</u> of the activities. The <u>nodes</u> of the network represent the activities.

3. PERT can be used to determine the earliest/latest start and finish times for each activity, the entire project completion time and the <u>slack time</u> for each activity. (See algorithm at the end of the Review.)

4. A <u>critical path</u> for the network is a path consisting of activities with <u>zero slack</u>.

5. In the <u>three-time estimate approach</u>, the time to complete an activity is assumed to follow a <u>Beta distribution</u>. Its mean is t = $(a + 4m + b)/6$, and its variance is $\sigma^2 = ((b-a)/6)^2$. Here a = the <u>optimistic</u> completion time estimate, b = the <u>pessimistic</u> completion time estimate, and m = the <u>most likely</u> completion time estimate.

6. In the three-time estimate approach, the <u>critical path</u> is determined as if the mean times for the activities were fixed times. The overall project completion time is assumed to have a normal distribution with mean equal to the sum of the means along the critical path and variance equal to the sum of the variances along the critical path.

7. In the <u>CPM</u> (Critical Path Method) approach to project scheduling, it is assumed that the normal time to complete an activity, t_j, which can be met at a normal cost, c_j, can be <u>crashed</u> to a reduced time, t_j', under maximum crashing for an increased cost, c_j'.

8. Using CPM, activity j's maximum <u>time reduction</u>, M_j, may be calculated by: $M_j = t_j - t_j'$. It is assumed that its cost per unit reduction, K_j, is linear and can be calculated by: $K_j = (c_j' - c_j)/M_j$.

9. <u>Linear programming</u> may be used to solve a CPM problem to minimize the crashing costs needed to complete a project within a specified time limit.

PERT/CPM CRITICAL PATH PROCEDURE

Step 1: Develop a list of the activities that make up the project.

Step 2: Determine the immediate predecessors for each activity in the project.

Step 3: Estimate the completion time for each activity.

Step 4: Draw a project network depicting the activities (on nodes) and immediate predecessors listed in Steps 1 and 2.

Step 5: Use the project network and the activity time estimates to determine the earliest start and the earliest finish time for each activity by making a forward pass through the network. The earliest finish time for the last activity in the project identifies the total time required to complete the project.

Step 6: Use the project completion time identified in Step 5 as the latest finish time for the last activity and make a backward pass through the network to identify the latest start and finish time for each activity.

Step 7: Use the difference between the latest start time and the earliest start time for each activity to determine the slack for the activity.

Step 8: Find the activities with zero slack; these are the critical activities.

Step 9: Use the information from Steps 5 and 6 to develop the activity schedule for the project.

FLOW CHART FOR
COMPUTING PROJECT COMPLETION TIME PROBABILITY

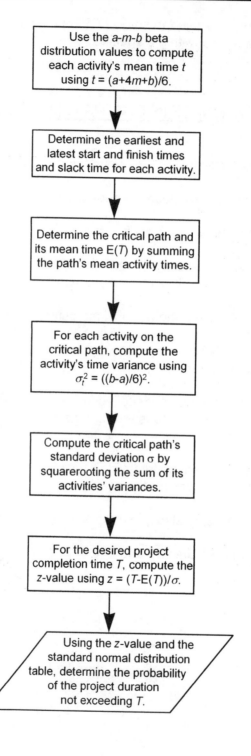

FLOW CHART FOR PROJECT CRASHING

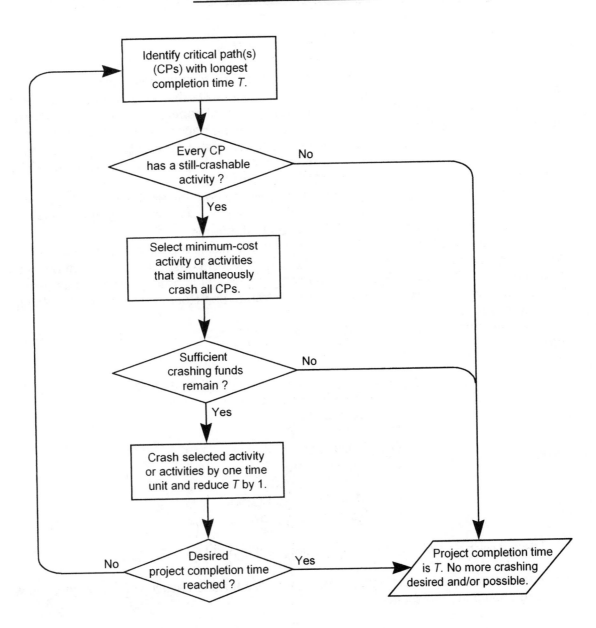

ILLUSTRATED PROBLEMS

PROBLEM 1

Kraft's Kustom Kars is in the business of producing custom automobile assemblies. In particular, Kraft operates a shop that builds and assembles the body and frame of the cars.

Kraft's operations begin with the processing of initial paperwork. This must be done before any other operations are commenced. Once the paperwork has been completed, the body of the car can be built in Room A and the frame of the car can be built in Room B. When the body is built, it is transferred to Room C for finishing work. Similarly, when the frame is built, it is transferred to Room D for finishing work.

When both are built, although not necessarily finished, the final paperwork can be completed. When both the body and frame are finished, they are transported to the assembly Room E, where the body is mounted to the frame.

In the frame building room, Room B, certain chemicals are used which must be completely eliminated by a thorough washdown to prevent gaseous fumes from becoming a health hazard. The project is considered complete when the final paperwork has been completed, the body has been mounted to the frame, and Room B has been completely washed down.

The table below gives the expected completion times in hours for each activity of the project.

Activity	Description	Completion Time
A	Initial Paperwork	3
B	Build Body	3
C	Build Frame	2
D	Finish Body	3
E	Finish Frame	7
F	Final Paperwork	3
G	Mount Body to Frame	6
H	Room B Washdown	2

a) Draw the PERT network that corresponds to this problem.

b) Find the earliest and latest start and finish times for each activity of the project. How long should the project take?

c) Which activities must not be delayed if the project is to be completed in the time calculated in part (b)?

d) Suppose the body finish operation (D) were delayed four hours. By how much would the entire project be delayed?

SOLUTION 1

Before constructing the PERT network, summarize in the following table the immediate predecessor activities for each activity.

Activity	Immediate Predecessors	Completion Times (Hr.)
A	--	3
B	A	3
C	A	2
D	B	3
E	C	7
F	B,C	3
G	D,E	6
H	C	2

To construct a PERT network, there must be a node for each activity. An activity's immediate predecessors are the nodes that immediately precede it.

The result is:

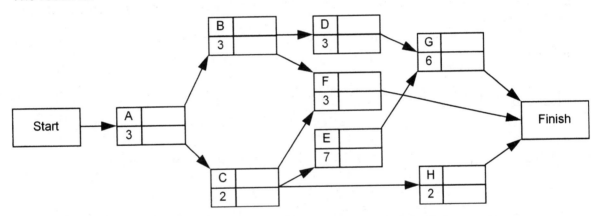

b) The earliest start time (ES) for activity A 0. Then the earliest finish time (EF) for an activity is given by: EF = ES + (completion time). Then ES for an activity = max (EF for all immediately preceding activities).

The forward pass to calculate ES and EF:

Activity	Earliest Start (ES)	Earliest Finish(EF)
A	0	0 + 3 = 3
B	3	3 + 3 = 6
C	3	3 + 2 = 5
D	6	6 + 3 = 9
E	5	5 + 7 = 12
H	5	5 + 2 = 7
F	MAX(5,6) = 6	6 + 3 = 9
G	MAX(9,12) = 12	12 + 6 = 18

The max(EF of the activities immediately preceding the Finish node) = 18, so the completion time of the project is 18.

The backward pass to calculate LF and LS:

Activity	Latest Finish (LF)	Latest Start (LS)
H	18	18 - 2 = 16
G	18	18 - 6 = 12
F	18	18 - 3 = 15
E	12	12 - 7 = 5
D	12	12 - 3 = 9
C	MIN(15,5,16) = 5	5 - 2 = 3
B	MIN(9,15) = 9	9 - 3 = 6
A	MIN(6,3) = 3	3 - 3 = 0

This gives the completed network below.

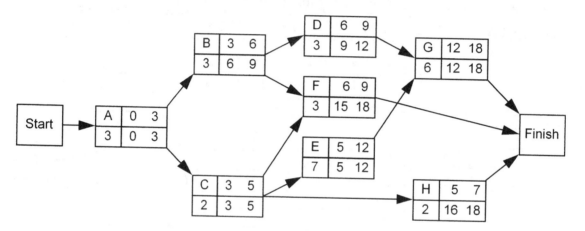

The slack time for each activity (LS - ES) is summarized below:

Activity	ES	EF	LS	LF	Slack
A	0	3	0	3	0
B	3	6	6	9	3
C	3	5	3	5	0
D	6	9	9	12	3
E	5	12	5	12	0
F	6	9	15	18	9
G	12	18	12	18	0
H	5	7	16	18	11

NOTE: One way to partially check the accuracy of your activity earliest/latest time calculations is to compute every activity's slack two ways: Slack = (LS - ES) = (LF - EF) If the preceding is not true, you have an error!   Also, the number of different values in your slack column should not exceed (but does not have to equal) the number of paths in the project network.

c) Activities A, C, E, G have 0 slack times -- they form the critical path.

d) Activity D has a slack of 3. Hence a 4 hour delay in D would delay the entire project 4 - 3 = 1 hour.

PROBLEM 2

Consider the following project:

Activity	Immediate Predecessors	Optimistic Time (Hr.)	Most Probable Time (Hr.)	Pessimistic Time (Hr.)
A	--	4	6	8
B	--	1	4.5	5
C	A	3	3	3
D	A	4	5	6
E	A	0.5	1	1.5
F	B,C	3	4	5
G	B,C	1	1.5	5
H	E,F	5	6	7
I	E,F	2	5	8
J	D,H	2.5	2.75	4.5
K	G,I	3	5	7

a) Construct the PERT network for this problem.

b) Solve for the expected earliest and latest start and finish times for each activity.

c) Identify the critical path and give the estimated project completion time.

d) What is the probability the project will be completed within one day (24 hours)?

SOLUTION 2

a) Nodes are needed for the start node, the finish node, and all of the activities.

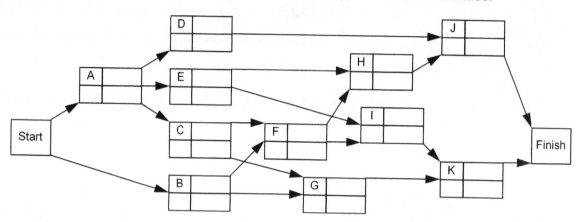

b) Calculate the expected times, *t*, and variances, σ^2, for each activity.

$$t = (a + 4m + b)/6 \qquad \sigma^2 = ((b-a)/6)^2$$

Activity	Expected Time	Variance
A	6	4/9
B	4	4/9
C	3	0
D	5	1/9
E	1	1/36
F	4	1/9
G	2	4/9
H	6	1/9
I	5	1
J	3	1/9
K	5	4/9

Thus, using the algorithm illustrated in problem 1, we have:

Activity	ES	EF	LS	LF	Slack
A	0	6	0	6	0
B	0	4	5	9	5
C	6	9	6	9	0
D	6	11	15	20	9
E	6	7	12	13	6
F	9	13	9	13	0
G	9	11	16	18	7
H	13	19	14	20	1
I	13	18	13	18	0
J	19	22	20	23	1
K	18	23	18	23	0

c) The critical path is the path of 0 slack = A-C-F-I-K. The estimated project completion time is the Max EF of the activities immediately preceding the Finish node = 23.

d) $z = (24 - 23)/\sigma$. Here, $\sigma^2 = \sigma^2_A + \sigma^2_C + \sigma^2_F + \sigma^2_I + \sigma^2_K$

$$= 4/9 + 0 + 1/9 + 1 + 4/9 = 2.$$

Hence, $\sigma = 1.414$. Thus $z = (24-23)/1.414 = .71$. From Appendix A,

$$P(z < .71) = .5 + .2612 = .7612.$$

PROBLEM 3

National Business Machines (NBM) has just developed a new microcomputer it plans to put into full scale production in a few months. The table and the PERT network below show the precedence relations and give the activity times and costs under normal operations and maximum crashing for a daily (22-hour) production of 1000 microcomputers at its local plant.

NBM wants to know the minimum cost of producing the 1000 microcomputers within the 22-hour period. Formulate and solve a linear program that will yield this information.

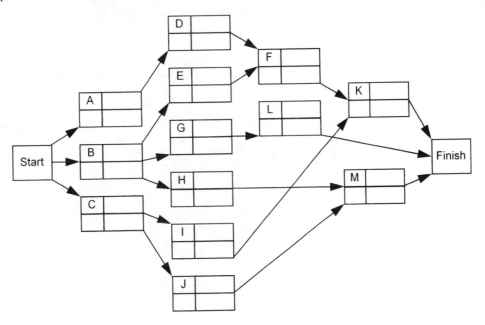

Activity	Normal Time (hr)	Normal Cost	Crash Crash Time (hr)	Cost
A	2	$2,000	1.5	$3,000
B	4	3,000	3	3,500
C	1	1,500	1	1,500
D	4	5,300	2.5	8,000
E	6	5,400	5	7,000
F	10	6,000	8	9,000
G	8	4,800	5	9,900
H	2	2,800	1	2,900
I	5	4,500	4	5,000
J	12	6,000	6	9,600
K	7	7,000	4	9,700
L	11	8,800	9	9,200
M	4	1,000	1	7,000

SOLUTION 3

First prepare a chart giving maximum crashing,

$$M = \text{(Normal Time)} - \text{(Time Under Maximum Crashing)}$$

and the marginal cost per hour for crashing,

$$K = (\text{[Cost Under Maximum Crashing]} - \text{[Normal Cost]})/M$$

Activity	M	K
A	0.5	2000
B	1	500
C	0	0
D	1.5	1800
E	1	1600
F	2	1500
G	3	1700
H	1	100
I	1	500
J)	6	600
K	3	900
L	2	200
M	3	2000

Let x_A = earliest finish time for Activity A, and y_A = amount of time Activity A is crashed.

The linear program must minimize the total extra cost:

$$\text{MIN } 2000y_A + 500y_B + 1800y_D + 1600y_E + 1500y_F + 1700y_G$$
$$+ 100y_H + 500y_I + 600y_J + 900y_K + 200y_L + 2000y_M$$

Subject to:
(1) The project must be completed within 22 hours: $x_K \leq 22$, $x_L \leq 22$, $x_M \leq 22$

(2) The amount an activity is crashed cannot exceed its maximum crashing:

$$
\begin{aligned}
y_A &\leq 0.5 \\
y_B &\leq 1 \\
y_D &\leq 1.5 \\
y_E &\leq 1 \\
y_F &\leq 2 \\
y_G &\leq 3 \\
y_H &\leq 1 \\
y_I &\leq 1 \\
y_J &\leq 6 \\
y_K &\leq 3 \\
y_L &\leq 2 \\
y_M &\leq 3
\end{aligned}
$$

(3) For each activity:
(Earliest Finish Time) $\geq$ (Earliest Finish Time of Preceding Activity)
+ [(Normal Activity Time) - (Amount of Time the Activity is crashed)]

$$
\begin{array}{lll}
x_A \geq 0 + (2 - y_A) & \text{or} & x_A + y_A \geq 2 \\
x_B \geq 0 + (4 - y_B) & \text{or} & x_B + y_B \geq 4 \\
x_C \geq 0 + (1 - 0) & \text{or} & x_C \geq 1
\end{array}
$$

$$
\begin{array}{lll}
x_D \geq x_A + (4 - y_D) & \text{or} & x_D + y_D - x_A \geq 4 \\
x_E \geq x_B + (6 - y_E) & \text{or} & x_E + y_E - x_B \geq 6 \\
x_G \geq x_B + (8 - y_G) & \text{or} & x_G + y_G - x_B \geq 8 \\
x_H \geq x_B + (2 - y_H) & \text{or} & x_H + y_H - x_B \geq 2 \\
x_I \geq x_C + (5 - y_I) & \text{or} & x_I + y_I - x_C \geq 5 \\
x_J \geq x_C + (12 - y_J) & \text{or} & x_J + y_J - x_C \geq 12
\end{array}
$$

$$
\begin{array}{lll}
x_F \geq x_D + (10 - y_F) & \text{or} & x_F + y_F - x_D \geq 10 \\
x_F \geq x_E + (10 - y_F) & \text{or} & x_F + y_F - x_E \geq 10 \\
x_L \geq x_G + (11 - y_L) & \text{or} & x_L + y_L - x_G \geq 11
\end{array}
$$

$$
\begin{array}{lll}
x_K \geq x_F + (7 - y_K) & \text{or} & x_K + y_K - x_F \geq 7 \\
x_K \geq x_I + (7 - y_K) & \text{or} & x_K + y_K - x_I \geq 7 \\
x_M \geq x_H + (4 - y_M) & \text{or} & x_M + y_M - x_H \geq 4 \\
x_M \geq x_J + (4 - y_M) & \text{or} & x_M + y_M - x_J \geq 4
\end{array}
$$

(4) Non-negativity of the variables:

$$
\begin{aligned}
x_i &\geq 0 \quad \text{for } I = A, B, C, \ldots, M \\
y_j &\geq 0 \quad \text{for } j = A, B, D, \ldots, M
\end{aligned}
$$

The Management Scientist provided the following solution output:

OBJECTIVE FUNCTION VALUE =   4700.000

VARIABLE	VALUE	REDUCED COSTS
XA	5.000	0.000
XB	3.000	0.000
XC	1.000	0.000
XD	9.000	0.000
XE	9.000	0.000
XF	18.000	0.000
XG	11.000	0.000
XH	13.000	0.000
XI	18.000	0.000
XJ	13.000	0.000
XK	22.000	0.000
XL	22.000	0.000
XM	17.000	0.000
YA	0.000	2000.000
YB	1.000	0.000
YD	0.000	1800.000
YE	0.000	100.000
YF	1.000	0.000
YG	0.000	1500.000
YH	0.000	100.000
YI	0.000	500.000
YJ	0.000	600.000
YK	3.000	0.000
YL	0.000	0.000
YM	0.000	2000.000

Summary:

Crash activity B one hour, activity F one hour, and activity K three hours. The 1000-unit daily production output will be achieved in 22 hours at a crashing cost of $4700.

PROBLEM 4

Given the following PERT network for Gus's Painters:

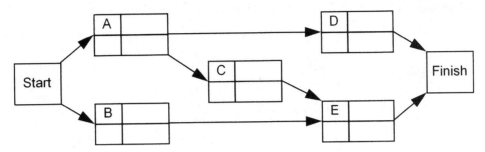

The following means and standard deviations were calculated for the activities:

Activity	t	σ
A	6	2
B	3	1
C	6	1
D	15	2
E	12	2

There is a $100,000 bonus for completing the project in 26 weeks. Currently activity E is assigned to Wilson Brothers. Gus has the option of hiring Jones Inc. for activity E. Their expected completion time for activity E is 8 weeks (with a standard deviation of 2), but they will cost Gus $15,000 more to do E than Wilson Brothers. Should Gus hire Jones?

SOLUTION 4

Analysis using Wilson Brothers to do E:

Activity	ES	EF	LS	LF
A	0	6	0	6
B	0	3	9	12
C	6	12	6	12
D	6	21	9	21
E	12	24	12	24

Hence the critical path is A - C - E and the overall expected project completion time is 24.

The variance of the critical path is:

$$\sigma^2 = \sigma^2_A + \sigma^2_C + \sigma^2_E = (2)^2 + (1)^2 + (2)^2 = 9. \text{ Thus } \sigma = 3.$$

To find the probability of completing the project in 26 weeks, calculate,

$$z = (26 - 24)/3 = .67.$$

Thus the probability of finishing in 26 weeks is $P(z < .67)$. From Appendix A, the table gives the $P(0 < z < .67) = .2486$. Therefore the probability of completing the project within 26 weeks is $.5 + .2486 = .7486$.

Thus the expected bonus using Wilson Brothers to do E is:

$$(.486)(100,000) + (.2514)(0) = \$74,860.$$

Analysis using Jones, Inc. to do E:

Activity	ES	EF	LS	LF
A	0	6	0	6
B	0	3	10	13
C	6	12	7	13
D	6	21	6	21
E	12	20	13	21

Hence the critical path is A - D and the overall expected project completion time is 21. The variance of the critical path is:

$$\sigma^2 = \sigma^2_A + \sigma^2_D = (2)^2 + (2)^2 = 8. \text{ Thus } \sigma = 2.828.$$

To find the probability of completing the project in 26 weeks, calculate,

$$z = (26 - 21)/2.828 = 1.77.$$

Thus the probability of finishing in 26 weeks is $P(z < 1.77)$. From Appendix A, the table gives the $P(0 < z < 1.77) = .4616$. Therefore the probability of completing the project within 26 weeks is $.5 + .4616 = .9616$.

Thus the expected bonus using Jones, Inc. to do E is:

$$(.9616)(100,000) + (.0384)(0) = \$96,160.$$

Decision:

The difference in expected returns between the two firms is: $\$96,160 - \$74,860 = \$21,300$. Since this is greater than the $\$15,000$ cost to hire Jones, Inc., Gus should hire Jones, Inc.

PROBLEM 5

For the project represented below, determine the earliest and latest start and finish times for each activity as well as the expected overall completion time.

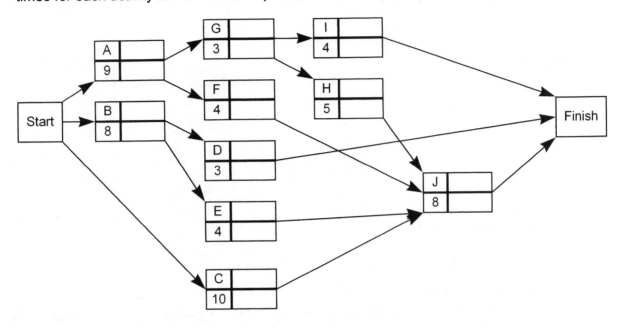

SOLUTION 5

a) Solving the PERT network for the ES, EF, LS, LF, and slack times by the method illustrated in problem 1, we can summarize:

Activity	ES	EF	LS	LF	Slack
A	0	9	0	9	0
B	0	8	5	13	5
C	0	10	7	17	7
D	8	11	22	25	14
E	8	12	13	17	5
F	9	13	13	17	4
G	9	12	9	12	0
H	12	17	12	17	0
I	12	16	21	25	9
J	17	25	17	25	0

The overall project completion time is 25 weeks.

ANSWERED PROBLEMS

PROBLEM 6

Consider a project that has been modeled as follows:

Activity	Immediate Predecessors	Completion Time (hr.)
A	---	7
B	---	10
C	A	4
D	A	30
E	A	7
F	B,C	12
G	B,C	15
H	E,F	11
I	E,F	25
J	E,F	6
K	D,H	21
L	G,J	25

a) Draw the PERT network for this project and determine project's expected completion time and its critical path.

> NOTE: If you are only interested in identifying the critical path and expected project completion time, there might be an easier approach than determining every activity's earliest start and finish times. List (if there are not too many) every path in the network and, for each one, sum the expected times of the activities on that path. You are looking for the path with the largest sum.

b) Can activities E and G be performed simultaneously without delaying the minimum project completion time?

c) Can one person perform A, G, and I without delaying the project?

d) By how much can activities G and L be delayed without delaying the entire project?

e) How much would the project be delayed if activity G was delayed by 7 hours and activity L was delayed by 4 hours? Explain.

PROBLEM 7

Given the following PERT network of tasks with completion times in hours for scheduling interns in a hospital:

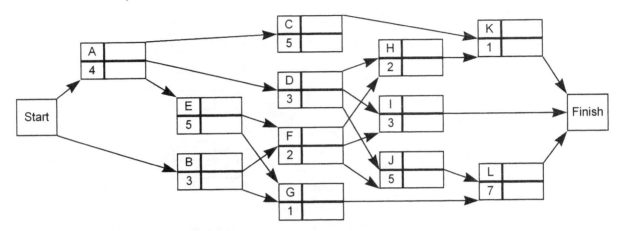

a) If interns start at midnight (00:00), determine each activity's ES, EF, LS, LF, and slack.

b) What is the critical path and project completion time?

c) If an intern can do any job and works a 24-hour shift, show that two interns can complete all the jobs. (Hint: One intern is assigned the critical path jobs.)

PROBLEM 8

A project consists of five activities. Naturally the paint mixing precedes the painting activities. Also, both ceiling painting and floor sanding must be done prior to floor buffing.

Activity	Optimistic Time (hr.)	Most Probable Time (hr.)	Pessimistic Time (hr.)
Floor sanding	3	4	5
Floor buffing	1	2	3
Paint mixing	0.5	1	1.5
Wall painting	1	2	9
Ceiling painting	1	5.5	7

a) Construct a PERT network for this problem.

b) What is the expected completion time of this project?

c) What is the probability that the project can be completed within 9 hr.?

PROBLEM 9

Given the following PERT network modeling new home construction by Bonanza Development:

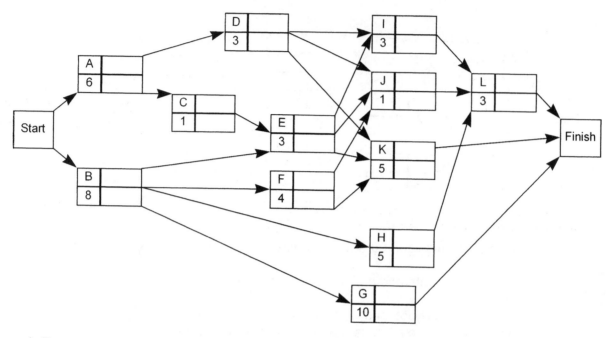

a) Prepare a table of the earliest and latest start and finish times and slack times for each activity in Bonanza's project.

b) What is the critical path and the expected project completion time?

c) Reliable Plumbers, the subcontractor performing activity J, is going to be delayed 5 weeks. If the project is delayed, it will cost Bonanza $2000 per week of delay of the entire project. Reliable is charging $3000 for the plumbing.

Bonanza has three options:

(1) Keep Reliable Plumbers.
(2) Cancel the contract with Reliable Plumbers and hire Local Plumbers, Inc. Local Plumbers, however, will take two weeks to do activity J, and will charge $7000.
(3) Bonanza can train its own employees who are currently performing activity E to do the work. This involves a two-week training period as soon as activity E is done. Then it is expected it will take them three weeks to perform activity J. The cost of the training is $800 per week and the cost of them doing activity J is $1,000 per week.

Which alternative do you recommend to Bonanza? Explain.

PROBLEM 10

Consider the following PERT network with estimated times in weeks. The project is scheduled to begin on May 1.

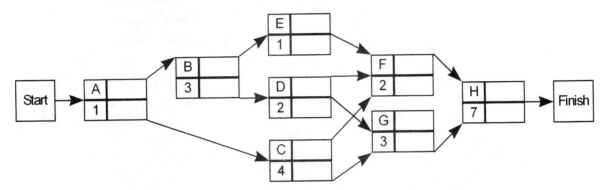

The three-time estimate approach was used to calculate the expected times and the following table gives the variance for each activity:

Activity	Variance	Activity	Variance
A	1.1	E	.3
B	.5	F	.6
C	1.2	G	.6
D	.8	H	1.0

a) Give the expected project completion <u>date</u> and the critical path.

b) By what <u>date</u> are you 99% sure the project will be completed?

c) The project has a target completion date of August 28 (17 weeks). If the project is completed by August 28, the profit on the project will be $10,000. If work is not completed by August 28, a $5,000 penalty will be incurred, reducing the project's profit to $5,000. For $2,000 more than is currently being spent for a firm to do activity H, a more experienced firm can complete the activity in just 5 weeks. Should this offer be accepted? (Assume the variance for H will not change.)

PROBLEM 11

Consider the following PERT network.

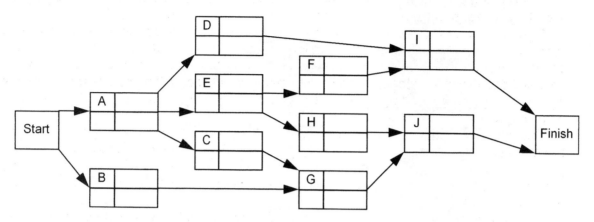

The following chart has been prepared giving the optimistic time (*a*), the most likely time (*m*), and the pessimistic time (*b*), in weeks for each activity.

Activity	*a*	*m*	*b*	Activity	*a*	*m*	*b*
A	2	8	14	F	2	3	10
B	3	12	21	G	3	9	15
C	2	5	8	H	7	8	9
D	4	5	12	I	3	11	13
E	1	3	17	J	7	10	13

a) Determine the critical path, expected project completion time, and standard deviation of the project completion time.

b) Management insists that the project be completed in 36 weeks and will be charged a $100,000 fine for any time overrun. If, at a cost of $3,000, the expected completion time of activity A could be reduced by 2 weeks, should the extra money be spent? (Assume A's variance does not change.)

c) Why is considering only critical path activities for project completion time not always a good assumption in probabilistic cases? (HINT: Consider activity E.)

PROBLEM 12

Plane, Inc. is a manufacturer of heavy equipment and is considering introducing a new line of small steamrollers. Development is to proceed as follows.

A feasibility study will first be performed. Upon receiving a successful feasibility report, a manufacturing building is to be secured and a project leader hired. Once the building is secured, Plane will be committed to the project. Therefore an advertising group will be selected and the raw materials for the manufacturing process will be purchased. When, in addition to securing the building, a project leader has been named, a manufacturing staff will be recruited.

After the manufacturing staff has been selected and the raw materials purchased, a prototype model of the steamroller will be produced. Following the completion of the prototype, work will begin on a production run of 100 steamrollers. When both the prototype model has been built and the advertising staff selected, an intensive advertising campaign will be launched.

The development phase of this project will be complete with the production of the first 100 steamrollers and the initiation of the advertising campaign.

Two separate cost analyses have been prepared. One is effective under current (normal) conditions, while the other is effective if the development phase of the activities is "crashed". These are summarized below. (Times are in weeks.)

	Normal		Crash	
Activity	Time	Cost	Time	Cost
Feasibility Study (A)	6	$ 80,000	5	$100,000
Building Purchased (B)	4	100,000	4	100,000
Project Leader Hired (C)	3	50,000	2	100,000
Advertising Staff Selected (D)	6	150,000	3	300,000
Materials Purchased (E)	3	180,000	2	250,000
Manufacturing Staff Hired (F)	10	300,000	7	480,000
Prototype Manufactured (G)	2	100,000	2	100,000
Production Run of 100 (H)	6	450,000	5	800,000
Advertising Campaign (I)	8	350,000	4	650,000

a) Draw the PERT network for this problem.

b) Formulate and solve a linear program for determining the minimum cost of completing this project in half a year (=26 weeks).

c) What assumptions are made in calculating the "marginal" costs for the activities?

d) Interpret the meaning of the shadow price that would be associated with the constraint that set the maximum completion time to 26 weeks.

PROBLEM 13

Joseph King has ambitions to be mayor of Williston, North Dakota. Joe has determined the breakdown of the steps to the nomination and has estimated normal and crash costs and times for the campaign as follows (times are in weeks):

Activity	Normal Time	Normal Cost	Crash Time	Crash Cost	Immediate Predecessors
A. Solicit Volunteers	6	$5,000	4	$9,000	----
B. Initial "Free" Exposure	3	$4,000	3	$4,000	----
C. Raise Money	9	$4,000	6	$10,000	A
D. Organize and Co-ordinate Schedule	4	$1,000	2	$2,000	A
E. Hire Advertising Firm	2	$1,500	1	$2,000	B
F. Arrange Major TV Interview	3	$4,000	1	$8,000	B
G. Advertising Campaign	5	$7,000	4	$12,000	C,E
H. Personal Campaigning	7	$8,000	5	$20,000	D,F

a) Joe King is not a wealthy man and would like to organize a four month (16 week) campaign at minimum cost. Write and solve a linear program to accomplish this task.

b) Dan Wetzel is an independent who is also trying to make a bid to become mayor of Williston. He has promised a clean campaign, one that he will initially finance on his own. He has $50,000 to invest in his campaign. Being a student of recent successful political campaigns, he knows that his best chance to win is be a "fresh new face" at nomination time. Hence he wishes to keep the entire campaign from beginning to end at a minimum. Write a linear program that, when solved, will minimize the total time of the campaign while keeping expenditures to a maximum of $50,000.

PROBLEM 14

For the project represented below, determine the earliest and latest start and finish times for each activity as well as the expected overall completion time.

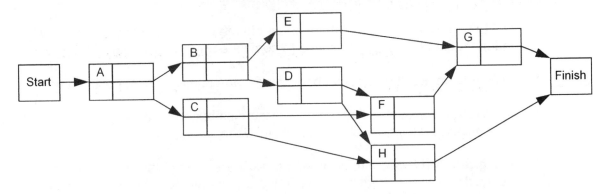

Activity	Time	ES	EF	LS	LF	Slack
A	4					
B	3					
C	4					
D	2					
E	5					
F	2					
G	5					
H	6					

TRUE/FALSE

____ 15. All activities on a critical path have zero slack time.

____ 16. In PERT, it is assumed that the amount of time to complete any one activity is independent of the amount of time to complete any other activity in the project.

____ 17. In PERT, an activity's most probable time is the same as its expected time.

____ 18. In PERT, it is assumed that the underlying distribution for each activity in the three-time estimate approach is a normal distribution.

____ 19. In a given PERT problem, activities F and G are on the critical path. If each is delayed two weeks, then in all cases, the project will be delayed four weeks.

____ 20. The difference between an activity's earliest finish and latest finish equals the difference between its earliest start and latest start.

____ 21. In a given PERT problem, activities F and G are not on the critical path and each has two weeks slack time. If both are delayed by two weeks each, then in all cases, the project will not be delayed.

____ 22. An activity can be started as soon as any one of the activities that immediately precedes it is finished.

____ 23. In a given PERT problem, activity F is on the critical path. If its time is reduced by five weeks, then in all cases, the overall project completion time will be reduced by five weeks.

____ 24. In PERT, the critical path is the path of longest distance through the network.

____ 25. In CPM, the marginal cost per week's saving of an activity's completion time is valid only between its normal time and the time after maximum crashing.

____ 26. It is possible to have more than one critical path at a time.

____ 27. In CPM, if activity B's normal completion time is 8 weeks and normal cost is $10,000, and its completion time after maximum crashing is 5 weeks at a cost of $15,000, then the assumption is that if $13,000 is spent on activity B, its completion time is 6.8 weeks.

____ 28. The project manager should monitor the progress of any activity with a large variance even if the expected times do not identify the activity as a critical activity.

____ 29. A critical activity can be part of a noncritical path.

CHAPTER 11

Inventory Models

KEY CONCEPTS

CONCEPT	ILLUSTRATED PROBLEMS	ANSWERED PROBLEMS
Economic Order Quantity Model	1	9,10,13,18
Economic Production Lot Size Model	2	10,11,18,19
Planned Shortage Model	3	12,13,20
Quantity Discount Model	4	14,24,25
EOQ Model With Stochastic Demand	5	15,26
Reorder Point Based on Service Level	5	15,21,26
Single Period Inventory Model:		
Normal Demand Distribution	6	16,22
Uniform Demand Distribution	8	23
Periodic Review Systems	7	17,27

REVIEW

1. The study of inventory models is concerned with <u>two basic questions</u>: (1) <u>how much</u> should be ordered each time, and (2) <u>when</u> should the reordering occur. The objective is to minimize total variable cost over a specified time period (assumed to be annual in the following review).

2. Potential variable costs include:

    (1) <u>Ordering cost</u> -- salaries and expenses of processing an order, regardless of the order quantity
    (2) <u>Holding cost</u> -- usually a percentage of the value of the item assessed for keeping an item in inventory (including finance costs, insurance, security costs, taxes, warehouse overhead, and other related variable expenses)
    (3) <u>Backorder cost</u> -- costs associated with being out of stock when an item is demanded (including lost goodwill)
    (4) <u>Purchase cost</u> -- the actual price of the items
    (5) Other Costs

3. The simplest inventory models assume demand and the other parameters of the problem to be deterministic and constant. The <u>deterministic models</u> covered in this chapter are: a) economic order quantity (EOQ), b) economic production lot size, c) EOQ with planned shortages, and d) EOQ with quantity discounts.

4. The most basic of the deterministic inventory models is the <u>economic order quantity (EOQ)</u>. The variable costs in this model are annual holding cost and annual ordering cost. For the EOQ, these two costs are equal.

5. The <u>economic production lot size</u> model is a variation of the basic EOQ model. A replenishment order is not received in one lump sum as it is in the basic EOQ model. Instead, inventory is replenished gradually as the order is produced (which requires the production rate to be greater than the demand rate). This model's variable costs are annual holding cost and annual set-up cost (equivalent to ordering cost). For the optimal lot size, these two costs are equal.

6. A <u>stockout</u> (or <u>shortage</u>) is a demand that cannot be immediately satisfied. A <u>backorder</u> is a stockout in which the customer waits until the next replenishment order arrives and then the demand is satisfied.

7. With the <u>EOQ with planned shortages</u> model, a replenishment order does not arrive at or before the inventory position drops to zero. Instead, shortages occur until a predetermined backorder quantity is reached, at which time the replenishment order arrives. The variable costs in this model are annual holding, backorder, and ordering. For the optimal order and backorder quantity combination, the sum of the annual holding and backordering costs equals the annual ordering cost

8. The <u>EOQ with quantity discounts</u> model is applicable where a supplier offers a lower purchase cost when an item is ordered in larger quantities. This model's variable costs are annual holding, ordering and purchase costs.

9. EOQ-based inventory models give results that are rather <u>insensitive to changes in the parameters</u>. Small and sometimes even moderate changes in costs, demands, etc. will have only minor effects on overall total costs.

10. The decision maker must determine if a set of <u>assumptions</u> is appropriate for his particular problem. If the assumptions are approximately correct, employing them will simplify the solution procedure, but the results should only be used as <u>guidelines</u> for an inventory policy.

11. There may be reasons, not built into the model, for <u>modifying the results of a model</u> (such as rounding a reorder time from 12.8 days to 2 weeks to simplify reordering and make bookkeeping control easier).

12. In many cases demand (or some other factor) is not known with a high degree of certainty and a probabilistic inventory model should actually be used. These models tend to be more complex than deterministic models. The <u>probabilistic models</u> covered in this chapter are: a) single-period order quantity, b) reorder-point quantity, and c) periodic-review order quantity.

13. A <u>single-period order quantity</u> model (sometimes called the <u>newsboy problem</u>) deals with a situation in which only one order is placed for the item and the demand is probabilistic. If the period's demand exceeds the order quantity, the demand is not backordered and revenue (profit) will be lost. If demand is less than the order quantity, the surplus stock is sold at the end of the period (usually for less than the original purchase price).

14. A firm's <u>inventory position</u> consists of the <u>on-hand inventory</u> plus <u>on-order</u> inventory (all amounts previously ordered but not yet received). An inventory item is reordered when the item's inventory position reaches a predetermined value, referred to as the <u>reorder point</u>.

15. The <u>reorder point</u> represents the quantity available to meet demand during lead time. <u>Lead time</u> is the time span starting when the replenishment order is placed and ending when the order arrives.

16. Under deterministic conditions, when both demand and lead time are constant, the reorder point associated with EOQ-based models is relatively simple to determine. The reorder point is set equal to <u>lead time demand</u>.

17. Under probabilistic conditions, when demand and/or lead time varies, the reorder point often includes safety stock. <u>Safety stock</u> is the amount by which the reorder point exceeds the expected (average) lead time demand.

18. The amount of safety stock in a reorder point determines the odds (chance) of a stockout during lead time. The complement of this chance is called the service level. <u>Service level</u>, in this context, is defined as the probability of not incurring a stockout during any one lead time. Also, it is the long-run proportion of lead times in which no stockouts occur.

19. A <u>periodic review system</u> is one in which the inventory level is checked and reordering is done only at specified points in time (at fixed intervals usually). Assuming the demand rate varies, the order quantity will vary from one review period to another. This is in contrast to the <u>continuous review system</u> in which inventory is monitored continuously and an order (of a fixed amount) can be placed whenever the reorder point is reached.

20. At the time a <u>periodic-review order quantity</u> is being decided, the concern is that the on-hand inventory and the quantity being ordered is enough to satisfy demand from the time this order is placed until the next order is received (not placed).

DETERMINISTIC INVENTORY MODELS -- ASSUMPTIONS/RESULTS

I. ECONOMIC ORDER QUANTITY (EOQ)

Assumptions

1. Demand is constant throughout the year at D items per year.
2. Ordering cost: $\$C_o$ per order.
3. Holding cost: $\$C_h$ per item in inventory per year.
4. Purchase cost per unit is constant (no quantity discount).
5. Delivery time (lead time) is constant.
6. Planned shortages are not permitted.

Results

1. Optimal order quantity: $Q^* = \sqrt{2DC_o/C_h}$

2. Number of orders per year: D/Q^*

3. Time between orders (cycle time): Q^*/D years

4. Total annual cost: [holding + ordering] = $[(1/2)Q^*C_h] + [DC_o/Q^*]$

II. ECONOMIC PRODUCTION LOT SIZE

Assumptions

1. Demand occurs at a constant rate of D items per year.
2. Production rate is P items per year (and $P>D$).
3. Set-up cost: $\$C_o$ per run.
4. Holding cost: $\$C_h$ per item in inventory per year.
5. Purchase cost per unit is constant (no quantity discount).
6. Set-up time (lead time) is constant.
7. Planned shortages are not permitted.

Results

1. Optimal production lot-size: $Q^* = \sqrt{2DC_o/[(1-D/P)C_h]}$

2. Number of production runs per year: D/Q^*

3. Time between set-ups (cycle time): Q^*/D years

4. Total annual cost: [holding + ordering] = $[(1/2)(1-D/P)Q^*C_h] + [DC_o/Q^*]$

III. PLANNED-SHORTAGE ORDER QUANTITY

Assumptions

1. Demand occurs at a constant rate of D items per year.
2. Ordering cost: $\$C_o$ per order.
3. Holding cost: $\$C_h$ per item in inventory per year.
4. Backorder cost: $\$C_b$ per item backordered per year.
5. Purchase cost per unit is constant (no quantity discount).
6. Set-up time (lead time) is constant.
7. Planned shortages are permitted (backordered demand units are withdrawn from a replenishment order when it is delivered).

Results

1. Optimal order quantity: $Q^* = \sqrt{2DC_o/C_h} \ \sqrt{(C_h+C_b)/C_b}$

2. Maximum number of backorders: $S^* = Q^*(C_h/(C_h+C_b))$

3. Number of orders per year: D/Q^*

4. Time between orders (cycle time): Q^*/D years

5. Total annual cost: $[C_h(Q^*-S^*)^2/2Q^*] + [DC_o/Q^*] + [S^{*2}C_b/2Q^*]$
   [holding + ordering + backordering]

IV. QUANTITY-DISCOUNT ORDER QUANTITY

Assumptions

1. Demand occurs at a constant rate of D items per year.
2. Ordering Cost: $\$C_o$ per order.
3. Holding Cost: $\$C_h = \$C_i I$ per item in inventory per year (note: holding cost is based on the cost of the item, C_i).
4. Purchase Cost: $\$C_1$ per item if the quantity ordered is between 0 and x_1, $\$C_2$ if the order quantity is between x_1 and x_2, etc.
5. Delivery time (lead time) is constant.
6. Planned shortages are not permitted.

Results

1. Optimal order quantity: use procedure on the next page to determine Q^*

2. Number of orders per year: D/Q^*

3. Time between orders (cycle time): Q^*/D years

4. Total annual cost: $[(1/2)Q^*C_h] + [DC_o/Q^*] + DC$
   [holding + ordering + purchase]

FLOW CHART OF
QUANTITY DISCOUNT PROCEDURE

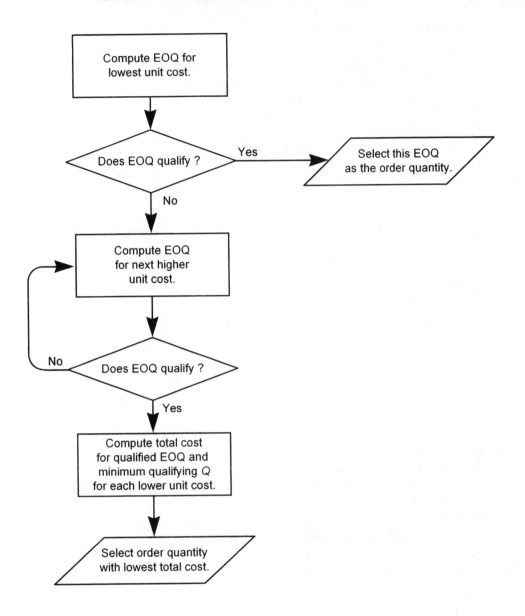

PROBABILISTIC INVENTORY MODELS -- ASSUMPTIONS/RESULTS

I. SINGLE-PERIOD ORDER QUANTITY

Assumptions

1. Period demand follows a known probability distribution.
   a. normal: mean is μ, standard deviation is σ
   b. uniform: minimum is a, maximum is b
2. Cost of overestimating demand: $\$c_o$
3. Cost of underestimating demand: $\$c_u$
4. Shortages are not backordered.
5. Period-end stock is sold for salvage (not held in inventory).

Results

1. Optimal probability of no shortage: $P(\text{demand} \leq Q^*) = c_u/(c_u+c_o)$

2. Optimal probability of shortage: $P(\text{demand} > Q^*) = 1 - c_u/(c_u+c_o)$

3. Optimal order quantity, based on demand distribution --
   a. normal: $Q^* = \mu + z\sigma$
   b. uniform: $Q^* = a + P(\text{demand} \leq Q^*)(b-a)$

II. REORDER POINT

Assumptions

1. Lead-time demand is normally distributed with mean μ and standard deviation σ.
2. Approximate optimal order quantity: EOQ
3. Service level is defined in terms of the probability of no stockouts during lead time and is reflected in z.
4. Shortages are not backordered.
5. Inventory position is reviewed continuously.

Results

1. Reorder point: $r = \mu + z\sigma$

2. Safety stock: $z\sigma$

3. Average inventory: $1/2(Q) + z\sigma$

4. Total annual cost: $[(1/2)Q^*C_h] + [z\sigma C_h] + [DC_o/Q^*]$
   $\qquad\qquad$ [holding(normal) + holding(safety) + ordering]

III. PERIODIC-REVIEW ORDER QUANTITY

Assumptions

1. Inventory position is reviewed at constant intervals (periods).
2. Demand during review period plus lead time period is normally distributed with mean μ and standard deviation σ.
3. Service level is defined in terms of the probability of no stockouts during a review period and is reflected in z.
4. On-hand inventory at ordering time: I
5. Shortages are not backordered.
6. Lead time is less than the length of the review period.

Results

1. Replenishment level: $M = \mu + z\sigma$

2. Order quantity: $Q = M - I$

ILLUSTRATED PROBLEMS

PROBLEM 1

Bart's Barometer Business (BBB) is a retail outlet that deals exclusively with weather equipment. Currently BBB is trying to decide on an inventory and reorder policy for home barometers.

These cost BBB $50 each and demand is about 500 per year distributed fairly evenly throughout the year. Reordering costs are $80 per order and holding costs are figured at 20% of the cost of the item. BBB is open 300 days a year (6 days a week and closed two weeks in August). Lead time is 60 working days.

a) Develop a total variable cost model for this system.

b) What is the optimal reorder quantity and reorder point?

c) How many times per year would BBB reorder?

d) What total annual variable cost does the model give?

e) Given your answer to (b) and (c), choose a more convenient order quantity. Compare the resulting total cost with (d) and comment.

SOLUTION 1

a) Total Costs = (Holding Cost) + (Ordering Cost) = $[C_h(Q/2)] + [C_o(D/Q)]$
   TC = $[.2(50)(Q/2)] + [80(500/Q)] = 5Q + (40,000/Q)$

b) $Q^* = \sqrt{2DC_o/C_h} = \sqrt{2(500)(80)/10} = 89.44 \approx 90$

   Lead time is $m = 60$ days, and daily demand is $d = 500/300$ or 1.667. Thus the reorder point $r = (1.667)(60) = 100$. Bart should reorder 90 barometers when his inventory position reaches 100, i.e. 10 on hand and one outstanding order.

c) Number of reorder times per year = $(500/90) = 5.56$ or once every $(300/5.56) = 54$ working days -- about every 9 weeks.

d) TC = $5(90) + (40,000/90) = 450 + 444 = \$894$.

e) It might be more convenient to order 100 at a time and order 5 times per year (every 10 weeks). This total cost is TC = $5(100) + (40,000/100) = 500 + 400 = \$900$. This $6 difference represents only a 0.6% change in total cost.

PROBLEM 2

   Non-Slip Tile Company (NST) has been using production runs of 100,000 tiles, 10 times per year to meet the demand of 1,000,000 tiles annually. The set-up cost is $5,000 per run and holding cost is estimated at 10% of the manufacturing cost of $1 per tile. The production capacity of the machine is 500,000 tiles per month. The factory is open 365 days per year.

a) Develop a model for the total annual variable cost for this problem.

b) What production schedule do you recommend?

c) How much is NST losing annually with their present production schedule?

d) How long is the machine idle between production runs?

e) What is the maximum number of tiles in inventory under the current policy? under the optimal policy?

f) What fraction of time is the machine producing tiles?

SOLUTION 2

This is an economic production lot size problem with
$$D = 1,000,000, P = 6,000,000, C_h = .10, C_o = 5,000.$$

a) $TC = [C_h(Q/2)(1 - D/P)] + [DC_o/Q] = .04167Q + 5,000,000,000/Q$

b) $Q^* = \sqrt{2DC_o/[C_h(1-D/P)]} = \sqrt{2(1,000,000)(5,000)/[.1(1-1/6)]} = 346,410$
   The number of runs per year = $D/Q^* = 2.89$ times per year

c) Optimal TC = .04167(346,410) + 5,000,000,000/346,410 = $28,868
   Current TC = .04167(100,000) + 5,000,000,000/100,000 = $54,167
   Difference = 54,167 - 28,868 = $25,299

d) There are 2.89 cycles per year, so each cycle lasts (365/2.89) = 126.3 days.
   The time to produce 346,410 per run = 346,410/6,000,000)365 = 21.1 days.
   The machine is idle 126.3 - 21.1 = 105.2 days between runs.

e) Current maximum inventory = $(1-D/P)Q^* = (1-1/6)100,000 = 83,333$.
   Optimal maximum inventory = (1-1/6)346,410 = 288,675.

f) The machine is producing tiles $D/P = 1/6$ of the time.

PROBLEM 3

Hervis Rent-a-Car has a fleet of 2,500 Rockets serving the Los Angeles area. All Rockets are maintained at a central garage. On the average, eight Rockets per month require a new engine. Engines cost $850 each. There is also a $120 order cost (independent of the number of engines ordered).

Hervis has an annual holding cost rate of 30% on engines. It takes two weeks to obtain the engines after they are ordered. For each week a car is out of service, Hervis loses $40 profit.

a) Determine Hervis' optimal order policy for engines.

b) How many days after receiving an order does Hervis run out of engines? How long is Hervis without any engines per cycle?

SOLUTION 3

This can be modeled as a planned shortage model with the following annual data:
$$D = 8 \times 12 = 96; C_o = \$120; C_h = .30(850) = \$255; C_b = 40 \times 52 = 2080.$$

a) $Q^* = \sqrt{2DC_o/C_h} \sqrt{(C_h+C_b)/C_b} = \sqrt{2(96)(120)/255} \sqrt{(255+2080)/2080} = 10.07 \approx 10$

   $S^* = Q^*(C_h/(C_h+C_b)) = 10(255/(255+2080)) = 1.09 \approx 1$

Demand is 8 per month or 2 per week. Since lead time is 2 weeks, lead time demand is 4. Thus, since the optimal policy is to order 10 to arrive when there is one backorder, the order should be placed when there are 3 engines remaining in inventory.

b) Inventory exists for $C_b/(C_b+C_h) = 2080/(255+2080) = .8908$ of the order cycle. (Note, $(Q^*-S^*)/Q^* = .8908$ also, before Q^* and S^* are rounded.) An order cycle is $Q^*/D = .1049$ years = 38.3 days. Thus, Hervis runs out of engines $.8908(38.3) = 34$ days after receiving an order. Hervis is out of stock for approximately $38 - 34 = 4$ days.

PROBLEM 4

Nick's Camera Shop carries Zodiac instant print film. The film normally costs Nick $3.20 per roll, and he sells it for $5.25. Zodiac film has a shelf life of 18 months. Nick's average sales are 21 rolls per week. His annual inventory holding cost rate is 25% and it costs Nick $20 to place an order with Zodiac.

If Zodiac offers a 7% discount on orders of 400 rolls or more, a 10% discount for 900 rolls or more, and a 15% discount for 2000 rolls or more, determine Nick's optimal order quantity.

SOLUTION 4

This can be modeled as a quantity discount problem with the following annual data:
$$D = 21(52) = 1092; \quad C_h = .25(C_i); \quad C_o = 20.$$

For each unit-price, starting with the lowest and working up, determine the most economical, <u>feasible</u> order quantity.

For $C_4 = .85(3.20) = \$2.72$:

To receive a 15% discount Nick must order at least 2,000 rolls. Unfortunately, the film's shelf life is 18 months. The demand in 18 months (78 weeks) is 78 X 21 = 1638 rolls of film, if he ordered 2,000 rolls he would have to scrap 372 of them. This would cost more than the 15% discount would save.

For $C_3 = .90(3.20) = \$2.88$:

$$Q_3^* = \sqrt{2DC_o/C_h} = \sqrt{2(1092)(20)/[.25(2.88)]} = 246.31 \text{ (not feasible)}$$

The most economical, feasible quantity for C_3 is $Q_3^* = 900$.

For $C_2 = .93(3.20) = \$2.976$:

$$Q_2^* = \sqrt{2DC_o/C_h} = \sqrt{2(1092)(20)/[.25(2.976)]} = 242.30 \text{ (not feasible)}$$

The most economical, feasible quantity for C_2 is $Q_2^* = 400$.

For $C_1 = 1.00(3.20) = \$3.20$ (no discount):

$$Q_1^* = \sqrt{2DC_o/C_h} = \sqrt{2(1092)(20)} = 233.67 \approx 234 \text{ (feasible, so we stop computing Qs.}$$
In this problem we have no more Qs anyway.)

Compute the total cost for the most economical, feasible order quantity in each price category for which a Q^* was computed.

$$TC_i = (1/2)(Q_i^* C_h) + (DC_o/Q_i^*) + DC_i$$
$$TC_3 = (1/2)(900)(.720) + ((1092)(20)/900) + (1092)(2.880) = \$3493$$
$$TC_2 = (1/2)(400)(.744) + ((1092)(20)/400) + (1092)(2.976) = \$3453$$
$$TC_1 = (1/2)(234)(.800) + ((1092)(20)/234) + (1092)(3.200) = \$3681$$

Comparing the total costs for 234, 400 and 900, the lowest total annual cost is $3453. Nick should order 400 rolls at a time.

PROBLEM 5

Robert's Drugs is a drug wholesaler supplying 55 independent drug stores. Roberts wishes to determine an optimal inventory policy for Comfort brand headache remedy. Sales of Comfort are relatively constant as the past 10 weeks of data indicate:

Week	Sales (cases)	Week	Sales (cases)
1	110	6	120
2	115	7	130
3	125	8	115
4	120	9	110
5	125	10	130

a) Each case of Comfort costs Roberts $10 and Roberts uses a 14% annual holding cost rate for its inventory. If the cost to prepare a purchase order for Comfort is $12, determine the optimal inventory ordering quantity for Comfort.

b) The lead time for a delivery of Comfort has averaged four working days. Lead time has therefore been estimated as having a normal distribution with a mean of 80 cases and a standard deviation of 10 cases. Roberts wants at most a 2% probability of selling out of Comfort during this lead time. What should be Roberts' reorder point?

c) On the basis of parts (a) and (b) determine the total annual inventory cost for Comfort.

SOLUTION 5

a) The average sales over the 10 week period is 120 cases. Hence
$D = 120 \times 52 = 6{,}240$ cases per year; $C_h = (.14)(10) = 1.40$; $C_o = 12$.

$$Q^* = \sqrt{2DCo/Ch} = \sqrt{2(6240)(12)/1.40} = 327$$

b) Lead time demand is normally distributed with $\mu = 80$, $\sigma = 10$. Since Roberts wants at most a 2% probability of selling out of Comfort, the corresponding z value (see Appendix A) is 2.06. That is, $P(z > 2.06) = .0197$ (about .02). Roberts should reorder Comfort when supply reaches $\mu + z\sigma = 80 + 2.06(10) = 101$ cases. The safety stock is 21 cases.

c) The total annual cost of this solution is:
Ordering: $(DC_o/Q^*) = ((6240)(12)/327)$	$= \$229$
Holding--Normal: $(1/2)Q^*C_o = (1/2)(327)(1.40)$	$= \$229$
Holding--Safety Stock: $C_h(21) = (1.40)(21)$	$= \$\underline{\ 29}$
Total	$= \$487$

PROBLEM 6

The publishers of the *Fast Food Restaurant Menu Book* wish to determine how many copies to print. There is a fixed cost of $5,000 to produce the book and the incremental profit per copy is $.45. Sales for this edition are estimated to be normally distributed. The most likely sales volume is 12,000 copies and they believe there is a 5% chance that sales will exceed 20,000.

a) If any unsold copies of the book can be sold at salvage at a $.55 loss, how many copies should be printed?

b) If any unsold copies of the book can be sold at salvage at a $.65 loss, how many copies should be printed? Comment.

SOLUTION 6

a) $\mu = 12{,}000$. To find σ note that $z = 1.65$ corresponds to a 5% tail probability. Therefore,
$$(20{,}000 - 12{,}000) = 1.65\sigma \text{ or } \sigma = 4848.$$

Using incremental analysis with $c_o = .55$ and $c_u = .45$,
$$(c_u/(c_u + c_o)) = .45/(.45 + .55) = .45.$$

Find Q^* such that $P(D \le Q^*) = .45$. From Appendix A, $z = -.12$ gives this probability. Thus,
$$Q^* = 12{,}000 - .12(4848) = 11{,}418 \text{ books.}$$

b) Using incremental analysis as above but with $c_0 = .65$,
$$(c_u/(c_u+c_0)) = .45/(.45 + .65) = .4091.$$

Find Q^* such that $P(D \le Q^*) = .4091$. From Appendix A, $z = -.23$ gives this probability.
Thus,
$$Q^* = 12,000 - .23(4848) = 10,885 \text{ books.}$$

However, since this is less than the breakeven volume of 11,111 books (= 5000/.45), no copies should be printed because if the company produced only 10,885 copies it will not recoup its $5,000 fixed cost of producing the book.

NOTE: A common mistake is thinking that the probability of having a stockout in some period is equivalent to the portion of the period's demand that will be backordered or lost, when demand is stochastic. A .10 stockout probability does NOT mean that ninety percent of demand will be satisfied. This point applies to all of the stochastic models in this chapter.

PROBLEM 7

Joe Walsh is a salesman for the Ace Brush Company. Every three weeks he contacts Dollar Department Store so that they may place an order to replenish their stock.

Weekly demand for Ace brushes at Dollar approximately follows a normal distribution with a mean of 60 brushes and a standard deviation of 9 brushes. Once Joe submits an order, the lead time until Dollar receives the brushes is one week.

Dollar would like at most a 2% chance of running out of stock during any replenishment period. If Dollar has 75 brushes in stock when Joe contacts them, how many should they order?

NOTE: When ordering with a periodic review system, we are concerned about having enough inventory NOT until we order again, but rather until the next order is received.

SOLUTION 7

This can be modeled as a periodic review problem with probabilistic demand. The review period plus the following lead time totals 4 weeks. This is the amount of time that will elapse before the next brush shipment arrives.

Weekly demand is normally distributed with:
  Mean weekly demand, $\mu = 60$
  Weekly standard deviation, $\sigma = 9$
  Weekly variance, $\sigma^2 = 81$

Thus the distribution of demand for 4 weeks is normal with:
  Mean demand over 4 weeks, $\mu = 4 \times 60 = 240$
  Variance of demand over 4 weeks, $\sigma^2 = 4 \times 81 = 324$
  Standard deviation over 4 weeks, $\sigma = (324)^{1/2} = 18$

NOTE: The standard deviation of the "whole" does not equal the sum of the standard deviations of the "parts". For example, if the standard deviation of daily demand equals 10, the standard deviation of two-day demand does not equal 20.

However, the variance of the "whole" does equal the sum of the variances of the "parts". So, for this example, the variance of two-day demand is $2(10)^2 = 200$ and the standard deviation of two-day demand equals $\sqrt{200} = 14.14$ or $\sqrt{2}$ days$(10) = 14.14$.

The replenishment level, M, is given by the formula $M = \mu + z\sigma$, where z is determined by the desired stockout probability. For a 2% stockout probability (2% tail area in Appendix A), $z = 2.05$. Thus, $M = 240 + 05(18) = 277$.

As the store currently has 75 brushes in stock, Dollar should order: $277 - 75 = \underline{202}$ brushes from Joe. The safety stock is $z\sigma = (2.05)(18) = 37$ brushes.

PROBLEM 8

Mark Hall manages a small greeting card shop that sells artificial Christmas trees during the six weeks prior to Christmas. Based on past experience and current circumstances, Mark estimates that he will sell somewhere between 20 and 80 trees and that the actual number is equally likely to fall anywhere in that range.

A tree costs Mark $28.00 and he sells it for $46.00. Due to very limited storage space, Mark is forced to sell any trees that remain after Christmas at half price ($23.00).

a) What is the optimal probability of stocking out (having more demand than supply)?

b) How many trees should Mark order?

c) Based on your order quantity in (b), what is the probability that Mark will have ten or more trees to sell at a discount after Christmas?

SOLUTION 8

This can be modeled as a single-period problem with uniform demand. The demand limits are $a = 20$ and $b = 80$. $c_u = 46 - 28 = \$18$; $c_o = 28 - 23 = \$5$.

a) Using incremental analysis, the optimal probability of NOT running out of stock is:
$$P(D \le Q^*) = c_u/(c_u+c_o) = 18/(18+5) = .7826$$
Thus, the optimal probability of stocking out is:
$$P(D > Q^*) = 1 - P(D \le Q^*) = 1 - .7826 = .2174$$

b) The optimal order quantity is:
$$Q^* = a + P(D \le Q^*)(b-a) = 20 + .7826(80-20) = 20 + 46.956 = 67 \text{ trees.}$$

c) If Mark orders 67 trees and later is left with ten or more of them, demand would have to be less than or equal to 57 trees. The probability of this is:
$$P(D \le 57) = (57-a)/(b-a) = (57-20)/(80-20) = 37/60 = .6167 \approx .62$$

ANSWERED PROBLEMS

PROBLEM 9

Terri's Tie Shop (TTS) is the exclusive retail outlet for Trophy Ties. Although Trophy Tie demand was slightly higher in December (Christmas) and June (Father's Day), it was relatively constant throughout last year:

Month	Demand	Month	Demand	Month	Demand	Month	Demand
Jan	75	Apr	76	Jul	68	Oct	70
Feb	70	May	69	Aug	75	Nov	76
Mar	72	Jun	85	Sep	74	Dec	90

The average cost of a Trophy Tie is $4 to TTS. TTS figures inventory costs at 15% yearly and reorder costs are $25 per order. There is no reason to assume demand will change much this year.

a) What is the average monthly demand?

b) Assume demand is constant throughout the year and the lead time is two months. Determine an optimal inventory policy for the model.

c) What is the total annual variable cost of the model?

d) Make some suggestions to modify the inventory policy of the model to fit the "real" problem. Comment.

PROBLEM 10

One decision faced by many manufacturing firms is whether to make or buy a particular component of the manufacturing process. Harrison Sound Corporation manufactures stereo systems. The company has a choice of either manufacturing the digital display unit for the Model 243 receiver themselves or purchasing the unit from Allied Electronics.
Allied will charge Harrison $7.50 per unit and Harrison estimates the cost of placing an order with Allied at $48. On the other hand, if Harrison manufactures the units themselves, there will be a set-up cost for production of $1,600, an annual production rate of 50,000 units a year is possible, and the per unit production cost will be $7.00.

a) If Harrison expects the annual demand for these display units to be about 10,000, and the holding cost rate is 20%, determine the total annual variable costs of both policies.

b) Which policy would you recommend to management? Why?

PROBLEM 11

National Business Machines (NBM) is trying to develop the effective use of one of its production lines which produces transistors for circuits of computers. In general, allowing for defectives, NBM needs 1,000,000 transistors per year for their NBM 470 series.

A production rate of 3,000,000 per year is possible if the production line were in continuous operation 24 hours a day, 365 days a year. The cost of storing a transistor is $1 per year. Production set-up costs $4,000 and takes two weeks.

a) What is the optimal number of transistors NBM should make per production run?

b) What is the duration of a production run?

c) If workers have (and must take) vacation between the end of one production run and the start-up of another, how much vacation time do they get per year? (Note they participate in the set-up).

PROBLEM 12

Andy's Auto Parts has been stocking an unusually fine grade of racing oil on which it makes a $.10 per quart profit. Demand has been 2,000 quarts per week. Storage costs are $.01 per quart per week. Reorder costs are $10 per order. If Andy allows backorders, he figures his demand will drop to 1,900 quarts per week. Andy will, however, give a $.03 per week discount per can backordered.

a) Derive an optimal inventory policy for Andy.

b) Based on your answer in (a), what is the maximum time a backordered customer would have to wait?

PROBLEM 13

Wiley's TV Town sells Apex large screen TV's. Weekly demand has averaged 20 Apex TV's per week. Wiley makes a gross profit of $50 per TV sold (not including inventory costs). Holding costs are $260 per TV per year and reorder costs are $32 per order. Lead time is 1 week.

a) Determine: (1) the optimal number of TV's Wiley should order; (2) his reorder point; and, (3) his yearly net profit.

b) Wiley is considering allowing backorders. Wiley intends to offer customers a discount of $20 per week for each week the customer must wait for his TV. Wiley estimates that this policy will result in a drop in demand to 19 TV's per week. Order and holding costs will remain the same. Should Wiley adopt this policy? Why or why not?

PROBLEM 14

Rosato's Pizza Parlor uses tomato sauce at a fairly constant rate of 3600 cans per year. It costs Rosato $40 to place an order for tomato sauce. The holding cost rate is 30 percent per can per year.

Rosato must pay shipping cost, based on weight, and a can of tomato paste weighs 15 pounds. Both the shipping cost and the purchase cost depend on the order quantity. Using the information below, determine the most economical number of cans to order at one time. (Hint: Start by converting the shipping cost discount schedule from pounds to cans.)

Shipping Cost		Purchase Cost	
Pounds	Cost/Pound	Quantity	Cost/Can
1 - 1799	$0.26	1 - 149	$17.80
1800 - 4499	0.23	150 - 349	17.50
4500 or more	0.20	350 or more	17.40

NOTE: A common mistake is to think that the EOQ equation (square-root equation) always determines the optimal order quantity. This is not true for quantity discount problems. Recall that an optimal solution must be a feasible solution. With quantity discounts, an EOQ-derived order quantity must be checked to see if it is feasible (falls in the required quantity range for the price being used).

PROBLEM 15

Kelly's Service Station does a large business in tune-ups. Demand has been averaging 210 spark plugs per week. Holding costs are $.01 per plug per week and reorder costs are estimated at $10 per order.

Kelly does not want to be out of stock on more than 1% of his orders. There is a one day delivery time. The standard deviation of demand is five plugs per day. Assume a normal distribution of demand during lead time and a 7-day work week.

a) What inventory policy do you suggest for Kelly's station?

b) What is the average amount of safety stock for the reorder point in (a)?

c) What are the total variable weekly costs including safety stock costs?

PROBLEM 16

Winkies Donuts is a small chain of donut shops in Lemon County. Winkies' success is built largely around its jelly donut. Recently, Winkies management has received a number of complaints concerning store #17 running out of jelly donuts late in the afternoon. Thus, Winkies has undertaken a study of the store's operations. The study has indicated the following:

(1) Afternoon demand for jelly donuts is approximately normally distributed with mean 150 and standard deviation 30 donuts.
(2) The cost to manufacture a jelly donut is $.09.
(3) The selling price is $.20.
(4) Donuts unsold at the end of the day are given to a charity which gives Winkies a tax savings of $.03 per donut.

Winkies management feels there is a goodwill loss of $.75 for each sale lost when it is out of stock of jelly donuts. Based on this information, how many jelly donuts should the baker prepare for the afternoon?

PROBLEM 17

A lawn and garden shop that is open for business seven days a week orders bags of grass seed every OTHER Monday. Lead time for seed orders is 5 days. On Monday, at ordering time, a clerk found 112 bags of seed in stock, and so he ordered 198 bags. Daily demand for grass seed is normally distributed with a mean of 15 bags and a standard deviation of four bags.

The manager would like to know what the probability is that a grass seed stockout will occur before the NEXT order arrives.

PROBLEM 18

Zak's Zippers is contemplating manufacturing their own zippers rather than distributing the zippers it receives from ZZZ, Inc. Zak's figures it must sell the zipper at the same price or else the yearly demand of 4,000 dozen zippers will be greatly affected.

Presently the purchase cost per dozen zippers is $10, whereas the proposed manufacturing cost for labor and raw materials is estimated at $8 per dozen. In any event, the holding costs are estimated at 20% of the purchase or manufacturing cost of the item. Reorder costs are currently $40 per order. Set-up costs for a production run are estimated at $400.

If Zak's can lease a machine capable of making 8,000 dozen zippers per year at an annual cost of $5,000, should Zak's make their own zippers?

PROBLEM 19

Rancher Jim's Luncheon Meat Company produces fresh luncheon meats. Demand is for 300,000 pounds of meat annually. Rancher Jim has his choice of two machines to process the meats. The annual lease costs and annual processing capacities are given below:

	Annual Lease Cost	Annual Processing Capacity
Machine I	$10,000	250,000 lb.
Machine II	$12,000	1,000,000 lb.

Set-up costs are $1,000 per run and holding costs are $.10 per pound per year. Rancher Jim's gross profit is $.20 per pound (not including annual lease, set-up or holding costs).

a) Show that Machine II gives the maximum profit for processing.

b) Why would you likely recommend machine I for Rancher Jim?

PROBLEM 20

Honest Archie's Appliance Co. has a policy of giving loaner TV's to customers who purchase a set from Archie when he is out of stock of they model they want. As soon as Archie gets the set in stock, he delivers it and picks up the loaner from the customer.

Demand at Archie's for the Apex 19-inch remote control TV is 5 units per week. The sets have an annual holding cost of $55. The cost to place an order for the sets is $80, and it typically takes three weeks for the sets to arrive after the order is placed.

a) If the loaner TV's cost Archie $3 per week to rent, determine his optimal order policy.

b) What is the total annual variable cost of this policy?

PROBLEM 21

Clearview Optical gives a customer a complimentary carrying case with each pair of eye glasses bought. Lead time demand for these cases is normally distributed with a mean of 230 cases and a standard deviation of 42 cases.

a) If Clearview reorders cases when inventory reaches 285 cases, what is the probability that there will be a stockout during lead time?

b) If Clearview desires a .05 probability of a stockout during lead time, what should the reorder point be for glass cases?

PROBLEM 22

Amazing Bakers sells bread to 40 supermarkets. It costs Amazing $1,250 per day to operate its plant. The profit per loaf of bread sold in the supermarket is $.025. Any unsold bread is returned to be sold at the Amazing Thrift store at a loss of $.015.

a) If sales follow a normal distribution with μ = 70,000 and σ = 5,000 per day, how many loaves should Amazing bake daily?

b) Amazing is considering a different sales plan for which the profit per loaf of bread sold in the supermarket is $.03 and the loss per loaf bread returned is $.018. If μ = 60,000 and σ = 4,000 per day, how many loaves should Amazing bake daily?

PROBLEM 23

Every year in early October Steven King buys pumpkins of one size from a farmer in Maine and then hires an artist to carve bewitching faces in them. He then tries to sell them at his produce stand in a public market in Boston.

The farmer charges Steven $2.50 per pumpkin and the artist is paid $2.00 per carved pumpkin. Steven sells a carved pumpkin for $8.00. Any pumpkins not sold by 5:00 p.m. on Halloween are donated to Steven's favorite children's hospital. Steven pays the artist $0.75 per pumpkin to rush the pumpkins to the hospital for the youngsters to enjoy.

Steven estimates the demand for his pumpkins this season to be uniformly distributed within a range of 30 to 70.

a) How many pumpkins should Steven have available for sale?

b) Based on your answer to (a), what is the probability that Steven will be short five or more pumpkins?

PROBLEM 24

Bank Drugs sells Jami Michelle lipstick. The Jami Michelle Company offers a 6% discount on orders of at least 500 tubes, a 10% discount on orders of at least 1,000 tubes, a 12% discount on orders of at least 1,800 tubes and a 15% discount on orders at least 2,500 tubes.

Bank sells an average of 40 tubes of Jami Michelle lipstick weekly. The normal price paid by Bank drugs is $1 per tube. If it costs Bank $30 to place an order, and Bank's annual holding cost rate is 27%, determine the optimal order policy for Bank Drugs.

PROBLEM 25

A company has the following choices for purchasing a product for which demand is 100 per week.

Option	Purchase Cost/Item	Quantity
I	$10.00	0 - 599
II	$ 9.80	600 or more
III	$ 9.90	exactly 100

Under option III, the ordering company will have no paperwork as the 100 items will be delivered every week automatically. Thus under option III, the only work associated with an order is in filing an invoice which is assumed to have zero cost. Otherwise reorder costs are $75 per order.

If holding costs are .5% per week, what is the optimal order quantity?

PROBLEM 26

Demand for the Kansas Systems Model 402 printer at the Computer Town chain of computer stores has averaged 35 units per week with a standard deviation of 10 units per week.

The units cost Computer Town $910 each and there is a $500 order cost. Computer Town's an annual holding cost rate is 20%.

The lead time for these printers is approximately a month with lead time demand being normally distributed with a mean of 140 units and a standard deviation of 20 units.

a) If Computer Town wants to experience an average of at most one stockout per year on these printers, determine an optimal inventory policy for the store.

b) Determine the annual cost of the policy for Computer Town.

c) If Computer Town was just starting to stock printers, use the data above to determine how many printers they should order.

PROBLEM 27

Chez Paul Restaurant orders special styrofoam "doggy bags" for its customers once a month and lead time is one week. Weekly demand for doggy bags is approximately normally distributed with an average of 120 bags and a standard deviation of 25.

Chez Paul wants at most a 3% chance of running out of doggy bags during the replenishment period. If he has 150 bags in stock when he places an order, how many additional bags should he order? What is the safety stock in this case?

____ 28. At the optimal order quantity, Q^*, in the EOQ model, annual order costs equal annual holding costs.

____ 29. If an item's per-unit backorder cost is greater than its per-unit holding cost, no intentional shortage should be planned.

____ 30. At the optimal order quantity for the quantity discount model, the sum of the annual holding and ordering costs is minimized.

____ 31. As lead time for an item increases, the cycle time increases.

____ 32. If an item's per-unit backorder cost equals one-half of its per-unit holding cost, it is optimal to plan to incur the first shortage one-third of the way through the order cycle.

____ 33. If the annual production rate for an item increases, then the optimal production lot size, Q^*, will also increase.

____ 34. When demand increases by 100 percent, the economic order quantity increases by less than 50 percent.

____ 35. If the cost of underestimating demand, c_u, is greater than the cost of overestimating demand, c_o, the optimal single-period order quantity is greater than expected demand.

____ 36. An assumption in the economic production lot size model is that there is storage capacity to hold the entire production lot.

____ 37. In the EOQ model, an item's optimal order quantity, Q^*, cannot be greater than its annual demand, D.

____ 38. The single-period inventory model is most applicable to items that are perishable or have seasonal demand.

____ 39. In the single-period inventory model, an increase in the item's salvage value will cause a decrease in the optimal quantity.

____ 40. To avoid a stockout of a periodic-review item, the item's order quantity plus inventory on hand at ordering time must last until the time the item can be ordered again.

____ 41. If the optimal production lot size decreases, average inventory increases.

____ 42. In the EOQ model, the doubling of both the ordering and holding costs would result in no change in the optimal order quantity.

CHAPTER 12

Waiting Line Models

KEY CONCEPTS

CONCEPT	ILLUSTRATED PROBLEMS	ANSWERED PROBLEMS
Poisson Arrival Process	1	10
Exponential Service Time Distribution	1	10
Queuing Systems		
M/M/1	1,4,5	10-15,17
M/M/k	2,3	11,15,16,18
M/M/1 w/Finite Calling Population	6	23
M/G/1	7	19
M/G/k w/Blocked Customers Cleared	8	20,21
M/D/1	9	22
Economic Analysis of Queuing Systems	3,4,5	11,14,16,17
Spreadsheet Example	1,2	

[*] Note: <u>Unless otherwise stated</u>, all problems in this chapter assume a Poisson arrival process, exponential service time distribution, first-come-first-served queue discipline and unlimited potential queue length.

$$\boxed{\text{REVIEW}}$$

1. Queuing theory is the study of waiting lines. Four characteristics of a queuing system are: (1) the manner in which customers arrive; (2) the time required for service; (3) the priority determining the order of service; and (4) the number and configuration of servers in the system.

2. In general, the arrival of customers into the system is a random event. Frequently the arrival pattern is modeled as a Poisson process. The Poisson distribution defines the probability of x arrivals during a specified time period as:

$$P(x) = \lambda^x e^{-\lambda}/(x!)$$

Here λ is the mean number of arrivals during the specified period and e = 2.71828...

Appendix D provides a table of the quantity $e^{-\lambda}$ for specified values of λ. Sample data should be collected to determine the appropriateness of using the Poisson distribution as well as estimating the value for λ.

3. Service time is also usually a random variable. A distribution commonly used to describe this time is the exponential distribution. The exponential distribution has a probability density function:

$$f(t) = \mu e^{-\mu t}$$

Here μ is the mean number of customers that can be served in a specified time period.

4. For the exponential distribution, the cumulative probability:

$$P(t \leq T) = 1 - e^{-\mu T}$$

Thus the probability of a service taking longer than T is $e^{-\mu T}$.

5. The most common queue discipline is first come, first served (FCFS). An elevator is an example of last come, first served (LCFS) queue discipline.

6. A three part code of the form A/D/k is used to describe various queuing systems. Here, A identifies the arrival distribution, D the service (departure) distribution and k the number of servers for the system.

   Frequently used symbols for the arrival and service processes are: M - Markov distributions (Poisson/exponential), D - Deterministic (constant) and G - General distribution (with a known mean and variance).

   Thus the notation, M/M/k refers to a queuing situation in which arrivals occur according to a Poisson distribution, service times follow an exponential distribution and there are k servers each working at an identical service rate.

7. In order for an M/M/*k* system not to have an <u>infinitely large queue</u>, λ must be less than $k\mu$, where λ is the mean arrival rate and μ is the mean service rate for each server.

8. For a single server system, one defines the ratio λ/μ as the <u>utilization factor</u> for the queue. This can be thought of as the long run proportion of time the server is busy, the probability there is someone in the system, or the probability that an arriving customer must wait for service.

9. In determining the most economical queuing system configuration or evaluating service parameters for the system, one is frequently interested in long run or <u>steady state</u> results. For steady state results to exist, $\lambda < \mu$ for an M/M/1 or an M/G/1 queue, and $\lambda < k\mu$ for an M/M/*k* queue.

10. Notation used for various queue measures are as follows:

P_0 = <u>probability</u> the service facility is idle
P_n = <u>probability</u> of n units in the system
P_w = <u>probability</u> an arriving unit must wait for service
L_q = average <u>number of units</u> in the queue awaiting service
L = average <u>number of units</u> in the system
W_q = average <u>time</u> a unit spends in the queue awaiting service
W = average <u>time</u> a unit spends in the system
λ = the average arrival <u>rate</u>
μ = the average service <u>rate</u> for each server
$1/\lambda$ = the average <u>time</u> between arrivals
$1/\mu$ = the average service <u>time</u>
σ = the standard deviation of the service <u>time</u>

11. For nearly all queuing systems, there is a relationship between the average time a unit spends in the system or queue and the average number of units in the system or queue. These relationships, known as <u>Little's flow equations</u> are:

$$L = \lambda W \quad \text{and} \quad L_q = \lambda W_q$$

12. When the queue discipline is FCFS, <u>analytical formulas</u> have been derived for several different queuing models including the following: M/M/1, M/M/*k*, M/G/1, M/G/*k* with blocked customers cleared, and M/M/1 with a finite calling population. These formulas are presented on the next few pages.

13. Analytical formulas are not available for all possible queuing systems. In this event, insights may be gained through a <u>simulation</u> of the system.

STEADY STATE RESULTS

Quantity	M/M/1 Queues	M/M/k Queues	M/G/1 Queues*
P_0	$1 - \dfrac{\lambda}{\mu}$	$\dfrac{1}{\displaystyle\sum_{n=0}^{k-1} \dfrac{(\lambda/\mu)^n}{n!} + \dfrac{(\lambda/\mu)^k}{k!}\left(\dfrac{k\mu}{k\mu-\lambda}\right)}$	$1 - \dfrac{\lambda}{\mu}$
P_n	$\left(\dfrac{\lambda}{\mu}\right)^n P_0$	$\dfrac{(\lambda/\mu)^n}{n!} P_0$ for $n \le k$ $\dfrac{(\lambda/\mu)^n}{k!\, k^{(n-k)}} P_0$ for $n > k$	No formula
L_q	$\dfrac{\lambda^2}{\mu(\mu-\lambda)}$	$\dfrac{\lambda\mu(\lambda/\mu)^k}{(k-1)!(k\mu-\lambda)^2} P_0$	$\dfrac{\lambda^2\sigma^2 + (\lambda/\mu)^2}{2(1-\lambda/\mu)}$
L	$L_q + \dfrac{\lambda}{\mu}$	$L_q + \dfrac{\lambda}{\mu}$	$L_q + \dfrac{\lambda}{\mu}$
W_q	$\dfrac{L_q}{\lambda}$	$\dfrac{L_q}{\lambda}$	$\dfrac{L_q}{\lambda}$
W	$W_q + \dfrac{1}{\mu}$	$W_q + \dfrac{1}{\mu}$	$W_q + \dfrac{1}{\mu}$
P_w	$\dfrac{\lambda}{\mu}$	$\dfrac{1}{k!}\left(\dfrac{\lambda}{\mu}\right)^k\left(\dfrac{k\mu}{k\mu-\lambda}\right) P_0$	$\dfrac{\lambda}{\mu}$

* Note: In the M/G/1 queue, if G is the exponential distribution, then $\sigma = 1/\mu$ and the above formulas reduce to those given for the M/M/1 queue.

STEADY STATE RESULTS

Quantity	M/D/1 Queues	M/G/k Queues with Blocked Customers Cleared	M/M/1 Queues* with Finite Calling Population (Size N)
P_0	$1 - \dfrac{\lambda}{\mu}$	$\dfrac{1}{\sum\limits_{i=0}^{k}(\lambda/\mu)^i / i!}$	$\dfrac{1}{\sum\limits_{n=0}^{N}\dfrac{N!}{(N-n)!}(\dfrac{\lambda}{\mu})^n}$
P_n	No formula	$\dfrac{(\lambda/\mu)^n / n!}{\sum\limits_{i=0}^{k}(\lambda/\mu)^i / i!}$	$\dfrac{N!}{(N-n)!}(\dfrac{\lambda}{\mu})^n P_0$
L_q	$\dfrac{(\lambda/\mu)^2}{2(1-\lambda/\mu)}$	No queue	$N - \dfrac{\lambda+\mu}{\lambda}(1-P_0)$
L	$L_q + \dfrac{\lambda}{\mu}$	$\dfrac{\lambda}{\mu}(1-P_k)$	$L_q + (1-P_0)$
W_q	$\dfrac{L_q}{\lambda}$	No queue	$\dfrac{L_q}{(N-L)\lambda}$
W	$W_q + \dfrac{1}{\mu}$	$\dfrac{1-P_k}{\mu}$	$W_q + \dfrac{1}{\mu}$
P_w	$\dfrac{\lambda}{\mu}$	No waiting	$1-P_0$

* Note: In the finite calling population model, λ represents the mean arrival rate for each unit.

ILLUSTRATED PROBLEMS

NOTE: Students frequently confuse <u>rates</u> and <u>times</u> in this chapter. They are not the same; they have an inverse relationship. The equations throughout the chapter assume λ and μ are <u>rates</u>. If you are given average interarrival time or average service time, use the inverse.

    Also, λ and μ should be stated in the same unit of time (per hour, for example). Finally, be careful converting the standard deviation of service times σ from one unit of time to another. (It might be easier to convert the arrival rate's time basis to that of the service rate.)

PROBLEM 1

    Joe Ferris is a stock trader on the floor of the New York Stock Exchange for the firm of Smith, Jones, Johnson, and Thomas, Inc. Stock transactions arrive at a mean rate of 20 per hour. Each order received by Joe requires an average of two minutes to process.

a) What is the probability that no orders are received within a 15-minute period?

b) What is the probability that exactly 3 orders are received within a 15-minute period?

c) What is the probability that more than 6 orders arrive within a 15-minute period?

d) What is the mean service rate per hour?

e) What percentage of the orders will take less than one minute to process?

f) What percentage of the orders will be completed in exactly 3 minutes?

g) What percentage of the orders will take more than 3 minutes to process?

h) What is the average time an order must wait from the time Joe receives the order until its processing is finished (i.e. its turnaround time)?

I) What is the average number of orders Joe has waiting to be processed?

j) What percentage of the time is Joe processing orders?

k) Develop a spreadsheet to find the values for the operating characteristics of this **M/M/1** queuing system.

SOLUTION 1

Orders arrive at a mean rate of 20 per hour or one order every 3 minutes. Therefore, in a 15 minute interval the average number of orders arriving will be λ = 15/3 = 5. From Appendix D note that e^{-5} = .0067.

a) $P(x = 0) = (5^0 e^{-5})/0! = e^{-5} = .0067.$

b) $P(x = 3) = (5^3 e^{-5})/3! = 125(.0067)/6 = .1396.$

c) $P(x > 6)$ = 1 - $P(x = 0)$ - $P(x = 1)$ - $P(x = 2)$ - $P(x = 3)$ - $P(x = 4)$ - $P(x = 5)$ - $P(x = 6)$
        = 1 - .762 = .238.

d) Since Joe Ferris' average processing time is 2 minutes (= 2/60 hr.), the mean service rate, μ, is μ = 1/(mean service time), or 60/2 = 30/hr.

e) Since the units are expressed in hours, $P(T \le 1$ minute) = $P(T \le 1/60$ hour). Using the exponential distribution, $P(T \le t) = 1 - e^{-\mu t}$. Hence,

$$P(T \le 1/60) = 1 - e^{-30(1/60)} = 1 - e^{-.5} = 1 - .6065 = .3935.$$

f) Since the exponential distribution is a continuous distribution, the probability a service time exactly equals any specific quantity is 0.

g) The percentage of orders requiring more than 3 minutes to process is:

$$P(T > 3/60) = e^{-30(3/60)} = e^{-1.5} = .2231.$$

h) This is an M/M/1 queue with λ = 20 per hour and μ = 30 per hour. The average time an order waits in the system is:

$$W = 1/(\mu - \lambda) = 1/(30 - 20) = 1/10 \text{ hour or 6 minutes.}$$

l) The average number of orders waiting in the queue is:

$$L_q = \lambda^2/[\mu(\mu - \lambda)] = (20)^2/[(30)(30-20)] = 400/300 = 4/3.$$

j) The percentage of time Joe is processing orders is equivalent to the utilization factor, λ/μ. Thus, the percentage of time he is processing orders is: λ/μ = 20/30 = 2/3 or 66 2/3%.

k) Spreadsheet showing data and formulas

	A	B	C	D	E	F	G	H
1	Poisson Arrival Rate						λ	20
2	Exponential Service Rate						μ	30
3		Operating Characteristics						
4	Probability of no orders in system						Po	=1-H1/H2
5	Average number of orders waiting						Lg	=H1^2/(H2*(H2-H1))
6	Average number of orders in system						L	=H5+H1/H2
7	Average time an order waits						Wq	=H5/H1
8	Average time an order is in system						W	=H7+1/H2
9	Probability an order must wait						Pw	=H1/H2

Spreadsheet showing computed values for operating characteristics

	A	B	C	D	E	F	G	H
1	Poisson Arrival Rate						λ	20
2	Exponential Service Rate						μ	30
3		Operating Characteristics						
4	Probability of no orders in system						Po	0.333
5	Average number of orders waiting						Lg	1.333
6	Average number of orders in system						L	2.000
7	Average time an order waits						Wq	0.067
8	Average time an order is in system						W	0.100
9	Probability an order must wait						Pw	0.667

PROBLEM 2

Smith, Jones, Johnson, and Thomas, Inc. (see problem 1) has begun a major advertising campaign which it believes will increase its business 50%. To handle the increased volume, the company has hired an additional floor trader, Fred Hanson, who works at the same speed as Joe Ferris.

a) Why will Joe Ferris alone not be able to handle the increase in orders?

b) What is the probability that neither Joe nor Fred will be working on an order at any point in time?

c) What is the average turnaround time for an order with both Joe and Fred working?

d) What is the average number of orders waiting to be filled with both Joe and Fred working?

SOLUTION 2

We first note that the new arrival rate of orders, λ, is 50% higher than that of problem 1. Thus, $\lambda = 1.5(20) = 30$ per hour.

a) Since Joe Ferris processes orders at a mean rate of $\mu = 30$ per hour, then $\lambda = \mu = 30$ and the utilization factor is 1. This implies the queue of orders will grow infinitely large. Hence, Joe alone cannot handle this increase in demand.

b) This is now an M/M/2 queuing system with $\lambda = 30$, $\mu = 30$, $k = 2$ and $\lambda/\mu = 1$. The probability that neither Joe nor Fred will be working is:

$$P_0 = \frac{1}{\sum_{n=0}^{k-1}\frac{(\lambda/\mu)^n}{n!} + \frac{(\lambda/\mu)^k}{k!}\left(\frac{k\mu}{k\mu-\lambda}\right)}$$

$$= \frac{1}{[(1 + (1/1!)(30/30)^1] + [(1/2!)(1)^2][2(30)/(2(30)-30)]}$$

$$= 1/(1 + 1 + 1)$$

$$= 1/3$$

(Note: Table 14.4 in the textbook shows $P_0 = .3333$ for $k = 2$ and $\lambda/\mu = 1$.)

c) The average turnaround time is the average waiting time in the system, W. $W = L/\lambda$ and $L = L_q + (\lambda/\mu)$. Now,

$$L_q = \frac{\lambda\mu(\lambda/\mu)^k}{(k-1)!(k\mu-\lambda)^2}P_0$$

$$= \frac{(30)(30)(30/30)^2}{(1!)((2)(30)-30))^2}(1/3)$$

$$= 1/3$$

Hence, $L = 1/3 + (30/30) = 4/3$. $W = (4/3)/30 = 4/90$ hr. $= 2.67$ min.

d) The average number of orders waiting to be filled is L_q. This was calculated above in part (c) as 1/3.

PROBLEM 3

The advertising campaign of Smith, Jones, Johnson and Thomas, Inc. (see problems 1 and 2) was so successful that business actually doubled. The mean rate of stock orders arriving at the exchange is now 40 per hour and the company must decide how many floor traders to employ. Each floor trader hired can process an order, on average, in 2 minutes.

Based on a number of factors the brokerage firm has determined the average waiting cost per minute for an order to be $.50. Floor traders hired will earn $20 per hour in wages and benefits. Using this information compare the total hourly cost of hiring 2 traders with that of hiring 3 traders.

NOTE: Economic analysis of queuing systems usually involves a tradeoff between the cost of service and the <u>cost of waiting</u>. To get the latter, you might be inclined to multiply the waiting cost per unit per time period, c_w, by the average wait time in the system, W. If you take this approach you are not finished until you also multiply by the average number of units entering the system per hour, λ. You get the same results by simply multiplying c_w by L, the average number of units in the system.

SOLUTION 3

Hourly Cost = (Total Hourly Salary Cost) + (Total Hourly Cost for Orders in the System)
    = ($20/trader/hour) x (Number of Traders)
        + ($30 waiting cost/hour) x (average number of orders in the system)
    = $20k + 30L$.

Thus, L must be determined for $k = 2$ traders and for $k = 3$ traders with $\lambda = 40$/hour and $\mu = 30$/hour (since the average service time is 2 minutes).

<u>$k = 2$</u>

$$P_0 = \frac{1}{\displaystyle\sum_{n=0}^{k-1} \frac{(\lambda/\mu)^n}{n!} + \frac{(\lambda/\mu)^k}{k!}\left(\frac{k\mu}{k\mu-\lambda}\right)}$$

$$= \frac{1}{[1+[(1/1!)(40/30)]+[(1/2!)(40/30)^2(60/(60-40))]]} = \frac{1}{1+(4/3)+(8/3)} = 1/5$$

Thus,

$$L_q = \frac{\lambda\mu(\lambda/\mu)^k}{(k-1)!(k\mu-\lambda)^2} P_0$$

$$= \frac{40(30)(40/30)^2}{1!(2(30)-40)^2} = 16/15$$

$L = L_q + (\lambda/\mu) = 16/15 + 4/3 = 12/5$.

Total Cost $= (20)(2) + 30(12/5) = \$112.00/hr$.

$k = 3$

$$P_0 = \frac{1}{[1+(1/1!)(40/30)+(1/2!)(40/30)^2] + [(1/3!)(40/30)^3(90/(90-40))]}$$

$$= \frac{1}{[1+ 4/3 + 8/9] + [32/45]} = 15/59$$

$$L_q = \frac{(30)(40)(40/30)^3}{(2!)(3(30)-40)^2} (15/59) = 128/885 \ (=.1446)$$

Thus, $L = 128/885 + 40/30 = 1308/885$ (= 1.4780).

Total Cost $= (20)(3) + 30(1308/885) = \$104.35$ per hour

Thus, the cost of having 3 traders is less than that of 2 traders.

PROBLEM 4

Frederick's Auto Company currently receives an average of 22 letters a day and has a typist who can type a letter in an average time of 20 minutes. It is considering taking some relief action to ease the typist's workload. It can either hire an additional typist (who also works at an average rate of one letter per 20 minutes) at a cost of $40 per day or it can lease one of three models of word processing systems listed below:

Model	Increase in Cost Per Day	Typist's Efficiency
I	$37	50%
II	$39	75%
III	$43	150%

Frederick's has determined that the cost of a letter waiting to be mailed is $.80/hour. If typists work 8 hours/day, what action should be taken?

SOLUTION 4

For each of the 5 alternatives, determine the average number of letters in the system and the total daily cost. The total daily cost = (extra typist cost or lease cost) + 6.40L, where $6.40 is $.80/hour times 8 hours/day.

Another Typist
This is an M/M/2 system with $\lambda = 22$, $\mu = 24$ and $k = 2$. Using the formulas from the review section we compute $P_0 = .3714$ and $L = 1.16$.
Hence total cost = 40 + (6.40)(1.16) = $47.42.

Lease Machine 1
This is an M/M/1 system with $\lambda = 22$ and $\mu = (1.5)(24) = 36$. Using the formulas from the review section for an M/M/1 system, $L = 22/(36\text{-}22) = 1.57$.
Total Cost = 37 + (6.40)(1.57) = $47.05.

Lease Machine 2
This is an M/M/1 system with $\lambda = 22$ and $\mu = (1.75)(24) = 42$. $L = 22/(42\text{-}22) = 1.1$.
Total cost = 39 + (6.40)(1.1) = 46.04.

Lease Machine 3
This is an M/M/1 system with $\lambda = 22$ and $\mu = (2.5)(24) = 60$. $L = 22/(60\text{-}22) = .58$.
Total cost = 43 + (6.40)(.58) = $46.71.

No Action
This is an M/M/1 system with $\lambda = 22$ and $\mu = 24$. $L = 22/(24\text{-}22) = 11$.
Total cost = 0 + (6.40)(11) = $70.40.

Conclusion
Thus, the best course of action is to lease Machine II.

PROBLEM 5

Jerry's Jewelry Store is seeking a salesman for its evening shift. Three applicants with former experience have applied for the position, each demanding different salaries. Jerry has contacted the former supervisor of each who has supplied him with information on average service times for each applicant. The applicant's salary demands and average service times are as follows:

Applicant	Hourly Wage	Average Service Time
Martha Miller	$ 6	6 min.
Ken Weeks	$10	5 min.
Eddie Smith	$14	4 min.

Customers arrive to the store at the average rate of 8 per hour and you have estimated the cost of having a customer in the store to be $4 per customer per hour (for security, customer relations, etc.) Which applicant should Jerry hire?

SOLUTION 5

For each applicant calculate the total hourly cost = (Hourly Wage) + 4L, where L is the average number of customers in the system. Each case is an M/M/1 system with $\lambda = 8$.

<u>Martha Miller</u>
Since the average service time is 6 min., the average service rate, $\mu = 1/6$ per minute or 10 per hour.

$L = 8/(10-8) = 4$.　　Total hourly cost = 6 + (4)(4) = $22.00.

<u>Ken Weeks</u>
Since the average service time is 5 min., the average service rate, $\mu = 1/5$ per minute or 12 per hour.

$L = 8/(12-8) = 2$.　　Total hourly cost = 10 + (4)(2) = $18.00.

<u>Eddie Smith</u>
Since the average service time is 4 min., the average service rate, $\mu = 1/4$ per minute or 15 per hour.

$L = 8/(15-8) = 8/7$.　Total hourly cost = 14 + (4)(8/7) = $18.56.

<u>Conclusion</u>　　　　　　Based on this study, hire Ken Weeks.

PROBLEM 6

Biff Smith is in charge of maintenance for four of the rides at the Algorithmland Amusement Park: the Pivot, the Traveling Salesman's Adventure, Minimax Regret, and the CPM Crash. On the average, each ride operates four hours before needing repair. When repair is needed, the average repair time is 10 minutes.

Assuming that the time between machine repairs and the service times follow exponential distributions, determine the following:

a) the proportion of time Biff is idle

b) the average time a ride is "down" for repairs

NOTE: For an M/M/1 system with a finite calling population, the arrival rate is the average number of times <u>one</u> unit from the finite population arrives per time period, not the average number of total arrivals per time period.

SOLUTION 6

This problem can be modeled as an M/M/1 queue with a finite calling population of size $N = 4$ (rides). Here

$\lambda = 1/(4$ hours) = .25 per hour.　$\mu = 60/(10$ minutes) = 6 per hour.　$\lambda/\mu = .25/6 = 1/24$.

a) The proportion of time Biff is idle is P_0:

$$P_0 = \frac{1}{\sum_{n=0}^{N} \frac{N!}{(N-n)!}(\frac{\lambda}{\mu})^n}$$

$$P_0 = \frac{1}{\frac{4!}{4!}(1/24)^0 + \frac{4!}{3!}(1/24)^1 + \frac{4!}{2!}(1/24)^2 + \frac{4!}{1!}(1/24)^3 + \frac{4!}{0!}(1/24)^4}$$

$$= \frac{1}{1 + 4(1/24)^1 + 12(1/24)^2 + 24(1/24)^3 + 24(1/24)^4} = .840825$$

Hence, Biff is idle approximately 84% of the time.

b) To find the average time a ride is "down" for repairs we need to calculate W. This is given by the formula:

$$W = W_q + \frac{1}{\mu} \quad \text{where } W_q = \frac{L_q}{(N-L)\lambda}, \quad L_q = N - \frac{\lambda+\mu}{\lambda}(1-P_0), \quad \text{and } L = L_q + (1-P_0)$$

Substituting the appropriate values gives:

L_q = 4 - ((.25+6)/.25)(1-.840825) = .020625

L = .020625 + (1-.840825) = .1798

W_q = .020625/((4-.1798).25) = .02159573

W = .02159573 + 1/6 = .18826 hours or 11.3 minutes

PROBLEM 7

The Bowmar University Student Union has one self service copying machine. On the average, 12 customers per hour arrive to make copies. (The arrival process follows a Poisson distribution.) The time to copy documents follows approximately a <u>normal</u> distribution with a mean of two and one-half minutes and a standard deviation of 30 seconds.

The Union president has received several complaints from students regarding the long lines at the copying machine. On the basis of this information determine:

a) the average number of customers waiting or using the copy machine.

b) the probability an arriving customer must wait in line.

c) the proportion of time the copy machine is idle.

d) the average time a customer must wait in line before using the copy machine.

SOLUTION 7

This situation can be modeled as an M/G/1 system with

$$\lambda = 12 \text{ per hour} = 12/60 = .2/\text{minute}$$
$$1/\mu = 2.5 \text{ minutes}$$
$$\mu = 1/(2.5) = .4 \text{ per minute}$$
$$\sigma = 30 \text{ seconds} = .5 \text{ minutes}$$

a) The average number of customers waiting or using the copy machine is:

$$L = L_q + \frac{\lambda}{\mu} \quad \text{where } L_q = \frac{\lambda^2 \sigma^2 + (\lambda/\mu)^2}{2(1-\lambda/\mu)}$$

Substituting the appropriate values gives:

$$L_q = \frac{(.2)^2(.5)^2 + (.2/.4)^2}{2(1-(.2/.4))} = .26 \quad \text{Thus } L = .26 + (.2/.4) = .76$$

b) The probability an arriving customer must wait in line is:
$$P_w = \lambda/\mu = .2/.4 = .5$$

c) The proportion of time the copy machine is idle is:
$$P_0 = 1 - \lambda/\mu = 1 - .2/.4 = .5$$

d) The average time a customer must wait in line before using the copy machine is:
$$W_q = L_q/\lambda = .26/.2 = 1.3 \text{ minutes}$$

PROBLEM 8

Several firms are over the counter (OTC) market makers of Probabillistics stock. A broker wishing to trade this stock for a client will call on these firms to execute the order. If the market maker's phone line is busy, a broker will immediately try calling another market maker to transact the order.

Richardson and Company is one such OTC market maker. It estimates that on the average, a broker will try to call to execute a stock transaction every two minutes. The time required to complete the transaction averages 75 seconds. The firm has four traders staffing its phones. Assume calls arrive according to a Poisson distribution.

a) What percentage of its potential business will be lost by Richardson?

b) What percentage of its potential business would be lost if only three traders staffed its phones?

SOLUTION 8

This problem can be modeled as an M/G/k system with block customers cleared with:

$1/\lambda = 2$ minutes $= 2/60$ hour
$\lambda = 60/2 = 30$ per hour
$1/\mu = 75$ seconds $= 75/60$ minutes $= 75/3600$ hours
$\mu = 3600/75 = 48$ per hour

a) As there are four traders staffing the phones, $k = 4$, and the system will be blocked when there are four customers in the system. Hence, the answer is P_4. To find P_4, first find P_0 by:

$$P_0 = \frac{1}{\sum\limits_{i=0}^{k}(\lambda/\mu)^i/i!} \quad \text{where } k = 4$$

$$= \frac{1}{1 + (30/48) + (30/48)^2/2! + (30/48)^3/3! + (30/48)^4/4!}$$

$$= \frac{1}{1 + (.625) + (.625)^2/2 + (.625)^3/6 + (.625)^4/24}$$

$$= .536$$

Now, $\quad P_4 = \dfrac{(\lambda/\mu)^4}{4!} P_0 = \dfrac{(30/48)^4}{24} (.536) = .003$

Thus with four traders 0.3% of the potential customers are lost.

b) In this case $k = 3$, and the answer is P_3. Recalculate P_0:

$$P_0 = \frac{1}{1 + (30/48) + (30/48)^2/2! + (30/48)^3/3!} = .537$$

Now, $\quad P_3 = \frac{(\lambda/\mu)^3}{3!} P_0 = \frac{(30/48)^3}{6} (.537) = .022$

Thus with three traders 2.2% of the potential customers are lost.

PROBLEM 9

The long distance viewing scope at the scenic rest stop on Interstate 20 provides two minutes of viewing for $.25. People wanting to use the scope arrive according to a Poisson distribution with a mean rate of 15 per hour.

a) What fraction of time is the scope idle?

b) What is the average number of sightseers waiting to use the scope?

c) What is the average time a sightseer waits to use the scope?

SOLUTION 9

This situation can modeled as an M/D/1 system with

$$\lambda = 15 \text{ per hour}$$
$$1/\mu = 2 \text{ minutes} = 2/60 \text{ hour}$$
$$\mu = 60/2 = 30 \text{ per hour}$$
$$\sigma = 0$$

a) The fraction of time the scope is idle is the complement of the utilization factor:

$$1 - \lambda/\mu = 1 - 15/30 = .5$$

b) The average number of customers waiting in line is:

$$L_q = \frac{(\lambda/\mu)^2}{2(1 - \lambda/\mu)} = \frac{(15/30)^2}{2(1 - 15/30)} = .25 \text{ people}$$

c) The average time a customer must wait to use the scope is:

$$W_q = L_q/\lambda = .25/15 = .01667 \text{ hours or } 1.0 \text{ minutes.}$$

PROBLEM 10

Customers arrive at the Roney Tax Preparation office at an average rate of one per hour. The average time it takes Ms. Roney to prepare a customer's income tax form is 45 minutes.

a) What is the probability of no customers arriving in 2 hours?

b) What is the probability that an income tax form is finished within 45 minutes from the time it is started?

c) What is the average time a customer spends waiting to see Ms. Roney?

d) What is the probability Ms. Roney has 3 customers in the office (i.e. 2 waiting customers plus the one being served)?

PROBLEM 11

Ms. Roney is contemplating a computer system to help her with her income tax preparation (see problem 10). She estimates that such a system will reduce the average time to prepare a return from 45 minutes to 30 minutes. The computer leases for $40 per day.

Ms. Roney estimates the average cost to her of having a waiting customer (due to good will, lost sales, etc.) is $3 per hour. She is open 10 hours per day.

a) Should she lease the computer?

b) If Ms. Roney has the option of hiring another tax preparer for $60 per day who works at the same speed she does, should she do this rather than lease the computer?

PROBLEM 12

The postmaster at the Oak Hill Post Office expects the mean arrival rate of people to her customer counter will soon increase by fifty percent due to a large apartment complex being built.

Currently, the mean arrival rate is 15 people per hour. The postmaster can serve an average of 25 people per hour.

By what percentage must the postmaster's mean service rate increase when the apartment complex is completed in order that the average time spent at the post office remains at its current value?

PROBLEM 13

Cars travel down Main Street at the rate of 20,000 per hour. The probability of any of these cars stopping at the drive-in window of the Burger Prince Restaurant is .002. Cars at Burger Prince are serviced at the mean rate of 60 per hour.

a) What is the average arrival rate to the drive-in window?

b) What is the average number of cars waiting to be served?

c) What is the average number of cars both being served and waiting to be served?

d) What is the probability an arriving car to the Burger Prince Restaurant must wait for service?

e) Management believes that if the number of cars waiting to be served was reduced to less than 1, the probability a car would stop at the drive-in window would increase to .003 and is contemplating implementing changes to speed up service. Given the increased arrival rate, what is the minimum value of the service rate that will meet management's objective?

PROBLEM 14

Cabinet Crafters manufactures specially designed kitchen cabinets and bathroom vanities. One piece of machinery used on most projects is a stationary router. The average number of times carpenters use the router daily is 20 and the average time required for each use is 15 minutes.

The company is planning to purchase a digital router which should reduce the average time required for each use to 12 minutes. The digital router will cost an additional $60 per day. If carpenters earn an average of $20 per hour and work 9 hours per day, determine whether or not Cabinet Crafters should purchase the digital router.

PROBLEM 15

Shear's Department Store has 2 catalog order desks, one at each entrance to the store. On the average, a customer arrives at each order desk every 12 minutes. The service rate at each order desk is an average of 8 customers per hour.

Shear's is considering consolidating its two desks into one location staffed by two order clerks. They would continue to serve customers at the mean rate of 8 customers per hour. Shear's figures it would not lose customers under this arrangement and hence arrivals to this single desk would occur every 6 minutes on the average.

For each configuration of the catalog order desks determine:

a) the average number of customers waiting to be served

b) the probability no customers are present in the entire system

c) the average time a customer spends at the order desk (waiting time plus service time)

d) the probability both clerks are busy

e) should Shear's consolidate its catalog order desks? Explain.

PROBLEM 16

The insurance department at Shear's has two agents, each working at a mean speed of 8 customers per hour. Customers arrive at the insurance desk at a mean rate of one every six minutes and form a single queue.

Management feels that some customers are going to find the wait at the desk too long and take their business to Word's, Shear's competitor. In order to reduce the time required by an agent to serve a customer Shear's is contemplating installing one of two minicomputer systems: System A which leases for $18 per day and will increase an agent's efficiency by 25%; or, System B which leases for $23 per day and will increase an agent's efficiency by 50%. Agents work 8-hour days.

If Shear's estimates its cost of having a customer in the system at $3 per hour, determine if Shear's should install a new minicomputer system, and if so, which one.

PROBLEM 17

A company has tool cribs where workmen draw parts. Two men have applied for the position of distributing parts to the workmen. George Fuller is fresh out of trade school and expects a $6 per hour salary. His average service time is 4 minutes. John Cox is a veteran who expects $12 per hour. His average service time is 2 minutes. A workman's time is figured at $10 per hour. Workmen arrive to draw parts at an average rate of 12 per hour.

a) What is the average waiting time a workman would spend in the system under each applicant?

b) Which applicant should be hired?

PROBLEM 18

Dollar Supermarkets currently has 5 checkout positions. On the average, one customer per minute enters the store and spends an average of 55 minutes choosing his items. Each checker can check out a customer in an average of 4 minutes.

a) What is the average time a customer will spend in the store?

b) Management is considering reducing the number of checkout positions to 3 and hiring baggers. This would reduce the average time required to check out a customer to 2.5 minutes. Would this reduce the average waiting time?

PROBLEM 19

Ted "Tank" Fuller operates a small Texxon gas station that has one gas pump. The arrival rate of vehicles to the pump follows a Poisson probability distribution having a mean of 10 per hour. The time it takes Tank to service a vehicle follows a normal distribution with a mean of 4 minutes and a standard deviation of 1.5 minutes.

a) What is the utilization factor for the gas pump?

b) What is the average length of time a gas customer spends waiting for service to begin?

c) What is the average number of full-service vehicles at the gas station?

d) What is the probability that the servicing of a vehicle will take no more than 7 minutes (excluding the queue wait)?

PROBLEM 20

Tom's Towing Service operates three tow trucks and relies solely on towing requests from the city police department. If Tom has a truck available when the police need one, Tom is always their first choice. However, if he does not have a truck available, the police will select an alternative company rather than wait.

On the average, the police request a tow truck once every 50 minutes. Tom estimates his average tow job takes 90 minutes.

a) Is Tom achieving at least 50 percent utilization of his fleet of tow trucks? (HINT: start by determining the average number of his trucks being used.)

b) What percentage of the police department's towing business is Tom losing because he has only three trucks?

PROBLEM 21

Quick Clean Rooter cleans out clogged drains. Due to the competitive nature of the drain cleaning business, if a customer calls Quick Clean and finds the line busy, they immediately try another company and Quick Clean loses the business.

Quick Clean management estimates that on the average, a customer tries to call Quick Clean every three minutes and the average time to take a service order is 200 seconds. The company wishes to hire enough operators so that at most 4% of its potential customers get the busy signal.

a) How many operators should be hired to meet this objective?

b) Given your answer to a), what is the probability that all the operators are idle?

PROBLEM 22

The Quick Snap photo machine at the Lemon County bus station takes four snapshots in <u>exactly</u> 75 seconds. Customers arrive at the machine according to a Poisson distribution at the mean rate of 20 per hour.

On the basis of this information, determine the following:

a) the average number of customers waiting to use the photo machine

b) the average time a customer spends in the system

c) the probability an arriving customer must wait for service.

PROBLEM 23

Andy Archer, Ph.D., is a training consultant for six mid-sized manufacturing firms. On the average, each of his six clients calls him for consulting assistance once every 25 days. Andy typically spends an average of five days at the client's firm during each consultation.

Assuming that the time between client calls follows an exponential distribution, determine the following:

a) the average number of clients Andy has on backlog

b) the average time a client must wait before Andy arrives to it

c) the proportion of the time Andy is busy.

TRUE/FALSE

____ 24. For an M/M/1 queue, the average time a customer spends in the system is equal to the average time a customer spends in the waiting line plus the average service time.

____ 25. In order to obtain analytical results for a queuing problem one must assume an exponential service time.

____ 26. For a single server queuing system, the average number of customers in the waiting line is one less than the average number in the system.

____ 27. In queuing notation L_q is the average time a customer spends in the waiting line.

____ 28. Little's flow equations apply to any queuing system regardless of the arrival distribution, service time distribution, and number of channels.

____ 29. For an M/M/1 queue, the sum of the utilization factor plus P_0 equals 1.

____ 30. Queue discipline refers to the assumption that a customer has the patience to remain in a slow moving queue.

____ 31. For an M/M/2 system, the probability that the system is empty plus the probability an arriving customer must wait for service equals 1.

____ 32. If some maximum number of customers are allowed in a queuing system at one time, the system has a finite calling population.

____ 33. Assuming the same arrival rates, the average number of customers in the system for an M/M/1 system is the same as that for an M/M/2 system if the average service time in the M/M/2 system is twice as long as for the M/M/1 system.

____ 34. For an M/M/k system, the average number of customers in the system equals the customer arrival rate times the average time a customer spends waiting in the system.

____ 35. Simulation may be used to obtain results for queuing systems.

____ 36. For an M/M/1 queuing system, if the service rate, μ, is doubled, the average wait in the system, W, is cut in half.

____ 37. A multiple-channel system has more than one waiting line.

____ 38. Even when the mean service rate of the queuing system cannot be increased, a reduction in the service time variation will reduce the average length of the waiting line.

CHAPTER 13

Simulation

KEY CONCEPTS

CONCEPT	ILLUSTRATED PROBLEMS	ANSWERED PROBLEMS
Simulation of:		
One Event	1,2	9
Two Events	3	7,8,10,11,14
Multiple Events	4	13,15
Comparison of Expected and Simulated Outcomes	1,6	9,10
Simulation of Decision Alternatives	2	7,10,11,14
Simulation Applications:		
Inventory Systems	2	10,11,13
Waiting Lines	3,4	8,12,15
Markov Processes	5	16
Project Times	6	9
Spreadsheet Example	1,5	

REVIEW

1. Computer simulation is one of the most frequently employed management science techniques. It is typically used to model random processes that are too complex to be solved by analytical methods.

2. One begins a computer simulation by developing a mathematical statement of the problem. The model should be realistic yet solvable within the speed and storage constraints of the computer system being used. Input values for the model as well as probability estimates for the random variables must then be determined.

3. Random variable values are utilized in the model through a technique known as Monte Carlo simulation. Here each random variable is mapped to a set of numbers so that each time one number in that set is generated, the corresponding value of the random variable is given as an input to the model. The mapping is done in such a way that the likelihood that a particular number is chosen is the same as the probability that the corresponding value of the random variable occurs.

4. Because a computer program generates random numbers for the mapping according to some formula, the numbers are not truly generated in a random fashion. However, using standard statistical tests, the numbers can be shown to appear to be drawn from a random process. Appendix B is a table of pseudo-random digits.

5. In a fixed-time simulation model, time periods are incremented by a fixed amount. For each time period a different set of data from the input sequence is used to calculate the effects on the model.

6. In a next-event simulation model, time periods are not fixed but are determined by the data values from the input sequence.

7. The computer program that performs the simulation is called a simulator. While this program can be written in any general purpose language (e.g. BASIC, FORTRAN, C++, etc.), special languages that reduce the amount of code which must be written to perform the simulation have been developed such as SIMSCRIPT, GPSS, SLAM, and Arena.

8. Validation/verification of both the model and the method used by the computer to carry out the calculations is extremely important. Models which do not accurately reflect real world behavior cannot be expected to generate meaningful results. Likewise, errors in programming can result in nonsensical results.

9. Validation/verification is generally done by having an expert review the model and the computer code for errors. If possible, the simulation should be run using actual past data. Predictions from the simulation model should be compared with historical results.

10. Experimental design is an important consideration in the simulation process. Issues such as the length of time of the simulation and the treatment of initial data outputs from the model must be addressed prior to collecting and analyzing output data.

11. Normally one is interested in results for the steady state (long run) operation of the system being modeled. Hence, the initial data inputs to the simulation generally represent a start-up period for the process and it may be important that the data outputs for this start-up period be ignored for predicting this long run behavior.

12. For each policy under consideration by the decision maker, the simulation is run by considering a long sequence of input data values (given by a pseudo-random number generator). Whenever possible, different policies should be compared by using the same sequence of input data.

13. Among the advantages of computer simulation is the ability to gain insights into the model solution which may be impossible to attain through other techniques. Also, once the simulation has been developed, it provides a convenient experimental laboratory to perform "what if" and sensitivity analysis.

14. Two major disadvantages of simulation are: (1) a large amount of time may be required to develop the simulation; and, (2) there is no guarantee that the solution obtained will actually be optimal. Simulation is, in effect, a trial-and-error method of comparing different policy inputs. It does not determine if some input which was not considered could have provided a better solution for the model.

FLOW CHART OF
COMPUTER SIMULATION PROCESS

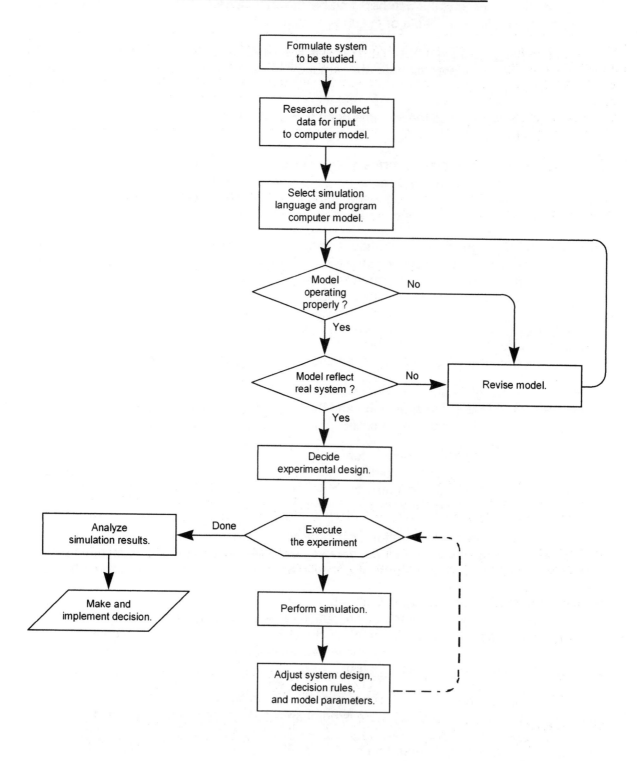

ILLUSTRATED PROBLEMS

NOTE: Several of the problems in this chapter relate to topics of other chapters such as inventory, waiting lines, markov processes, and projects. Where applicable, you are encouraged to compare your simulation results with those of analytic procedures covered in other chapters. However, you might find significant differences that are due most likely to the small number of simulation trials performed.

PROBLEM 1

The price change of shares of Probablistics, Inc. has been observed over the past 50 trades. The frequency distribution is as follows:

Price Change	Frequency (Number of Trades)
-3/8	4
-1/4	2
-1/8	8
0	20
+1/8	10
+1/4	3
+3/8	2
+1/2	1
	Total = 50

a) Develop a relative frequency distribution for this data.

b) If the current price per share of Probablistics is 23, use random numbers to simulate the price per share over the next 20 trades. (For random numbers, use the first two numbers at the bottom of column 1 of Appendix B and move up.)

c) Compare the simulated price after 20 trades (from part b) with the expected price one would obtain based on the probability distribution.

d) Using a spreadsheet, simulate 10 trades.

SOLUTION 1

a) To develop a relative frequency distribution for this data, divide the frequency of each price by the total number of trades. The results are shown in the table below.

b) To develop a simulation for the future prices, assign a random number to each price change so that the probability of seeing a certain price corresponds to its probability (relative frequency).

One such assignment of numbers is:

Price Change	Relative Frequency	Random Numbers
-3/8	.08	00 - 07
-1/4	.04	08 - 11
-1/8	.16	12 - 27
0	.40	28 - 67
+1/8	.20	68 - 87
+1/4	.06	88 - 93
+3/8	.04	94 - 97
+1/2	.02	98 - 99

According to the instructions, the first random number will be 62, the second 32, etc. The simulated results are:

Trade Number	Rand. Number	Price Change	Stock Price
1	62	0	23
2	32	0	23
3	71	+1/8	23 1/8
4	94	+3/8	23 1/2
5	04	-3/8	23 1/8
6	97	+3/8	23 1/2
7	58	0	23 1/2
8	67	0	23 1/2
9	78	+1/8	23 5/8
10	14	-1/8	23 1/2
11	54	0	23 1/2
12	48	0	23 1/2
13	84	+1/8	23 5/8
14	66	0	23 5/8
15	73	+1/8	23 3/4
16	13	-1/8	23 5/8
17	91	+1/4	23 7/8
18	10	-1/4	23 5/8
19	62	0	23 5/8
20	32	0	23 5/8

c) Based on the probability distribution, the expected price change per trade can be calculated by: $(.08)(-3/8) + (.04)(-1/4) + (.16)(-1/8) + (.40)(0) + (.20)(1/8) + (.06)(1/4) + (.04)(3/8) + (.02)(1/2) = .005$

The expected price change for 20 trades is $(20)(.005) = .10$. Hence, the expected stock price after 20 trades is $23 + .10 = 23.10$. This is lower than the simulated price of 23.625 (or 23 5/8).

d) Spreadsheet for the stock price simulation

	A	B	C	D	E	F
1	**Lower**	**Upper**		**Trade**	**Price**	**Stock**
2	**Random**	**Random**	**Price**	**Number**	**Change**	**Price**
3	**Number**	**Number**	**Change**	1	0.000	23.000
4	0.00	0.08	-0.375	2	0.000	23.000
5	0.08	0.12	-0.250	3	-0.125	22.875
6	0.12	0.28	-0.125	4	-0.375	22.500
7	0.28	0.68	0.000	5	0.125	22.625
8	0.68	0.88	0.125	6	0.000	22.625
9	0.88	0.94	0.250	7	0.000	22.625
10	0.94	0.98	0.375	8	0.125	22.750
11	0.98	1.00	0.500	9	0.125	22.875
12				10	0.125	**23.000**

=VLOOKUP(RAND(),$A$4:$C$11,3) ⬏

PROBLEM 2

Shelly's Supermarket has just installed a postage stamp vending machine. Based on one month of operation, Shelly's estimates the number of postage stamps sold per day can be approximated by the following distribution:

Number Sold Per Day	Probability
20	.10
30	.15
40	.20
50	.25
60	.20
70	.10

Shelly's makes a $.02 profit per postage stamp. The vending machine holds 230 stamps and it costs Shelly's $2.00 in labor to fill the machine.

a) Determine the mean number of stamps sold per day.

b) Determine the mean time until the machine is empty.

c) Assume that Shelly's adopts the following policy. Shelly's will fill the machine at the beginning of every n-th day, where n is the answer found in part (b). Conduct a 20-day simulation and determine the expected profit per day. Assume the machine must be filled on the first day. (Use the first two numbers of column 3 of Appendix B, beginning at the top for the random numbers.)

d) Suppose Shelly's fills the machine every (n-1)-th day. Repeat the 20-day simulation and compare the answer with that of part (c). Which policy would you recommend?

SOLUTION 2

The flow chart on the next page can assist in setting up the simulations.

a) The mean number of stamps sold daily =
   (.10)(20)+(.15)(30)+(.20)(40)+(.25)(50)+(.20)(60)+(.10)(70) = 46.

b) The mean time until the machine is empty is:
   (Machine capacity)/(Mean number of stamps sold per day) = 230/46 = 5 days.

Flow Chart of Vending Machine Simulation

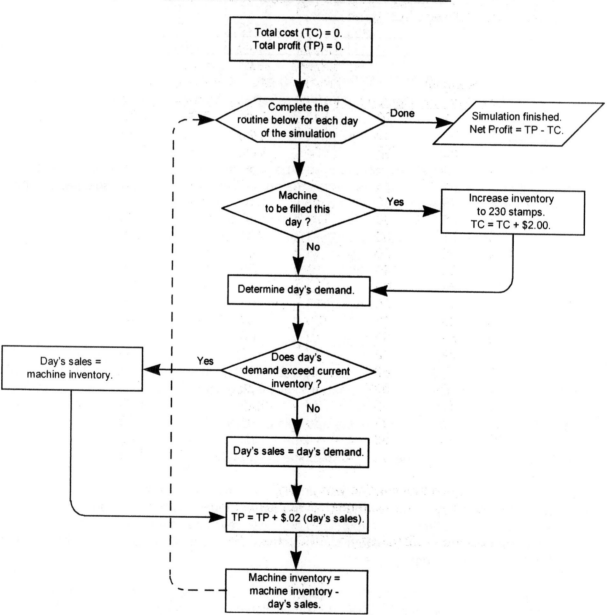

Assuming Shelly's fills the machine every fifth day, determine a set of random numbers corresponding to each sales level.

Number Sold Per Day	Range Of Numbers
20	00 - 09
30	10 - 24
40	25 - 44
50	45 - 69
60	70 - 89
70	90 - 99

Following the instructions of using the first two numbers in column 3 of Appendix B generates the following simulation:

Day	Random Number	Demand	Number Of Stamps Left In Machine	Profit From Sale Of Stamps	Cost Of Refilling Machine	Daily Profit
1	71	60	170	1.20	2.00	- .80
2	95	70	100	1.40	--	1.40
3	83	60	40	1.20	--	1.20
4	44	40	0	.80	--	.80
5	34	40	0	0*	--	0
6	49	50	180	1.00	2.00	-1.00
7	88	60	120	1.20	--	1.20
8	56	50	70	1.00	--	1.00
9	05	20	50	.40	--	.40
10	39	40	10	.80	--	.80
11	75	60	170	1.20	2.00	- .80
12	12	30	140	.60	--	.60
13	03	20	120	.40	--	.40
14	59	50	70	1.00	--	1.00
15	29	40	30	.80	--	.80
16	77	60	170	1.20	2.00	- .80
17	76	60	110	1.20	--	1.20
18	57	50	60	1.00	--	1.00
19	15	30	30	.60	--	.60
20	53	50	0	.60**	--	.60

Total Profit = $9.60

*   0 since the machine was empty

** .60 since there were only 30 stamps left in the machine

Expected Profit per Day = (9.60)/20 = $.48.

d) In order to compare the two policies, the same set of input data should be generated. Thus the simulation below has the same input for daily demand as that of part (c). In this part, the machine is to be filled every fourth day.

Day	Random Number	Demand	Number Of Stamps Left In Machine	Profit From Sale Of Stamps	Cost Of Refilling Machine	Daily Profit
1	71	60	170	1.20	2.00	- .80
2	95	70	100	1.40	--	1.40
3	83	60	40	1.20	--	1.20
4	44	40	0	.80	--	.80
5	34	40	190	0	2.00	-1.20
6	49	50	140	1.00	--	1.00
7	88	60	80	1.20	--	1.20
8	56	50	30	1.00	--	1.00
9	05	20	210	.40	2.00	-1.60
10	39	40	170	.80	--	.80
11	75	60	110	1.20	--	1.20
12	12	30	80	.60	--	.60
13	03	20	210	.40	2.00	-1.60
14	59	50	160	1.00	--	1.00
15	29	40	120	.80	--	.80
16	77	60	60	1.20	--	1.20
17	76	60	170	1.20	2.00	- .80
18	57	50	120	1.00	--	1.00
19	15	30	90	.60	--	.60
20	53	50	40	.60	--	1.00

Total Profit = $8.80

Expected Daily Profit = $ .44

Based on the results of this simulation, Shelly's should fill the machine every fifth day rather than every fourth day.

PROBLEM 3

Wayne International Airport primarily serves domestic air traffic. Occasionally, however, a chartered plane from abroad will arrive with passengers bound for Wayne's two great amusement parks, Algorithmland and Giffith's Cherry Preserve.

Whenever an international plane arrives at the airport the two customs inspectors on duty set up operations to process the passengers.

Incoming passengers must first have their passports and visas checked. This is handled by one inspector. The time required to check a passenger's passports and visas can be described by the following probability distribution:

Time Required to Check a Passenger's Passport and Visa	Probability
20 seconds	.20
40 seconds	.40
60 seconds	.30
80 seconds	.10

After having their passports and visas checked, the passengers next proceed to the second customs official who does baggage inspections. Passengers form a single waiting line with the official inspecting baggage on a first come, first served basis.

The time required for baggage inspection has the following probability distribution:

Time Required For Baggage Inspection	Probability
No Time	.25
1 minute	.60
2 minutes	.10
3 minutes	.05

a) If a chartered plane from abroad lands at Wayne Airport with 80 passengers, use simulation to determine how long it will take for the first 20 passengers to clear customs. (From Appendix B, use the first two digits in column 8 for passport control and the first two digits in column 9 for baggage inspection.)

b) What is the average length of time a customer waits before having his bags inspected after he clears passport control? How is this estimate biased?

NOTE: The value of a decision variable is an input to a simulation model, whereas it is an output to an optimization model (like a linear programming model). A simulation model does not decide the value of a decision variable, it evaluates the result, in terms of some objective, of a given value of a decision variable.

SOLUTION 3

The problem is easiest to set up as a next-event simulation model. The random number mappings are:

Time Required to Check a Passenger's Passport and Visa	Probability	Random Numbers
20 seconds	.20	00 - 19
40 seconds	.40	20 - 59
60 seconds	.30	60 - 89
80 seconds	.10	90 - 99

Time Required For Baggage Inspection	Probability	Random Numbers
No Time	.25	00 - 24
1 minute	.60	25 - 84
2 minutes	.10	85 - 94
3 minutes	.05	95 - 99

For each passenger the following information must be recorded:
 (1) When his service begins at the passport control inspection
 (2) The length of time of this service
 (3) When his service begins at the baggage inspection
 (4) The length of time of this service

Note the following relationships:
 (1) Time a passenger begins service by the passport inspector =
      (Time the previous passenger started passport service)
       + (Time of previous passenger's passport service)

 (2) Time a passenger begins being served by the baggage inspector depends on whether or not the passenger must wait in line for this service.
      If passenger does not wait in line for baggage inspection:
       Time a passenger begins being served by the baggage inspector =
       (Time passenger completes service with the passport control inspector)
      If the passenger does wait in line for baggage inspection:
       Time a passenger begins being served by the baggage inspector =
       (Time previous passenger completes service with the baggage inspector)

 (3) Time a customer completes service at the baggage inspector =
      (Time customer begins service with baggage inspector) +
      (Time required for baggage inspection).

The following table describes the simulation: (service times in minutes)

Passenger Number	Passport Control				Baggage Inspections			
	Time Begin	Random Number	Service Time	Time End	Time Begin	Random Number	Service Time	Time End
1	0:00	93	1:20	1:20	1:20	13	0:00	1:20
2	1:20	63	1:00	2:20	2:20	08	0:00	2:20
3	2:20	26	:40	3:00	3:00	60	1:00	4:00
4	3:00	16	:20	3:20	4:00	13	0:00	4:00
5	3:20	21	:40	4:00	4:00	68	1:00	5:00
6	4:00	26	:40	4:40	5:00	40	1:00	6:00
7	4:40	70	1:00	5:40	6:00	40	1:00	7:00
8	5:40	55	:40	6:20	7:00	27	1:00	8:00
9	6:20	72	1:00	7:20	8:00	23	0:00	8:00
10	7:20	89	1:00	8:20	8:20	64	1:00	9:20
11	8:20	49	:40	9:00	9:20	36	1:00	10:20
12	9:00	64	1:00	10:00	10:20	56	1:00	11:20
13	10:00	91	1:20	11:20	11:20	25	1:00	12:20
14	11:20	02	:20	11:40	12:20	88	2:00	14:20
15	11:40	52	:40	12:20	14:20	18	0:00	14:20
16	12:20	69	1:00	13:20	14:20	74	1:00	15:20
17	13:20	29	:40	14:00	15:20	75	1:00	16:20
18	14:00	96	1:20	15:20	16:20	29	1:00	17:20
19	15:20	95	1:20	16:40	17:20	80	1:00	18:20
20	16:40	84	1:00	17:40	18:20	25	1:00	19:20

For example, passenger 1 begins being served by the passport control inspector immediately. His service time is 1:20 (80 seconds) at which time he goes to the baggage inspector who waves him through without inspection.

Passenger 2 begins service with passport inspector 1:20 minutes (80 seconds) after arriving there (as this is when passenger 1 is finished) and requires 1:00 minute (60 seconds) for passport inspection. He is waved through baggage inspection as well. The process continues in this manner.

a) Passenger 20 clears customs after 19 minutes 20 seconds.

b) For each passenger calculate his waiting time (in seconds):

(Baggage Inspection Begins) - (Passport Control Ends) =
0+0+0+40+0+20+20+40+40+0+20+20+0+40+120+60+80+60+40+40 = 640 seconds.

This gives an average of 640/20 = 32 seconds per passenger. This is a biased estimate because we assume that the simulation began with the system empty, resulting in underestimated average waiting time.

PROBLEM 4

Attendees at the National Management Science Society (NMSS) Conference register by first standing in line to pay their fees. They then proceed to a designated line based on the first letter of their last name to collect their conference materials.

At the conference, it is planned to have three different parallel lines for the collection of materials: one each for people whose last names begin with A-H, I-Q, and R-Z respectively.

During each minute of the morning registration period it is anticipated that attendees will arrive to pay their fees according to the following distribution:

Number of Arrivals	Probability
0	.30
1	.30
2	.30
3	.10

The time to pay one's fees is either one minute or two minutes depending upon whether one uses a check or credit card. The probability of a one-minute time is .60.

After paying his fees, an attendee then goes to the correct line for the conference materials. At this year's conference 35% of the attendees have last names beginning with A-H, 36% with last names beginning with I-Q, and 29% with last names beginning with R-Z. The time required to pick up conference materials is fixed at 2 minutes.

a) Simulate the waiting line for the first 30 attendees during the morning registration. From Appendix B, use column 3 to generate the number of arrivals in any given minute, column 4 to generate registration fee service time, and column 5 to generate the first letter of the last name. Assume registration begins at 8:00 AM.

b) What is the average size of the waiting line to pay fees (not including the person being served), and the average customer waiting time to pay fees based on this simulation?

c) What is the percentage of time each of the three individuals who distribute conference materials is working?

SOLUTION 4

a) For each minute, record the number of arrivals at the fee desk. Then for each arrival determine how long he must wait in line to pay fees, his service time to pay fees, which conference material line is joined, and his waiting and service time in that material line. Random numbers are needed for the number of arrivals in a given minute to the fee line, the length of service time in the fee line, and first letter of the last name to determine to which conference material line the attendee will proceed. The random number mappings are:

Number of Arrivals	Probability	Random Numbers
0	.30	00 - 29
1	.30	30 - 59
2	.30	60 - 89
3	.10	90 - 99

Service Time To Pay Fees	Probability	Random Numbers
1 minute	.60	00 - 59
2 minutes	.40	60 - 99

First Letter Of Last Name	Probability	Random Numbers
A-H	.35	00 - 34
I-Q	.36	35 - 70
R-Z	.29	71 - 99

The simulation then flows chronologically through the events listed as headings on the simulation chart on the next page:
1. Time period begins with Q customers waiting to pay fees. (Q can be determined from the number of previous customers with end times in the fee pay line greater than this time period.)
2. Determine the number of arrivals in the period, #.
3. For each distinct arrival, I, determine wait, begin and end times in the fee pay line.
4. For each distinct arrival, determine the last name and the wait, begin and end times in the conference material line.
5. Repeat until 30 customers have arrived.

b) The average length of the waiting line to pay fees is the average of the entries in the column Q over the 26 time intervals observed, including the 10 at the beginning of 8:26. This is 181/26 = 6.96. The average time a customer waits to pay his fees is the average of the entries in the Fee Pay Wait column over the 30 arrivals = 248/30 = 8.267 minutes.

c) To determine the percentage of time each of the three people who are distributing conference materials are working, take the total amount of time each works and divide by the total length of the simulation (= 42 minutes since 8:41 is the earliest the next arrival could want material service.)

ARRIVALS

Time	RN	#	Q
8:00	71	2	0
8:01	95	3	1
8:02	83	2	3
8:03	44	1	5
8:04	34	1	5
8:05	49	1	5
8:06	88	2	6
8:07	56	1	7
8:08	05	0	7
8:09	39	1	6
8:10	75	2	6
8:11	12	0	8
8:12	03	0	7
8:13	59	1	6
8:14	29	0	6
8:15	77	2	6
8:16	76	2	7
8:17	57	1	9
8:18	15	0	9
8:19	53	1	8
8:20	37	1	8
8:21	46	1	9
8:22	85	2	9
8:23	24	0	10
8:24	53	1	9
8:25	72	2	9
8:26			10
TOTAL 26		30	181

FEE PAY

I	Wait	Begin	RN	Time	End
1	0	8:00	51	1	8:01
2	1	8:01	79	2	8:03
3	2	8:03	09	1	8:04
4	3	8:04	67	2	8:06
5	5	8:06	15	1	8:07
6	5	8:07	58	1	8:08
7	6	8:08	04	1	8:09
8	6	8:09	78	2	8:11
9	7	8:11	30	1	8:12
10	7	8:12	56	1	8:13
11	7	8:13	75	2	8:15
12	9	8:15	75	2	8:17
13	10	8:17	05	1	8:18
14	9	8:18	49	1	8:19
15	9	8:19	70	2	8:21
16	11	8:21	25	1	8:22
17	9	8:22	26	1	8:23
18	8	8:23	10	1	8:24
19	9	8:24	46	1	8:25
20	9	8:25	16	1	8:26
21	10	8:26	64	2	8:28
22	11	8:28	72	2	8:30
23	11	8:30	50	1	8:31
24	11	8:31	15	1	8:32
25	11	8:32	79	2	8:34
26	12	8:34	22	1	8:35
27	13	8:35	51	1	8:36
28	12	8:36	01	1	8:37
29	12	8:37	47	1	8:38
30	13	8:38	88	2	8:40
TOTAL	248			40	

CONFERENCE MATERIAL

RN	Name	Wait	Begin	End
15	A-H	0	8:01	8:03
08	A-H	0	8:03	8:05
19	A-H	1	8:05	8:07
45	I-Q	0	8:06	8:08
76	R-Z	0	8:07	8:09
42	I-Q	0	8:08	8:10
38	I-Q	1	8:10	8:12
47	I-Q	1	8:12	8:14
82	R-Z	0	8:12	8:14
37	I-Q	1	8:14	8:16
49	I-Q	1	8:16	8:18
43	I-Q	1	8:18	8:20
37	I-Q	2	8:20	8:22
11	A-H	0	8:19	8:21
45	I-Q	1	8:22	8:24
55	I-Q	2	8:24	8:26
89	R-Z	0	8:23	8:25
09	A-H	0	8:24	8:26
67	I-Q	1	8:26	8:28
84	R-Z	0	8:26	8:28
51	I-Q	0	8:28	8:30
67	I-Q	0	8:30	8:32
14	A-H	0	8:31	8:33
10	A-H	1	8:33	8:35
52	I-Q	0	8:34	8:36
03	A-H	0	8:35	8:37
02	A-H	1	8:37	8:39
09	A-H	2	8:39	8:41
13	A-H	3	8:41	**8:43**
42	I-Q	0	8:40	8:42
TOTAL 21				

---------------------------- Simulation Over ----------------------------

In 43 minutes (8:00-8:43) the number of minutes busy were A-H: 20, I-Q: 29, R-Z: 8

A-H worker = 20/43 = 46.5%, I-Q worker = 29/43 = 67.4%, R-Z worker = 8/43 = 18.6%.

PROBLEM 5

Mark is a specialist at repairing large metal-cutting machines that use laser technology. His repair territory consists of the cities of Austin, San Antonio, and Houston. His day-to-day repair assignment locations can be modeled as a Markov process (covered in Chapter 17). The transition matrix is as follows:

		Next Day's Location		
		Austin	San Antonio	Houston
This Day's Location	Austin	.60	.15	.25
	San Antonio	.20	.75	.05
	Houston	.15	.05	.80

a) Show the random number assignments that can be used to simulate Mark's next day location when his current location is Austin, San Antonio, and Houston.

b) Assume Mark is currently in Houston. Simulate where Mark will be over the next 25 days. What percentage of time will Mark be in each of the three cities? (Use column 8 of Appendix B.)

c) Repeat the simulation in part b with Mark currently in Austin. (Use column 9 of Appendix B.) Compare the percentages with those found in part (b).

d) Using a spreadsheet, simulate where Mark will be over the next 20 days.

SOLUTION 5

a)

Currently in Austin		Currently in San Antonio		Currently in Houston	
Next-Day Location	Random Numbers	Next-Day Location	Random Numbers	Next-Day Location	Random Numbers
Austin	00 - 59	Austin	00 - 19	Austin	00 - 14
San Ant.	60 - 74	San Ant.	20 - 94	San Ant.	15 - 19
Houston	75 - 99	Houston	95 - 99	Houston	20 - 99

b) <u>Starting in Houston</u>

Day	Random Number	Day's Location
1	93	Houston
2	63	Houston
3	26	Houston
4	16	San Ant.
5	21	San Ant.
6	26	San Ant.
7	70	San Ant.
8	55	San Ant.
9	72	San Ant.
10	89	San Ant.
11	49	San Ant.
12	64	San Ant.
13	91	San Ant.
14	02	Austin
15	52	Austin
16	69	San Ant.
17	29	San Ant.
18	96	Houston
19	95	Houston
20	84	Houston
21	61	Houston
22	09	Austin
23	06	Austin
24	00	Austin
25	63	San Ant.

Austin	= 5/25	= 20%
San Antonio	= 13/25	= 52%
Houston	= 7/25	= 28%

c) <u>Starting in Austin</u>

Day	Random Number	Day's Location
1	13	Austin
2	08	Austin
3	60	San Ant.
4	13	Austin
5	68	San Ant.
6	40	San Ant.
7	40	San Ant.
8	27	San Ant.
9	23	San Ant.
10	64	San Ant.
11	36	San Ant.
12	56	San Ant.
13	25	San Ant.
14	88	San. Ant.
15	18	Austin
16	74	San Ant.
17	75	San Ant.
18	29	San Ant.
19	80	San Ant.
20	25	San Ant.
21	05	Austin
22	64	San Ant.
23	71	San Ant.
24	83	San Ant.
25	74	San Ant.

Austin	= 5/25	= 20%
San Antonio	= 20/25	= 80%
Houston	= 0/25	= 0%

d) Partial Spreadsheet with Variable Look-up Table

	A	B	C	D	E	F	G	H	I
1	Current Location								
2	Aus.			S.A.			Hou.		
3	LRN	URN	NDL	LRN	URN	NDL	LRN	URN	NDL
6	0.00	0.60	Aus.	0.00	0.20	Aus.	0.00	0.15	Aus.
7	0.60	0.75	S.A.	0.20	0.95	S.A.	0.15	0.20	S.A.
8	0.75	1.00	Hou.	0.95	1.00	Hou.	0.20	1.00	Hou.
9									

LRN = Lower Random Number
URN = Upper Random Number
NDL = Next-Day Location

Partial Spreadsheet with Simulation Table

	A	B	C	D	E	F
11	Current		Random		Next-Day	
12	Location		Number		Location	
13	Aus.		0.89		Hou.	
14	Hou.		0.12		Aus.	
15	Aus.		0.45		Aus.	
16	Aus.		0.57		Aus.	
17	Aus.		0.53		Aus.	
18	Aus.		0.89		Hou.	
19	Hou.		0.56		Hou.	
20	Hou.		0.84		Hou.	
21	Hou.		0.93		Hou.	
22	Hou.		0.16		S.A.	
23	S.A.		0.64		S.A.	
24	S.A.		0.30		S.A.	
25	S.A.		0.67		S.A.	
26	S.A.		0.46		S.A.	
27	S.A.		0.37		S.A.	
28	S.A.		0.75		S.A.	
29	S.A.		0.45		S.A.	
30	S.A.		0.37		S.A.	
31	S.A.		0.28		S.A.	
32	S.A.		0.22		S.A.	

IF(A13=$A$2,VLOOKUP(C13,$A$6:$C$8,3),
    IF(A13=$D$2,VLOOKUP(C13,$D$6:$F$8,3),
        VLOOKUP(C13,$G$6:$I$8,3)))

PROBLEM 6

Consider the following house renovation project.

Job and Description	Expected Completion Time (in days)
A - Remove old roof shingles	2
B - Plaster walls and ceilings	4
C - Lay new roof shingles	3
D - Paint exterior	5
E - Paint walls and ceilings	4
F - Hang new gutters	2
G - Install exterior lights	2
H - Lay wall-to-wall carpet	2

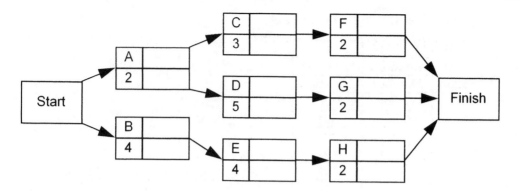

For each job the probabilities of being completed 1 day earlier than expected, on time, 1 day later than expected, and 2 days later than expected are .2, .5, .2, and .1, respectively.

a) Determine the critical path(s) and the project's expected completion time.

b) Do a five trial simulation using the last digit of column 4 of Appendix B for the random numbers to determine the average completion time of the project. Compare this result with your answer to part (a).

SOLUTION 6

a) A path in this context is a set of successive jobs that lead from the project network's starting node (node 1) to the finish node (node 7). There are three different paths in the network. They are A-C-F, A-D-G, and B-E-H. The critical (longest) path consists of jobs B-E-H. The project's expected completion time is the sum of the expected completion times of the jobs on the critical path. Thus, the expected project completion time is 4 + 4 + 2 = 10 days.

> Note: Project Scheduling is covered in Chapter 10. The critical path method (CPM) and other techniques are demonstrated.

b) The random number mappings are as follows. Note only single digit random numbers need be generated.

Job Completion Time	Probability	Random Numbers
Expected time minus 1 day	.2	0,1
Expected time	.5	2,3,4,5,6
Expected time plus 1 day	.2	7,8
Expected time plus 2 days	.1	9

The table on the following page describes the simulation. Note that due to the randomness of job times, a path other than B-E-H was critical in four out of the five trials.

Job	RN	Job's Exp. Time	Time Adjustment	Job's Act. Time	Critical Path and Proj. Compl. Time
A	2	2	0	2	
B	5	4	0	4	
C	1	3	-1	2	
D	2	5	0	5	
E	0	4	-1	3	
F	7	2	+1	3	
G	8	2	+1	3	
H	1	2	-1	1	A-D-G = 10
A	7	2	+1	3	
B	5	4	0	4	
C	8	3	+1	4	
D	5	5	0	5	
E	5	4	0	4	
F	1	2	-1	1	
G	5	2	0	2	
H	0	2	-1	1	A-D-G = 10
A	8	2	+1	3	
B	8	4	+1	5	
C	2	3	0	3	
D	5	5	0	5	
E	6	4	0	4	
F	7	2	+1	3	
G	4	2	0	2	
H	4	2	0	2	B-E-H = 11
A	7	2	+1	3	
B	2	4	0	4	
C	3	3	0	3	
D	6	5	0	5	
E	7	4	+1	5	
F	6	2	0	2	
G	3	2	0	2	
H	4	2	0	2	A-D-G = 12
A	8	2	+1	3	
B	5	4	0	4	
C	1	3	-1	2	
D	2	5	0	5	
E	2	4	0	4	
F	5	2	0	2	
G	9	2	+2	4	
H	6	2	0	2	A-D-G = 12

Average project completion time is (10+10+11+12+12)/5 = 11 days.

ANSWERED PROBLEMS

PROBLEM 7

Susan Winslow has two alternative routes to travel from her home in Olport to her office in Lewisburg. She can travel on Freeway 5 to Freeway 57 or on Freeway 55 to Freeway 91. The time distributions are as follows:

Freeway 5		Freeway 57		Freeway 55		Freeway 91	
Time	Relative Frequency	Time	Relative Frequency	Time	Relative Frequency	Time	Relative Frequency
5	.30	4	.10	6	.20	3	.30
6	.20	5	.20	7	.20	4	.35
7	.40	6	.35	8	.40	5	.20
8	.10	7	.20	9	.20	6	.15
		8	.15				

Do a five-day simulation of each of the two combinations of routes using columns 1, 2, 3, and 4 of Appendix B for the random numbers. Based on this simulation, which routes should Susan take if her objective is to minimize her total travel time?

PROBLEM 8

The Rumson Post Office serves a small rural town. In any one minute interval during a Saturday morning either 0, 1, 2, or 3 customers arrive with the following probabilities: $P(0) = .40$; $P(1) = .30$; $P(2) = .20$; $P(3) = .10$.

The only clerk working on Saturday at the post office is Mrs. Smith. Her service time per customer is also a random variable with the following distribution of 1, 2, or 3 minutes per service: $P(1) = .80$; $P(2) = .15$; $P(3) = .05$.

If the system starts empty, simulate the waiting line over a 10 minute interval. Use Appendix B, column 1 to generate the number of arrivals and column 2 to generate service times. What is the average number of customers waiting in line for service?

PROBLEM 9

Consider the following PERT problem.

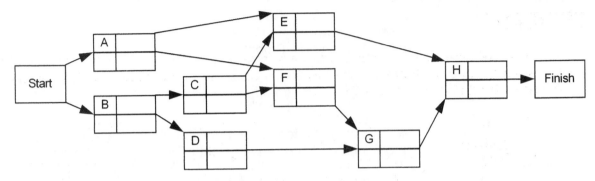

The expected completion time for each job is given below:

Job	Expected Completion Time in Weeks
A	7
B	4
C	3
D	6
E	5
F	3
G	3
H	4

a) Determine the critical path(s) and expected completion time of this project.

b) Suppose that each job has a 25% chance of being completed in a week less than its expected completion time and a 25% chance of being completed in a week more than its expected completion time. Do a five-trial simulation using the last two digits of column 6 of Appendix B for the random numbers to determine the average completion time of this project. Compare this answer to part (a).

PROBLEM 10

Demand for mopeds at the Easy Rider Bike Shop is either 0, 1, 2, or 3 per day with the following probability distribution:

Demand	Probability
0	.15
1	.25
2	.35
3	.25

Each working day a moped remains in inventory costs Easy Rider $2 per moped. It costs Easy Rider $30 to process an order.

The delivery time required to obtain new mopeds from the wholesaler is also random with the following distribution:

Delivery Time (in Working Days)	Probability
1	.20
2	.60
3	.20

Easy Rider has adopted the policy of offering customers an $8 per day discount for each working day they must wait for a moped if Easy Rider is out of stock.

a) Assume Easy Rider is open 200 days per year and delivery time is exactly two working days. Further, assume that although demand varies, it is actually constant at the level of average demand. What would be the optimal order policy?

b) Do a 20-day simulation using the answer you obtained in part (a) assuming a current inventory of 6 mopeds and that delivery time and demand follow the distributions given above. Use the first two digits in column 2 of Appendix B to generate demands and the first two digits of column 3 to generate lead times. What is the average inventory cost per day, where inventory holding costs are assessed on ending inventory?

PROBLEM 11

Miller's Carpets runs a store that carries a certain style of carpet. Over the weeks Miller's has collected data concerning the demand for the number of rolls of this brand of carpet:

Weekly Demand	Probability
0	.10
1	.20
2	.20
3	.20
4	.20
5	.10

Miller's policy has been to reorder 8 rolls whenever its inventory reached 4 rolls or less at the end of the week. Current inventory is 5 rolls. Reordering costs are $40 per order and holding costs are $2 per roll per week. Stockout costs are $10 per occurrence and these sales are lost.

Lead time for an order has been observed to be:

Weeks	Probability
1	.40
2	.50
3	.10

a) Conduct an 8-week simulation of Miller's situation and determine the total cost for this period. Use column 4 of Appendix B for demand and column 6 for lead times.

b) Miller's has been offered a new policy. The wholesaler will automatically deliver 3 rolls to Miller's at the end of each week for a weekly service charge of $12. This eliminates reorder costs and lead times. Should Miller's accept this new policy or keep its current policy?

PROBLEM 12

Customers at Winkies Donuts can either eat their doughnut purchase on the premises or carry it out. Winkies estimates that 35% of its morning business customers enjoy their doughnuts on the premises.

Customers eating their doughnuts on the premises either buy one or two doughnuts and nearly always order a beverage. Winkies estimates the following profits and probabilities hold for service times of the on-the-premises customers:

Service Times	Probability	Expected Profit
25 seconds	.15	$ .08
50 seconds	.60	$ .23
75 seconds	.25	$ .34

Carry-out customers typically purchase a couple of doughnuts or a dozen. Winkies estimates the following profits and probabilities hold for the service times of carry-out customers:

Service Times	Probability	Expected Profit
50 seconds	.30	$ .15
100 seconds	.70	$ .90

During any 25 second interval, either 0, 1, or 2 customers will arrive at Winkies with the following probability distribution:

Customers	Probability
0	.75
1	.16
2	.09

Winkies has only one morning sales clerk on duty.

a) Conduct a 10-minute simulation of sales at Winkies. Using Appendix B, use column 1 for number of arrivals in 25 seconds, column 2 for the eat-in/carry-out decision, column 3 for on-the-premises and carry-out service times.

b) What is the expected profit during this period?

c) What percentage of the time is the server busy?

d) What is the average number of customers at Winkies?

PROBLEM 13

Honest Archie's Appliance Company has decided to cease selling microwave ovens. Archie has slashed prices on the three models he has in stock -- Amana, Litton, and Tappan. He currently has 3 Amanas, 2 Littons, and 4 Tappans left in stock.

Because of his low prices, Archie expects to have from one to four customers come into his store each day inquiring about the ovens. Archie believes the following daily probabilities hold:

Customers	Probability
1	.50
2	.30
3	.10
4	.10

For each inquiry, Archie believes the following probabilities hold: P(not interested in any purchase) = .30; P(desires Amana) = .30; P(desires Litton) = .25; P(desires Tappan) = .15.

If a customer desires a particular brand of oven that Archie is sold out of, Archie will try to sell the customer the brand of oven in which his current stock is the largest. (If there is a tie, he chooses the one that had the largest initial stock.) Archie believes there is a 25% chance he will be successful in convincing the person to switch to that brand and a 75% chance of losing the sale.

Do a simulation to determine the number of days it will take Archie to sell out his stock of microwave ovens. Use column 7 of Appendix B for arriving customers, column 8 for oven preference, and column 9 for brand switching.

PROBLEM 14

As the owner of a rent-a-car agency you have determined the following statistics:

Potential Rentals Daily	Probability	Rental Duration	Probability
0	.10	1 day	.50
1	.15	2 days	.30
2	.20	3 days	.15
3	.30	4 days	.05
4	.25		

The gross profit is $40 per car per day rented. When there is demand for a car when none is available there is a goodwill loss of $80 and the rental is lost. Each day a car is unused costs you $5 per car. Your firm initially has 4 cars.

a) Conduct a 10-day simulation of this business using column 1 of Appendix B for demand and column 2 for rental length.

b) If your firm can obtain another car for $200 for 10 days should you take the extra car?

PROBLEM 15

Scooper Dooper is a small ice cream parlor located next to the Lemonville exit of the Metropolitan Subway Line. Arriving customers to Scooper Dooper purchase either ice cream cones, malts, or sundaes. The following table gives the approximate service time required, expected profit, and the probability of each type of purchase:

Purchase	Probability	Service Time Required	Expected Profit
Ice Cream Cone	.75	30 seconds	$.12
Malt	.15	60 seconds	$.22
Sundae	.10	90 seconds	$.30

The store is small, holding a maximum of four customers. Customers who find the store full go elsewhere for their ice cream. Management estimates that during the lunch hour in each 30 second interval there will be either 0, 1, 2, or 3 arrivals with the following probability distribution:

Number of Arrivals	Probability
0	.30
1	.40
2	.20
3	.10

Simulate the operation of the Scooper Dooper ice cream parlor for a 15-minute period during the lunch hour. From Appendix B, use column 1 to generate the number of arrivals and column 2 to determine the type of purchase.

a) What is the expected profit earned during this period?

b) What percentage of the customers are lost due to a full store?

c) What is the average size of the waiting line?

PROBLEM 16

Three airlines compete on the route between New York and Los Angeles. Stanton Marketing has performed an analysis of first class business travelers to determine their airline choice. Stanton has modeled this choice as a Markov process and has determined the following transition probabilities.

		Next Airline		
		A	B	C
	A	.50	.30	.20
Last Airline	B	.30	.45	.25
	C	.10	.35	.55

a) Show the random number assignments that can be used to simulate the first class business traveler's next airline when her last airline is A, B, and C.

b) Assume the traveler used airline C last. Simulate which airline the traveler will be using over her next 25 flights. What percentage of her flights are on each of the three airlines? (Use column 3 of Appendix B.)

TRUE/FALSE

___ 17. Given the accuracy of computers, it is not necessary to validate a simulation program.

___ 18. Using the next event simulation approach, the time between system updates is variable.

___ 19. A random number mapping always maps a set of occurrences to numbers between 00 and 99.

___ 20. Computer simulation requires a special purpose simulation language.

___ 21. In comparing different policies using simulation, one should use the same set of random numbers whenever possible.

___ 22. Flowcharts are useful in designing a simulation program.

___ 23. In Monte Carlo simulation, outcomes are determined by choosing a random number and selecting the outcome corresponding to that number.

___ 24. A computer simulator is a device which acts like a computer but is not a computer.

___ 25. One is guaranteed an optimal solution to a problem using simulation.

___ 26. A typical way to avoid start-up problems in simulation is to run the program for a specified time without recording any data corresponding to the simulation.

___ 27. Probabilistic inputs to a Monte Carlo simulation must follow a discrete probability distribution.

___ 28. If there are no probabilistic components in a problem, there is no reason to use computer simulation to solve it.

___ 29. Simulation is a trial-and-error approach to problem solving.

___ 30. If a computer simulator is correctly programmed, there will be no difference between the simulated and real distributions for a probabilistic component.

___ 31. If a computer simulator is properly programmed, different random number sequences will not cause different output results.

CHAPTER 14

Decision Analysis

KEY CONCEPTS

CONCEPT	ILLUSTRATED PROBLEMS	ANSWERED PROBLEMS
Payoff Tables	1,2,3	8-16
Nonprobabilistic Decision Criteria: Optimistic, Conservative, Minimax Regret Approaches	1,2	8,9,10,12,15
Spreadsheet Approach	1	
Probabilistic Decision Criteria: Expected Monetary Value, Expected Opportunity Loss	1-4	8-16
Spreadsheet Approach	3	
Decision Trees	1,3,4	10-16
Expected Value of Perfect Information	1,3	9,10,11,13,14,16
Spreadsheet Approach	3	
Bayes' Rule: Revising Probabilities	3,4	11,13,14,16,19
Spreadsheet Approach	3	
Expected Value of Sample Information	3	11,13,14,16
Efficiency of Sample Information	3	11,13
Sensitivity Analysis	5	11,19
Influence Diagrams	3	
Decision Making Using Utility	6,7	17,18,19

REVIEW

1. A <u>decision problem</u> is characterized by decision alternatives, states of nature, and resulting payoffs.

2. The <u>decision alternatives</u> are the different strategies the decision maker can employ.

3. The <u>states of nature</u> refer to future events, not under the control of the decision maker, which may occur. States of nature should be defined so that they are mutually exclusive and collectively exhaustive.

4. For each decision alternative and state of nature, there is a resulting <u>payoff</u>. These are often represented in matrix form called a <u>payoff table</u>.

5. A decision is said to <u>dominate</u> another decision if the payoffs for every state of nature for one is at least equal to the corresponding payoffs for the other and is greater for at least one state of nature.

6. One way to solve a complex decision problem is by the use of a <u>decision tree</u>. This is a <u>chronological representation</u> of the decision problem.

7. Each decision tree has two types of nodes. <u>Round nodes</u> correspond to the states of nature while <u>square nodes</u> correspond to the decision alternatives. The branches leaving each round node represent the different states of nature while the branches leaving each square node represent the different decision alternatives.

8. At the end of each limb of a decision tree are the payoffs attained from the series of branches making up that limb. To solve the problem one "<u>folds back the tree</u>", working backwards from the ends of the branches towards the root node of the tree.

9. <u>Decision making under certainty</u> occurs when the decision maker knows with certainty which state of nature will occur.

10. If the decision maker does not know with certainty which state of nature will occur, then he is said to be doing <u>decision making under uncertainty</u>.

11. Three <u>commonly used criteria</u> for decision making under uncertainty when probability information regarding the likelihood of the states of nature is unavailable are: (1) the optimistic, (2) the conservative, and (3) the minimax regret approach.

12. The <u>optimistic approach</u> would be used by an optimistic decision maker. The decision with the largest possible payoff is chosen. (If the payoff table were in terms of costs, the decision that had the lowest cost would be chosen.)

13. The <u>conservative approach</u> would be used by a conservative decision maker. For each decision the minimum payoff is listed. Then the decision corresponding to the maximum of these minimum payoffs is selected. Hence, the minimum possible payoff is maximized. (If the payoffs were in terms of costs, the maximum costs would be determined for each decision. The decision having the minimum of these maximum costs would be selected.)

14. The <u>minimax regret approach</u> requires the construction of a <u>regret table</u> or an <u>opportunity loss table</u>. This is done by calculating for each state of nature the difference between each payoff and the largest payoff for that state of nature. Then, using this regret table, the maximum regret for each possible decision is listed. The decision chosen is the one corresponding to the minimum of the maximum regrets.

15. If probabilistic information regarding he states of nature is available, one may use the <u>expected value (EV)</u> approach. Here the expected return for each decision is calculated by summing the products of the payoff under each state of nature and the probability of the respective state of nature occurring. The decision yielding the best expected return is chosen.

16. <u>Risk analysis</u> is the study of the possible payoffs associated with a decision alternative or a decision strategy. A tool used in risk analysis is graphically depicting the <u>risk profile</u> for a decision alternative. The risk profile shows the possible payoffs for the decision alternative along with their associated probabilities. Sometimes a review of the risk profile associated with an optimal decision alternative may cause the decision maker to choose another decision alternative even though the expected value of the other alternative is not as good.

17. <u>Sensitivity analysis</u> can be used to determine the probability range over which a decision will remain optimal. Such an analysis can provide a better perspective on management's original judgment regarding the state of nature probabilities.

18. Frequently information is available which can improve the probability estimates for the states of nature. The <u>expected value of perfect information (EVPI)</u> is the <u>increase</u> in the expected profit that would result if one knew with certainty which state of nature would occur. This quantity provides an upper bound on the expected value of any sample or survey information. EVPI can be calculated as follows:
    (1) determine the optimal return corresponding to each state of nature;
    (2) compute the expected value of these optimal returns;
    (3) subtract the EV of the optimal decision from the amount determined in step (2).

19. Knowledge of sample or survey information can be used to revise the probability estimates for the states of nature. Prior to obtaining this information, the probability estimates for the states of nature are called <u>prior probabilities</u>. With knowledge of <u>conditional probabilities</u> for the outcomes or indicators of the sample or survey information, these prior probabilities can be revised by employing <u>Bayes' Theorem</u>. The outcomes of this analysis are called <u>posterior probabilities</u>.

20. Posterior probabilities are calculated as follows:
    (1) For each state of nature, multiply the prior probability by its conditional probability for the indicator -- this gives the joint probabilities for the states and indicator.
    (2) Sum these joint probabilities over all states -- this gives the marginal probability for the indicator.
    (3) For each state, divide its joint probability by the marginal probability for the indicator -- this gives the posterior probability distribution.

21. The expected value of sample information (EVSI) is the additional expected profit possible through knowledge of the sample or survey information. EVSI is calculated as follows:
    (1) determine the optimal decision and its expected return for the possible outcomes of the sample or survey using the posterior probabilities for the states of nature;
    (2) compute the expected value of these optimal returns;
    (3) subtract the EV of the optimal decision obtained without using the sample information from the amount determined in step (2).

22. Efficiency of sample information is the ratio of EVSI to EVPI. As the EVPI provides an upper bound for the EVSI, efficiency is always a number between 0 and 1.

23. An influence diagram is a graphical device that shows the relationship among decisions, chance events, and consequences for a decision problem. Such a device is particularly useful in understanding and analyzing more-complex decision problems.

24. Utility is a measure of the total worth of a particular outcome, reflecting the decision maker's attitude towards a collection of factors. Some of these factors may be profit, loss, and risk. Utilities are used when the decision criteria must be based on more than just expected monetary values. While determining utility values is not an easy task, such an analysis should be performed in cases where payoffs can assume extremely high or extremely low values.

25. Once a utility function has been determined, the optimal decision can be chosen using the expected utility approach. Here, for each decision alternative, the utility corresponding to each state of nature is multiplied by the probability for that state of nature. The sum of these products for each decision alternative represents the expected utility for that alternative. The decision alternative with the highest expected utility is chosen.

26. Utility values are influenced by the attitude of the decision maker towards risk. A risk avoider will have a concave utility function when utility is measured on the vertical axis and monetary value is measured on the horizontal axis. Individuals purchasing insurance exhibit risk avoidance behavior.

27. A risk taker, such as a gambler, pays a premium to obtain risk. His/her utility function is convex. This reflects the decision maker's increasing marginal value of money.

28. A risk-neutral decision maker has a linear utility function. In this case, the expected value approach can be used.

29. Most individuals are risk avoiders for some amounts of money, risk neutral for other amounts of money, and risk takers for still other amounts of money. This explains why the same individual will purchase both insurance and also a lottery ticket.

FLOW CHART FOR
DECISION MAKING WITHOUT PROBABILITIES

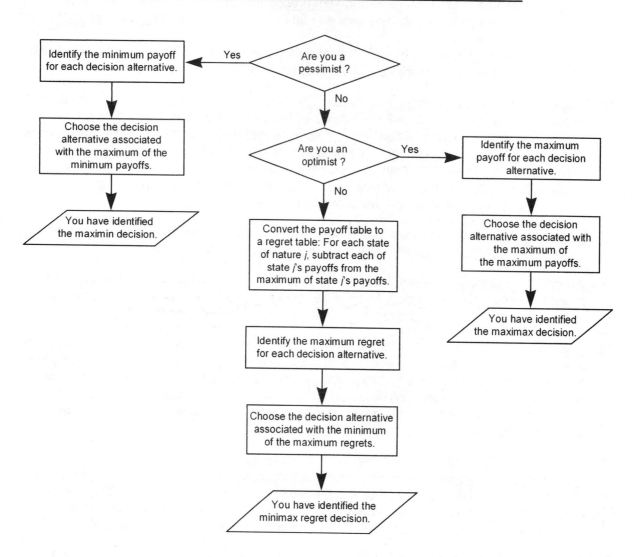

FLOW CHART FOR
DECISION MAKING WITH PROBABILITIES (PART A)

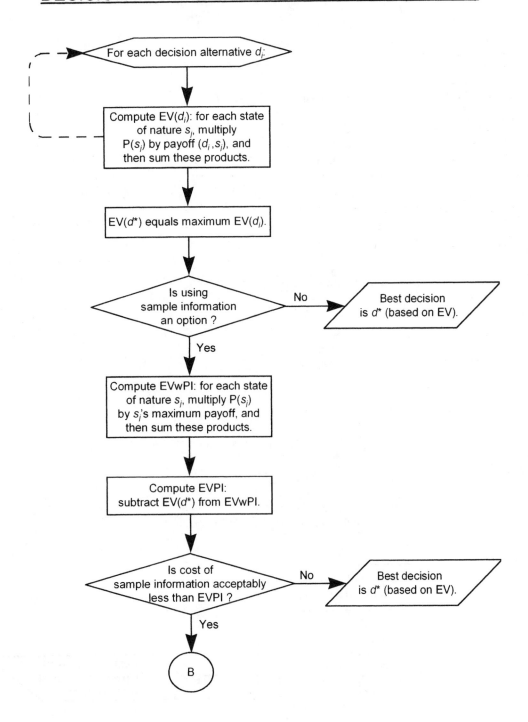

FLOW CHART FOR
DECISION MAKING WITH PROBABILITIES (PART B)

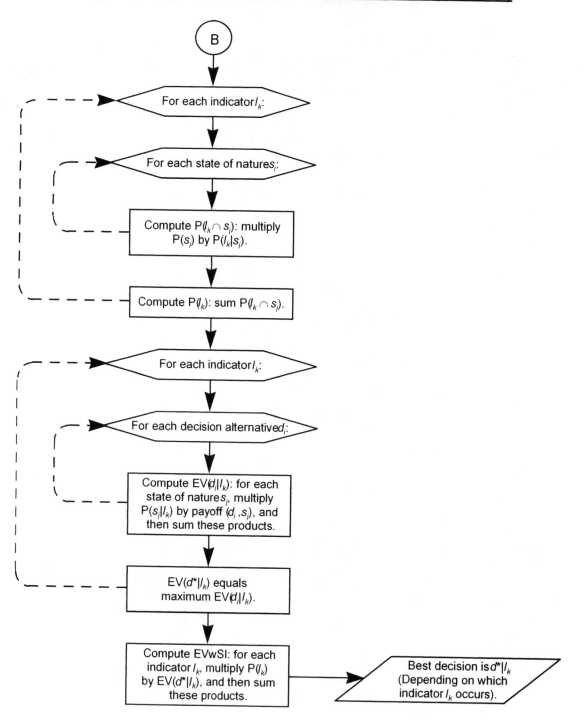

FLOW CHART FOR
DECISION MAKING WITH UTILITY

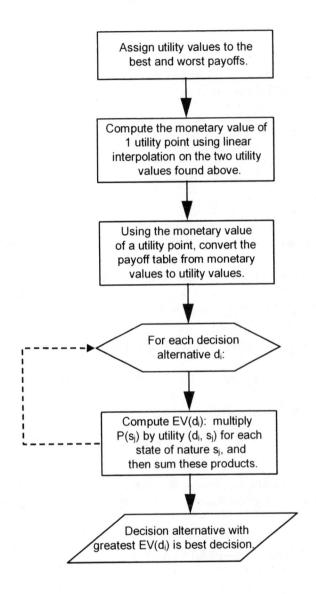

ILLUSTRATED PROBLEMS

PROBLEM 1

Consider the following problem with three decision alternatives and three states of nature with the following payoff table representing profits:

		States of Nature	
	s_1	s_2	s_3
d_1	4	4	-2
d_2	0	3	-1
d_3	1	5	-3

(with "Decisions" labeling the rows d_1, d_2, d_3)

a) What is the optimal decision if the decision maker were conservative?

b) What is the optimal decision if the decision maker were optimistic?

c) What is the optimal decision using the minimax regret approach?

d) Use spreadsheets to find the optimal decisions in parts a), b), and c) above.

e) Use a decision tree to find the optimal decision if $P(s_1) = .20$, $P(s_2) = .50$, $P(s_3) = .30$.

f) Given the probabilities in (d), calculate the EVPI.

SOLUTION 1

a) A conservative decision maker would use the conservative approach. List the minimum payoff for each decision. Choose the decision with the maximum of these minimum payoffs.

Decision	Minimum Payoff
d_1	-2
d_2	-1 (maximum, choose d_2)
d_3	-3

b) An optimistic decision maker would use the optimistic approach. All we really need to do is to choose the decision that has the largest single value in the payoff table. This largest value is 5, and hence the optimal decision is d_3.

c) For the minimax regret approach, first compute a regret table by subtracting each payoff in a column from the largest payoff in that column. In this example, in the first column subtract 4, 0, and 1 from 4; in the second column, subtract 4, 3, and 5 from 5; etc. The resulting regret table is:

$$\begin{array}{c|ccc} & s_1 & s_2 & s_3 \\ \hline d_1 & 0 & 1 & 1 \\ d_2 & 4 & 2 & 0 \\ d_3 & 3 & 0 & 2 \end{array}$$

Then, for each decision list the maximum regret. Choose the decision with the minimum of these values:

Decision	Maximum Regret
d_1	1 (minimum, choose d_1)
d_2	4
d_3	3

d) Conservative Approach

Formula Spreadsheet for Conservative Approach

	A	B	C	D	E	F
1	PAYOFF TABLE					
2						
3	**Decision**	**State of Nature**			**Minimum**	**Recommended**
4	**Alternative**	s1	s2	s3	**Payoff**	**Decision**
5	d1	4	4	-2	=MIN(B5:D5)	=IF(E5=$E$9,A5,"")
6	d2	0	3	-1	=MIN(B6:D6)	=IF(E6=$E$9,A6,"")
7	d3	1	5	-3	=MIN(B7:D7)	=IF(E7=$E$9,A7,"")
8						
9			**Best Payoff**		=MAX(E5:E7)	

Solution Spreadsheet for Conservative Approach

	A	B	C	D	E	F
1	PAYOFF TABLE					
2						
3	**Decision**	**State of Nature**			**Minimum**	**Recommended**
4	**Alternative**	s1	s2	s3	**Payoff**	**Decision**
5	d1	4	4	-2	-2	
6	d2	0	3	-1	-1	**d2**
7	d3	1	5	-3	-3	
8						
9			**Best Payoff**		-1	

Optimistic Approach

Formula Spreadsheet for Optimistic Approach

	A	B	C	D	E	F
1	PAYOFF TABLE					
2						
3	Decision	State of Nature			Maximum	Recommended
4	Alternative	s1	s2	s3	Payoff	Decision
5	d1	4	4	-2	=MAX(B5:D5)	=IF(E5=$E$9,A5,"")
6	d2	0	3	-1	=MAX(B6:D6)	=IF(E6=$E$9,A6,"")
7	d3	1	5	-3	=MAX(B7:D7)	=IF(E7=$E$9,A7,"")
8						
9			Best Payoff		=MAX(E5:E7)	

Solution Spreadsheet for Optimistic Approach

	A	B	C	D	E	F
1	PAYOFF TABLE					
2						
3	Decision	State of Nature			Maximum	Recommended
4	Alternative	s1	s2	s3	Payoff	Decision
5	d1	4	4	-2	4	
6	d2	0	3	-1	3	
7	d3	1	5	-3	5	d3
8						
9			Best Payoff		5	

Minimax Regret Approach

Formula Spreadsheet for Minimax Regret Approach

	A	B	C	D	E	F
1	PAYOFF TABLE					
2	Decision	State of Nature				
3	Altern.	s1	s2	s3		
4	d1	4	4	-2		
5	d2	0	3	-1		
6	d3	1	5	-3		
7						
8	OPPORTUNITY LOSS TABLE					
9	Decision	State of Nature			Maximum	Recommended
10	Altern.	s1	s2	s3	Regret	Decision
11	d1	=MAX($B$4:$B$6)-B4	=MAX($C$4:$C$6)-C4	=MAX($D$4:$D$6)-D4	=MAX(B11:D11)	=IF(E11=$E$14,A11,"")
12	d2	=MAX($B$4:$B$6)-B5	=MAX($C$4:$C$6)-C5	=MAX($D$4:$D$6)-D5	=MAX(B12:D12)	=IF(E12=$E$14,A12,"")
13	d3	=MAX($B$4:$B$6)-B6	=MAX($C$4:$C$6)-C6	=MAX($D$4:$D$6)-D6	=MAX(B13:D13)	=IF(E13=$E$14,A13,"")
14		Minimax Regret Value			=MIN(E11:E13)	

Solution Spreadsheet for Minimax Regret Approach

	PAYOFF TABLE					
1	PAYOFF TABLE					
2	**Decision**	**State of Nature**				
3	**Alternative**	s1	s2	s3		
4	d1	4	4	-2		
5	d2	0	3	-1		
6	d3	1	5	-3		
7						
8	OPPORTUNITY LOSS TABLE					
9	**Decision**	**State of Nature**			**Maximum**	**Recommended**
10	**Alternative**	s1	s2	s3	**Regret**	**Decision**
11	d1	0	1	1	1	**d1**
12	d2	4	2	0	4	
13	d3	3	0	2	3	
14		**Minimax Regret Value**			1	

e) The tree diagram looks as follows:

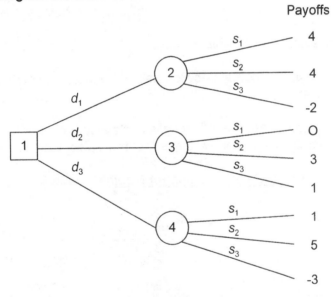

Payoffs

To calculate the expected values at nodes 2, 3, and 4, multiply the payoffs by the corresponding probabilities and then sum. The decision with the maximum expected value of 2.2, d_1, is then chosen.

$$EV(\text{Node 2}) = .20(4) + .50(4) + .30(-2) = 2.2 \text{ (maximum, choose } d_1)$$
$$EV(\text{Node 3}) = .20(0) + .50(3) + .30(-1) = 1.2$$
$$EV(\text{Node 4}) = .20(1) + .50(5) + .30(-3) = 1.8$$

NOTE: The optimal decision based on minimizing expected regret will always be the same as the optimal decision based on maximizing expected payoff. If you compute the expected regret for each decision, using the regret table in part (c), you will find that d_1 is optimal just as it is in part (d) above.

f) The EVPI is calculated by multiplying the maximum payoff for each state by the corresponding probability, summing these values, and then subtracting the expected value of the optimal decision from this sum.

Thus, the EVPI = [.20(4) + .50(5) + .30(-1)] - 2.2 = .8

NOTE: There is an alternative approach to computing the EVPI. EVPI also equals the expected regret associated with the minimax decision. If you compute the expected regret associated with d_1, using the regret table in part (c), you will see that it agrees with the answer to part (e) above.

PROBLEM 2

Jim has been employed at Gold Key Realty at a salary of $2,000 per month during the past year. Because Jim is considered to be a top salesman, the manager of Gold Key is offering him one of three salary plans for the next year: (1) a 25% raise to $2,500 per month; (2) a base salary of $1,000 plus $600 per house sold; or, (3) a straight commission of $1,000 per house sold. Over the past year, Jim has sold up to 6 homes in a month.

a) Compute the monthly salary payoff table for Jim.

b) For this payoff table find Jim's optimal decision using: (1) the conservative approach, (2) minimax regret approach.

c) Suppose that during the past year the following is Jim's distribution of home sales. If one assumes that this a typical distribution for Jim's monthly sales, which salary plan should Jim select?

Home Sales	Number of Months
0	1
1	2
2	1
3	2
4	1
5	3
6	2

SOLUTION 2

a) There are three decision alternatives (salary plans) and seven states of nature (the number of houses sold monthly).

Number of Homes Sold

	0	1	2	3	4	5	6
Plan I	2500	2500	2500	2500	2500	2500	2500
Plan II	1000	1600	2200	2800	3400	4000	4600
Plan III	0	1000	2000	3000	4000	5000	6000

b) (1) Conservative Approach

Decision	Minimum Payoff
Plan I	2500 (maximum; choose Plan I)
Plan II	1000
Plan III	0

(2) Minimax Regret Approach

Construct a regret table by subtracting all numbers in a column from the maximum number in the column:

Regret Table

Number of Homes Sold

	0	1	2	3	4	5	6
Plan I	0	0	0	500	1500	2500	3500
Plan II	1500	900	300	200	600	1000	1400
Plan III	2500	1500	500	0	0	0	0

Choose the decision with the minimum of the maximum regrets.

Decision	Maximum Regret
Plan I	3500
Plan II	1500 (minimum; choose Plan II)
Plan III	2500

c) Use the relative frequency method for determining the probabilities:

Homes Sold	Frequency	Probability
0	1	1/12
1	2	2/12
2	1	1/12
3	2	2/12
4	1	1/12
5	3	3/12
6	2	2/12

Use the expected value (EV) approach:

$$EV(\text{Plan I}) = 1/12(2500) + 2/12(2500) + 1/12(2500) + 2/12(2500)$$
$$+ 1/12(2500) + 3/12(2500) + 2/12(2500) = 2500$$

$$EV(\text{Plan II}) = 1/12(1000) + 2/12(1600) + 1/12(2200) + 2/12(2800)$$
$$+ 1/12(3400) + 3/12(4000) + 2/12(4600) = 3050$$

$$EV(\text{Plan III}) = 1/12(0) + 2/12(1000) + 1/12(2000) + 2/12(3000)$$
$$+ 1/12(4000) + 3/12(5000) + 2/12(6000) = 3417$$

Choose Plan III, the plan with the highest EV.

PROBLEM 3

Burger Prince Restaurant is contemplating opening a new restaurant on Main Street. It has three different models, each with a different seating capacity. Burger Prince estimates that the average number of customers per hour will be 80, 100, or 120. The payoff table for the three models is as follows:

	Average Number of Customers Per Hour		
	$s_1 = 80$	$s_2 = 100$	$s_3 = 120$
Model A	$10,000	$15,000	$14,000
Model B	$ 8,000	$18,000	$12,000
Model C	$ 6,000	$16,000	$21,000

Burger Prince estimates the probability of 80 customers per hour is the same as the probability of 120 customers per hour and twice as much as the probability of 100 customers per hour.

a) What is the optimal decision using the expected value approach?

b) What is the expected value of perfect information?

c) Answer parts a) and b) above using a spreadsheet.

d) Contrast the risk profiles of the Model A and Model C decision alternatives.

e) Burger Prince must decide whether or not to purchase a marketing survey from Stanton Marketing for $1,000. The results of the survey are "favorable" or "unfavorable". The conditional probabilities are:

$$P(\text{favorable} \mid 80 \text{ customers per hour}) = .2$$
$$P(\text{favorable} \mid 100 \text{ customers per hour}) = .5$$
$$P(\text{favorable} \mid 120 \text{ customers per hour}) = .9$$

Should Burger Prince have the survey performed by Stanton Marketing?

f) Answer part e) above using a spreadsheet.

g) What is the efficiency of the survey?

h) Construct an influence diagram for this problem.

SOLUTION 3

a) (1) Determine the probabilities for 80, 100, and 120 customers:
    Given: $P(80) = P(120)$
    $P(80) = 2P(100)$.
    $P(80) + P(100) + P(120) = 1$
    Thus: $P(80) + .5P(80) + P(80) = 1$
    $2.5P(80) = 1 \longrightarrow P(80) = .4 \longrightarrow P(100) = .2, P(120) = .4.$

(2) Calculate the expected value for each decision. The following decision tree can assist in this calculation. Here d_1, d_2, d_3 represent the decision alternatives of models A, B, C, and s_1, s_2, s_3 represent the states of nature of 80, 100, and 120.

PAYOFFS

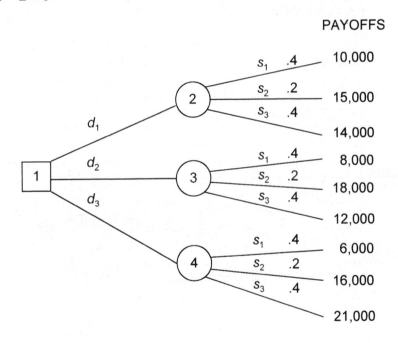

Calculating the expected value for each decision gives:

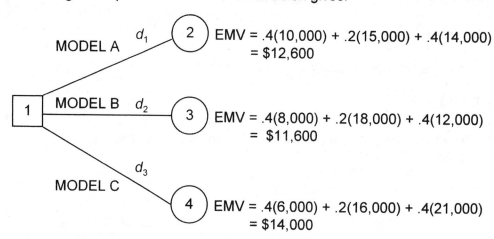

$$\text{EMV} = .4(10,000) + .2(15,000) + .4(14,000)$$
$$= \$12,600$$

$$\text{EMV} = .4(8,000) + .2(18,000) + .4(12,000)$$
$$= \$11,600$$

$$\text{EMV} = .4(6,000) + .2(16,000) + .4(21,000)$$
$$= \$14,000$$

(3) Choose the model with largest EV -- Model C.

b) Calculate the expected value for the optimum payoff for each state of nature and subtract the EV of the optimal decision: EVPI= .4(10,000) + .2(18,000) + .4(21,000) - 14,000 = $2,000.

c) Using a spreadsheet:

Formula Spreadsheet for Expected Value Approach

	A	B	C	D	E	F
1	PAYOFF TABLE					
2						
3	Decision	State of Nature			Expected	Recommended
4	Alternative	s1 = 80	s2 = 100	s3 = 120	Value	Decision
5	Model A	10,000	15,000	14,000	=$B$8*B5+$C$8*C5+$D$8*D5	=IF(E5=$E$9,A5,"")
6	Model B	8,000	18,000	12,000	=$B$8*B6+$C$8*C6+$D$8*D6	=IF(E6=$E$9,A6,"")
7	Model C	6,000	16,000	21,000	=$B$8*B7+$C$8*C7+$D$8*D7	=IF(E7=$E$9,A7,"")
8	Probability	0.4	0.2	0.4		
9		Maximum Expected Value			=MAX(E5:E7)	

Spreadsheet for Expected-Value Decision and EVPI

	A	B	C	D	E	F
1	PAYOFF TABLE					
2						
3	**Decision**	**State of Nature**			**Expected**	**Recommended**
4	**Alternative**	s1 = 80	s2 = 100	s3 = 120	**Value**	**Decision**
5	d1 = Model A	10,000	15,000	14,000	12600	
6	d2 = Model B	8,000	18,000	12,000	11600	
7	d3 = Model C	6,000	16,000	21,000	14000	d3 = Model C
8	**Probability**	0.4	0.2	0.4		
9		**Maximum Expected Value**			14000	
10						
11		**Maximum Payoff**			EVwPI	EVPI
12		10,000	18,000	21,000	16000	2000

d) Risk profile for Model A alternative: Risk profile for Model C alternative:

A decision maker <u>might</u> prefer the more equal payoffs associated the Model A decision alternative, even thought its expected value is less than that of the Model C alternative.

e) Find the posterior probabilities:

Favorable

State	Prior	Conditional	Joint	Posterior*
80	.4	.2	.08	.148
100	.2	.5	.10	.185
120	.4	.9	.36	.667
		Total	.54	1.000

Unfavorable

State	Prior	Conditional	Joint	Posterior*
80	.4	.8	.32	.696
100	.2	.5	.10	.217
120	.4	.1	.04	.087
		Total	.46	1.000

Note: * Posterior probability = (Joint Probability)/(Sum of Joint Probabilities)

The decision tree for this problem:

Calculate expected values

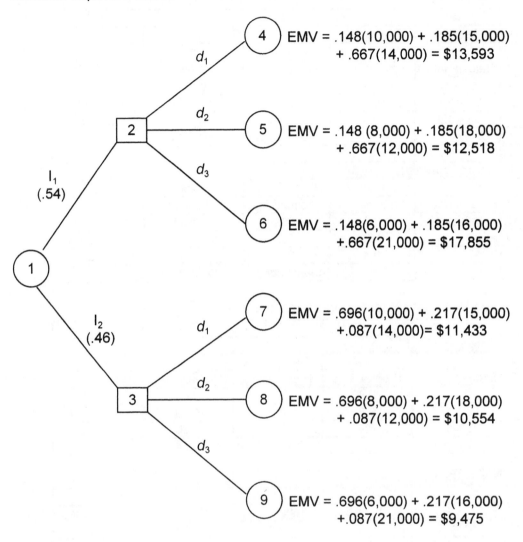

EMV = .148(10,000) + .185(15,000) + .667(14,000) = $13,593

EMV = .148 (8,000) + .185(18,000) + .667(12,000) = $12,518

EMV = .148(6,000) + .185(16,000) +.667(21,000) = $17,855

EMV = .696(10,000) + .217(15,000) +.087(14,000)= $11,433

EMV = .696(8,000) + .217(18,000) + .087(12,000) = $10,554

EMV = .696(6,000) + .217(16,000) +.087(21,000) = $9,475

Hence, if the outcome of the survey is "favorable" choose Model C. If it is unfavorable, choose model A.

$$\text{EVSI} = .54(\$17,855) + .46(\$11,433) - \$14,000 = \$900.88$$

Since this is less than the cost of the survey, the survey should not be purchased.

f) Formula Spreadsheet for Posterior Probabilities

	A	B	C	D	E
1	Market Research Favorable				
2		Prior	Conditional	Joint	Posterior
3	State of Nature	Probabilities	Probabilities	Probabilities	Probabilities
4	s1 = 80	0.4	0.2	=B4*C4	=D4/$D$7
5	s2 = 100	0.2	0.5	=B5*C5	=D5/$D$7
6	s3 = 120	0.4	0.9	=B6*C6	=D6/$D$7
7			P(Favorable) =	=SUM(D4:D6)	
8					
9	Market Research Unfavorable				
10		Prior	Conditional	Joint	Posterior
11	State of Nature	Probabilities	Probabilities	Probabilities	Probabilities
12	s1 = 80	0.4	0.8	=B12*C12	=D12/$D$15
13	s2 = 100	0.2	0.5	=B13*C13	=D13/$D$15
14	s3 = 120	0.4	0.1	=B14*C14	=D14/$D$15
15			P(Unfavorable) =	=SUM(D12:D14)	

Solution Spreadsheet for Posterior Probabilities

	A	B	C	D	E
1	Market Research Favorable				
2		Prior	Conditional	Joint	Posterior
3	State of Nature	Probabilities	Probabilities	Probabilities	Probabilities
4	s1 = 80	0.4	0.2	0.08	0.148
5	s2 = 100	0.2	0.5	0.10	0.185
6	s3 = 120	0.4	0.9	0.36	0.667
7			P(Favorable) =	0.54	
8					
9	Market Research Unfavorable				
10		Prior	Conditional	Joint	Posterior
11	State of Nature	Probabilities	Probabilities	Probabilities	Probabilities
12	s1 = 80	0.4	0.8	0.32	0.696
13	s2 = 100	0.2	0.5	0.10	0.217
14	s3 = 120	0.4	0.1	0.04	0.087
15			P(Favorable) =	0.46	

g) The efficiency = EVSI/EVPI = ($900.88)/($2000) = .4504.

h) Influence diagram:

PROBLEM 4

The past few years have seen a general decline in the economic conditions of the resort community of Pacific City. Certain town officials, as well as other interested parties from Las Vegas, believe that the legalization of casino gambling will greatly improve the city's future. They have succeeded in having a gambling referendum placed on the ballot in next month's special election.

One effect of the declining economic condition of Pacific City has been the bankruptcy last year of the St. Carlton Inn, the city's largest hotel. The St. Carlton is scheduled to be sold at a sealed bid auction next week. The terms of the auction call for an immediate 10% down payment by the highest bidder, with the remaining balance due in two months.

One party interested in bidding on the St. Carlton is Justin Thyme, a real estate promoter and publisher of Fantasy Magazine. Justin has learned from associates that there are at least three other parties interested in the property, including a syndicate from Chicago.

Justin has decided that if he submits a bid it will be for $5 million for the property. If he bids $5 million, he estimates that he has a 40% chance of winning the auction. He also estimates that if the gambling referendum passes, he can sell the property for $7.5 million. If the initiative fails, he will sacrifice his 10% deposit.

Justin believes, based on polls taken to date, that the gambling referendum has a 30% chance of passing. He is considering hiring the noted pollster, Harris Gallup, before the auction to give his opinion on the outcome of the referendum. Based on Gallup's past record, Justin estimates that the probability Gallup will correctly predict the outcome is .8. Gallup's fee is $100,000.

What should Justin do?

SOLUTION 4

To solve this problem, first construct a tree diagram with possible courses of actions and outcomes properly sequenced.

Justin's first decision is whether or not to hire Gallup. If he does, then he will either obtain a prediction from him that the referendum will pass or fail. At that point, or if he does not hire Gallup, he must decide whether or not to bid.

Following this, he will learn if his bid is a winning one. If it is, then he will next be concerned with whether the referendum passes or not. If it does, he sells his property for $7.5 million. If it does not pass, he sacrifices his $.5 million deposit.

The tree diagram for this problem:

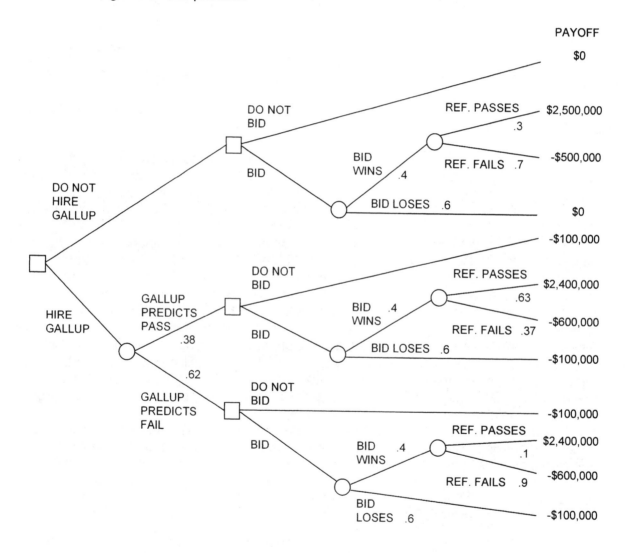

Beginning at the ends of the tree and working towards the root gives the expected returns on the following page:

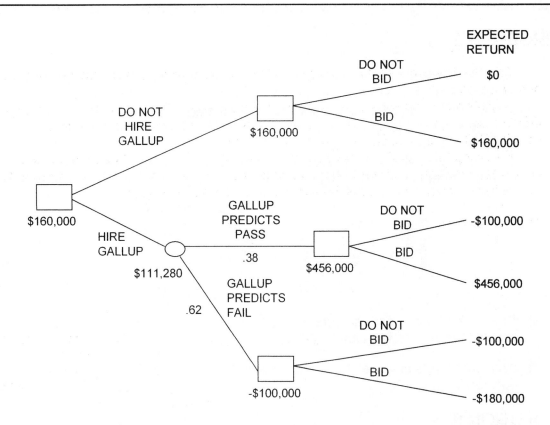

Therefore, if Justin does not hire Gallup, he should bid. If he does hire Gallup, he should bid if Gallup predicts the referendum will pass, and he should not bid if Gallup predicts the referendum will fail.

The expected return if Justin hires Gallup is: .38(456,000) + .62(-100,000) = $111,280 The expected return if Justin does not hire Gallup = $160,000. Thus, his optimal strategy is not to hire Gallup and submit a $5 million bid.

The probabilities for the Pass/Fail branches were obtained as follows:

Indicator Information I_1 -- <u>Gallup Predicts Pass</u>

State	Prior	Conditional	Joint	Posterior
Referendum Passes	.30	.80	.24	.63
Referendum Fails	.70	.20	.14	.37
		Total	.38	1.00

Indicator Information I_2 -- <u>Gallup Predicts Fail</u>

State	Prior	Conditional	Joint	Posterior
Referendum Passes	.30	.20	.06	.10
Referendum Fails	.70	.80	.56	.90
		Total	.62	1.00

PROBLEM 5

East West Distributing is in the process of trying to determine where they should schedule next year's production of a popular line of kitchen utensils that they distribute. Manufacturers in four different countries have submitted bids to East West. However, a pending trade bill in Congress will greatly affect the cost to East West due to proposed tariffs, favorable trading status, etc.

After careful analysis, East West has determined the following cost breakdown for the four manufacturers (in $1,000's) based on whether or not the trade bill passes:

	Bill Passes	Bill Fails
Country A	260	210
Country B	320	160
Country C	240	240
Country D	275	210

a) If East West estimates that there is a 40% chance of the bill passing, which country should they choose for manufacturing?

b) Over what range of values for the "bill passing" will the solution in part (a) remain optimal?

SOLUTION 5

a) Using the expected value approach, calculate the expected value for each country. Note that country D's costs are dominated by country A's costs (whether the bill passes or not, production is at least as expensive in country D as in country A) and therefore country D need not be considered. (Note that the probability that the bill will fail is $1 - .4 = .6$.)

$$EV(A) = .4(260) + .6(210) = 230$$
$$EV(B) = .4(320) + .6(160) = 224$$
$$EV(C) = .4(240) + .6(240) = 240$$

East West should choose the country with the lowest expected cost: country B.

b) To determine the range for the probability of the bill passing over which country B will be optimal, compare choosing country B versus country A, and then compare choosing country B versus country C. Now let,

$$p = \text{the probability of the trade bill passing.}$$

Country B would be preferred to country A as long as:

$$EV(B) \le EV(A)$$
or
$$p(320) + (1-p)160 \le p(260) + (1-p)(210)$$
$$160p + 160 \le 50p + 210$$
$$110p \le 50$$
$$p \le .455$$

Similarly, Country B would be preferred to C as long as EV(B) ≤ EV(C). Using the same approach as above, this is equivalent to $p(320) + (1-p)160 \leq 240$. Solving, $p \leq .50$.

Thus as long as the probability of the bill passing is less than .455, then East West should choose Country B. The following graph illustrates the expected value of the decisions as a function of p:

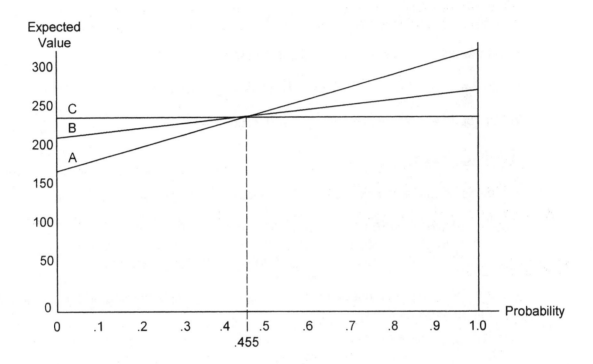

PROBLEM 6

Consider the following three-state, four-decision problem with the following payoff table in dollars:

	s_1	s_2	s_3
d_1	+100,000	+40,000	-60,000
d_2	+50,000	+20,000	-30,000
d_3	+20,000	+20,000	-10,000
d_4	+40,000	+20,000	-60,000

The probabilities for the three states of nature are: $P(s_1) = .1$, $P(s_2) = .3$, and $P(s_3) = .6$.

a) If the decision maker is risk neutral, what is the optimal decision?

b) Suppose two decision makers have the following utility values:

Amount	Utility Decision Maker I	Decision Maker II
$100,000	100	100
$50,000	94	58
$40,000	90	50
$20,000	80	35
-$10,000	60	18
-$30,000	40	10
-$60,000	0	0

Graph the utility curves for the two decision makers.

c) Classify each of the decision makers as either a risk avoider, a risk taker, or risk neutral.

d) Find the optimal decision for each of the decision makers.

SOLUTION 6

a) If the decision maker is risk neutral the expected value approach is applicable.

$$EV(d_1) = .1(100,000) + .3(40,000) + .6(-60,000) = -\$14,000$$
$$EV(d_2) = .1(\ 50,000) + .3(20,000) + .6(-30,000) = -\$\ 7,000$$
$$EV(d_3) = .1(\ 20,000) + .3(20,000) + .6(-10,000) = +\$\ 2,000$$

Note the EV for d_4 need not be calculated as decision d_4 is dominated by decision d_2. The optimal decision is d_3.

b)

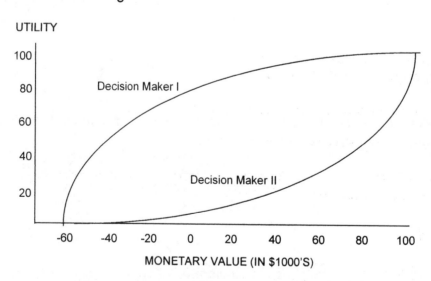

c) Decision Maker I has a concave utility function - he is a risk avoider. Decision Maker II has convex utility function - he is a risk taker.

d) Note again that d_4 is dominated by d_2 and hence is not considered. For the remaining decisions, compute the expected utility for each decision maker using the probabilities given.

Utility Table I

	s_1	s_2	s_3	Expected Utility
d_1	100	90	0	37.0
d_2	94	80	40	57.4
d_3	80	80	60	**68.0**
Probability	.1	.3	.6	

The largest expected utility is 68.0. Decision Maker I should make decision d_3.

Utility Table II

	s_1	s_2	s_3	Expected Utility
d_1	100	50	0	**25.0**
d_2	58	35	10	22.3
d_3	35	35	18	24.8
Probability	.1	.3	.6	

The largest expected utility is 25.0. Decision Maker II should make decision d_1.

PROBLEM 7

In Problem 6, suppose the probabilities for the three states of nature are changed to: $P(s_1) = .5$, $P(s_2) = .3$, and $P(s_3) = .2$.

a) Find the optimal decision for a risk neutral decision maker.

b) Find the optimal decisions for Decision Maker I and II.

c) What is the value of this decision problem to Decision Maker I and Decision Maker II? What conclusion can you draw?

SOLUTION 7

a) Use the EV approach for a risk neutral decision maker:

$$EV(d_1) = .5(100,000) + .3(40,000) + .2(-60,000) = 50,000$$
$$EV(d_2) = .5(\ 50,000) + .3(20,000) + .2(-30,000) = 25,000$$
$$EV(d_3) = .5(\ 20,000) + .3(20,000) + .2(-10,000) = 14,000$$

Hence, the risk neutral optimal decision is d_1.

b) Use the expected utility criterion for each decision maker:

Decision Maker I

$EU(d_1) = .5(100) + .3(90) + .2(0) = 77.0$
$EU(d_2) = .5(94) + .3(80) + .2(40) = 79.0$
$EU(d_3) = .5(80) + .3(80) + .2(60) = 76.0$

Hence, Decision Maker I's optimal decision is d_2.

Decision Maker II

$EU(d_1) = .5(100) + .3(50) + .2(0) = 65.0$
$EU(d_2) = .5(58) + .3(35) + .2(10) = 41.5$
$EU(d_3) = .5(35) + .3(35) + .2(18) = 31.6$

Hence, Decision Maker II's optimal decision is d_1.

c) To determine the value of the decision problem to a decision maker, find the amount that corresponds to the expected utility of the optimal decision.

For Decision Maker I, the optimal expected utility is 79. He assigned a utility of 80 to +$20,000, and a utility of 60 to -$10,000. Linearly interpolating in this range 1 point is worth $30,000/20 = $1,500. Thus a utility of 79 is worth about $20,000 - 1,500 = $18,500.

For Decision Maker II, the optimal expected utility is 65. He assigned a utility of 100 to $100,000, and a utility of 58 to $50,000. In this range, 1 point is worth $50,000/42 = $1190. Thus a utility of 65 is worth about $50,000 + 7(1190) = $58,330.

Conclusion: The decision problem is worth more to Decision Maker II.

ANSWERED PROBLEMS

PROBLEM 8

Mark Investment Advisors has just completed an analysis on the returns of five utility stocks for next year. Mark hypothesizes that next year the economy will either be in a depression (s_1), a recession (s_2), an upward period (s_3), or a major expansionary period (s_4). The per dollar growth for the five stocks corresponding to each state of the economy are:

	s_1	s_2	s_3	s_4
Stock A	-.40	-.20	+.10	+.60
Stock B	-.30	-.10	0	+.30
Stock C	-.10	0	+.05	+.30
Stock D	0	+.05	+.10	+.15
Stock E	+.05	+.15	-.10	-.20

a) If you could purchase shares of Stock B or Stock C, which would you purchase? Why?

b) Find the best stock to purchase under each approach: (1) optimistic; (2) minimax regret; (3) conservative.

c) Suppose Mark's financial outlook for next year is $P(s_1) = .2$; $P(s_2) = .4$; $P(s_3) = .2$; and $P(s_4) = .2$. Using the expected value approach, which stock would Mark recommend?

PROBLEM 9

Transrail is bidding on a project that it figures will cost $400,000 to perform. Using a 25% markup, it will charge $500,000, netting a profit of $100,000. However, it has been learned that another company, Rail Freight, is also considering bidding on the project. If Rail Freight does submit a bid, it figures to be a bid of about $470,000.

Transrail really wants this project and is considering a bid with only a 15% markup to $460,000 to ensure winning regardless of whether or not Rail Freight submits a bid.

a) Prepare a profit payoff table from Transrail's point of view.

b) What decision would be made if Transrail were conservative?

c) If Rail Freight is known to submit bids on only 25% of the projects it considers, what decision should Transrail make?

d) Given the information in (c), how much would a corporate spy be worth to Transrail to find out if Rail Freight will bid?

PROBLEM 10

The Super Cola Company must decide whether or not to introduce a new diet soft drink. Management feels that if it does introduce the diet soda it will yield a profit of $1 million if sales are around 100 million, a profit of $200,000 if sales are around 50 million, or it will lose $2 million if sales are only around 1 million bottles. If Super Cola does not market the new diet soda, it will suffer a loss of $400,000.

a) Construct a payoff table for this problem.

b) Construct a regret table for this problem.

c) Should Super Cola introduce the soda if the company: (1) is conservative; (2) is optimistic; (3) wants to minimize its maximum disappointment?

d) An internal marketing research study has found P(100 million in sales) = 1/3; P(50 million in sales) = 1/2; P(1 million in sales) = 1/6. Should Super Cola introduce the new diet soda?

e) A consulting firm can perform a more thorough study for $275,000. Should management have this study performed?

PROBLEM 11

Super Cola is also considering the introduction of a root beer drink. The company feels that the probability that the product will be a success is .6. The payoff table is as follows:

	Success (s_1)	Failure (s_2)
Produce (d_1)	$250,000	-$300,000
Do Not Produce (d_2)	-$ 50,000	-$ 20,000

The company has a choice of two research firms to obtain information for this product. Stanton Marketing has market indicators, I_1 and I_2 for which $P(I_1 \mid s_1) = .7$ and $P(I_1 \mid s_2) = .4$. New World Marketing has indicators J_1 and J_2 for which $P(J_1 \mid s_1) = .6$ and $P(J_1 \mid s_2) = .3$.

a) What is the optimal decision if neither firm is used? Over what probability of success range is this decision optimal?

b) What is the EVPI?

c) Find the EVSIs and efficiencies for Stanton and New World.

d) If both firms charge $5,000, which firm should be hired?

e) If Stanton charges $10,000 and New World charges $4,000, which firm should Super Cola hire? Why?

PROBLEM 12

Metropolitan Cablevision is investigating the installation of a cable TV system in town. The engineering department estimates the cost of the system (in present worth dollars) to be $700,000. The sales department has investigated four pricing plans. For each pricing plan the marketing division has estimated the revenue per household in present worth dollars to be:

Plan	Revenue Per Household
I	$15
II	$18
III	$20
IV	$24

The sales department estimates the number of household subscribers would be approximately either 10,000, 20,000, 30,000, 40,000, 50,000 or 60,000.

a) Construct a payoff table for this problem.

b) What is the company's optimal decision under (1) the optimistic approach; (2) the conservative approach; and (3) the minimax regret approach?

c) Suppose the sales department has determined that the number of subscribers will be a function of the pricing plan. The probability distributions for the pricing plans are given below. Use decision tree analysis to determine which pricing plan is optimal under the expected value approach.

Number of Subscribers	Probability under Pricing Plan			
	I	II	III	IV
10,000	0	.05	.10	.20
20,000	.05	.10	.20	.25
30,000	.05	.20	.20	.25
40,000	.40	.30	.20	.15
50,000	.30	.20	.20	.10
60,000	.20	.15	.10	.05

PROBLEM 13

Dicom Corporation has developed a new high speed computer that it intends to sell for $150,000. Dicom's salesmen have scheduled demonstrations with four clients next month. For each client, Dicom estimates there is a 40% chance of his purchasing the computer.

Dicom plans to make at least one computer next month but could make as many as four. Production costs are $100,000 for producing one computer, $190,000 for two, $260,000 for three, and $310,000 for four.

Any unsold computers produced will be sold at $60,000. Also, if a client wants to purchase a computer, but all computers produced have been sold, the company estimates it loses $20,000.

a) Determine a payoff table for this problem.

b) What is the optimal strategy using the expected monetary value criterion? (HINT: Use the binomial distribution to determine the probabilities for the states of nature.)

c) Dicom can have a survey performed to indicate the market impression of the new computer -- favorable or unfavorable. The following probabilities are believed to hold:

P(favorable | 0 sold) = .1   P(favorable | 3 sold) = .9
P(favorable | 1 sold) = .2   P(favorable | 4 sold) = 1.0
P(favorable | 2 sold) = .6

How much should Dicom pay for this survey and what is its efficiency?

PROBLEM 14

Dollar Department Stores has just acquired the chain of Wenthrope and Sons Custom Jewelers. Dollar has received an offer from Harris Diamonds to purchase the Wenthrope store on Grove Street for $120,000.

Dollar has determined probability estimates of the store's future profitability, based on economic outcomes, as: P($80,000) = .2, P($100,000) = .3, P($120,000) = .1, and P($140,000) = .4.

a) Should Dollar sell the store on Grove Street?

b) What is the EVPI?

c) Dollar can have an economic forecast performed, costing $10,000, that produces indicators I_1 and I_2, for which P(I_1 | 80,000) = .1; P(I_1 | 100,000) = .2; P(I_1 | 120,000) = .6; P(I_1 | 140,000) = .3. Should Dollar purchase the forecast?

PROBLEM 15

Cashman Co. will be leasing a new copier and is considering four plans.

Plan	Monthly Lease	Unit Copy Cost
I	$100	$.020 for the first 10,000; $.016 thereafter
II	$200	$.012 for all copies
III	$150	first 5,000 free; $.022 thereafter
IV	$300	$.005 for all copies

The company has determined it will make either 12,600, 14,400, 16,200, 18,000, 19,800, 21,600 copies per month with probabilities of .05, .10, .15, .25, .25, and .20 respectively.

a) Construct a monthly payoff table for Cashman in terms of costs.

b) What is the optimal plan if the company uses the (1) optimistic approach or (2) the conservative approach?

c) What is the optimal plan using the expected value approach?

PROBLEM 16

An appliance dealer must decide how many (if any) new microwave ovens to order for next month. The ovens cost $220 and sell for $300. Because the oven company is coming out with a new product line in two months, any ovens not sold next month will have to be sold at the dealer's half price clearance sale. Additionally, the appliance dealer feels he suffers a loss of $25 for every oven demanded when he is out of stock. On the basis of past months' sales data, the dealer estimates the probabilities of monthly demand (D) for 0, 1, 2, or 3 ovens to be .3, .4, .2, and .1, respectively.
The dealer is considering conducting a telephone survey on the customers' attitudes towards microwave ovens. The results of the survey will either be favorable (F), unfavorable (U) or no opinion (N). The dealer's probability estimates for the survey results based on the number of units demanded are:

$$P(F \mid D = 0) = .1 \quad P(F \mid D = 2) \ .3 \qquad P(U \mid D = 0) = .8 \quad P(U \mid D = 2) = .1$$
$$P(F \mid D = 1) = .2 \quad P(F \mid D = 3) \ .9 \qquad P(U \mid D = 1) = .3 \quad P(U \mid D = 3) = .1$$

a) What is the dealer's optimal decision without conducting the survey?

b) What is the EVPI?

c) Based on the survey results what is the optimal decision strategy for the dealer?

d) What is the maximum amount he should pay for this survey?

PROBLEM 17

Burger Prince Restaurant is considering the purchase of a $100,000 fire insurance policy. The fire statistics indicate that in a given year the probability of property damage in a fire is as follows:

Fire Damage	Probability	Fire Damage	Probability
$0	.980	$50,000	.004
$10,000	.005	$75,000	.002
$25,000	.003	$100,000	.006

a) If Burger Prince were risk neutral, how much would they be willing to pay for fire insurance?

b) If Burger Prince has the utility values given below, approximately how much would they be willing to pay for fire insurance?

			Amount of Loss ($)				
	100,000	75,000	50,000	25,000	10,000	5,000	0
Utility	0	30	60	85	95	99	100

PROBLEM 18

Dollar Department Stores has the opportunity of acquiring 3, 5, or 10 leases from the bankrupt Granite Variety Store chain. Dollar estimates the profit potential of the leases depends on the state of the economy over the next five years.

There are four possible states of the economy as modeled by Dollar Department Stores and its president estimates $P(s_1) = .4$, $P(s_2) = .3$, $P(s_3) = .1$, and $P(s_4) = .2$. The utility has also been estimated. Given the payoff and utility tables below which decision should Dollar make?

Payoff Table

	State of the Economy Over the Next 5 Years			
	s_1	s_2	s_3	s_4
d_1 (buy 10 leases)	10	5	0	-20
d_2 (buy 5 leases)	5	0	-1	-10
d_3 (buy 3 leases)	2	1	0	-1
d_4 (do not buy)	0	0	0	0

Utility Table

Payoff ($billions)	+10	+5	+2	0	-1	-10	-20
Utility	+10	+5	+2	0	-1	-20	-50

PROBLEM 19

Super Cola is considering the introduction of a new 8 oz. root beer. The probability that the root beer will be a success is believed to equal .6. The payoff table is as follows:

	Success (s_1)	Failure (s_2)
Produce	$250,000	-$300,000
Do Not Produce	-$50,000	-$20,000

Company management has determined the following utility values:

Amount	Utility
$250,000	100
-$ 20,000	60
-$ 50,000	55
-$300,000	0

a) Is the company a risk taker, risk averse, or risk neutral?

b) What is Super Cola's optimal decision? Over what range of the probability of success will this decision remain optimal?

c) Stanton Marketing has market indicators, I_1 and I_2 for which $P(I_1|s_1) = .7$ and $P(I_1|s_2) = .4$. New World Marketing has market indicators J_1 and J_2 for which $P(J_1|s_1) = .6$ and $P(J_2|s_2) = .3$. If both indicators are available for free, which one should be selected?

TRUE/FALSE

20. The expected value of sample information can never be less than the expected value of perfect information.

21. The expected value of perfect information must always be nonnegative.

22. The expected value of sample information is the difference between the expected value with perfect information and the expected value without perfect information.

23. Using the optimistic and conservative approaches will never give the same optimal decision.

24. The $P(I_k \mid s_j)$ must equal $P(s_j / I_k)$.

25. For each indicator, I_k, the joint probabilities must sum to 1.

26. Posterior probabilities are calculated by dividing each joint probability by the sum of the joint probabilities for that indicator.

27. The sum of $P(I_k \mid s_j)$ for all s_j is 1.0.

28. Sample information with an efficiency rating of 100% is perfect information.

29. Sensitivity analysis on state-of-nature probability estimates cannot be performed on problems with more than two states-of-nature.

30. If the expected value of sample information exceeds the cost of purchasing the sample information, one should not attempt to obtain the sample information.

31. The states of nature in a decision problem must be mutually exclusive and collectively exhaustive.

32. Maximizing the expected payoff and minimizing the expected opportunity loss result in the same recommended decision.

33. The expected value approach is more appropriate for a one-time decision than a repetitive decision.

34. $P(I_k \mid s_j)$ is a posterior probability.

CHAPTER 15

Multicriteria Decisions

KEY CONCEPTS

CONCEPT	ILLUSTRATED PROBLEMS	ANSWERED PROBLEMS
Goal Programming		
Formulations	1-3	9-11
Graphical Solution	1	10
Computer Solution	2	10
Scoring Model	4	12
Analytic Hierarchy Process		
Pairwise Comparison Matrices	5-8	13-17
Priority Vectors	5-8	13-17
Overall Priorities	7,8	14-17
Consistency	5	14,15
Hierarchy Construction	8	15,16

REVIEW

1. Multicriteria decision making involves two or more criteria that typically are in conflict. A trade-off among the criteria is usually necessary.

2. Goal programming may be used to solve linear programs with multiple objectives. Each objective may be viewed as a "goal".

3. An approach to goal programming is to satisfy goals in a priority sequence. Second-priority goals are pursued without reducing the first-priority goals; third-priority goals are pursued without reducing first- or second-priority goals, etc.

4. In goal programming, d_i^+ and d_i^- are the amounts a targeted goal i is overachieved or underachieved, respectively. Usually only one of d_i^+ or d_i^- is considered detrimental.

5. For each priority level, the objective function is to minimize the (weighted) sum of the goal deviations. Previous "optimal" achievements of goals are added to the constraint set so that they are not degraded while trying to achieve lesser priority goals. The goals themselves are added to the constraint set with d_i^+ and d_i^- acting as the surplus and slack variables.

6. Infeasible linear programming problems can be reformulated as goal programs so that some reasonable solution may be attained.

7. A scoring model is a quick and relatively easy way to identify the most desired decision alternative in a multicriteria decision problem.

8. The steps required to develop a scoring model are: (1) list the decision-making criteria; (2) assign a weight to, indicating the importance of, each criterion; (3) rate how well each decision alternative satisfies each criterion; (4) compute the score for each decision alternative; and (5) order the decision alternatives from highest score to lowest. The alternative with the highest score is the recommended alternative.

9. The Analytic Hierarchy Process (AHP), is a procedure designed to quantify managerial judgments of the relative importance of each of several conflicting criteria used in the decision making process.

10. Computer packages can be used for evaluating AHPs. The AHP developed in this chapter is based on one such package, EXPERT CHOICE.

GOAL PROGRAMMING APPROACH

Assuming all of the objectives (goals) and functional constraints in the problem have been identified:

1. Decide the priority level of each goal.

2. If a priority level has more than one goal, for each goal i decide the weight, w_i, to be placed on the deviation(s), d_i^+ and/or d_i^-, from the goal.

3. Set up the initial linear program as follows:

   (Assume d_1^+ and d_2^- are the detrimental deviations from first priority goals 1 and 2, respectively.)

$$\text{MIN } w_1 d_1^+ + w_2 d_2^-$$

   s.t.   Functional Constraints, and
          Goal Constraints

4. Solve this linear program. (Assume that the optimal value of the objective function is k.) If there is a lower priority level, go to step 5; otherwise, a final optimal solution has been reached.

5. Consider the next-lower priority level goals and formulate a new objective function based on these goals. Add a constraint requiring the achievement of the next-higher priority level goals to be maintained. The new linear program is:

   (Assume d_3^+ and d_4^- are the detrimental deviations associated with the current priority level goals.)

$$\text{MIN } w_3 d_3^+ + w_4 d_4^-$$

   s.t.   Functional Constraints,
          Goal Constraints, and
          $w_1 d_1^+ + w_2 d_2^- = k$

Go to step 4. (Repeat steps 4 and 5 until all priority levels have been examined. Each time, solve a linear program with a lesser priority goal for the objective function and with the optimal achieved amounts of higher priority goals as added constraints.)

FLOW CHART FOR
GOAL PROGRAMMING SOLUTION PROCESS

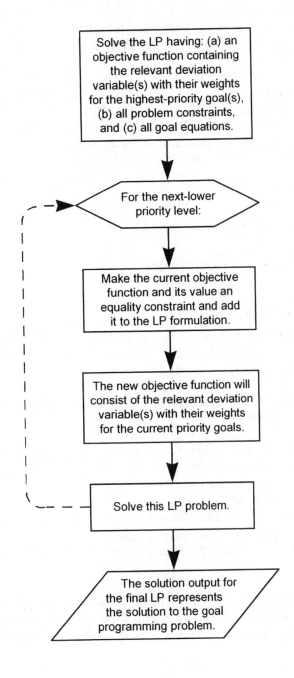

ANALYTIC HIERARCHY PROCESS

1. The first step is:
   (a) list an <u>overall goal</u> for the process;
   (b) list <u>criteria</u> that make up the relevant factors that contribute to achieving the goal;
   (c) list the <u>(n) possible decision alternatives</u> for each of the individual criterion.

   *** For each criterion, perform steps 2 through 5 ***

2. Develop a <u>pairwise comparison matrix</u> for a criterion by rating the relative importance between each pair of decision alternatives. The matrix lists the alternatives horizontally and vertically and has the numerical ratings comparing the horizontal (first) alternative with the vertical (second) alternative. Ratings are given as follows:

Compared to the second alternative, the first alternative is:	Numerical rating
extremely preferred	9
very strongly preferred	7
strongly preferred	5
moderately preferred	3
equally preferred	1

   Intermediate numeric ratings of 8, 6, 4, 2 can be assigned. A reciprocal rating (i.e. 1/9, 1/8, 1/7, etc.) is assigned when the second alternative is preferred to the first. The value of 1 is always assigned when comparing an alternative with itself.

3. Develop the <u>normalized matrix</u> by dividing each number in a column of the pairwise comparison matrix by its column sum.

4. Develop the <u>priority vector for the criterion</u> by averaging each row of the normalized matrix. These row averages form the <u>priority vector</u> of alternative preferences with respect to the particular criterion. The values in this vector sum to 1.

5. The consistency of the subjective input in the pairwise comparison matrix can be measured by calculating a <u>consistency ratio</u>. (See details below.) A consistency ratio of less than .1 is good. For consistency ratios which are greater than .1, the subjective input should be re-evaluated.

6. After steps 2 through 5 has been performed for all criteria, the results of step 4 are summarized in a <u>priority matrix</u> by listing the decision alternatives horizontally and the criteria vertically. The column entries are the priority vectors for each criterion.

7. Develop a <u>criteria pairwise development matrix</u> in the same manner as that used to construct alternative pairwise comparison matrices by using subjective ratings (step 2). Similarly, normalize the matrix (step 3) and develop a <u>criteria priority vector</u> (step 4).

8. Develop an <u>overall priority vector</u> by multiplying the criteria priority vector (from step 7) by the priority matrix (from step 6).

Determining the Consistency Ratio

1. For each row of the pairwise comparison matrix, determine a weighted sum by summing the multiples of the entries by the priority of its corresponding (column) alternative.

2. For each row, divide its weighted sum by the priority of its corresponding (row) alternative.

3. Determine the average, λ_{max}, of the results of step 2.

4. Compute the <u>consistency index</u>, CI, of the n alternatives by:

$$CI = (\lambda_{max} - n)/(n - 1).$$

5. Determine the <u>random index</u>, RI, from the the following chart:

Number of Decision Alternatives, n	Random Index, RI
3	0.58
4	0.90
5	1.12
6	1.24
7	1.32
8	1.41

6. Determine the <u>consistency ratio</u>, CR, as follows:

$$CR = CR/RI.$$

FLOW CHART OF
ANALYTIC HIERARCHY PROCESS

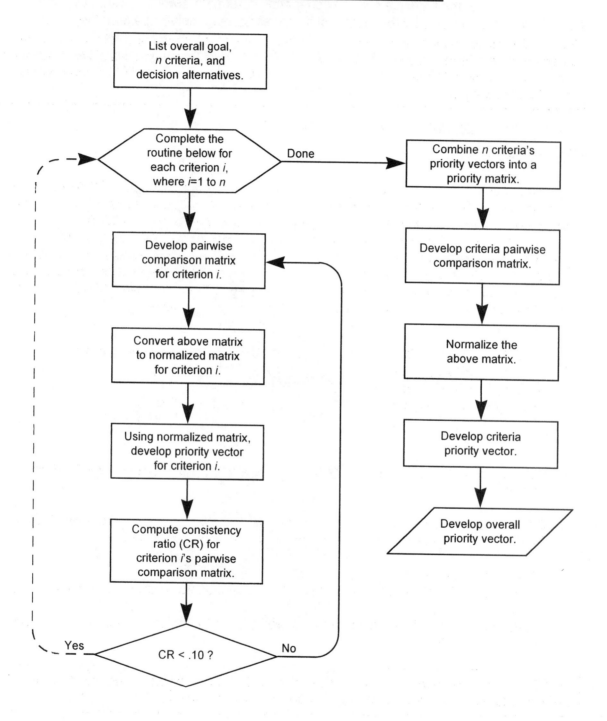

ILLUSTRATED PROBLEMS

NOTE: Priorities and weights are not synonymous in goal programming. Think of priorities as absolute, firm, preemptive. No tradeoffs occur in the achievement of goals with different priorities. However, tradeoffs can occur in the achievement of goals with the same priority and different weights.

PROBLEM 1

Conceptual Products is a computer manufacturer that produces the CP2860 and the CP3860 computers. It takes one hour to manufacture a CP2860 and its profit is $200 and it takes one and one-half hours to manufacture a CP3860 and its profit is $500.

The two computer models differ in many ways, but they have two components in common, case and hard drive. The CP2860 model uses two hard drives and no DVD drive whereas the CP3860 models use one hard drive and one DVD drive.   The hard drives, DVD drives, and cases are bought from vendors. There are 1000 hard drives, 500 DVD drives, and 600 cases available to Conceptual Products on a weekly basis

The company has four goals which are given below.

Priority 1: Meet a state contract of 200 CP2860 machines weekly. (Goal 1)
Priority 2: Make at least 500 total computers weekly. (Goal 2)
Priority 3: Make at least $250,000 weekly. (Goal 3)
Priority 4: Use no more than 400 man-hours per week. (Goal 4)

a) Formulate this problem as a goal program.

b) Solve graphically for the solution that best meets the goals of Conceptual Products as stated above.

c) Suppose Conceptual Products combined goals 3 and 4 into one priority level, Priority 3. What would be the recommendation under the following conditions:

   (1) Each goal was equally desirable.
   (2) Each $1000 underachieved from its profit goal was three times as important as an extra man-hour.
   (3) Each $1000 underachieved from its profit goal was five times as important as an extra man-hour.

NOTE: A goal constraint is expressed as an equality (=) constraint having exactly one d^+ variable and one d^- variable (and one or more decision variables).

SOLUTION 1

a) <u>Variables</u>

x_1 = the number of CP2860 computers produced weekly
x_2 = the number of CP3860 computers produced weekly

<u>Functional Constraints</u>

Availability of hard drives: $2x_1 + x_2 \le 1000$

Availability of DVD drives: $x_2 \le 500$

Availability of cases: $x_1 + x_2 \le 600$

<u>Goals</u>

Define: d_i^- = the amount the right hand side of goal i is deficient
d_i^+ = the amount the right hand side of goal i is exceeded

(1) 200 CP2860 computers weekly: $x_1 \qquad + d_1^- - d_1^+ = 200$

(2) 500 total computers weekly: $x_1 + \quad x_2 + d_2^- - d_2^+ = 500$

(3) \$250 (in thousands) profit: $.2x_1 + \ .5x_2 + d_3^- - d_3^+ = 250$

(4) 400 total man-hours weekly: $x_1 + 1.5x_2 + d_4^- - d_4^+ = 400$

<u>Non-negativity</u>: $x_1, x_2, d_i^-, d_i^+ \ge 0$ for all i

<u>Objective Functions</u>

Priority 1: Minimize the amount the state contract is not met: MIN d_1^-

Priority 2: Minimize the number under 500 computers produced weekly: MIN d_2^-

Priority 3: Minimize the amount under \$250,000 earned weekly: MIN d_3^-

Priority 4: Minimize the man-hours over 400 used weekly: MIN d_4^+

Summary

Using the notation P_j to denote the priority level of the objective functions, the problem becomes:

MIN $P_1(d_1^-) + P_2(d_2^-) + P_3(d_3^-) + P_4(d_4^+)$

s. t. $2x_1 \quad +x_2 \qquad\qquad\qquad\qquad\qquad\qquad\quad \leq 1000$

$\qquad\qquad\quad x_2 \qquad\qquad\qquad\qquad\qquad\qquad\quad \leq \ 500$

$\qquad\quad x_1 \quad +x_2 \qquad\qquad\qquad\qquad\qquad\qquad \leq \ 600$

$\qquad\quad x_1 \qquad\qquad +d_1^- -d_1^+ \qquad\qquad\qquad\quad = \ 200$

$\qquad\quad x_1 \quad +x_2 \qquad\qquad +d_2^- -d_2^+ \qquad\qquad = \ 500$

$\qquad\quad .2x_1 \ +.5x_2 \qquad\qquad\qquad +d_3^- -d_3^+ \qquad = \ 250$

$\qquad\quad x_1 +1.5x_2 \qquad\qquad\qquad\qquad +d_4^- -d_4^+ \ = \ 400$

$\qquad\quad x_1, x_2, d_1^-, d_1^+, d_2^-, d_2^+, d_3^-, d_3^+, d_4^-, d_4^+ \geq 0$

b) To solve graphically, first graph the functional constraints as below. Then graph the first goal: $x_1 = 200$ and note that there is a set of points that exceeds $x_1 = 200$, i.e. where $d_1^- = 0$.

Now add goal 2: $x_1 + x_2 = 500$ as below. Note there is still a set of points satisfying the first goal that also satisfies this second goal, i.e. where $d_2^- = 0$.

Now add goal 3: $.2x_1 + .5x_2 = 250$ as below. Note that no points satisfy the previous functional constraints and goals as well as this constraint. Thus to MIN d_3^-, this minimum value is achieved when we MAX $.2x1 + .5x2$. We note that this occurs at $x_1 = 200$, $x_2 = 400$, so that $.2x_1 + .5x_2 = 240$ or $d_3^- = 10$.

Since this is the only point the meets goal three with only a $10 (thousand) deficiency, priority 4's objective becomes irrelevant. This is because if we add the constraint: $.2x_1 + .5x_2 = 240$, there is only one feasible point.

This is our recommendation of $x_1 = 200$, $x_2 = 400$. Thus the recommendations is to make 200 CP2860 computers and 400 CP3860 computers weekly.

c) The first two priorities were met by a set of points and it was shown that there was no point that met the first two goals and goal 3. Similarly, by looking at the top graph on the previous page, it is seen that there are no points that meet the first two priorities and goal 4. Since both will not be achieved,

$$d_3^- = 250 - .2x_1 - .5x_2$$
$$d_4^+ = x_1 + 1.5x_2 - 400.$$

Case (1): MIN $\;\; d_3^- + d_4^+ \;\;$ = MIN $.8x_1 + x_2 - 150$
Case (2): MIN $\;\; 3d_3^- + d_4^+ \;\;$ = MIN $.4x_1 + 350$
Case (3): MIN $\;\; 5d_3^- + d_4^+ \;\;$ = MIN $-x_2 + 850$

Ignoring the constant in each of the above, it can be seen in the next three graphs that:

Case (1) is minimized at $x_1 = 500$, $x_2 = 0$
Case (2) is minimized by all points on the line $x_1 = 200$ between $x_2 = 300$ and $x_2 = 400$
Case (3) is minimized where x_2 takes on its maximum value, i.e. at $x_1 = 200$, $x_2 = 400$

CASE (1)

CASE (2)

2X1 + X2 ≤ 1000

Case 2: MIN .4X1

Goal 1: X1 = 200

Optimal Points:
(200,300) to (200,400)

X1 + X2 ≤ 600

X2 ≤ 500

Points Satisfying Both
Goal 1 and Goal 2
with $d_1^- = 0$ and $d_2^- = 0$

Goal 2: X1 + X2 ≥ 500

CASE (3)

2X1 + X2 ≤ 1000

Goal 1: X1 = 200

Optimal Point: (200,400)

X1 + X2 ≤ 600

X2 ≤ 500

Points Satisfying Both
Goal 1 and Goal 2
with $d_1^- = 0$ and $d_2^- = 0$

Goal 2: X1 + X2 ≥ 500

Case 3: MIN -X2
or MAX X2

PROBLEM 2

Suppose in problem 1, Conceptual Products made a third computer, the CP4860 which requires two hard drives and a DVD drive. It takes two hours to manufacture and the profit is $900. Use a computer program such as *The Management Scientist* to solve the goal program of Case (3) in part (c) of problem 1.

NOTE: A goal programming problem with p preemptive goal priorities can be solved as a series of p linear programming problems.

NOTE: When we solve a goal programming problem as a series of LPs, the objective functions (always to be <u>minimized</u>) will include only relevant deviation variables and <u>not</u> decision variables.

SOLUTION 2

The goal programming formulation is now:

$$\text{MIN } P_1(d_1^-) + P_2(d_2^-) + P_3(5d_3^-) + P_3(d_4^+)$$

s.t.	$2x_1 + x_2 + 2x_3$	≤ 1000	(hard drives)
	$x_2 + x_3$	≤ 500	(DVD drives)
	$x_1 + x_2 + x_3$	≤ 600	(cases)

(Priority 1) $x_1 \qquad\qquad + d_1^- - d_1^+ = 200$ (Goal 1: contract)

(Priority 2) $x_1 + x_2 + x_3 + d_2^- - d_2^+ = 500$ (Goal 2: total)

(Priority 3) $.2x_1 + .5x_2 + .9x_3 + d_3^- - d_3^+ = 250$ (Goal 3: profit)

(Priority 3) $x_1 + 1.5x_2 + 2x_3 + d_4^- - d_4^+ = 400$ (Goal 4: man-hours)

$$x_1, x_2, d_i^-, d_i^+ \geq 0 \text{ for all } i$$

Priority 1 Program

The following was input into *The Management Scientist*:

$$\text{MIN} \quad D1MINUS$$

$$
\begin{aligned}
\text{S.T.} \quad 2X1 + \quad X2 + 2X3 & & < 1000 \\
X2 + \quad X3 & & < \ \ 500 \\
X1 + \quad X2 + \quad X3 & & < \ \ 600 \\
X1 \qquad\qquad\qquad + D1MINUS - D1PLUS & = 200 \\
X1 + \quad X2 + \quad X3 + D2MINUS - D2PLUS & = 500 \\
.2X1 + \ .5X2 + .9X3 + D3MINUS - D3PLUS & = 250 \\
X1 + 1.5X2 + \ 2X3 + D4MINUS - D4PLUS & = 400
\end{aligned}
$$

The following output was attained:

OBJECTIVE FUNCTION VALUE = 0.000

VARIABLE	VALUE	REDUCED COSTS
X1	200.000	0.000
X2	0.000	0.000
X3	233.333	0.000
D1MINUS	0.000	1.000
D1PLUS	0.000	0.000
D2MINUS	66.667	0.000
D2PLUS	0.000	0.000
D3MINUS	0.000	0.000
D3PLUS	0.000	0.000
D4MINUS	0.000	0.000
D4PLUS	266.667	0.000

Thus the priority 1 objective is met since the value of the objective function, D1MINUS = 0.

Priority 2 Program

Add to the constraints on the previous page a constraint requiring the priority 1 objective to be maintained at 0: D1MINUS = 0, <u>and</u> change the objective to the priority 2 objective: MIN D2MINUS.

The following output is generated:

OBJECTIVE FUNCTION VALUE =		0.000
VARIABLE	**VALUE**	**REDUCED COSTS**
X1	285.714	0.000
X2	0.000	0.000
X3	214.286	0.000
D1MINUS	0.000	0.000
D1PLUS	85.714	0.000
D2MINUS	0.000	1.000
D2PLUS	0.000	0.000
D3MINUS	0.000	0.000
D3PLUS	0.000	0.000
D4MINUS	0.000	0.000
D4PLUS	314.286	0.000

The priority 2 objective is met since the value of the objective function, D2MINUS, = 0.

Priority 3 Program

Add to the previous constraints, a constraint requiring that the priority 2 objective to be maintained at 0: D2MINUS = 0, and change the objective to the priority 3 objective: MIN 5 D3MINUS + D4PLUS.

The following output is generated:

OBJECTIVE FUNCTION VALUE =		314.286
VARIABLE	**VALUE**	**REDUCED COSTS**
X1	285.714	0.000
X2	0.000	0.071
X3	214.286	0.000
D1MINUS	0.000	0.000
D1PLUS	85.714	0.000
D2MINUS	0.000	0.000
D2PLUS	0.000	0.714
D3MINUS	0.000	3.571
D3PLUS	0.000	1.429
D4MINUS	0.000	1.000
D4PLUS	314.286	0.000

Thus the optimal recommendation is to produce 285.714286 CP2860 computers weekly and 214.285714 CP4860 computers weekly. All goals will be met except goal 4. 314.285714 extra man-hours or a total of 714.285714 man-hours will be used.

PROBLEM 3

The campaign headquarters of Jerry Black, a candidate for the Board of Supervisors, has 100 volunteers. With one week to go in the election, there are three major strategies remaining: media advertising, door-to-door canvassing, and telephone campaigning. It is estimated that each phone call will take approximately four minutes and each door-to-door personal contact will average seven minutes. These times include time between contacts for breaks, transportation, dialing, etc. Volunteers who work on advertising will not be able to handle any other duties. Each ad will utilize the talents of three workers for the entire week.

Volunteers are expected to work 12 hours per day during the final seven days of the campaign. At a minimum, Jerry Black feels he needs 30,000 phone contacts, 20,000 personal contacts, and three advertisements during the last week. However, he would like to see 50,000 phone contacts and 50,000 personal contacts made and five advertisements developed. It is felt that advertising is 50 times as important as personal contacts which in turn is twice as important as phone contacts.

Formulate and solve this goal programming problem with a single weighted priority to determine how the work should be distributed during the final week of the campaign.

SOLUTION 3

Define variables

x_1 = number of volunteers doing phone work during the week
x_2 = number of volunteers making personal contacts during week
x_3 = number of volunteers preparing advertising during the week

Define goals

1) 50,000 phone contacts:
d_1^+ and d_1^- = the amount this quantity is overachieved and underachieved, respectively

2) 50,000 personal contacts:
d_2^+ and d_2^- = the amount this quantity is overachieved and underachieved, respectively

3) 5 advertisements:
d_3^+ and d_3^- = the amount this quantity is overachieved and underachieved, respectively

Define objective

It would not hurt Jerry Black if his goals were exceeded, however since the importance of his goals are in the ratio 1:2:100, the goal programming objective function would be:

MIN $d_1^- + 2d_2^- + 100d_3^-$

Define constraints

There are (7 days) x (12 hours per day) x (60 minutes per hour) = 5040 minutes per worker. Thus a phone worker could make 5040/4 = 1260 phone calls in the week. And a door-to-door canvasser could make 5040/7 = 720 personal contacts during the week.

Linear Programming Constraints

1) At least 30,000 phone contacts: $\qquad$ $1260x_1 \geq 30,000$

2) At least 20,000 personal contacts: $\qquad$ $720x_2 \geq 20,000$

3) At least 3 advertisements: $\qquad$ $(1/3)x_3 \geq 3$

4) 100 volunteers: $\qquad$ $x_1 + x_2 + x_3 = 100$

Goal Constraints

5) Make 50,000 phone contacts: $\qquad$ $1260x_1 - d_1^+ + d_1^- = 50,000$

6) Make 50,000 personal contacts: $\qquad$ $720x_2 - d_2^+ + d_2^- = 50,000$

7) Design 5 advertisements: $\qquad$ $(1/3)x_3 - d_3^+ + d_3^- = 5$

Non-negativity of Variables

$x_1, x_2, x_3, d_1^+, d_1^-, d_2^+, d_2^-, d_3^+, d_3^- \geq 0$

PROBLEM 4

John Harris is interested in purchasing a new Harley-Davidson motorcycle. He has narrowed his choice to one of three models: Sportster Classic, Heritage Softtail, and Electra Glide. After much consideration, John has determined his decision-making criteria, assigned a weight to each criterion, and rated how well each model alternative satisfies each criterion.

| | | Decision Alternative | | |
Criterion	Weight	Sportster Classic	Heritage Softtail	Electra Glide
Wind protection	5	3	6	8
Fuel tank mileage	3	5	7	6
Passenger comfort	2	5	6	8
Seat height	3	8	5	6
Acceleration	4	8	5	3
Weight	3	8	6	3
Storage capacity	3	4	5	8

Using a scoring model, determine the recommended motorcycle model for John.

SOLUTION 4

Step 4: Compute the score for each decision alternative.

$$S_j = \sum_i w_i\, r_{ij}$$

$$S_1 = 5(3)+3(5)+2(5)+3(8)+4(8)+3(8)+3(4) = 132$$

$$S_2 = 5(6)+3(7)+2(6)+3(5)+4(5)+3(6)+3(5) = 131$$

$$S_3 = 5(8)+3(6)+2(8)+3(6)+4(3)+3(3)+3(8) = \underline{137}$$

Step 5: Order the decision alternatives from highest score to lowest score. The alternative with the highest score is the recommended alternative.

The <u>Electra Glide model</u> has the highest score and is the <u>recommended decision alternative</u>. Note that both the Sportster and the Electra Glide ranked first in 3 of 7 criteria, but due to the weights of the criteria the Electra Glide prevailed.

Spreadsheet showing data

	A	B	C	D	E
2			Sportster	Heritage	Electra
3	Criteria	Weight	Classic	Softtail	Glide
4	Wind protection	5	3	6	8
5	Fuel tank mileage	3	5	7	6
6	Passenger comfort	2	5	6	8
7	Seat height	3	8	5	6
8	Acceleration	4	8	5	3
9	Weight	3	8	6	3
10	Storage capacity	3	4	5	8

Spreadsheet showing formulas

12	A	B	C	D	E	
13	SCORING CALCULATIONS					
14			Sportster	Heritage	Electra	
15	Criteria		Classic	Softtail	Glide	
16	Wind protection		=B4*C4	=B4*D4	=B4*E4	
17	Fuel tank mileage		=B5*C5	=B5*D5	=B5*E5	
18	Passenger comfort		=B6*C6	=B6*D6	=B6*E6	
19	Seat height		=B7*C7	=B7*D7	=B7*E7	
20	Acceleration		=B8*C8	=B8*D8	=B8*E8	
21	Weight		=B9*C9	=B9*D9	=B9*E9	
22	Storage capacity		=B10*C10	=B10*D10	=B10*E10	
23	Score		=sum(C16:C22)			
24				=sum(D16:D22)		
25					=sum(E16:E22)	

Spreadsheet showing solution

12	A	B	C	D	E
13	SCORING CALCULATIONS				
14			Sportster	Heritage	Electra
15	**Criteria**		**Classic**	**Softtail**	**Glide**
16	Wind protection		15	30	40
17	Fuel tank mileage		15	21	18
18	Passenger comfort		10	12	16
19	Seat height		24	15	18
20	Acceleration		32	20	12
21	Weight		24	18	9
22	Storage capacity		12	15	24
23	**Score**		**132**	**131**	**137**

PROBLEM 5

Designer Gill Glass must decide which of three manufacturers will develop his "signature" toothbrushes. Three factors seem important to Gill: (1) his costs; (2) reliability of the product; and, (3) delivery time of the orders.

The three manufacturers are Cornell Industries, Brush Pik, and Picobuy. Cornell Industries will sell toothbrushes to Gill Glass for $100 per gross, Brush Pik for $80 per gross, and Picobuy for $144 per gross. Gill has decided that in terms of price, Brush Pik is moderately preferred to Cornell and very strongly preferred to Picobuy. In turn Cornell is strongly to very strongly preferred to Picobuy.

a) Form the pairwise comparison matrix for cost.

b) Calculate the normalized matrix for cost.

c) Determine the priority vector for cost.

d) Are Gill Glass's responses to cost consistent? Explain.

SOLUTION 5

a) Because Brush Pik is moderately preferred to Cornell, Cornell's entry in the Brush Pik row is 3 and Brush Pik's entry in the Cornell row is 1/3. Because Brush Pik is very strongly preferred to Picobuy, Picobuy's entry in the Brush Pik row is 7 and Brush Pik's entry in the Picobuy row is 1/7. Because Cornell is strongly to very strongly preferred to Picobuy, Picobuy's entry in the Cornell row is 6 and Cornell's entry in the Picobuy row is 1/6.

All diagonal entries are 1. Hence:

Pairwise comparison matrix for cost

	Cornell	Brush Pik	Picobuy
Cornell	1	1/3	6
Brush Pik	3	1	7
Picobuy	1/6	1/7	1

b) To determine normalized matrix, divide each entry in the matrix by its corresponding column sum. For Cornell the column sum = 1 + 3 + 1/6 = 25/6. For Brush Pik the column sum is 1/3 + 1 + 1/7 = 31/21. For Picobuy the column sum is 6 + 7 + 1 = 14. This gives:

Normalized matrix for cost

	Cornell	Brush Pik	Picobuy
Cornell	6/25	7/31	6/14
Brush Pik	18/25	21/31	7/14
Picobuy	1/25	3/31	1/14

c) The priority vector is determined by averaging the row entries in the normalized matrix. Converting to decimals we get:

Priority vector for cost

$$
\begin{array}{ll}
\text{Cornell:} & (\ 6/25 + \ 7/31 + 6/14)/3 = \\
\text{Brush Pik:} & (18/25 + 21/31 + 7/14)/3 = \\
\text{Picobuy:} & (\ 1/25 + \ 3/31 + 1/14)/3 =
\end{array}
\begin{bmatrix} .298 \\ .632 \\ .069 \end{bmatrix}
$$

d) To check consistency,

(1) Multiply each column of the pairwise comparison matrix by its priority:

$$
.298\begin{bmatrix} 1 \\ 3 \\ 1/6 \end{bmatrix} + .632\begin{bmatrix} 1/3 \\ 1 \\ 1/7 \end{bmatrix} + .069\begin{bmatrix} 6 \\ 7 \\ 1 \end{bmatrix} = \begin{bmatrix} .923 \\ 2.009 \\ .209 \end{bmatrix}
$$

(2) Divide these number by their priorities to get:

$$
\begin{array}{l}
.923/.298 = 3.097 \\
2.009/.632 = 3.179 \\
.209/.069 = 3.029
\end{array}
$$

(3) Average the above results to get λ_{max}.

$$\lambda_{max} = (3.097 + 3.179 + 3.029)/3 = 3.102$$

(4) Compute the consistence index, CI, for two terms by:

$$CI = (\lambda_{max} - n)/(n - 1) = (3.102 - 3)/2 = .051.$$

(5) Compute the consistency ratio, CR, by CI/RI, where RI = .58 for 3 factors:

$$CR = CI/RI = .051/.58 = .088$$

Since the consistency ratio, CR, is less than .10, this is well within the acceptable range for consistency.

PROBLEM 6

Referring to problem (4), Gill Glass has determined that for reliability, Cornell is very strongly preferable to Brush Pik and equally to moderately preferable to Picobuy. Also, Picobuy is strongly preferable to Brush Pik.

Regarding delivery time, Cornell is equally preferred with Picobuy. Both Cornell and Picobuy are very strongly to extremely preferable to Brush Pik.

a) Construct pairwise comparison matrices for reliability and for delivery time.

b) Construct priority vectors for reliability and delivery time.

SOLUTION 6

a) <u>Pairwise comparison matrix for reliability</u>

	Cornell	Brush Pik	Picobuy
Cornell	1	7	2
Brush Pik	1/7	1	5
Picobuy	1/2	1/5	1

<u>Pairwise comparison matrix for delivery time</u>

	Cornell	Brush Pik	Picobuy
Cornell	1	8	1
Brush Pik	1/8	1	1/8
Picobuy	1	8	1

b) For reliability the column sums are 23/14, 41/5, and 8. Dividing each entry by its corresponding column sum, we get:

  Normalized matrix for reliability

	Cornell	Brush Pik	Picobuy
Cornell	14/23	35/41	2/8
Brush Pik	2/23	5/41	5/8
Picobuy	7/23	1/41	1/8

Priority vector for reliability

$$
\begin{array}{lll}
\text{Cornell:} & (14/23 + 35/41 + 2/8)/3 = & \begin{bmatrix} .571 \\ .278 \\ .151 \end{bmatrix} \\
\text{Brush Pik:} & (\ 2/23 + 5/41\ + 5/8)/3 = & \\
\text{Picobuy:} & (\ 7/23 + 1/41\ + 1/8)/3 = &
\end{array}
$$

For delivery time the column sums are 17/8, 17, and 17/8 respectively. Dividing each entry by its corresponding column sum gives:

Normalized matrix for delivery time

	Cornell	Brush Pik	Picobuy
Cornell	8/17	8/17	8/17
Brush Pik	1/17	1/17	1/17
Picobuy	8/17	8/17	8/17

Priority vector for delivery time

$$
\begin{array}{lll}
\text{Cornell:} & (8/17 + 8/17 + 8/17)/3 = & \begin{bmatrix} .471 \\ .059 \\ .471 \end{bmatrix} \\
\text{Brush Pik:} & (1/17 + 1/17 + 1/17)/3 = & \\
\text{Picobuy:} & (8/17 + 8/17 + 8/17)/3 = &
\end{array}
$$

PROBLEM 7

The accounting department at Gill Glass (problems (4) and (5)) has determined that in terms of criteria, cost is extremely preferred to delivery time and very strongly preferred to reliability, and that reliability is very strongly preferred to delivery time.

a) Construct a pairwise comparison matrix for the criteria.

b) Construct a normalized pairwise matrix for the criteria.

c) Determine a priority vector for the criteria.

d) Determine an overall priority vector for the decision alternatives based on the criteria of the accounting dept.

SOLUTION 7

a) Pairwise comparison matrix for criteria

	Cost	Reliability	Delivery
Cost	1	7	9
Reliability	1/7	1	7
Delivery	1/9	1/7	1

b) The column sums are 79/63, 57/7, and 17 respectively. Dividing each entry by its corresponding column sum gives:

Normalized matrix for criteria

	Cost	Reliability	Delivery
Cost	63/79	49/57	9/17
Reliability	9/79	7/57	7/17
Delivery	7/79	1/57	1/17

c) Average the rows of the normalized matrix to get:

Priority vector for criteria

$$\begin{array}{ll} \text{Cost:} & (63/79 + 49/57 + 9/17)/3 = \\ \text{Reliability:} & (\;9/79 + \;7/57 + 7/17)/3 = \\ \text{Delivery:} & (\;7/79 + \;1/57 + 1/17)/3 = \end{array} \begin{bmatrix} .729 \\ .216 \\ .055 \end{bmatrix}$$

d) The overall priorities are determined by multiplying the priority vector of the criteria by the priorities for each decision alternative for each objective:

Priority Vector
for criteria -> [.729   .216   .055   ]

	Cost	Reliability	Delivery
Cornell	.298	.571	.471
Brush Pik	.632	.278	.059
Picobuy	.069	.151	.471

(Priority Matrix)

Overall priority vector

$$\begin{array}{ll} \text{Cornell:} & (.729)(.298) + (.216)(.571) + (.055)(.471) = \\ \text{Brush Pik:} & (.729)(.632) + (.216)(.278) + (.055)(.059) = \\ \text{Picobuy:} & (.729)(.069) + (.216)(.151) + (.055)(.471) = \end{array} \begin{bmatrix} .366 \\ .524 \\ .109 \end{bmatrix}$$

Thus, Brush Pik appears to be the overall recommendation.

PROBLEM 8

A student has one quantitative elective left to select to complete his graduation requirements. The two quantitative electives that are available are an advanced management science class (MS) and an advanced statistics class (STAT). Two factors which are important to the student in his selection process are relevance (R) and difficulty (D). The student formulated the following pairwise consistency matrices:

Criteria	R	D
R	1	1/3
D	3	1

Relevance	MS	STAT
MS	1	1/3
STAT	3	1

Difficulty	MS	STAT
MS	1	5
STAT	1/5	1

a) Draw the hierarchy for this decision problem.

b) Compute the priorities for each of the pairwise comparison matrices.

c) Determine an overall priority for the course selection process.

SOLUTION 8

a) First, list the overall goal: Select the best course. Then, list the evaluation criteria: Relevance, Difficulty. Last, list the alternatives: Management Science, Statistics.

b) Priority Vectors:

Relevance

The column sums are 4 and 4/3 respectively. Dividing the entries by the column sums yields the following <u>normalized matrix</u>:

	MS	STAT
MS	1/4	1/4
STAT	3/4	3/4

Averaging the rows gives the following <u>priority vector</u> for relevance:

$$\begin{matrix} \text{MS} \\ \text{STAT} \end{matrix} \begin{bmatrix} 1/4 \\ 3/4 \end{bmatrix}$$

Difficulty

The column sums are 6/5 and 6 respectively. Dividing the entries by the column sums yields the following <u>normalized matrix</u>:

	MS	STAT
MS	5/6	5/6
STAT	1/6	1/6

Averaging the rows gives the following <u>priority vector</u> for difficulty:

$$\begin{matrix} \text{MS} \\ \text{STAT} \end{matrix} \begin{bmatrix} 5/6 \\ 1/6 \end{bmatrix}$$

<u>Criteria</u>

The column sums are 4 and 4/3 respectively. Dividing the entries by the column sums yields the following <u>normalized matrix</u>:

	Rel.	Dif.
Rel.	1	1/3
Dif.	3	1

Averaging the rows gives the following <u>priority vector</u> for criteria:

$$\begin{matrix} \text{Relevance} \\ \text{Difficulty} \end{matrix} \begin{bmatrix} 1/4 \\ 3/4 \end{bmatrix}$$

c) Determine the overall priorities for MS and STAT by multiplying their relevance and difficulty vectors by their priority:

Priority vector
for criteria --> [1/4   3/4]

	Rel.	Dif.
Rel.	1/4	5/6
Dif.	3/4	1/6

(Priority Matrix)

<u>Overall priority vector</u>

$$\begin{matrix} \text{MS:} \\ \text{STAT:} \end{matrix} \begin{matrix} (.25)(.25) + (.75)(.833) = \\ (.25)(.75) + (.75)(.167) = \end{matrix} \begin{bmatrix} .6875 \\ .3125 \end{bmatrix}$$

Thus, MS appears to be the overall recommendation.

PROBLEM 9

Alfax Industries is trying to promote a new product which it recently developed. It wishes to restrict advertising to television and radio ads. Television ads cost $50,000 each to produce and radio ads $15,000 each. Each television ad will require the use of three Alfax marketing employees and each radio ad will require one. There are 24 persons in the marketing department. Management requires a minimum of six total ads monthly.

Alfax has set the following goals for the production of ads:

(1) Do not exceed a monthly advertising budget of $250,000.
(2) Do not use more than 50% of its marketing personnel on this project.
(3) Produce at least 4 television ads monthly.
(4) Produce at least 4 radio ads monthly.

a) Using the goals as simple constraints, formulate the constraint set for this problem and show it is infeasible.

b) Solve the above goal program graphically with four levels of priority.

c) Suppose goals (3) and (4) were within the same priority level but with the goal of producing at least 4 television ads monthly deemed twice as important as making 4 radio ads. Resolve this problem with three levels of priority.

PROBLEM 10

Barry College has received a $200,000 donation for its scholarship fund to be used for $3000 athletic scholarships, $2500 minority scholarships and $2000 women's scholarships. The donor, an avid sports fan, has stipulated at least 20 athletic scholarships must be awarded.

The Board of Trustees of Barry College has three levels of priority for awarding the scholarships:

(1) It would like at least 80 total scholarships.
(2) It would like no more than 25% of the scholarships to be athletic scholarships.
(3) It would like at least 25 athletic scholarships, 40 minority scholarships, and 30 women's scholarships. (Meeting the target for minorities is viewed as three times as important as meeting the target for athletes or women.)

Formulate a goal program for Barry College and solve by a computer package such as the Management Scientist.

PROBLEM 11

Universal Electric (UE) has facilities all over the United States. Currently UE has 150,000 employees, 5,000 of which are in management positions. The government contends that UE is delinquent in its Affirmative Action policies and will take action if UE does not rectify the situation.

Although UE currently has 12,000 minority employees (8% of its total), only 50 are in management positions (or 1% of the management positions). UE has submitted a plan to the federal government which expresses that UE has a target of 20% minority employees by the end of the year. In negotiating with various minority groups, UE has promised that by the end of the year, at least 10% of its management positions will be held by minorities.

Attrition rates of all employees (both management and otherwise) are 8% for non-minorities, 4% for minorities. Because of a good year, UE will create 6,000 new positions, 200 of which will be in management. However, the mandate from the top is that it would be unwise from a community relations point of view, if more than 2/3 of the new employee positions and more than 2/3 of the promotions to management positions be minorities.

Assume all management positions will be filled in-house and hence all hiring will be for non-management positions. Further assume violations of the company mandate have the same weight as not meeting the goal of 10% minority management positions. However, not meeting federal standards is considered three times more serious.

Formulate and solve this problem as a goal program with a single weighted priority.

PROBLEM 12

Rudy's Barbecue is in need of an office management software package. After considerable research, Rudy has narrowed his choice to one of three packages: SoftTrack, VersaSuite, and N-able. He has determined his decision-making criteria, assigned a weight to each criterion, and rated how well each alternative satisfies each criterion.

| | | Decision Alternative | | |
| | | Soft- | Versa- | N- |
Criterion	Weight	Track	Suite	Able
Ease of use	4	3	5	8
Report generation	3	8	7	6
Functional integration	5	5	8	6
On-line help	3	8	6	4
Entry error-checking	2	8	3	4
Price	4	4	7	5
Support cost	3	6	5	7

Using a scoring model, determine the recommended software package for Rudy's.

PROBLEM 13

Consider a beauty pageant in which there are three finalists. They are to be judged on (1) evening gown; (2) swim suit; and, (3) answering a corny question posed by an equally corny MC. The three finalists are Miss Northern State, Miss Central State, and Miss Southern State.

It is known that Judge Jones believes that swim suit is strongly more important than evening gown appearance and extremely more important than answering the question. Further, he feels that the evening gown appearance is very strongly more important than answering the question.

In the evening gown competition, Miss Central State performed very strongly compared to Miss Southern State and strongly compared to Miss Northern State. Miss Northern State compared equally to moderately more strongly than Miss Southern State.

In the swim suit competition, Miss Southern State was extremely preferred to both Miss Northern State or Miss Central State and Miss Northern State was moderately preferred to Miss Central State.

In the question competition, Miss Northern State was extremely preferred to Miss Southern State and strongly preferred to Miss Central State. Miss Central State was moderately preferred to Miss Southern State.

Judge Jones has 100 points to distribute among the three finalists. Using his observations and preferences, how should he divide his 100 points between the three finalists?

PROBLEM 14

The Drezners have a choice of three neighborhood supermarkets: Gamma Delta, Bill's, and Hewes. Five factors are important to the Drezners: (1) Location; (2) Overall Prices; (3) Cleanliness; (4) Ease of Parking; and, (5) Selection/Quality. The pairwise comparison matrices are shown below:

Location:

	GD	B	H
GD	1	1/2	4
B	2	1	3
H	1/4	1/3	1

Overall Prices:

	GD	B	H
GD	1	1/2	4
B	2	1	3
H	1/4	1/3	1

Cleanliness:

	GD	B	H
GD	1	1/2	4
B	2	1	3
H	1/4	1/3	1

Ease of Parking:

	GD	B	H
GD	1	1/2	4
B	2	1	3
H	1/4	1/3	1

Selection/Quality:

	GD	B	H
GD	1	1/2	4
B	2	1	3
H	1/4	1/3	1

a) Determine the priority vector for each of the criteria.

b) If all five criteria were equally important, what would be the overall supermarket priority vector?

Now assume the Drezners feel that:
1) Location and ease of parking have equal priority.
2) Overall price is moderately more important than cleanliness or selection, and is very strongly more important than location or ease of parking.
3) Cleanliness is strongly more important than ease of parking, very strongly more important than location, and moderately more important than selection.
4) Selection/quality are moderately more important than location and very strongly more important than parking.

c) Given these preferences, construct a criteria pairwise comparison matrix.

d) Calculate the consistency ratio for the criteria and comment.

e) Determine the overall priority vector for the Drezners.

PROBLEM 15

Abraham L. Ford is a lifelong Republican who has a dilemma in the upcoming election. In general, Mr. Ford very strongly prefers Republicans over Democrats and strongly prefers Republicans over Independents. He moderately favors Independents over Democrats.

However, in the upcoming election, on the issues he strongly to very strongly favors Democrat Fritz Carter over Republican Ron Nixon and strongly favors Fritz Carter over Independent George Anderson. He moderately favors Anderson over Nixon. He has decided that issues are moderately to strongly more important to him than party.

a) Determine the hierarchy for this problem.

b) Determine the pairwise comparison matrix for each alternative.

c) Determine the priority vector for the alternatives for each criterion.

d) Determine the consistency ratio for the issues criterion.

e) Determine a priority vector for the criteria.

f) Determine Mr. Ford's overall priority vector for the candidates.

PROBLEM 16

Terry's Trucking is trying to determine which database package to purchase for its microcomputer. It has narrowed its choices to BASE 8 and DATA RECORD. BASE 8 is very strongly to extremely preferred in price, but DATA RECORD is strongly to very strongly preferred for ease of use.

a) Determine the hierarchy for Terry's Trucking's decision.

b) Construct the pairwise comparison matrix for each criterion.

c) Determine the priority vector for the alternatives for each criterion.

d) Determine the overall priority vector if:
   (1) price is extremely preferred to ease of use; or if
   (2) ease of use is extremely preferred to price; or if
   (3) price and ease of use are equally preferred.

e) Approximately what relation between price and ease of use would give BASE 8 and DATA RECORD equal priority in an overall priority vector?

PROBLEM 17

Consider the following military application regarding the so called "star wars" or "strategic defense initiative". The overall goal is to maintain peace.
The criteria are: (1) strong defense; (2) international image; (3) U.S. - Soviet relations. The decision alternatives are: (1) continue with "star wars" development; (2) scale down "star wars" development; (3) abandon "star wars" development.

a) Make up your own preferences and feelings regarding the criteria and alternatives. Determine an overall priority vector of the alternatives.

b) Comment on a possible limitation of this model with regard to the scale used for the pairwise comparison matrices.

TRUE/FALSE

___ 18. A goal programming problem will always have more than one priority level.

___ 19. The number of linear programs that must be sequentially solved to develop the solution to a goal program is determined by the number of goals in the objective function.

___ 20. For each goal in a goal program, two variables are added: one for underachieving the goal and one for overachieving the goal.

___ 21. It is not possible to have two penalties for the same goal, one for underachieving the goal and another for overachieving it.

___ 22. For a particular goal program, the Phase 1 objective was Minimize d_1^+. The objective was not satisfied but underachieved by an amount of 50. Any solution to the Phase 2 problem of Minimize d_2^- must have $d_1^+ = 50$.

___ 23. In the process of satisfying second-priority goals, improvement in the satisfaction of first-priority goals sometimes occurs.

___ 24. Trade-offs among goals at the same priority level will not occur unless the goals have the same relative weight.

___ 25. In the analytic hierarchy process, if the entry in row A for decision B is 2, the entry in row B for decision A is 1/2.

___ 26. In the analytic hierarchy process, a consistency ratio of .99 is extremely good.

___ 27. If the consistency index is .90, the consistency ratio is .90.

___ 28. The analytic hierarchy process utilizes pairwise comparisons to establish priority measures for both the criteria and the decision alternatives.

___ 29. The criteria priority vector for gum is: Price: .3, Taste: .7. For Price, BRAND A's priority is .8 and BRAND B's is .2. For Taste, BRAND A's priority is .4 and BRAND B's is .6. Overall BRAND A has a higher priority than BRAND B.

___ 30. On the 1-to-9 pairwise comparison scale, a numerical rating of 9 means extremely preferred and 5 means equally preferred.

___ 31. In the analytic hierarchy process, the hierarchy from top to bottom is overall goal, decision alternatives, and criteria.

___ 32. A consistency ratio measures the consistency of a decision alternative's relative rank from one criterion to another.

CHAPTER 16

Forecasting

KEY CONCEPTS

CONCEPT	ILLUSTRATED PROBLEMS	ANSWERED PROBLEMS
Smoothing Methods		
Moving Average	1	9
Weighted Moving Average	2	6
Exponential Smoothing	1	6,7
Linear Trend Projection	2	10,12
Multiplicative Time Series Model	3,4	8,11,13
Regression Analysis	5	14
Mean Squared Error	1	6,7,9

REVIEW

1. A time series is a set of observations measured at successive points in time or over successive periods of time. A time series is analyzed so that one may determine good forecasts or predictions of future values for the time series.

2. While a time series may consist of numerous components, a usual assumption is that four separate components combine to affect the values of a time series. These four components are: (1) a trend component; (2) a cyclical component; (3) a seasonal component; and, (4) irregular components.

3. The trend component accounts for the gradual shifting of the time series over a long period of time.

4. Any regular pattern of sequences of values above and below the trend line is attributable to the cyclical component of the series.

5. The seasonal component of the series accounts for regular patterns of variability within certain time periods, such as over a year.

6. The irregular component of the series is caused by short-term, unanticipated and non-recurring factors that affect the values of the time series. One cannot attempt to predict its impact on the time series in advance.

7. In cases in which the time series is fairly stable and has no significant trend, seasonal, or cyclical effects, one can use <u>smoothing methods</u> to average out the irregular components of the time series.

8. The <u>moving average</u> smoothing method consists of computing an average of the most recent n data values for the series and using this average for forecasting the value of the time series for the next period.

9. The <u>centered moving average</u> method consists of computing an average of n periods' data and associating it with the midpoint of the periods. For example, the average for periods 5, 6, and 7 is associated with period 6. This methodology is useful in the process of computing season indexes.

10. In the <u>weighted moving average</u> smoothing method for computing the average of the most recent n periods, the more recent observations are typically given more weight than older observations. (For convenience, the weights usually sum to 1.)

11. One difficulty of both the moving average and the weighted moving average methods is that n historical data points must be stored in order to compute the forecast for the next period. In <u>exponential smoothing</u> only two pieces of information are needed to compute the forecast: (1) the forecasted value for the current period, and (2) the actual value for the current period.

12. Using <u>exponential smoothing</u>, the forecast is calculated by:
$$\alpha[\text{the actual value for the current period}]$$
$$+ (1-\alpha)[\text{the forecasted value for the current period}],$$
where the <u>smoothing constant</u>, α, is a number between 0 and 1.

13. Another way to view <u>exponential smoothing</u> is that the forecast for the next period is equal to the forecast for the current period plus a proportion (α) of the forecast error in the current period.

14. It is essential that forecasts be as accurate as possible. One measure of <u>forecast accuracy</u> is known as the <u>mean squared error</u>. In this measure the average of the squared forecast errors for the historical data is calculated. The forecasting method or parameter(s) which minimize this mean squared error is then selected.

15. An alternative measure for the performance of a forecasting technique is the <u>mean absolute deviation (MAD)</u>. In this measure, the mean of the absolute values of all forecast errors is calculated, and the forecasting method or parameter(s) which minimize this measure is selected. The mean absolute deviation measure is less sensitive to individual large forecast errors than the mean squared error measure.

16. If a time series exhibits a linear trend, the <u>method of least squares</u> may be used to determine a trend line (projection) for future forecasts. This statistical technique, also used in regression analysis, determines the unique trend line forecast which minimizes the mean square error between the trend line forecasts and the actual observed values for the time series.

17. Using the method of least squares, the formula for the <u>trend projection</u> is: $T_t = b_0 + b_1 t$.
Here,

T_t = the trend forecast for time period t
b_1 = the slope of the trend line
b_0 = the trend line projection for time 0

Where

$$b_1 = \frac{n\sum tY_t - \sum t \sum Y_t}{n\sum t^2 - (\sum t)^2} \qquad b_0 = \bar{Y} - b_1\bar{t}$$

Here, Y_t = the observed value of the time series at time period t

$\bar{Y}$ = the average of the observed values for Y_t

$\bar{t}$ = the average time period for the n observations

18. In the case of <u>nonlinear trend</u>, a more advanced statistical technique might possibly be used to develop the forecasting curve.

19. The <u>multiplicative time series model</u> assumes that the actual time series value, Y_t, is equal to the product of the four time series components: (1) trend (T_t); (2) cyclical (C_t); (3) seasonal (S_t); and (4) irregular (I_t). Thus, $Y_t = T_t C_t S_t I_t$.

20. In situations in which no historical data is available or when historical data will not give an accurate picture of the future, <u>nonquantitative techniques</u> for forecasting may be used.

21. An example of a nonquantitative forecasting technique is the <u>delphi approach</u>. A panel of experts, each of whom is physically separated from the others and is anonymous, is asked to respond to a sequential series of questionnaires. After each questionnaire, the responses are tabulated and the information and opinions of the entire group are made known to each of the other panel members so that they may revise their previous forecast response. The process continues until some degree of consensus is achieved.

22. Another nonquantitative approach, <u>scenario writing</u>, consists of developing a conceptual scenario of the future based on a well defined set of assumptions. After several different scenarios have been developed, the decision maker determines which is most likely to occur in the future and makes decisions accordingly.

23. <u>Subjective</u> or <u>interactive qualitative approaches</u>, commonly known as "brainstorming sessions" are another way to perform a nonquantitative forecast. It is important in such sessions that any ideas or opinions be permitted to be presented without regard to its relevancy and without fear of criticism.

MULTIPLICATIVE TIME SERIES PROCEDURE

1. Calculate the centered moving averages (CMAs).
    The centered moving average represents the combined trend and cyclical components of the series. Calculate K-period moving averages (where K is the number of seasons, i.e. quarterly data would have four seasons whereas monthly data would have twelve seasons.)

2. Center the CMAs on integer-valued periods.
    Associate each moving average with the middle period of the K data points comprising the average. When K is an even number there is no distinct middle period. In this case, taking the average of two successive moving averages (one centered just above the period and one centered just below the period) gives the moving average associated with that period.

3. Determine the seasonal and irregular factors ($S_t I_t$).
    For each centered moving average found in step 2, divide this value into the observed value, Y_t. This quotient represents the seasonal and irregular factors.

4. Determine the average seasonal factors.
    For each season, average the corresponding quotients found in step 3 to smooth out the irregular component and isolate the seasonal factors.

5. Scale the seasonal factors (S_t).
    To ensure that the seasonal factors average to 1, adjust the seasonal factors by dividing each by the average seasonal factor value.

6. Determine the deseasonalized data.
    Divide each data value, Y_t, by its seasonal factor.

7. Determine a trend line of the deseasonalized data.
    Use the method of least squares on this data set to identify the trend line for the data.

8. Determine the deseasonalized predictions.
    Determine the trend forecast(s) associated with the future period(s) by using the trend line equation found in step 7.

9. Take into account the seasonality.
    Multiply each deseasonalized prediction by the appropriate seasonal factor.

FLOW CHART OF
MULTIPLICATIVE TIME SERIES PROCEDURE

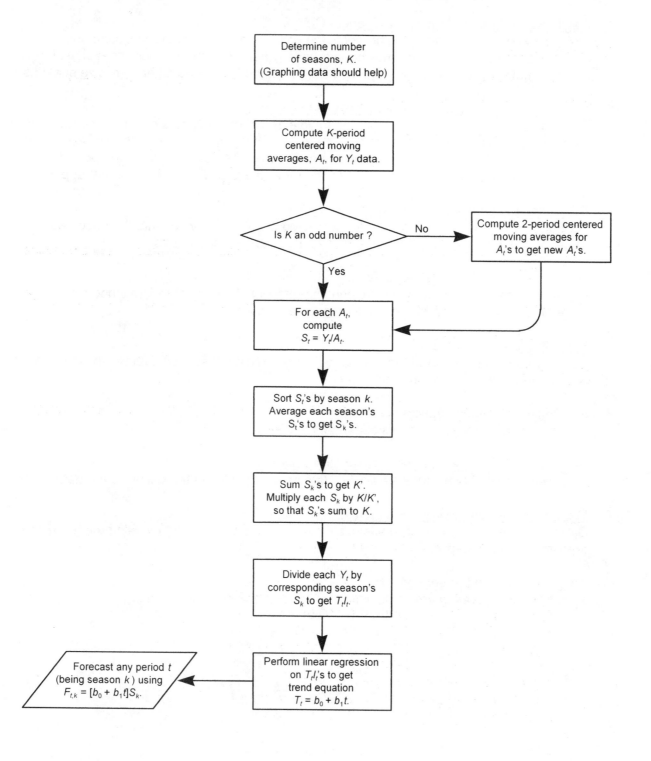

ILLUSTRATED PROBLEMS

PROBLEM 1

During the past ten weeks, sales of cases of Comfort brand headache medicine at Robert's Drugs have been as follows:

Week	Sales	Week	Sales
1	110	6	120
2	115	7	130
3	125	8	115
4	120	9	110
5	125	10	130

a) If Robert's uses exponential smoothing to forecast sales, which value for the smoothing constant α, $\alpha = .1$ or $\alpha = .8$, gives better forecasts?

b) Using your value for α in part (a) that gave better forecasts, forecast sales for week 11.

c) Forecast sales in week 11 using a three-week moving average.

SOLUTION 1

a) To evaluate the two smoothing constants, determine how the forecasted values would compare with the actual historical values in each case. Let

Y_t = actual sales in week t
F_t = forecasted sales in week t

<u>For $\alpha = .1$, $1 - \alpha = .9$</u>

$F_1 = Y_1 = 110$. For other weeks, $F_{t+1} = .1Y_t + .9F_t$

$$
\begin{aligned}
F_2 &= .1Y_1 + .9F_1 = .1(110) + .9(110) &= 110 \\
F_3 &= .1Y_2 + .9F_2 = .1(115) + .9(110) &= 110.5 \\
F_4 &= .1Y_3 + .9F_3 = .1(125) + .9(110.5) &= 111.95 \\
F_5 &= .1Y_4 + .9F_4 = .1(120) + .9(111.95) &= 112.76 \\
F_6 &= .1Y_5 + .9F_5 = .1(125) + .9(112.76) &= 113.98 \\
F_7 &= .1Y_6 + .9F_6 = .1(120) + .9(113.98) &= 114.58 \\
F_8 &= .1Y_7 + .9F_7 = .1(130) + .9(114.58) &= 116.12 \\
F_9 &= .1Y_8 + .9F_8 = .1(115) + .9(116.12) &= 116.01 \\
F_{10} &= .1Y_9 + .9F_9 = .1(110) + .9(116.01) &= 115.41
\end{aligned}
$$

For $\alpha = .8$, $1 - \alpha = .2$

F_1 $= 110$
$F_2 = .8(110) + .2(110)$ $= 110$
$F_3 = .8(115) + .2(110)$ $= 114$
$F_4 = .8(125) + .2(114)$ $= 122.80$
$F_5 = .8(120) + .2(122.80)$ $= 120.56$
$F_6 = .8(125) + .2(120.56)$ $= 124.11$
$F_7 = .8(120) + .2(124.11)$ $= 120.82$
$F_8 = .8(130) + .2(120.82)$ $= 128.16$
$F_9 = .8(115) + .2(128.16)$ $= 117.63$
$F_{10} = .8(110) + .2(117.63)$ $= 111.53$.

In order to determine which smoothing constant gives the better performance, calculate, for each, the mean squared error for the nine weeks of forecasts, weeks 2 through 10 by:

$$[(Y_2-F_2)^2 + (Y_3-F_3)^2 + (Y_4-F_4)^2 + ... + (Y_{10}-F_{10})^2] / 9$$

Week	Y_t	$\alpha = .1$ F_t	$(Y_t - F_t)^2$	$\alpha = .8$ F_t	$(Y_t - F_t)^2$
1	110				
2	115	110.00	25.00	110.00	25.00
3	125	110.50	210.25	114.00	121.00
4	120	111.95	64.80	122.80	7.84
5	125	112.76	149.94	120.56	19.71
6	120	113.98	36.25	124.11	16.91
7	130	114.58	237.73	120.82	84.23
8	115	116.12	1.26	128.16	173.30
9	110	116.01	36.12	117.63	58.26
10	130	115.41	212.87	111.53	341.27
		Sum	974.22	Sum	847.52
	MSE	Sum/9	108.25	Sum/9	94.17

Hence, based on the mean squared error criterion, using $\alpha = .8$ gives a slightly better forecast than using $\alpha = .1$.

b) If $\alpha = .8$, then the forecast for week 11 will be

$$.8Y_{10} + .2F_{10} = .8(130) + .2(111.53) = 126.31$$

c) Using a three week moving average, the forecast for week 11 will be the average of the preceding three weeks: weeks 8, 9, and 10.

$$F_{11} = (115 + 110 + 130)/3 = 118.33$$

PROBLEM 2

The number of plumbing repair jobs performed by Auger's Plumbing Service in each of the last nine months are listed below.

Month	Jobs	Month	Jobs	Month	Jobs
March	353	June	374	September	399
April	387	July	396	October	412
May	342	August	409	November	408

a) Assuming a linear trend function, forecast the number of repair jobs Auger's will perform in December using the least squares method.

b) What is your forecast for December using a three-period weighted moving average with weights of .6, .3, and .1? How does it compare with your forecast from part (a)?

SOLUTION 2

NOTE: The method of least squares requires time periods to be numbered. If your periods are labeled with words (e.g. February or Thursday) or the number labels are large (e.g. 1983), simply assign the first period in your data set the value 1, etc. Determine the value of the time period you want to forecast accordingly. For example, if 1983 is period 1, then 1998 is period 16.

a) The trend line is $T_t = b_0 + b_1 t$. The least squares method gives:

(month) t	Y_t	tY_t	t^2
(Mar.) 1	353	353	1
(Apr.) 2	387	774	4
(May) 3	342	1026	9
(June) 4	374	1496	16
(July) 5	396	1980	25
(Aug.) 6	409	2454	36
(Sep.) 7	399	2793	49
(Oct.) 8	412	3296	64
(Nov.) 9	408	3672	81
Sum 45	3480	17844	285

Thus, $\bar{t} = 5$ $\bar{Y} = 386.667$

$$b_1 = \frac{n\Sigma tY_t - \Sigma t \Sigma Y_t}{n\Sigma t^2 - (\Sigma t)^2} = \frac{(9)(17844) - (45)(3480)}{(9)(285) - (45)^2} = 7.4$$

$$b_0 = \bar{Y} - b_1\bar{t} = 386.667 - 7.4(5) = 349.667$$

$$T_{10} = 349.667 + (7.4)(10) = 423.667$$

b) Using a three-month weighted moving average, the forecast for December will be the weighted average of the preceding three months: September, October, and November.

$$F_{10} = .1Y_{Sep.} + .3Y_{Oct.} + .6Y_{Nov.} = .1(399) + .3(412) + .6(408) = 408.3$$

Due to the positive trend component in the time series, the least squares method produced a forecast that is more in tune with the trend that exists. The weighted moving average, even with heavy (.6) placed on the current period, produced a forecast that is lagging behind the changing data.

PROBLEM 3

Quarterly revenues (in $1,000,000's) for a national restaurant chain for a five year period were as follows:

			Year		
Quarter	1	2	3	4	5
1	33	42	54	70	85
2	36	40	53	67	82
3	35	42	54	70	87
4	38	47	62	77	99

Forecast the revenues for the next four quarters.

SOLUTION 3

Assume the data values are a multiplicative function of the data's trend, cyclical, seasonal, and irregular factors, i.e.

$$Y_t = T_t * C_t * S_t * I_t$$

Step 1: Calculate the centered moving averages (CMAs).
  First, use a moving average over the four quarters to mask the effects of the seasonal and irregular factors. For each four quarter period, calculate the moving average and associate it with the "middle period". For example, the first moving average is: (33+36+35+38)/4 = 35.5. The second equals = 37.75, etc.

Step 2: Center the CMAs on integer-valued periods.
  When the number of quarters is even, there is no integer valued "middle period" (the middle of the first four quarters would be quarter 2.5). In order to have the moving average "centered" at a particular quarter, average the half-period moving average preceding this quarter and the half-period moving average succeeding this quarter. For example, the moving averages of quarters 2.5 and 3.5 are 35.5 and 37.75, respectively. Thus, the centered moving average for quarter 3 is (35.5 + 37.75)/2 = 36.625.

Year	Quarter	Revenues	Four Quarter Moving Average	Centered Moving Average
1	1	33		
	2	36		
	(2.5)		35.50	
	3	35		36.625
	(3.5)		37.75	
	4	38		38.250
	(4.5)		38.75	
2	1	42		39.625
	(1.5)		40.50	
	2	40		41.625
	(2.5)		42.75	
	3	42		44.250
	(3.5)		45.75	
	4	47		47.375
	(4.5)		49.00	
3	1	54		50.500
	(1.5)		52.00	
	2	53		53.875
	(2.5)		55.75	
	3	54		57.750
	(3.5)		59.75	
	4	62		61.500
	(4.5)		63.25	
4	1	70		65.250
	(1.5)		67.25	
	2	67		69.125
	(2.5)		71.00	
	3	70		72.875
	(3.5)		74.75	
	4	77		76.625
	(4.5)		78.50	
5	1	85		80.625
	(1.5)		82.75	
	2	82		85.500
	(2.5)		88.25	
	3	87		
	4	99		

Step 3: Determine the seasonal and irregular factors ($S_t I_t$).

The centered moving averages represent the combine effects of the trend and cyclical factors ($T_t C_t$). Since $Y_t = T_t C_t S_t I_t$, $S_t I_t = Y_t/(T_t C_t) = Y_t/$(centered moving average for period t). So, dividing each data point by its centered moving average gives an estimate of $S_t I_t$.

For example for period 3 (year 1, quarter 3), the data point, $Y_3 = 35$, and its centered moving average $T_3 C_3 = 36.625$. Thus, for this period, $S_3 I_3 = 35/36.625 = .956$

Continue this procedure for determining $S_t I_t$ for all periods:

Year	Quarter	Revenues (Y_t)	Average (T_tC_t)	$S_t I_t$
1	3	35	36.625	.956
	4	38	38.250	.993
2	1	42	39.625	1.060
	2	40	41.625	.961
	3	42	44.250	.949
	4	47	47.375	.992
3	1	54	50.500	1.069
	2	53	53.875	.984
	3	54	57.750	.935
	4	62	61.500	1.008
4	1	70	65.250	1.073
	2	67	69.125	.969
	3	70	72.875	.961
	4	77	76.625	1.005
5	1	85	80.625	1.054
	2	82	85.500	.959

Step 4: Determine the average seasonal factors.

To eliminate the irregular effects, take the average of the $S_t I_t$ over the four years. That is, to find the average of $S_t I_t$ for quarter 1, average the quarter 1 values for years 2, 3, 4 and 5. Do the same for quarter 2. For quarters 3 and 4, the average would be over years 1, 2, 3, and 4. This gives:

$$S_1 = (1.060 + 1.069 + 1.073 + 1.054) / 4 \quad = 1.064$$
$$S_2 = (.961 + .984 + .969 + .959) / 4 \quad = .968$$
$$S_3 = (.956 + .949 + .935 + .961) / 4 \quad = .950$$
$$S_4 = (.993 + .992 + 1.008 + 1.005) / 4 \quad = 1.000$$

Step 5: Scale the seasonal factors (S_t).

Each seasonal average must be adjusted by the average of the seasonal factors, $(1.064 + .968 + .950 + 1.000) / 4 = .9955$, giving:

$$S_1 = 1.064/.9955 = 1.069$$
$$S_2 = .968/.9955 = .973$$
$$S_3 = .950/.9955 = .954$$
$$S_4 = 1.000/.9955 = 1.004$$

Step 6: Determine the deseasonalized data.

The seasonal factors (S_t) can now be removed from the data by dividing each data point by its seasonal factor. This gives deseasonalized data which will only be a function of trend, cyclical and irregular factors.

Year	Quarter	Y_t	Deseasonalized (Y_t/S_t)
1	1	33	33/1.069 = 30.87
	2	36	36/0.973 = 37.00
	3	35	35/0.954 = 36.69
	4	38	38/1.004 = 37.84
2	1	42	42/1.069 = 39.29
	2	40	40/0.973 = 41.11
	3	42	42/0.954 = 44.03
	4	47	47/1.004 = 46.44
3	1	54	54/1.069 = 50.51
	2	53	53/0.973 = 54.47
	3	54	54/0.954 = 56.60
	4	62	62/1.004 = 61.75
4	1	70	70/1.069 = 65.48
	2	67	67/0.973 = 68.86
	3	70	70/0.954 = 73.38
	4	77	77/1.004 = 76.69
5	1	85	85/1.069 = 79.51
	2	82	82/0.973 = 84.28
	3	87	87/0.954 = 91.19
	4	99	99/1.004 = 98.61

Step 7: Determine a trend line of the deseasonalized data.

Now, label the periods $t = 1$ through $t = 20$ and use the regression trend analysis (see problem 2) to determine the following trend line describing the seasonally adjusted data over the 20 quarters:

$$T_t = 23.436 + 3.361t$$

Step 8: Determine the deseasonalized predictions.

Use this trend line to determine the trend predictions for the four quarters of year 6.

Step 9: Take into account the seasonality.

Then adjust these quarterly predictions by multiplying each by its seasonal adjustment factor.

Quarter	Period t	Trend Prediction (T_t=23.436+3.361t)	Seasonally Adjusted Forecast ($T_t S_t$)
1	21	94.02	(94.02)(1.069) = 100.50
2	22	97.38	(97.38)(0.973) = 94.72
3	23	100.74	(100.74)(0.954) = 96.15
4	24	104.10	(104.10)(1.004) = 104.53

PROBLEM 4

Business at Terry's Tie Shop can be viewed as falling into three distinct seasons: (1) Christmas (November-December); (2) Father's Day (late May - mid-June); and (3) all other times. Average weekly sales (in $'s) during each of these three seasons during the past four years has been as follows:

	Year			
Season	1	2	3	4
1	1856	1995	2241	2280
2	2012	2168	2306	2408
3	985	1072	1105	1120

Determine a forecast for the average weekly sales in year 5 for each of the three seasons.

SOLUTION 4

The table on the next page summarizes the computations in steps 1-6.

Step 1: Calculate the centered moving averages.
   There are three distinct seasons in each year. Hence, take a three season moving average to eliminate seasonal and irregular factors. For example the first moving average is: $(1856 + 2012 + 985)/3 = 1617.67$.

Step 2: Center the CMAs on integer-valued periods.
   The first moving average computed in step 1 (1617.67) will be centered on season 2 of year 1. Note that the moving averages from step 1 center themselves on integer-valued periods because n is an odd number.

Step 3: Determine the seasonal and irregular factors $(S_t I_t)$.
   Isolate the trend and cyclical components. For each period t, this is given by $Y_t/$(Moving Average for period t).

Step 4: Determine the average seasonal factors.
   Averaging all $S_t I_t$ values corresponding to that season:

Season 1: $(1.163 + 1.196 + 1.181) / 3$	$= 1.180$
Season 2: $(1.244 + 1.242 + 1.224 + 1.244) / 4$	$= 1.238$
Season 3: $(.592 + .587 + .582) / 3$	$= .587$

Step 5: Scale the seasonal factors (S_t).
   Average the seasonal factors $= (1.180 + 1.238 + .587)/3 = 1.002$. Divide each seasonal factor by the average of the seasonal factors.

Season 1:	$1.180/1.002$	$= 1.178$
Season 2:	$1.238/1.002$	$= 1.236$
Season 3:	$.587/1.002$	$= .586$
	Total	$= 3.000$

Step 6: Determine the deseasonalized data.
Divide the data point values, Y_t, by S_t.

Year	Season	Dollar Sales (Y_t)	Moving Average	$S_t l_t$	Scaled S_t	Y_t/S_t
1	1	1856		1.178		1576
	2	2012	1617.67	1.244	1.236	1628
	3	985	1664.00	.592	.586	1681
2	1	1995	1716.00	1.163	1.178	1694
	2	2168	1745.00	1.242	1.236	1754
	3	1072	1827.00	.587	.586	1829
3	1	2241	1873.00	1.196	1.178	1902
	2	2306	1884.00	1.224	1.236	1866
	3	1105	1897.00	.582	.586	1886
4	1	2280	1931.00	1.181	1.178	1935
	2	2408	1936.00	1.244	1.236	1948
	3	1120			.586	1911

Step 7: Determine a trend line of the deseasonalized data.
Use the linear regression method illustrated in problem 2. For t = 1, 2, ..., 12, this gives:

$$T_t = 1580.11 + 33.96t.$$

Step 8: Determine the deseasonalized predictions for quarters (13, 14, 15).
Substitute t = 13, 14, and 15 into the above equation:

$$T_{13} = 1580.11 + (33.96)(13) = 2022$$
$$T_{14} = 1580.11 + (33.96)(14) = 2056$$
$$T_{15} = 1580.11 + (33.96)(15) = 2090$$

Step 9: Take into account the seasonality.
Multiply each deseasonalized prediction by its seasonal factor to give the following forecasts for year 5:

Season 1: (1.178)(2022) = 2382
Season 2: (1.236)(2056) = 2541
Season 3: (.586)(2090) = 1225

PROBLEM 5

Connie Harris, in charge of office supplies at First Capital Mortgage Corp., would like to predict the quantity of paper used in the office photocopying machines per month. She believes that the number of loans originated in a month influence the volume of photocopying performed. She has compiled the following recent monthly data:

Number of Loans Originated in Month	Sheets of Photocopy Paper Used (000's)
25	16
25	13
35	18
40	25
40	21
45	22
50	24
60	25

a) Develop the least-squares estimated regression equation that relates sheets of photocopy paper used to loans originated.

b) Use the regression equation developed in part (a) to forecast the amount of paper used in a month when 65 loan originations are expected.

SOLUTION 5

a) The regression equation is $y = b_0 + b_1x$. The least squares method gives:

Month (i)	y_i	x_i	x_iy_i	x_i^2
1	16	25	400	625
2	13	25	325	625
3	18	35	630	1225
4	25	40	1000	1600
5	21	40	840	1600
6	22	45	990	2025
7	24	50	1200	2500
8	25	60	1500	3600
Totals	164	320	6885	13800

$$b_1 = \frac{\Sigma x_i y_i - (\Sigma x_i \Sigma y_i)/n}{\Sigma x_i^2 - (\Sigma x_i)^2/n}$$

$$= \frac{6885 - (320)(164)/8}{13800 - (320)^2/8}$$

$$= 325/1000 = 0.325$$

$b_0 = y - b_1x = \Sigma y_i/n - b_1(\Sigma x_i/n) = 164/8 - .325(320/8) = 20.5 - 13 = 7.5$
Thus, the estimated regression equation is $y = 7.5 + .325x$

b) The forecast is $y = 7.5 + .325x = 7.5 + .325(65) = 28,625$ sheets.

ANSWERED PROBLEMS

PROBLEM 6

The monthly electricity bill at the Chez Paul Restaurant over the past 12 months has been as follows:

Month	Amount	Month	Amount
Jan	$271.90	Jul	$330.70
Feb	305.70	Aug	300.10
Mar	306.40	Sep	275.50
Apr	297.30	Oct	301.30
May	315.30	Nov	279.40
Jun	297.20	Dec	306.60

Paul is considering using exponential smoothing with $\alpha = .5$ or a four period weighted moving average with weights of .4, .3, .2, and .1 to forecast future electricity costs.

a) Which forecasting technique will give the smallest mean square error?

b) Give next January's forecast for each method.

PROBLEM 7

Sales (in thousands) of the new Thorton Model 506 convection oven over the eight week period since its introduction have been as follows:

Week	Sales
1	18.6
2	21.4
3	25.2
4	22.4
5	24.6
6	19.2
7	21.7
8	23.8

a) Which exponential smoothing model provides better forecasts, one using $\alpha = .6$ or $\alpha = .2$? Compare them using mean squared error.

b) Using the two forecast models in part (a), what are the forecasts for week 9?

PROBLEM 8

Forecast the sales of Jami Michelle skin cream for year 6 given the following quarterly sales (in thousands) over the past five years:

	Year				
Quarter	1	2	3	4	5
1	34	38	43	47	49
2	27	33	37	39	45
3	49	51	60	68	72
4	27	28	29	32	40

PROBLEM 9

Weekly sales of the Weber La Guillotine food processor for the past ten weeks have been:

Week	Sales	Week	Sales
1	980	6	990
2	1040	7	1030
3	1120	8	1260
4	1050	9	1240
5	960	10	1100

a) Determine, on the basis of minimizing the mean square error, whether a three period or four period simple moving average model gives a better forecast for this problem.

b) For each model, forecast sales for week 11.

PROBLEM 10

Four months ago, the Bank Drug Company introduced Jeffrey William brand designer bandages. Advertised using the slogan, "What the best dressed cuts are wearing", weekly sales for this period (in 1000's) have been as follows:

Week	Sales	Week	Sales	Week	Sales
1	12.8	7	20.6	12	23.8
2	14.6	8	18.5	13	25.1
3	15.2	9	19.9	14	24.7
4	16.1	10	23.6	15	26.5
5	15.8	11	24.2	16	28.9
6	17.2				

a) Plot a graph of sales vs. weeks. Does linear trend appear reasonable?

b) Assuming linear trend, forecast sales for weeks 17, 18, 19, and 20.

PROBLEM 11

The number of haircuts performed each day at KwikKuts in the last four weeks are listed below:

Week	Monday	Tuesday	Wednesday	Thursday	Friday
1	122	122	103	133	98
2	127	130	106	137	97
3	126	131	111	151	104
4	135	135	110	146	107

a) Plot the sales data. Do you see both trend and seasonality components in the data?

b) Forecast the number of haircuts to be performed in each workday of week 6.

PROBLEM 12

At a local car dealership the following is a record of sales for the past 12 months:

Month	Sales	Month	Sales
Jan	36	Jul	25
Feb	34	Aug	22
Mar	28	Sep	26
Apr	30	Oct	22
May	27	Nov	21
Jun	24	Dec	19

a) Using the method of least squares, determine a trend line for forecasting future sales.

b) Using your model in part (a), determine how long it will be before zero sales are forecasted.

c) Consider your answer to part (b). What will be the forecasted sales for the month after that? Does this make sense? Comment on the validity of the model. What assumption about the model appears to be in error?

PROBLEM 13

A 24-hour coffee/donut shop makes donuts every eight hours. The manager must forecast donut demand so that the bakers have the fresh ingredients they need. Listed below is the actual number of glazed donuts (in dozens) sold in each of the preceding 13 eight-hour shifts.

Date	Shift	Demand (dozens)
June 3	Day	59
	Evening	47
June 4	Night	35
	Day	64
	Evening	43
June 5	Night	39
	Day	62
	Evening	46
June 6	Night	42
	Day	64
	Evening	50
June 7	Night	40
	Day	69

Forecast the demand for glazed donuts for the three shifts of June 8 and the three shifts of June 9.

PROBLEM 14

Scott Bell Builders would like to predict the total number of labor hours spent framing a house based on the square footage of the house. The following data has been compiled on ten houses recently built.

Square Footage (100's)	Framing Labor Hours	Square Footage (100's)	Framing Labor Hours
20	195	27	225
21	170	29	240
23	220	31	225
23	200	32	275
26	230	35	260

a) Develop the least-squares estimated regression equation that relates framing labor hours to house square footage.

b) Use the regression equation developed in part (a) to predict framing labor hours when the house size is 3350 square feet.

TRUE/FALSE

____ 15. If a time series has a trend component, then one should not use a moving average to forecast.

____ 16. In forecasting with trend and seasonal components using a multiplicative model, one computes moving averages in order to isolate the combined seasonal and irregular components.

____ 17. If the random variability in a time series is great, a high α value should be used to exponentially smooth out the fluctuations.

____ 18. In exponential smoothing, one typically chooses the smoothing constant as that value which minimizes the mean squared error.

____ 19. Forecasting errors are always less using exponential smoothing than a weighted moving average.

____ 20. A forecaster would choose trend projection using the least squares method over exponential smoothing if the data exhibited a trend component.

____ 21. To forecast using the multiplicative model, one must adjust the trend component by the seasonal factor.

____ 22. In a weighted moving average, the most recent occurrence is typically given the least weight.

____ 23. In using the Delphi technique, one attempts to obtain a group consensus.

____ 24. One advantage of exponential smoothing over moving averages is that fewer data points are used in the forecast.

____ 25. An α equal to 0.2 will cause an exponential smoothing forecast to react more quickly to a sudden drop in demand than will an α equal to 0.4.

____ 26. Exponential smoothing with $\alpha = .2$ and a moving average with $n = 5$ put the same weight on the actual value for the current period.

____ 27. The sum of the seasonal indexes should be adjusted, if necessary, to equal 1.

____ 28. With fewer periods in a moving average, it will take longer to adjust to a new level of demand.

____ 29. A causal forecasting method is most effective when demand data exhibit fluctuations caused by seasonal influences.

CHAPTER 17

Markov Processes

KEY CONCEPTS

CONCEPT	ILLUSTRATED PROBLEMS	ANSWERED PROBLEMS
Transition Probabilities	1-4	5-13
Probabilities at Stage n	1,2,3	8,10,11,12,13
Steady State Probabilities	1,2	6,7,8,9,12
Fundamental Matrix	3,4	5,10,11,13
Markov Chain Applications	1-4	5-13

REVIEW

1. Markov process models are useful in studying the evolution of systems over repeated trials or sequential time periods or stages.

2. Transition probabilities govern the manner in which the state of the system changes from one stage to the next. These are often represented in a transition matrix, P.

3. A system has a finite Markov chain with stationary transition probabilities if:
    1) there are a finite number of states,
    2) the transition probabilities remain constant from stage to stage, and
    3) the probability of the process being in a particular state at stage $n+1$ is completely determined by the state of the process at stage n (and not the state at stage $n-1$). This is referred to as the memory-less property.

4. The state probabilities at any stage of the process can be recursively calculated by multiplying the initial state probabilities by the state of the process at stage n.

5. The probability of the system being in a particular state after a large number of stages is called a steady-state probability. Steady-state probabilities are independent of the initial state of the system.

6. Steady state probabilities can be found by solving the system of equations $\Pi P = \Pi$ together with the condition for probabilities that $\Sigma \pi_i = 1$. Here the matrix P is the transition probability matrix and the vector Π is the vector of steady state probabilities.

8. If a Markov chain has both absorbing and non-absorbing states, the states may be rearranged so that the transition matrix can be written as the following composition of <u>four</u> <u>submatrices</u>: *I*, *0*, *R*, and *Q*:

$$\begin{bmatrix} I & O \\ R & Q \end{bmatrix}$$

where:
  I = an identity matrix indicating one always remains in an absorbing state once it is reached,
  0 = a zero matrix representing 0 probability of transitioning from the absorbing states to the non-absorbing states,
  R = the transition probabilities from the non-absorbing states to the absorbing states, and
  Q = the transition probabilities between the non-absorbing states.

9. The <u>fundamental matrix</u>, *N*, is the inverse of the difference between the identity matrix and the *Q* matrix, i.e.

$$N = (I - Q)^{-1}$$

10. The <u>NR matrix</u>, the product of the fundamental matrix and the *R* matrix, gives the probabilities of eventually moving from each non-absorbing state to each absorbing state. Multiplying any vector of initial non-absorbing state probabilities by *NR* gives the vector of probabilities for the process eventually reaching each of the absorbing states. Such computations enable economic analyses of systems and policies.

FLOW CHART OF
MARKOV PROCESS CALCULATIONS

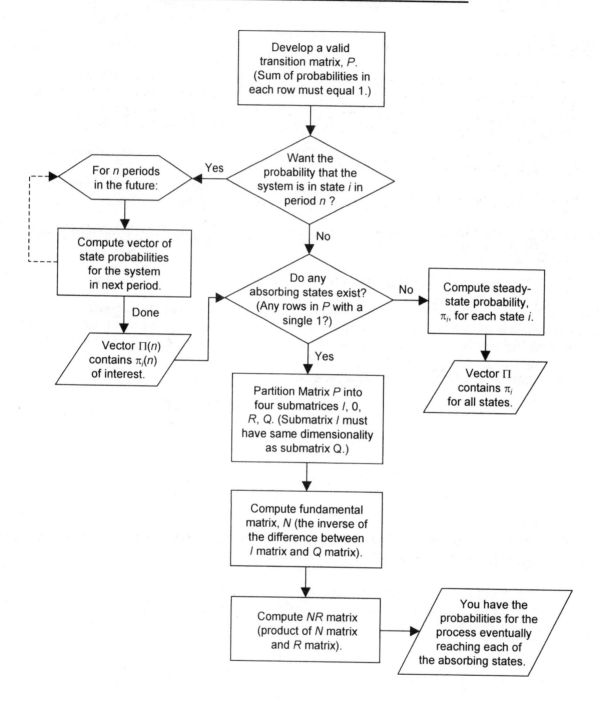

ILLUSTRATED PROBLEMS

PROBLEM 1

Henry, a persistent salesman, calls North's Hardware Store once a week hoping to speak with the store's buying agent, Shirley. If Shirley does not accept Henry's call this week, the probability she will do the same next week is .35. On the other hand, if she accepts Henry's call this week, the probability she will not do so next week is .20.

a) Construct the transition matrix for this problem.

b) How many times per year can Henry expect to talk to Shirley?

c) What is the probability Shirley will accept Henry's next two calls if she does not accept his call this week?

d) What is the probability of Shirley accepting exactly one of Henry's next two calls if she accepts his call this week?

SOLUTION 1

a) The transition matrix is:

		Next Week's Call	
		Refuses	Accepts
This Week's Call	Refuses	.35	.65
	Accepts	.20	.80

b) To find the expected number of accepted calls per year, find the long-run probability of a call being accepted and multiply it by 52 weeks.

Let π_1 = the long run proportion of refused calls

π_2 = the long run proportion of accepted calls

Then,

$$[\pi_1 \ \pi_2]\begin{bmatrix} .35 & .65 \\ .20 & .80 \end{bmatrix} = [\pi_1 \ \pi_2]$$

Thus,

$$.35\pi_1 + .20\pi_2 = \pi_1 \quad (1)$$
$$.65\pi_1 + .80\pi_2 = \pi_2 \quad (2)$$

and,

$$\pi_1 + \pi_2 = 1 \quad (3)$$

Solving using equations (2) and (3), (equation 1 is redundant), substitute $\pi_1 = 1 - \pi_2$ into (2) to give:

$$.65(1 - \pi_2) + .80\pi_2 = \pi_2$$

This gives $\pi_2 = .76471$. Substituting back into (3) gives $\pi_1 = .23529$.

Thus the expected number of accepted calls per year is $(.76471)(52) = 39.76$ or about 40.

c) The tree diagram for this problem is:

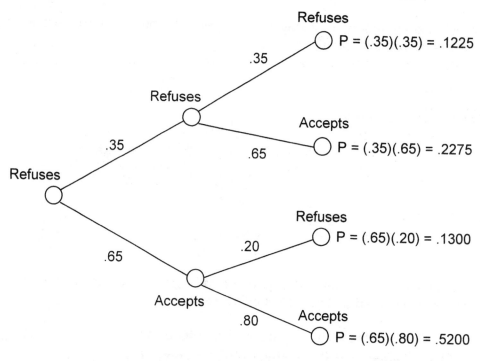

Hence, the probability the next two calls are accepted given that this week's call is refused is $.65(.80) = .52$.

d) The probability of exactly one of the next two calls being accepted if this week's call is accepted can be found by adding the probabilities of (accept next week and refuse the following week) and (refuse next week and accept the following week) = $.13 + .16 = .29$.

PROBLEM 2

Joe Ferris, a stock trader at the brokerage firm of Smith, Jones, Johnson, and Thomas, Inc. has noticed that price changes in the shares of Dollar Department Stores at each trade are dependent upon the previous trade's price change. His observations can be summarized by the following transition matrix.

		Next Price Change		
		+1/8	0	-1/8
	+1/8	.7	.2	.1
Current Price Change	0	.3	.4	.3
	-1/8	.2	.1	.7

a) What is the long-run average change in the value of a share of Dollar Department Stores' stock per trade?

b) If the shares of Dollar Department Stores are currently traded at $18 and the last trade was at 17 7/8, what is the probability the shares will sell at 18 in two trades?

SOLUTION 2

a) Let, p_1 = the long-run probability of a +1/8 stock price change

p_2 = the long-run probability of a 0 stock price change

p_3 = the long-run probability of a -1/8 stock price change

To determine the long-run (steady state) probabilities, solve:

$$[\pi_1 \ \pi_2 \ \pi_3] \begin{bmatrix} .7 & .2 & .1 \\ .3 & .4 & .3 \\ .2 & .1 & .7 \end{bmatrix} = [\pi_1 \ \pi_2 \ \pi_3]$$

This gives the following set of equations

$$.7\pi_1 + .3\pi_2 + .2\pi_3 = \pi_1 \quad (1)$$
$$.2\pi_1 + .4\pi_2 + .1\pi_3 = \pi_2 \quad (2)$$
$$.1\pi_1 + .3\pi_2 + .7\pi_3 = \pi_3 \quad (3)$$
$$\pi_1 + \pi_2 + \pi_3 = 1 \quad (4)$$

Note, that any one of (1), (2) or (3) can be considered redundant. Delete (1) and solve (2), (3), and (4). From (4) substitute $\pi_1 = 1 - \pi_2 - \pi_3$. This leaves the following two equations in two unknowns:

$$.2(1 - \pi_2 - \pi_3) + .4\pi_2 + .1\pi_3 = \pi_2$$

and $\quad .1(1 - \pi_2 - \pi_3) + .3\pi_2 + .7\pi_3 = \pi_3$

or $\qquad\qquad .8\pi_2 + .1\pi_3 = .2$

and $\qquad\qquad -.2\pi_2 + .4\pi_3 = .1$

Solving these two gives $\pi_2 = 7/34$ and $\pi_3 = 12/34$. Substituting into (4) gives $\pi_1 = 15/34$. Hence, the long run average change per trade is:

$$(15/34)(1/8) + (7/34)(0) + (12/34)(-1/8) = \$.011.$$

b) The fact that the last trade was 17 7/8 means that the last price change was +1/8. The tree diagram for the problem is:

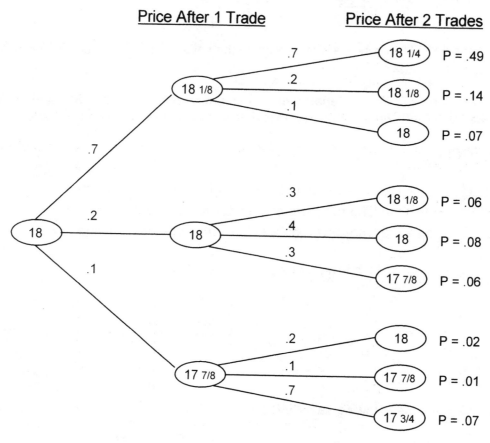

The probability that the stock will sell at 18 after 2 trades is .07 + .08 + .02 = .17.

PROBLEM 3

Joe Isley, the owner of Big I HiFi, believes that the store's inventory can be modeled as a Markov process. If items are either classified as in stock, out of stock, discontinued from stock or put on clearance sale, then the following transition matrix has been estimated:

		Next Month			
		In Stock	Out of Stock	Discontinued from Stock	Put On Clearance Sale
This Month	In Stock	.67	.20	.05	.08
	Out of Stock	.48	.42	.10	0
	Discontinued	0	0	1	0
	Clearance Sale	0	0	0	1

a) Rewrite the transition matrix for the problem in the form of I, O, R, and Q submatrices.

b) Compute the fundamental matrix for this problem.

c) What is the probability of an item currently in stock being out of stock in two months?

d) What is the probability of an item currently out of stock eventually being discontinued from stock?

SOLUTION 3

a) Rearranging the states gives:

		Next Month			
		Discontinued	Clearance	In Stock	Out Of Stock
This Month	Discontinued	1	0	0	0
	Clearance	0	1	0	0
	In Stock	.05	.08	.67	.20
	Out of Stock	.10	0	.48	.42

Note,
$$R = \begin{bmatrix} .05 & .08 \\ .10 & 0 \end{bmatrix} \quad \text{and} \quad Q = \begin{bmatrix} .67 & .20 \\ .48 & .42 \end{bmatrix}$$

b)

$$N = (I - Q)^{-1} = \begin{bmatrix} .33 & -.20 \\ -.48 & .58 \end{bmatrix}^{-1}$$

To compute $(I - Q)^{-1}$, first calculate its determinant,

$$d = a_{11}a_{22} - a_{21}a_{12} = (.33)(.58) - (-.48)(-.20) = .0954$$

Then,

$$N = \begin{bmatrix} (.58/.0954) & (.20/.0954) \\ (.48/.0954) & (.33/.0954) \end{bmatrix} = \begin{bmatrix} 6.08 & 2.10 \\ 5.03 & 3.46 \end{bmatrix}$$

c) The tree diagram is:

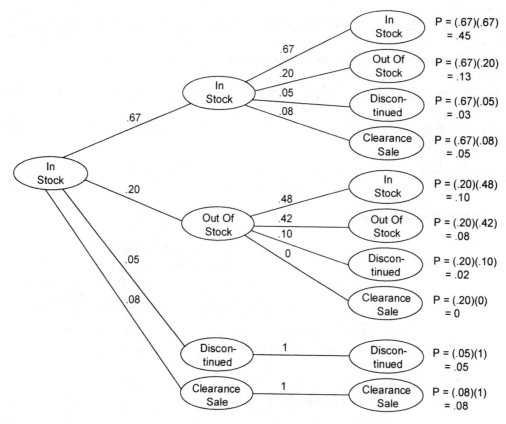

Therefore, the probability of an item currently in stock being out of stock in two months is .13 + .08 = .21.

d) The probability of eventually moving into each of the absorbing states from the nonabsorbing states is given by:

$$NR = \begin{bmatrix} 6.08 & 2.10 \\ 5.03 & 3.46 \end{bmatrix} \times \begin{bmatrix} .05 & .08 \\ .10 & 0 \end{bmatrix}$$

$$= \begin{array}{c} \text{In Stock} \\ \\ \text{Out Of Stock} \end{array} \begin{array}{cc} \text{Discontinued} & \text{Clearance Sale} \\ \begin{bmatrix} .51 & .49 \\ \\ .60 & .40 \end{bmatrix} \end{array}$$

Hence, the probability of an item currently out of stock eventually being discontinued is .60.

NOTE: If there is more than one absorbing state, a steady-state condition independent of initial state conditions does not exist. For example, in the above problem we cannot state what percentage of all inventory items eventually is discontinued or what percentage is put on clearance.

PROBLEM 4

The vice president of personnel at Jetair Aerospace has noticed that yearly shifts in personnel can be modeled by a Markov process. The transition matrix is:

		Next Year				
		Same Position	Promotion	Retire	Quit	Fired
	Same Position	.55	.10	.05	.20	.10
	Promotion	.70	.20	0	.10	0
Current Year	Retire	0	0	1	0	0
	Quit	0	0	0	1	0
	Fired	0	0	0	0	1

a) Write the transition matrix in the form of I, O, R, and Q submatrices.:

b) Compute the fundamental matrix, N, for this problem.

c) What is the probability of an employee who was just promoted eventually retiring? Quitting? Being fired?

SOLUTION 4

a) Because the identity matrix must be in the upper right corner, rewrite the transition matrix as follows:

<u>Next Year</u>

		Retire	Quit	Fired	Same	Promotion
	Retire	1	0	0	0	0
	Quit	0	1	0	0	0
<u>Current Year</u>	Fired	0	0	1	0	0
	Same	.05	.20	.10	.55	.10
	Promotion	0	.10	0	.70	.20

Note,

$$Q = \begin{bmatrix} .55 & .10 \\ .70 & .20 \end{bmatrix} \qquad R = \begin{bmatrix} .05 & .20 & .10 \\ 0 & .10 & 0 \end{bmatrix}$$

b)

$$N = (I - Q)^{-1} = \begin{bmatrix} 1 & 0 \\ 0 & 1 \end{bmatrix} - \begin{bmatrix} .55 & .10 \\ .70 & .20 \end{bmatrix}^{-1} = \begin{bmatrix} .45 & -.10 \\ -.70 & .80 \end{bmatrix}^{-1}$$

The determinant, $d = a_{11}a_{22} - a_{21}a_{12} = (.45)(.80) - (-.70)(-.10) = .29$

Thus,

$$N = \begin{bmatrix} .80/.29 & .10/.29 \\ .70/.29 & .45/.29 \end{bmatrix} = \begin{bmatrix} 2.76 & .34 \\ 2.41 & 1.55 \end{bmatrix}$$

c) The probabilities of eventually moving to the absorbing states from the nonabsorbing states are given by:

$$NR = \begin{bmatrix} 2.76 & .34 \\ 2.41 & 1.55 \end{bmatrix} \times \begin{bmatrix} .05 & .20 & .10 \\ 0 & .10 & 0 \end{bmatrix}$$

$$= \begin{array}{c} \\ \text{Same} \\ \\ \text{Promotion} \end{array} \begin{array}{ccc} \text{Retire} & \text{Quit} & \text{Fired} \\ \begin{bmatrix} .14 & .59 & .28 \\ .12 & .64 & .24 \end{bmatrix} \end{array}$$

The probability of someone just being promoted eventually being in one of the absorbing states is given by the bottom row of this probability matrix. The answers are therefore:

Eventually Retiring   =   .12
Eventually Quitting   =   .64
Eventually Being Fired   =   .24

ANSWERED PROBLEMS

PROBLEM 5

Rent-To-Keep rents household furnishings by the month. At the end of a rental month a customer can: a) rent the item for another month, b) buy the item, or c) return the item. The matrix below describes the month-to-month transition probabilities for 32-inch stereo televisions the shop stocks.

		Next Month		
		Rent	Buy	Return
	Rent	.72	.10	.18
This Month	Buy	0	1	0
	Return	0	0	1

What is the probability that a customer who rented a TV this month will eventually buy it?

PROBLEM 6

The evening television news broadcast that individuals view on one evening is influenced by which broadcast they viewed previously. An executive at the C network has determined the following transition probability matrix describing this phenomenon.

		Next Network News Watched		
		A	C	N
Current	A	.80	.12	.08
Network				
News	C	.08	.85	.07
Watched				
	N	.08	.09	.83

a) Which network has the most loyal viewers?

b) What are the three networks' long-run market shares?

c) Suppose each of the three networks earns $1,250 in daily profit from advertising revenue for each 1,000,000 viewers it has. If on the average 40,000,000 people watch the evening television news, compute the long run average daily profit each network generates from its evening news broadcast.

PROBLEM 7

On any particular day an individual can take one of two routes to work. Route A has a 25% chance of being congested, whereas route B has a 40% chance of being congested.
The probability of the individual taking a particular route depends on his previous day's experience. If one day he takes route A and it is not congested, he will take route A again the next day with probability .8. If it is congested, he will take route B the next day with probability .7.
On the other hand, if on a day he takes route B and it is not congested, he will take route B again the next day with probability .9. Similarly if route B is congested, he will take route A the next day with probability .6.

a) Construct the transition matrix for this problem. (HINT: There are 4 states corresponding to the route taken and the congestion. The transition probabilities are products of the independent probabilities of congestion and next day choice.)

b) What is the long-run proportion of time that route A is taken?

PROBLEM 8

Mark is a specialist at repairing large metal-cutting machines that use laser technology. His repair territory consists of the cities of Austin, San Antonio, and Houston. His day-to-day repair assignment locations can be modeled as a Markov process. The transition matrix is as follows:

		Next Day's Location		
		Austin	San Antonio	Houston
This	Austin	.35	.35	.30
Day's	San Antonio	.25	.50	.25
Location	Houston	.10	.20	.70

a) Determine the probability of Mark working the next three days in Houston (where his girlfriend lives) if today he is working in Austin.

b) Find the long-run proportions of time Mark will work in each of the three cities.

PROBLEM 9

There are currently only two fast food restaurants in the Main Street area, Burger Prince and Feisty Fowl. The probability of a customer eating at one restaurant is dependent upon which restaurant he ate at previously. The probabilities can be summarized by the following transition matrix.

		Next Restaurant	
		Burger Prince	Feisty Fowl
Last	Burger Prince	.7	.3
Restaurant	Feisty Fowl	.4	.6

Colonel Mustard's Hot Dogs is planning to open a new restaurant next to Burger Prince. Burger Prince's management estimates the new restaurant will result in the transition matrix below. By how much will the long-run market share of Burger Prince and Feisty Fowl change with the opening of Colonel Mustard's.

		Next Restaurant		
		Burger Prince	Feisty Fowl	Colonel Mustard's
Last Restaurant	Burger Prince	.5	.3	.2
	Feisty Fowl	.3	.5	.2
	Col. Mustard's	.3	.3	.4

PROBLEM 10

Precision Craft, Inc. manufactures ornate pedestal sinks. On any day, the status of a given sink is either: a) somewhere in the normal manufacturing process, b) being reworked because of a detected flaw, c) finished successfully, or d) scrapped because a flaw could not be corrected. The transition matrix is:

		Tomorrow's Status			
		In-Process	Rework	Finished	Scrapped
Today's	In-Process	.30	.15	.50	.05
Status	Rework	.40	.10	.30	.20
	Finished	0	0	1	0
	Scrapped	0	0	0	1

a) What is the probability of a sink eventually being finished if it is currently in process?

b) What is the probability of a sink eventually being scrapped if it is currently in rework?

c) What is the probability that a sink currently in rework will have a "finished" status either tomorrow or the next day? (HINT: there are three ways this can happen.)

PROBLEM 11

Southside College has modeled its student loan program as a Markov process. Each year a student with a prior loan borrows again, defers repayment for a year, makes payments, pays the loan balance in full, or defaults on repayment. The transition matrix is as follows:

		Next Year				
		Borrowing	Deferring	Paying	Paid-Off	Default
	Borrowing	.60	.30	0	.10	0
	Deferring	.15	0	.65	.10	.10
This Year	Paying	0	0	.75	.15	.10
	Paid-Off	0	0	0	1	0
	Defaulted	0	0	0	0	1

a) If currently a student is making payments on his/her loan, what is the probability the loan will be paid in full eventually?

b) Is the probability of eventually defaulting greater for a student who is currently borrowing more or a student who is making payments?

c) What is the probability a student who is borrowing this year will repay the loan balance in full in two years or less?

PROBLEM 12

Three airlines compete on the route between New York and Los Angeles. Stanton Marketing has performed an analysis of first class business travelers to determine their airline choice. Stanton has modeled this choice as a Markov process and has determined the following transition probabilities.

		Next Airline		
		A	B	C
	A	.50	.30	.20
Last Airline	B	.30	.45	.25
	C	.10	.35	.55

a) Determine the long-run share for each of the three airlines.

b) Determine the probability of a passenger flying on three different airlines on his next three flights if his next flight is on: (1) A   (2) B   (3) C

c) The weekly profit of each airline is estimated to be $(y - .28)$ millions of dollars, where y is the airline's market share of the New York - Los Angeles traffic. Airline A is considering an advertising campaign that it believes will result in new business. Stanton Marketing has projected that such a campaign will result in the following transition probability matrix.

		Next Airline		
		A	B	C
	A	.50	.25	.25
Last Airline	B	.35	.45	.20
	C	.15	.30	.55

What is the maximum that should be spent per week on this advertising campaign?

PROBLEM 13

A recent study done by an economist for the Small Business Administration investigated failures of small business. Failures were either classified as due to poor financing, poor management, or a poor product. The failure rates differed for new businesses (under one year old) versus established businesses (over one year old.)

As the result of the economist's study, the following probabilities were determined. For new businesses the probability of failure due to financing was .15, due to management .20, and due to product .05. The corresponding probabilities for established businesses were .10, .06, and .03 respectively.

a) Determine a five-state Markov Chain transition matrix with states for new, established, and each of the three failure states. Write it in the form of I, O, R, and Q submatrices.

b) Determine the probability that a new business will survive during the next three years.

c) What proportion of new businesses eventually fail due to:
   (1) poor financing?   (2) poor management?   (3) poor product?

TRUE/FALSE

___ 14. The sum of the probabilities in a transition matrix equals the number of rows in the matrix.

___ 15. All Markov chains have steady-state probabilities.

___ 16. If the initial state probability distribution equals the Markov chain's steady-state probability distribution then all states will have this probability distribution.

___ 17. The steady-state probability distribution is a function of the initial state probability distribution.

___ 18. All Markov chain transition matrices have the same number of rows as columns.

___ 19. The fundamental matrix is used to calculate the probability of the process moving into each absorbing state.

___ 20. A state, i, is an absorbing state if, when $i = j$, $p_{ij} = 1$.

___ 21. A Markov chain cannot consist of all absorbing states.

___ 22. If a Markov chain has at least one absorbing state, steady-state probabilities cannot be calculated.

___ 23. In a Markov chain, p_{ij} must equal p_{ji}.

___ 24. Transition probabilities are joint probabilities.

___ 25. The sum of the "from" probabilities in any "to" column in a transition matrix must equal 1.

___ 26. The probability p_{ij}, when $i = j$, is a steady-state probability.

___ 27. The "memory-less" property of first-order Markov processes refers to not needing to know the state of the system prior to the current state in order to predict the future state.

___ 28. State j is an absorbing state if $p_{ij} = 1$.

CHAPTER 18

Dynamic Programming

KEY CONCEPTS

CONCEPT	ILLUSTRATED PROBLEMS	ANSWERED PROBLEMS
Formulations Using Dynamic Programming	2,3,4	5,6,8,9,10,11,12
Shortest Route Problems	1	7,10
Knapsack Problems	3	5,8,9
Inventory Control Problems	4	6,11,12

REVIEW

1. Dynamic programming is an approach to problem solving which permits decomposing of the original problem into a series of several smaller sub-problems.

2. To successfully apply dynamic programming, the original problem must be viewed as a multistage decision problem. Defining the stages is sometimes obvious, but at other times this requires subtle reasoning.

3. Generally, a dynamic programming problem is solved by starting at the final stage and working backwards to the initial stage. This is called backward recursion.

4. At each stage, n, of the dynamic program, there is a state variable, x_n, and an optimal decision variable, d_n. One way to identify the data needed to be included in the state variable is to imagine being called in as a consultant to help solve the problem at a particular stage. The information one would have to know to finish solving the problem is the state information.

5. For each value of x_n and d_n at stage n, there is a return function value, $r_n(x_n, d_n)$.

6. The output of the process at stage n is x_{n-1}, the state variable for stage n-1. It is calculated by a stage transformation function, $t_n(x_n, d_n)$.

7. The optimal value function, $f_n(x_n)$, is the cumulative return starting at stage n in state x_n and proceeding to stage 1 under an optimal policy (strategy).

8. The power of dynamic programming is that one need solve only a small portion of all sub-problems. This is due to Bellman's <u>principle of optimality.</u> It states that regardless of what decisions were made at previous stages, if the decision to be made at stage n is to be part of an overall optimal solution, then the decision made at stage n must be optimal for all remaining stages.

9. The following <u>recursion relation</u> can be used to operationalize the principle of optimality:

$$f_n(x_n) = \max_{d_n} \{r_n(x_n,d_n) + f_{n-1}(t_n(x_n,d_n))\}$$

10. A problem is solved beginning at stage 0 with the <u>boundary condition</u> $f_0(x_0) = 0$, and working backwards to the last stage, N.

11. Three classes of problems which conveniently lend themselves to dynamic programming are: (1) the <u>shortest route problem</u>, (2) the <u>knapsack or cargo loading problem</u>, and (3) <u>production and inventory control problems</u>.

12. In solving a <u>shortest route problem</u> using dynamic programming, one should consider the network as a series of stages with a unique subset of nodes corresponding to each stage. The state variables correspond to the different nodes at each stage.

13. The <u>knapsack problem</u> seeks to determine the optimal number of each of N items (which must not be fractional) to select in order to maximize profit subject to an overall capacity constraint. In solving a knapsack problem using dynamic programming, the stages correspond to the different items being placed into a knapsack. The state variables correspond to the capacity available at the stage.

14. In <u>production and inventory control problems</u>, the stages correspond to time periods and the state variables generally will refer to the amounts of inventory on hand at the beginning of each stage.

FLOW CHART FOR
DYNAMIC PROGRAMMING SOLUTION PROCESS

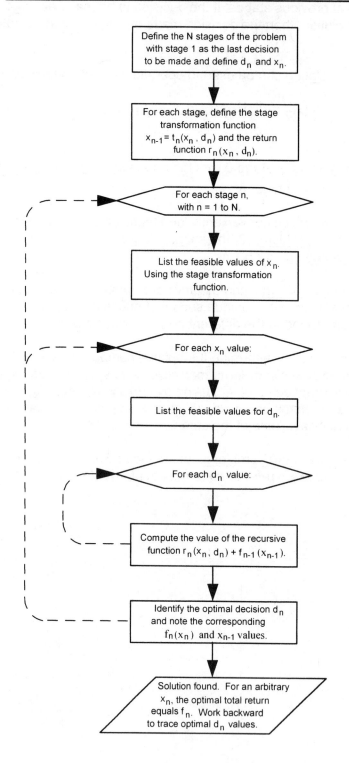

ILLUSTRATED PROBLEMS

PROBLEM 1

Use dynamic programming to determine the shortest path(s) from node 1 to node 15 assuming travel is only permitted from left to right in the network.

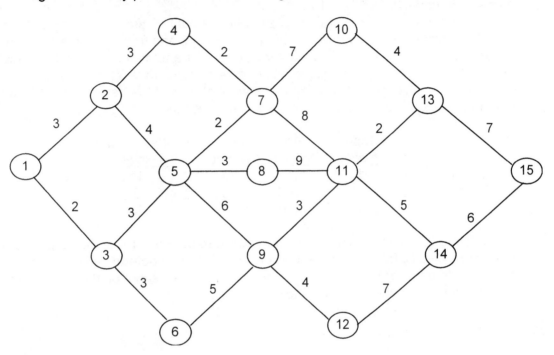

SOLUTION 1

This problem can be viewed as a six stage decision problem. Working backward through the network, let stage 1 correspond to nodes 13 and 14; stage 2 correspond to nodes 10, 11, and 12; stage 3 correspond to nodes 7, 8, and 9; stage 4 correspond to nodes 4, 5, and 6; stage 5 correspond to nodes 2 and 3; and stage 6 correspond to node 1.

At each stage a decision will be made as to how to move from the particular state to the final state (node 15) in the shortest possible distance.

Stage 1

At stage 1 there are two states: nodes 13 and 14. Because there is no choice of how to reach node 15 from either of these nodes, each decision is automatic. This is summarized as:

Input Nodes	Arc Decision	Shortest Distance
13	13-15	7
14	14-15	6

In the table, column 1 gives the particular states of this stage, column 2 gives the optimal arc decision, and column 3 gives the shortest distance to reach the final node. The information in this third column is used at the next stage and the information in the second column is used to determine the optimal strategy.

Stage 2

At stage 2 there are three states: nodes 10, 11, and 12. From nodes 10 and 12 there is no decision required to determine the shortest path. However a decision must be made at node 11.

From node 11 there are two possibilities: travel on arc 11-13 to node 13 or on arc 11-14 to node 14. The distance of arc 11-13 is 2 and from the table at stage 1, the distance from node 13 to node 15 is 7 (column 3) for a total of 9. Similarly the distance of arc 11-14 is 5 and the distance from node 14 to node 15 is 6 for a total of 11. Since 9 is less than 11, the optimal decision if one were at node 11 is travel on arc 11-13 to reach node 13. These analyses can be summarized as:

Input Nodes	Arc Decision	Output Nodes	Shortest Distance To Node 15
10	10-13	13	11
11	11-13	13	9
12	12-14	14	13

Note that a new column has been added to the table to list the output node. For this problem this information is redundant since it can be determined by the arc decision. In many problems, however, the output node cannot be determined from the arc decision easily and therefore should be listed.

Stage 3

At stage 3 a decision must be made at nodes 7 and 9 regarding the best route. From node 7 one could either move to node 10 or node 11. The distance from node 7 to node 10 is 7 and from stage 2, the distance from node 7 to 15 (column 4) is 11 for a total of 18. Similarly, the total distance from node 7, taking the 7-11 arc, can be determined to be 17. Hence, the best decision from node 7 is to travel 7-11. The complete results for stage 3 are summarized by:

Input Nodes	Arc Decision	Output Nodes	Shortest Distance To Node 15
7	7-11	11	17
8	8-11	11	18
9	9-11	11	12

Writing the shortest distance to node 15 above each node calculated thus far gives:

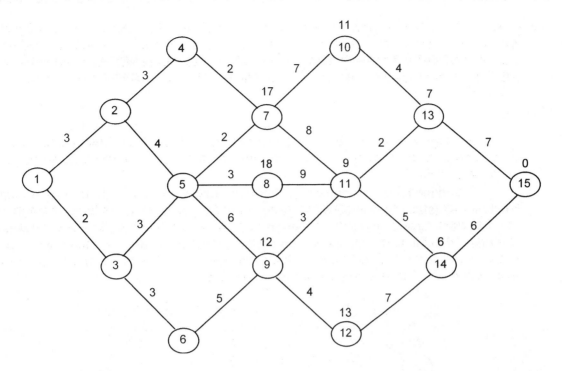

Stage 4

At stage 4, there are three possible arcs to travel on from node 5. The best decision is found in a similar manner to previous stages by calculating the minimum of (the arc distance from 5) + (the shortest distance to node 15 from the resulting node). This equals minimum of {(2 + 17), (3 + 18), (6 + 12)} = 18 by traveling on the arc 5-9. Note there are no comparisons for nodes 4 and 6.

Summarizing the results for stage 4,

Input Nodes	Arc Decision	Output Nodes	Shortest Distance To Node 15
4	4-7	7	19
5	5-9	9	18
6	6-9	9	17

Stage 5

At stage 5 decisions must be made at both nodes 2 and 3. Node 2: Min {(3 + (distance from node 4)), (4 + (distance from node 5))} = Min {(3 + 19), (4 + 18)}. Both give 22. Similarly, for node 3: Min {(3 + 18), (3 + 17)} = 20.

Summarizing,

Input Nodes	Arc Decision	Output Nodes	Shortest Distance To Node 15
2	2-4 or 2-5	2 or 5	22
3	3-6	6	20

Stage 6

At stage 6 a decision must be made to travel on 1-2 or 1-3. Choose the minimum {(3 + 22), (2 + 20)} = 22. Hence, the minimum distance from node 1 to node 15 is 22.

Input Nodes	Arc Decision	Output Nodes	Shortest Distance To Node 15
1	1-3	3	22

Working forwards through the network (backwards through the stages) the best route is 1-3 (stage 6), then 3-6 (stage 5), then 6-9 (stage 4), then 9-11 (stage 3), then 11-13 (stage 2) and finally 13-15 (stage 1) or 1-3-6-9-11-13-15. The final network, including the shortest distance to node 15 at each node is given on the next page.

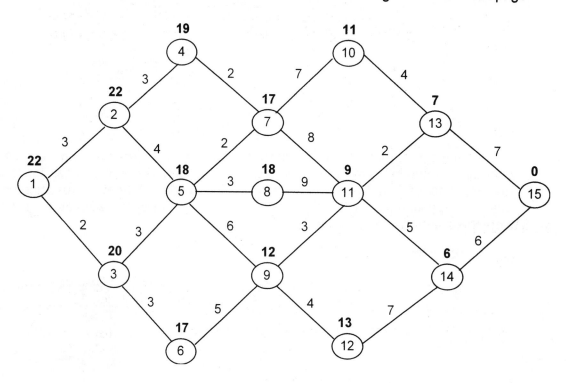

PROBLEM 2

Dollar Department Stores has four operating divisions: Dollar Stores, Wenthrope Jewelry, Fidelity Insurance, and the newly acquired Burger Prince Restaurants. Dollar management is currently planning its yearly budget and has decided to allocate $20,000,000 to the four divisions.

The four division vice presidents have prepared various requests for funds together with the estimated future discounted, after tax profitability to Dollar. These amounts (in $1,000,000's) are summarized in the table below. Note that the maximum requests from the divisions vary. If each division must receive at least $3,000,000 in funds, how should the money be allocated to each division to maximize Dollar's total future discounted, after tax profitability?

	Future Discounted After-Tax Profitability of Requests			
Request	Dollar Stores	Wenthrope Jewelry	Fidelity Insurance	Burger Prince Restaurants
3	5	7	2	7
4	7	10	5	10
5	8	13	10	15
6	11	15	14	19
7	13	18	17	23
8	14	22	20	25
9	16	--	23	29
10	18	--	26	--
11	--	--	28	--

SOLUTION 2

Stage 1

At stage 1, we consider allocating to Dollar stores only. Letting x_1 = the amount allocated to stage 1, and $f_1(x_1)$ be the maximum return of allocating to stages 1 to 1, and $d_1{}^*$ be the optimal allocation to stage 1 we have:

x_1	$f_1(x_1)$	$d_1{}^*$
0-2	$-\infty$	---
3	5	3
4	7	4
5	8	5
6	11	6
7	13	7
8	14	8
9	16	9
10-20	18	10

Stage 2

At stage 2 consider allocation to both Wenthrope Jewelry and Dollar Stores;

$ avail. x_2	d_2 to Wenthrope 3	4	5	6	7	8	d_2^*	$f_2(x_2)$	$x_2 - d_2^*$ = x_1
0-5								-∞	
6	**12**	-∞	-∞	-∞			3	12	3
7	14	**15**	-∞	-∞	-∞		4	15	3
8	15	17	**18**	-∞	-∞	-∞	5	18	3
9	18	18	**20**	**20**	-∞	-∞	5,6	20	4,3
10	20	21	21	22	**23**	-∞	7	23	3
11	21	23	24	23	25	**27**	8	27	3
12	23	24	26	26	26	**29**	8	29	4
13	25	26	27	28	29	**30**	8	30	5
14	25	28	29	29	31	**33**	8	33	6
15	25	28	31	31	32	**35**	8	35	7
16	25	28	31	33	34	**36**	8	36	8
17	25	28	31	33	36	**38**	8	38	9
18-20	25	28	31	33	36	**40**	8	40	10

(Sample Calculation: With $x_2 = \$11$, if $d_2 = \$7$ is allocated to Wenthrope there is a return of 18. This leaves (11-7) = \$4 to be allocated to stage 1. Look at chart for stage 1. This value is a return of 7, for a total of 7 + 18 = 25, which is the corresponding number in the $x_2 = 11$ row, $d_2 = 7$ column.)

Stage 3

At this stage consider allocation of funds to Fidelity Insurance, Wenthrope Jewelry, and Dollar Stores.

$ avail. x_3	d_3 to Fidelity Insurance 3	4	5	6	7	8	9	10	11	d_3^*	$f_3(x_3)$	$x_3-d_3^*$ = x_2
0-8											-∞	
9	**14**	-∞	-∞	-∞	-∞	-∞				3	14	6
10	**17**	**17**	-∞	-∞	-∞	-∞	-∞	-∞		3,4	17	7,6
11	20	20	**22**	-∞	-∞	-∞	-∞	-∞	-∞	5	22	6
12	22	23	25	**26**	-∞	-∞	-∞	-∞	-∞	6	26	6
13	25	25	28	**29**	**29**	-∞	-∞	-∞	-∞	6,7	29	7,6
14	29	28	30	**32**	**32**	**32**	-∞	-∞	-∞	6,7,8	32	8,7,6
15	31	32	33	34	**35**	**35**	**35**	-∞	-∞	7,8,9	35	8,7,6
16	32	34	37	37	37	**38**	**38**	**38**	-∞	8,9,10	38	8,7,6
17	35	35	39	**41**	40	40	**41**	**41**	40	6,9,10	41	11,8,7
18	37	38	40	43	**44**	43	43	**44**	43	7,10	44	11,8
19	38	40	43	44	46	**47**	46	46	46	8	47	11
20	40	41	45	47	47	49	**50**	49	48	9	50	11

Stage 4

At stage 4 consider allocating funds to all four divisions. However, we know that we only have to consider allocating $x_4 = \$20$.

$ avail. x_4	d_4 to Burger Prince							d_4^*	$f_4(x_4)$	$x_4-d_4^*$ $= x_3$
	3	4	5	6	7	8	9			
20	48	48	50	51	**52**	51	51	7	52	13

The optimal discounted after tax profitability is $52,000,000. To see how this is determined, retrace the decisions through the various stages.

The optimal allocation for stage 4 is $d_4^* = 7$, leaving $x_3 = 13$ for stages 1 to 3. The optimal allocation at stage 3 of 13 is $d_3^* = 6$ or $d_3^* = 7$. This leaves $x_2 = 7$ or 6 respectively for stages 1 to 2. The optimal allocation at stage 2 of 7 is $d_2^* = 4$ and of 6 is $d_2^* = 3$. In either case this leaves 3 for stage 1. Thus the following are optimal allocations:

	Give	Return		Give	Return
Burger Prince	7	23		7	23
Fidelity Insurance	6	14	or	7	17
Wenthrope Jewelry	4	10		3	7
Dollar Stores	3	5		3	5
	Total	52			52

PROBLEM 3

The Dreyfus Advertising Agency is currently handling the Super-Cola account. Super-Cola has earmarked $15,000 for next month's advertising of Burple powdered soft drink.

Dreyfus has determined a value, in terms of long term profit, for each form of advertising. Also, Super-Cola has placed restrictions on the maximum number of times a particular advertising medium can be used. This is summarized below. How should Dreyfus spend the $15,000 to maximize the total value rating?

Medium	Cost Per Use	Value Per Use	Maximum # of Uses
TV	$ 7,000	11	2
Radio	$ 2,000	5	3
Newspaper	$ 1,000	2	6
Burple Challenge	$12,000	18	1
Magazine	$ 4,000	9	2

SOLUTION 3

This problem is a knapsack problem. The different advertising media correspond to the items going into the knapsack. As there are five different media, the problem will have five stages. At stage 1, determine the number of TV ads to buy, at stage 2, determine the number of radio ads to buy, etc.

d_n = the number of times advertising medium n is used

x_n = the number of advertising dollars (in $1,000's) remaining at stage n to allocate to media 1 through n

The stage transformation functions for this problem give the amount of money remaining to allocate the previous stages after a certain number of ads of type n are selected at stage n. Specifically,

$$\text{Stage 5: } x_4 = t_5(x_5, d_5) = x_5 - 4d_5$$
$$\text{Stage 4: } x_3 = t_4(x_4, d_4) = x_4 - 12d_4$$
$$\text{Stage 3: } x_2 = t_3(x_3, d_3) = x_3 - d_3$$
$$\text{Stage 2: } x_1 = t_2(x_2, d_2) = x_2 - 2d_2$$
$$\text{Stage 1: } x_0 = t_1(x_1, d_1) = x_1 - 7d_1$$

The return function at each stage gives the return for only allocating d_n ads to medium n. Specifically,

$$\text{Stage 5: } r_5(x_5, d_5) = 9d_5$$
$$\text{Stage 4: } r_4(x_4, d_4) = 18d_4$$
$$\text{Stage 3: } r_3(x_3, d_3) = 2d_3$$
$$\text{Stage 2: } r_2(x_2, d_2) = 5d_2$$
$$\text{Stage 1: } r_1(x_1, d_1) = 11d_1$$

Stage 1

At stage 1, compute the value associated with allocating up to $15,000 to TV commercials (in units of $1,000's). For each amount (value of x_1) compute the optimal allocation, d_1^*, and the resulting return from this action, $f_1(x_1)$. These are summarized below.

x_1	d_1^*	$f_1(x_1)$
0-6	0	0
7-13	1	11
14-15	2	22

Stage 2

At stage 2, determine how many radio commercials to purchase. The input at stage 2, x_2, will be the number of thousand of dollars available to be spent on both radio (stage 2) and TV (stage 1). Again this amount may be any amount between $0 and $15,000.

The decision, d_2^*, will be the optimal number of radio ads to purchase. Since there is an upper limit of 3 radio ads, d_2 can only be 0, 1, 2, or 3. For each possible value of d_2, calculate: $r_2(x_2,d_2) + f_1(x_1) = 5d_2 + f_1(x_2-2d_2)$

The value of d_2 that maximizes this function is designated as d_2^* and the corresponding value of the function is designated as $f_2(x_2)$. The values of this function and the analysis for d_2^* and $f_2(x_2)$ are summarized below:

x_2	d_2 0	1	2	3	d_2^*	$f_2(x_2)$	$x_2 - 2d_2^*$ $= x_1$
0	0				0	0	0
1	0				0	0	1
2	0	5			1	5	0
3	0	5			1	5	1
4	0	5	10		2	10	0
5	0	5	10		2	10	1
6	0	5	10	15	3	15	0
7	11	5	10	15	3	15	1
8	11	5	10	15	3	15	2
9	11	16	10	15	1	16	7
10	11	16	10	15	1	16	8
11	11	16	21	15	2	21	7
12	11	16	21	15	2	21	8
13	11	16	21	26	3	26	7
14	22	16	21	26	3	26	8
15	22	16	21	26	3	26	9

A sample calculation for the previous table for row $x_2 = 14$, column $d_2 = 1$: The return from $d_2 = 1$ is $r_2(x_2,d_2) = 5d_2 = 5(1) = 5$. This leaves $x_1 = t_2(x_2,d_2) = x_2 - 2d_2 = 14 - 2 = 12$ to be allocated to the previous stages. The optimal value from the previous chart of f1(12) = 11. Adding these two numbers (5 and 11) together gives the entry of 16 for this row and column.

Stage 3

At stage 3 the recurrence relation is: $f_3(x_3) = \text{MAX } \{2d_3 + f_2(x_3 - d_3)\}$
$d_3 \leq 6$

The resulting table is:

x_3	0	1	2	3	4	5	6	d_3^*	$f_3(x_3)$	$x_3 - d_3^* = x_2$
0	**0**							0	0	0
1	0	**2**						1	2	0
2	**5**	2	4					0	5	2
3	**5**	**7**	4	6				1	7	2
4	**10**	7	9	6	8			0	10	4
5	10	**12**	9	11	8	10		1	12	4
6	**15**	12	14	11	13	10	12	0	15	6
7	15	**17**	14	16	13	15	12	1	17	6
8	15	17	**19**	16	18	15	17	2	19	6
9	16	17	19	**21**	18	20	17	3	21	6
10	16	18	19	21	**23**	20	22	4	23	6
11	21	18	20	21	23	**25**	22	5	25	6
12	21	23	20	22	23	25	**27**	6	27	6
13	26	23	25	22	24	25	**27**	6	27	7
14	26	**28**	25	27	24	26	27	1	28	13
15	26	28	**30**	27	29	26	28	2	30	13

A sample calculation for the previous table for row $x_3 = 14$, column $d_3 = 3$: The return from $d_3 = 3$ is $r_3(x_3, d_3) = 2d_3 = 2(3) = 6$. This leaves $x_2 = t_3(x_3, d_3) = x_3 - d_3 = 14 - 3 = 11$ to be allocated to the previous stages. The optimal value from the previous chart of $f_2(11) = 21$. Adding these two numbers (6 and 21) together gives the entry of 27 for this row and column.

Stage 4

The recurrence relation for this stage is: $f_4(x_4) = \text{MAX} \{18d_4 + f_3(x_4 - 12d_4)\}$
$$d_4 \leq 1$$

The resulting table is as follows:

x_4	d_4 0	d_4 1	d_4^*	$f_4(x_4)$	$x_4 - 12d_4^*$ $= x_3$
0	**0**		0	0	0
1	**2**		0	2	1
2	**5**		0	5	2
3	**7**		0	7	3
4	**10**		0	10	4
5	**12**		0	12	5
6	**15**		0	15	6
7	**17**		0	17	7
8	**19**		0	19	8
9	**21**		0	21	9
10	**23**		0	23	10
11	**25**		0	25	11
12	**27**	18	0	27	12
13	**27**	20	0	27	13
14	**28**	23	0	28	14
15	**30**	25	0	30	15

A sample calculation for the previous table for row $x_4 = 14$, column $d_4 = 1$: The return from $d_4 = 1$ is $r_4(x_4, d_4) = 18d_4 = 18$. This leaves $x_3 = t_4(x_4, d_4) = x_4 - 12d_4 = 14 - 12 = 2$ to be allocated to the previous stages. The optimal value from the previous chart of $f_3(2) = 5$. Adding these two numbers (18 and 5) together gives the entry of 23 for this row and column.

Stage 5

The recurrence relation for this stage is: $f_5(x_5) = \text{MAX} \{9d_5 + f_4(x_5 - 4d_5)\}$
$$d_5 \leq 2$$

At this stage the only calculation needed is for $x_5 = 15$ as Dreyfus wants to spend the entire \$15,000. The resulting table is:

x_5	0	1	2	d_5^*	$f_5(x_5)$	$x_5 - 4d_5^*$ $= x_4$
15	30	34	**35**	2	35	7

The optimal value is 35. Working back through the network, select 2 magazine ads (stage 5), leaving 7 for stage 4 giving 0 Burple Challenges, leaving 7 for stage 3 giving 1 newspaper ad, leaving 6 for stage 2 giving 3 radio ads, leaving 0 for TV.

PROBLEM 4

Dicom Corporation wishes to determine a production schedule for its new Model 44/12 virtual memory computer. Because of differences in parts availability and spare production capacity, the cost of producing the machines will vary from month to month.

The following table gives these costs together with the sales demand over the next 5 months as well as the maximum possible production level per month.

Month	Cost of Production Per Machine (in $100,000's)	Maximum Production Level for Month	Sales Demand (in Units)
July	42	5	3
August	32	4	2
September	18	3	1
October	26	4	5
November	45	5	3

The holding cost for each unsold machine still in inventory at the end of the month is $500,000. Corporate policy dictates that the maximum number of machines allowed in inventory at the end of any month is 8.

Determine an optimal 5-month production schedule for the Dicom Model 44/12.

SOLUTION 4

This is an $N = 5$ period dynamic programming problem with each period corresponding to one month. Working backward, let stage one correspond to November, stage 2 to October, etc. The following data can be inferred from above:

Month (n)	Demand D_n	Production Capacity P_n	Storage Capacity W_n	Production Cost Per Unit C_n	Holding Cost Per unit H_n
1	3	5	8	45	5
2	5	4	8	26	5
3	1	3	8	18	5
4	2	4	8	32	5
5	3	5	8	42	5

(Costs are in $100,000's)

If, at some month between July and November, a consultant was called in to solve this problem, besides the above data he would have to know how many computers were currently in inventory.

Hence, define the state variable x_n = the number of computers in inventory at the beginning of month n. Since the computer is new, there will be no inventory at the start of July ($x_5 = 0$). Also define d_n = the production quantity for month n. Then the stage transformations for months 0 through 4 can be defined by: (Previous month's inventory) + (production this month) - (demand this month), or

$$x_{n-1} = x_n + d_n - D_n$$

The return (cost) at each stage, $r_n(x_n, d_n)$, is the sum of the production and holding costs for the month. The production cost is the production cost per unit multiplied by the number of units produced (d_n). The holding cost is the ending inventory for the month multiplied by the holding cost per unit.

Hence, $$r_n(x_n, d_n) = C_n d_n + H_n(x_n + d_n - D_n)$$

This gives: $r_1(x_1, d_1) = 50d_1 + 5x_1 - 15$ $r_4(x_4, d_4) = 37d_4 + 5x_4 - 10$

$r_2(x_2, d_2) = 31d_2 + 5x_2 - 25$ $r_5(x_5, d_5) = 47d_5 + 5x_5 - 15$

$r_3(x_3, d_3) = 23d_3 + 5x_3 - 5$

There are, however, certain restrictions on x_n and d_n:

1) Since backordering is not allowed, we must be able to meet the sales demand. That is, for month n:

$$x_n + d_n \geq D_n. \qquad (1)$$

2) Because there is a maximum storage of W_n at each stage n, the total inventory at the end of any month cannot exceed W_n. Hence, for each month it must be true that $x_n + d_n - D_n \leq W_n$, or

$$x_n + d_n \leq W_n + D_n. \qquad (2)$$

3) The amount produced in any given month cannot exceed the production capacity for that month, or

$$d_n \leq P_n. \qquad (3)$$

Define the optimal value function, $f_n(x_n)$ to be the optimal return (minimal cost) for stages 1 through n given one starts stage n with x_n computers in inventory. Then,

$$f_n(x_n) = \underset{d_n}{\text{MIN}} \{r_n(x_n, d_n) + f_{n-1}(x_{n-1})\}$$

where the d_n is constrained by restrictions (1), (2), and (3).

<u>Stage 1</u>

Starting at stage 1 (November), since $f_0(x_0) = 0$ is a boundary condition, then,

$$f_1(x_1) = \text{MIN } r_1(x_1, d_1)$$
$$d_1$$

Using the expression for $r_1(x_1, d_1)$ and restrictions (1), (2), and (3),

$$f_1(x_1) = \text{MIN } 5x_1 + 50d_1 - 15$$
$$\text{s.t. } x_1 + \quad d_1 \geq 3 \quad (1)$$
$$x_1 + \quad d_1 \leq 11 \quad (2)$$
$$d_1 \leq 5 \quad (3)$$
$$\text{and, } \quad d_1 \geq 0$$

Thus the restrictions are that $0 \leq d_1 \leq 5$, and from (2), $x_1 \leq 11$. Tabulating the values for $50d_1 + 5x_1 - 15$ for feasible values gives:

x_1	0	1	2	3	4	5	$d_1{}^*$	$f_1(x_1)$
0				135	185	235	3	135
1			90	140	190	240	2	90
2		45	95	145	195	245	1	45
3	0	50	100	150	200	250	0	0

Note that having $x_1 > 3$ would result in Dicom having computers in inventory at the end of November, which is undesirable and will actually cause an increase in costs.

<u>Stage 2</u>

At stage 2 the recurrence relation is: $f_2(x_2) = \text{MIN } 5x_2 + 31d_2 - 25 + f_1(x_1)$
$$d_2$$

Given the restrictions, the sub-problem is:

$$f_2(x_2) = \text{MIN } 5x_2 + 31d_2 - 25 + f_1(x_2 + d_2 - 5)$$
$$\text{s.t. } x_2 + \quad d_2 \geq 5 \quad (1)$$
$$x_2 + \quad d_2 \leq 13 \quad (2)$$
$$d_2 \leq 4 \quad (3)$$
$$\text{and} \quad d_2 \geq 0$$

The table for the values of $5x_2 + 31d_2 - 25 + f_1(x_1)$ is:

			d_2					$x_2 + d_2^* - 5$
x_2	0	1	2	3	4	d_2^*	$f_2(x_2)$	$= x_1$
1					**239**	4	239	0
2				213	**199**	4	199	1
3			187	173	**159**	4	159	2
4		161	147	133	**119**	4	119	3
5	135	121	107	**93**		3	93	3
6	95	81	**67**			2	67	3
7	55	**41**				1	41	3
8	**15**					0	15	3

Note that $x_2 = 0$ is infeasible and therefore there is no row corresponding to $x_2 = 0$.

Stage 3

The recurrence relation for stage 3 is:

$$f_3(x_3) = \text{MIN} \quad 5x_3 + 23d_3 - 5 + f_2(x_3 + d_3 - 1)$$

$$\text{s.t.} \quad x_3 + \quad d_3 \geq \ 1 \qquad \qquad (1)$$
$$x_3 + \quad d_3 \leq \ 9 \qquad \qquad (2)$$
$$d_3 \leq \ 3 \qquad \qquad (3)$$
$$\text{and} \quad \ d_3 \geq \ 0$$

The table for the values of $5x_3 + 23d_3 - 5 + f_2(x_3 + d_3 - 1)$ is:

			d_3				$x_3 + d_3^* - 1$
x_3	0	1	2	3	d_3^*	$f_3(x_3)$	$= x_2$
0			280	**263**	3	263	2
1		263	245	**228**	3	228	3
2	244	227	210	**193**	3	193	4
3	209	192	175	**172**	3	172	5
4	174	157	154	**151**	3	151	6
5	139	136	133	**130**	3	130	7
6	118	115	112	**109**	3	109	8
7	97	94	**91**		1	91	8
8	76	**73**			1	73	8

Stage 4

The recurrence relation for stage 4 is:

$$f_4(x_4) = \text{MIN}\ \ 5x_4 + 37d_4 - 10 + f_3(x_4 + d_4 - 2)$$

$$\text{s.t.}\quad x_4 + \quad d_4 \geq 2 \qquad (1)$$
$$x_4 + \quad d_4 \leq 10 \qquad (2)$$
$$d_4 \leq 4 \qquad (3)$$
$$\text{and}\quad d_4 \geq 0$$

The table for the values of $5x_4 + 37d_4 - 10 + f_3(x_4 + d_4 - 2)$ is:

			d_4					x_4+d_4*-2
x_4	0	1	2	3	4	d_4*	$f_4(x_4)$	$= x_3$
0			**327**	329	331	2	327	0
1		**295**	297	299	315	1	295	0
2	**263**	265	267	283	299	0	263	0
3	**233**	235	251	267	283	0	233	1
4	**203**	219	235	251	267	0	203	2
5	**187**	203	219	235	254	0	187	3
6	**171**	187	203	220	241	0	171	4
7	**155**	171	190	209		0	155	5
8	**139**	158	177			0	139	6

Stage 5

The recurrence relation for stage 5 is:

$$f_5(x_5) = \text{MIN}\ \ 5x_5 + 47d_5 - 15 + f_4(x_5 + d_5 - 3)$$

$$\text{s.t.}\quad x_5 + \quad d_5 \geq 3 \quad (1)$$
$$x_5 + \quad d_5 \leq 11 \quad (2)$$
$$d_5 \leq 5 \quad (3)$$
$$\text{and}\quad d_5 \geq 0$$

Since July starts with $x_5 = 0$ inventory on hand, compute the table for $5x_5 + 47d_5 - 15 + f_4(x_5 + d_5 - 3)$ only for $x_5 = 0$.

			d_5					x_5+d_5*-3
x_5	0	1	2	3	4	5	d_5* $f_5(x_5)$	$= x_4$
0				**453**	468	483	3 453	0

Working backwards through the tables, one can determine the optimal solution that gives the minimum cost of $453 x 100,000 = $43,500,000.

Stage	Month	Produce ($d_n{}^*$)	Inventory On-Hand Beginning Next Month x_{n-1}
5	July	3	0
4	August	2	0
3	September	3	2
2	October	4	1
1	November	2	0

ANSWERED PROBLEMS

PROBLEM 5

Ajax Sound is in the business of fabricating phonograph connection wire. They purchase 30 foot spools of wire from National Electric at $3.00 per spool and cut the wire into various lengths.

Each length of wire is fitted with phono connector jacks at both ends and then packaged. The phono connector jacks cost $.40 per pair (one pair is used in each package of wire). Packaging and labor together cost $.20 per package.

Because of Ajax's superior marketing skills they are in the enviable position of being able to sell all the phonograph connection wire they produce. They are currently contemplating offering four different sized packages of wire:

Size	Wholesale Package Price
5'	$1.30
8'	$1.80
12'	$2.50
16'	$3.30

If unused wire from a spool can be sold for scrap at $.03 per foot, how many packages of each size wire should Ajax make from a 30-foot spool?

PROBLEM 6

Unidyde Corporation is currently planning the production of red dye number 56 for the next four months. Production and handling costs, as well as production and storage capacity, vary from month to month. This data is given in the table below.

Production and holding costs are in ($1,000's per batch) and production levels and storage capacities are in batches. Holding costs are based on inventory on hand at the end of the month. The number of orders for batches the sales department has received over the four-month period are also given.

Month	Production Cost	Maximum Production	Holding Cost	Storage Capacity	Orders Received
Febr.	11	3	3	4	2
March	15	4	2	3	4
April	16	3	2	5	2
May	9	2	1	2	3

Unidyne does not wish to have any inventory of the dye at the end of May. Its current inventory is 2 batches.

Determine a production schedule for the next four months.

PROBLEM 7

Given the following shortest path problem in which travel is only permitted from left to right. Use dynamic programming to determine the shortest path from node 1 to:

a) Node 15.

b) Node 14.

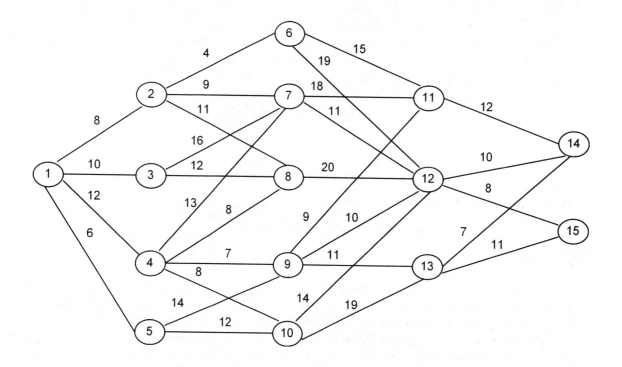

PROBLEM 8

Marvelous Marvin is planning his annual "Almost Everything Must Go" inventory clearance sale. Marvin has decided to allocate 18 shelf feet to the cooking section. He is considering offering up to five items for sale in this category:

Item	Shelf Feet Required	Expected Profit
A	1	$ 10
B	2	$ 25
C	3	$ 40
D	5	$ 70
E	7	$100

If Marvin wants at least one item A and one item B on sale, what stock should he have on sale and what is the total expected profit?

PROBLEM 9

Mission Bay Development Corporation is engaged in developing an exclusive 25 acre parcel of property. They have received bids from five builders to purchase construction lots. Because of the different nature of the builders, they desire different sized lots. The data is as follows:

Builder	Lot Size Requested	Offered Price Per Lot	Maximum Number Of Lots Desired
1	3 acre	$ 50,000	6
2	1 acre	$ 15,000	5
3	6 acre	$105,000	8
4	20 acre	$350,000	1
5	5 acre	$ 91,000	2

How should Mission Bay sell their land to maximize total sales revenue?

PROBLEM 10

Universal Telephone and Television has $6,000,000 earmarked for investment among three divisions which are having earnings difficulties. The three divisions are Bolivia Telephone Company, Camden Insurance Corporation, and Host Baking Company.

The company is considering either giving Bolivia Telephone 0, 2, 4, or 6 million dollars or selling it for 2 million dollars. It is also considering giving Camden Insurance 0, 2, 4, or 6 million dollars but it is not contemplating selling this division. Finally, it is considering either giving Host Baking 0, 4, or 6 million dollars or selling it for 4 million dollars.

The table below gives estimates of the long term present value return of each action. All figures are in $1,000,000's.

Action	Bolivia Telephone	Camden Insurance	Host Baking
Sell	$ 2	---	$ 4
Give $0	$-1	$ 1	$ 3
Give $2	$ 4	$ 5	---
Give $4	$ 7	$ 8	$ 5
Give $6	$10	$12	$ 8

By careful modeling of the problem, it can be shown that the network on the next page corresponds to this investment problem. The arc distances are the long term results associated with each investment alternative.

Use dynamic programming to find the longest path(s) through this network and determine how Universal Telephone and Television should disperse the $6,000,000.

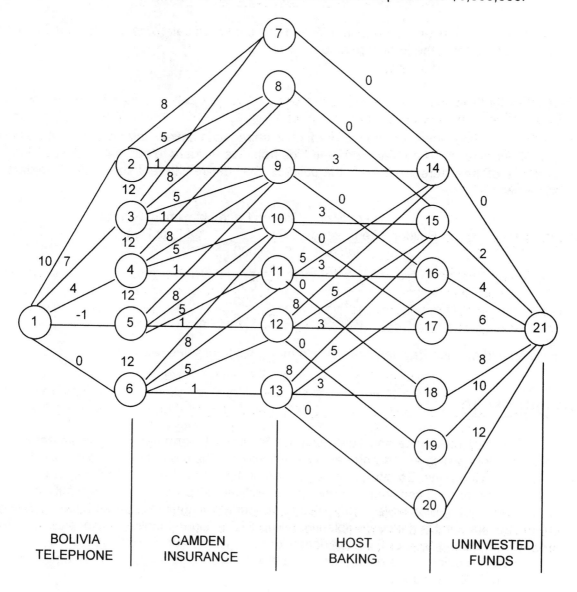

PROBLEM 11

Franklin Plate Company is in the business of manufacturing commemorative plates for holidays. The company is currently planning its production schedule for this year's Thanksgiving plate.

Discussions with the sales manager have indicated that sales of the plate will run from August through November. The production manager has determined the manufacturing cost per plate for each of these months as well as the sales demand (in 1000's) and manufacturing capacity (in 1000's). The data is as follows:

Month	Demand	Manufacturing Cost Per Plate	Maximum Production
August	2	2	6
September	4	3	6
October	6	3	4
November	3	4	3

It is also known that the maximum inventory level possible at the end of any month is 5,000 plates. The storage cost per plate for each plate in inventory at the end of the month is $.50.

Franklin has no inventory on hand at the beginning of August and wishes to have no inventory left after November. Use dynamic programming to determine an optimal production schedule.

PROBLEM 12

Walt's Custom Boats manufactures luxury yachts. Walt is phasing out production of his 42-foot Sportfisher that he plans to replace with a 44-foot Sportfisher. Walt currently has orders for the next four months for the 42-foot model after which he will cease production. The following data (with costs in $1,000's) is given for the next four months:

Mon.	Production Cost Per Boat	Maximum Production Level	Holding Cost Per Boat In Inventory At End Of Month	Maximum Storage Capacity	# Boats To Be Delivered In Month
May	25	4	1	6	1
June	27	3	1	5	3
July	30	2	2	3	3
Aug.	29	3	1	4	4

If Walt's current inventory of 42-foot Sportfishers is 1 boat, how should Walt schedule production of the 42-foot Sportfisher over the next four months to minimize the total production and inventory holding costs?

TRUE/FALSE

13. In order to use dynamic programming one must be able to view the problem as a multistage decision problem.

14. The stage transformation function identifies which state one reaches at the next stage for a given decision.

15. At each stage of a dynamic programming problem one must solve a separate subproblem.

16. The stages of a dynamic programming problem must all have the same number of states.

17. In a knapsack problem, the stages can correspond to the different types of items.

18. The subscripts used in dynamic programming notation refer to states.

19. In a knapsack problem, if one adds another item, one must completely resolve the problem in order to find a new optimal solution.

20. In a production and inventory control problem, the states can correspond to the amount of inventory on hand at the beginning of each period.

21. In a dynamic programming problem the number of stages must equal the number of states.

22. The stage transformation function is a function of all previous decisions.

23. The principle of optimality states that regardless of which decisions were made at previous stages, if the decision made at stage n is to be part of an overall optimal solution, then the decision must be optimal for all remaining stages.

24. Stage 1 in a dynamic programming problem involves finding the best choice for the final decision to actually be made.

25. Using dynamic programming, total enumeration of all possible solutions to a problem is performed.

26. Dynamic programming, like linear programming, is a specific technique that can be applied in a consistent manner to a wide variety of problems.

27. Finding the optimal solution at each stage of a dynamic programming problem will lead to an optimal solution to the total problem.

Answers
to Problems
and True/False

CHAPTER 1

6) a) Management science can provide a quantitative methodology for deciding the job-machine pairings so that total job processing time is minimized.
   b) How long it takes to process each job on each machine, and any job-machine pairings that are unacceptable.
   c) Decision variables: one for each job-machine pairing, taking on a value of 1 if the pairing is used and 0 otherwise.
   Objective function: minimize total job processing time.
   Constraints: each job is assigned to exactly one machine, and each machine be assigned no more than one job.
   d) Stochastic: job processing times vary due to varying machine set-up times, variable operator performance, and more.
   e) Assume that processing times are deterministic (known/fixed).

7) a) The company because of its size and the newness of its product should probably select the simplified model because of the reduced costs and the time period for attaining results. This first pass at the problem most likely will give a "ballpark" figure. The model can then be refined as more experience with production and demand is attained.
   b) Because of the large volume and the national distribution, perhaps the more complete study should be done in this case. Additionally, since the firm is a conglomerate, a more complete justification of its policy to the stockholders may be required.

8) a)
$$\text{MAX} \quad 10s_1 + 10s_2 + 25s_3$$
$$\begin{aligned}
\text{S.T.} \quad 25s_1 &&&\leq 5{,}000 \\
50s_2 &&&\leq 5{,}000 \\
&100s_3 &&\leq 5{,}000 \\
25s_1 &&&\geq 1{,}000 \\
50s_2 &&&\geq 1{,}000 \\
&100s_3 &&\geq 1{,}000 \\
25s_1 + 50s_2 &+ 100s_3 &&\leq 10{,}000 \\
&s_1, s_2, s_3 \geq 0
\end{aligned}$$

   b)
$$\text{MAX} \quad 1.4x_1 + 1.2x_2 + 1.25x_3$$
$$\begin{aligned}
\text{S.T.} \quad x_1 &&&\leq 5{,}000 \\
x_2 &&&\leq 5{,}000 \\
&x_3 &&\leq 5{,}000 \\
x_1 &&&\geq 1{,}000 \\
x_2 &&&\geq 1{,}000 \\
&x_3 &&\geq 1{,}000 \\
x_1 + x_2 &+ x_3 &&\leq 10{,}000 \\
&x_1, x_2, x_3 \geq 0
\end{aligned}$$

   c) Both give the same result.

9) a) $N = L/25$; $C = 8C_gN$; $C = .32C_gL$
   b) $TC = C_n + .32C_gL$; if $L = 50$, $TC = \$260$; if $L = 65$, $N = 2.6$ guards, so it must be decided whether to use 2 or 3 guards during the day.

10) a) X_1 = number of seats CPI manufactures in quarter 1
    X_2 = number of seats subcontracted in quarter 1
    X_3 = number of seats held in inventory from quarter 1 to quarter 2
    X_4 = number of seats CPI manufactures in quarter 2
    X_5 = number of seats subcontracted in quarter 2
    b) Minimize $10.25X_1 + 12.50X_2 + 1.50X_3 + 10.25X_4 + 13.75X_5$

CHAPTER 1 continued

11) a) $X_1 \leq 3800$ (1)
   $X_4 \leq 3800$ (2)
   $X_1 + X_2 - X_3 = 3700$ (3)
   $X_3 \leq 300$ (4)
   $X_3 + X_4 + X_5 = 4200$ (5)

   b) The real problem is stochastic

   c) Three decision variables must be introduced:
   X_6 = number of seats held in inventory from quarter 2 to quarter 3
   X_7 = number of seats CPI manufactures in quarter 3
   X_8 = number of seats subcontracted in quarter 3
   Addition to objective function: $+1.50X_6 + 10.25X_7 + 13.75X_8$
   Adjustment to constraint (5) above: $X_3 + X_4 + X_5 - X_6 = 4200$
   Three additional constraints:
   $X_6 \leq 300$
   $X_7 \leq 3800$
   $X_6 + X_7 + X_8 =$ 3rd quarter demand

12) a) $50s + 30c \leq 800$
   $s \geq 5$
   $c \geq 5$

   b) (1) Max $s + c$; (2) Max $.03s + .05c$; (3) Max $6s + 5c$

13) a) Variable costs: Assembly labor = \$8, Packaging labor = \$1,
                   Packaging material = \$11, Components = \$630
   Fixed costs: Lease, utilities, etc. = \$5,000
   Cost function: $c(x) = 650x + 5,000$

   b) $r(x) = 700x$
   c) 100
   d) \$650
   e) \$20,000

14) False	15) True	16) True	17) True	18) False
19) True	20) False	21) False	22) False	23) False
24) False	25) False	26) True	27) True	28) False

CHAPTER 2

9) $X_1 = 0$, $X_2 = 4$; $Z = 48$

10) a) $X_1 = 4$, $X_2 = 3/2$; $Z = 19$ b) All points on line $2X_1 + X_2 = 6$ between (3,0) and (24/13,30/13).

11) a-b) extreme points: (0,4), (1,2), (3,1) -- feasible region is unbounded.
   c)   (1) optimal solution $X_1 = 3$, $X_2 = 1$, $Z = 1$
        (2) alternate optimal solutions on $X_1 - 2X_2 = 1$ above (3,1)
        (3) unbounded linear program

CHAPTER 2 | continued

12) a) $X_1 = 3$, $X_2 = 4$; $Z = 29$ b) No change. If only a single point is feasible, objective function's slope is inconsequential.

13) a) $X_1 = 10$, $X_2 = 15$, $Z = 230$
   b) Any point satisfying all the other constraints will also satisfy constraint 1
   c) $X_1 = 20$, $X_2 = 15$, $Z = 310$

14) a) MAX $60X_1 + 43X_2$
      S.T. $X_1 + 3X_2 - S_1 \qquad = 9$
               $6X_1 - 2X_2 \qquad\quad = 12$
               $X_1 + 2X_2 \quad + S_3 = 10$
               $X_1, X_2, S_1, S_3 \geq 0$
   b) line segment of $6X_1 - 2X_2 = 12$ between (22/7,24/7) and (27/10,21/10).
   c) Extreme points: (22/7,24/7) and (27/10,21/10). First one is optimal giving $Z = 336$.

15) a) (35,0) $Z = \$630,000$ b) (5,12) $Z = \$630,000$ c) (10,10) $Z = \$630,000$

16) a) 100 dozen childs, 66 2/3 doz. adults, profit = $12,333.33; both slack variables = 0.
   b) this point is an interior point in the original formulation

17) True	18) True	19) True	20) False	21) False
22) False	23) False	24) False	25) False	26) True
27) True	28) True	29) False	30) True	31) False

CHAPTER 3

7) a) 1500 shares of airlines stock, 800 shares of insurance stock; the expected return is $5400
  b) Between $0 and $2.40

8) a) 6 product 1, 4 product 2, Profit = $540
  b) Between $50 and $75; at $70 the profit is $580
  c) No – total % change is 83 1/3% < 100%
  d) Dual prices are the shadow prices for the resources; since there was unused copper (because $S_2 = 2$), extra copper is worth $0
  e) $30
  f) $10; this is the amount extra man-hours are worth
  g) The shadow price is the "premium" for aluminum -- would be willing to pay up to $10 + $30 = $40 for extra aluminum

9) a) Standard -- 33 1/3, Slim-Line -- 266 2/3, $Z = \$1100$
  b) $5.60
  c) Standard -- 86 2/3, Slim-Line -- 213 1/3, $Z = \$1180$

10) a) No   b) No   c) Yes -- Sum of % changes > 100%   d) $10 -- Value of extra man-hours
   e) $1 -- this is the "premium" value for the boxes; hence extra boxes are worth $1.25
   f) They will stay the same -- Sum of % changes < 100%

CHAPTER 3 continued

11) a) 200 shares of James, 20 shares of QM, 40 shares of Delic. Total gain = $3200
   b) Each dollar increase in the allowed minimum investment in QM will result in a $.05 decrease in the total $ gain.
   c) Constraint #1 dual price (.25) X 1000 = $250
   d) No. It would be James Ind. (only stock with + dual price)
   e) Constraint #2 dual price (.15) X 1000 = $150
   f) Allowed max. investment could be raised to $8000
   g) No, cumulative change does not exceed 100%

12) a) $X_1 = 2$, $X_2 = 4$, $Z = 32$ b) $5 \leq C_1 \leq 10$; $3 \leq C_2 \leq 6$ c) $X_1 = 0$, $X_2 = 6$
   d) 1; improvement in the objective function for an extra unit of iron
   e) Zinc's shadow price = 0 as long as this line does not determine the optimal point (its RHS $\leq$ 2).

13) a) 120 containers of jade figurines, 60 containers of linen placemats; Profit = $13,200
   b) Between $30 and $120   c) (1) $6.67; (2) $16.67; (3) $0

14) a) 105 minivans, 75 trailers; $673,500 profit
   b) $2812.50 $\leq$ minivan profit $\leq$ no upper limit, no lower limit $\leq$ trailer profit $\leq$ $5120.00
   c) Dual price for yardman hours is $1600. Thus, an increase of $1600 in monthly profit can be gained for each hour increase in the monthly availability of yardmen!

15) a) 10,000 mi. on Harley; 35,000 mi. on Hauler   b) $15.00   c) 7.5 cents

16) True   17) True   18) True   19) True   20) False
21) False   22) True   23) True   24) True   25) True
26) True   27) True   28) True   29) False   30) True

CHAPTER 4

11) a) MAX $2X_1 + X_2 + .75X_3 + .5X_4 + .75X_5 + 1.5X_6$
   S.T. $20X_1 + 16X_2 + 13X_3 + 9X_4 + 12X_5 + 17X_6 \leq 550$
   $X_1 + X_2 + X_3 + X_4 + X_5 + X_6 \geq 40$
   $X_1 + X_2 + X_3 - 2X_4 - 2X_5 - 2X_6 \geq 0$
   $X_1 + X_2 + X_5 + X_6 \geq 20$
   $X_j \geq 0$ j = 1,...,6

   Solution: $X_1 = 5.833$, $X_2 = 0.833$, $X_3 = 20$, $X_4 = 0$, $X_5 = 13.333$, $X_6 = 0$; Total = 37.5 tons

   b) The variables must be integers.

12) P_i = the number of producers in month i (where i = 1,2,3)
      T_i = the number of trainers in month i (where i = 1,2)
      A_i = the number of apprentices in month i (where i = 2,3)
      R_i = the number of recruits in month i (where i = 1,2)

   MIN $3000P_1 + 3300T_1 + 2200R_1 + 3000P_2 + 3300T_2 + 2600A_2 + 2200R_2 + 3000P_3 + 2600A_3$

CHAPTER 4 continued

12) continued

    s.t. $.6P_1 + .3T_1 + .05R_1 \geq 20$
              $.6P_1 + .3T_1 + .05R_1 + .6P_2 + .3T_2 + .4A_2 + .05R_2 \geq 44$
              $.6P_1 + .3T_1 + .05R_1 + .6P_2 + .3T_2 + .4A_2 + .05R_2 + .6P_3 + .4A_3 \geq 74$
                $P_1 - P_2 + T_1 - T_2 = 0$
                $P_2 - P_3 + T_2 + A_2 = 0$
                $A_2 - R_1 = 0$
                $A_3 - R_2 = 0$
                $2T_1 - R_1 \geq 0$
                $2T_2 - R_2 \geq 0$
                $P_1 + T_1 = 100$
                $P_3 + A_3 \geq 140$
                $P_j, T_j, A_j, R_j \geq 0$ for all j

    Solution: $P_1 = 100$, $T_1 = 0$, $R_1 = 0$, $P_2 = 80$, $T_2 = 20$, $A_2 = 0$, $R_2 = 40$, $P_3 = 100$, $A_3 = 40$
              Total cost = $1,098,000.

13) X_j = the number of instrument j produced; where j = 1(deluxe trumpet); 2(prof. trumpet);
                                      3(deluxe cornet); 4(prof. cornet)

    MAX $80X_1 + 160X_2 + 60X_3 + 120X_4$
    s.t. $2X_1 + 1.5X_2 + 1.5X_3 + X_4 \leq 2000$
            $X_1 + 1.5X_2 + X_3 + 1.5X_4 \leq 1800$
            $X_1 \geq 500$
                      $X_3 \geq 300$
               $X_2 \leq 150$
                          $X_4 \leq 100$
        $X_1 + X_2 - 2X_3 - 2X_4 = 0$
                $X_j \geq 0$ $j = 1,...,4$

    Solution: $X_1 = 620$, $X_2 = 150$, $X_3 = 300$, $X_4 = 85$; Total profit = $101,800.

14) a) MAX $5X_1 + 12X_2 + 25X_3 + 4X_4 + 10X_5 + 18X_6 + 9X_7 + 16X_8$
       S.T. $1.8X_1 + 2.2X_2 + 3X_3 + .74X_4 + 1.6X_5 + 2.2X_6 + X_7 + 1.5X_8 \leq 300$
               $1.8X_1 + 2.2X_2 + 3X_3 \geq 75$
               $1.8X_1 + 2.2X_2 + 3X_3 \leq 120$
                        $.74X_4 + 1.6X_5 + 2.2X_6 \geq 75$
                        $.74X_4 + 1.6X_5 + 2.2X_6 \leq 120$
                                  $X_7 + 1.5X_8 \geq 30$
                                  $X_7 + 1.5X_8 \leq 75$
      $.75X_1 - .25X_2 - .25X_3 + .75X_4 - .25X_5 - .25X_6 - .25X_7 - .25X_8 \geq 0$
                                      $X_j \geq 0$ $j = 1,...,8$
  b) $X_1 = 0$, $X_2 = 0$, $X_3 = 40$, $X_4 = 41.28$, $X_5 = 0$, $X_6 = 33.84$, $X_7 = 0$, $X_8 = 50$, $Z = 2,574.28$
  c) The variables must be integers.

15) X_{11} = pounds of chocolate used in Chompers
        X_{21} = pounds of chocolate used in Smerks
        X_{31} = pounds of chocolate used in Delicious Chocolate
        X_{12} = pounds of caramel used in Chompers
        X_{22} = pounds of caramel used in Smerks

CHAPTER 4 continued

15) continued

X_{23} = pounds of peanuts used in Smerks
Y_1 = number of one ounce Chompers bars produced daily
Y_2 = number of one ounce Smerks bars produced daily
Y_3 = number of one ounce Delicious Choc. bars produced daily
Y_4 = number of one pound Delicious Choc. bags produced daily

MAX $.128Y_1 + .148Y_2 + .138Y_3 + 2.261Y_4 - 1.60X_{11} - 1.60X_{21} - 1.60X_{31} - .95X_{12} - .95X_{22} - 1.40X_{23}$
s.t.
$$(1/16)Y_3 + Y_4 = X_{31}$$
$$(1/16)Y_1 = X_{11} + X_{12}$$
$$(1/16)Y_2 = X_{21} + X_{22} + X_{23}$$
$$X_{12} \geq .18(X_{11} + X_{12})$$
$$X_{12} \leq .28(X_{11} + X_{12})$$
$$X_{22} = X_{23}$$
$$X_{21} \geq .20(X_{21} + X_{22} + X_{23})$$
$$X_{21} \leq .40(X_{21} + X_{22} + X_{23})$$
$$Y_1 + Y_2 + Y_3 \leq 20,000$$
$$Y_4 \leq 1,000$$
$$Y_1 \geq 3,000$$
$$Y_2 \geq 3,000$$
$$Y_3 \geq 3,000$$
$$Y_1 - Y_2 \leq .10(Y_1 + Y_2)$$
$$Y_2 - Y_1 \leq .10(Y_1 + Y_2)$$
$$X_{11} + X_{21} + X_{31} \geq 1,000$$
$$X_{12} + X_{22} = 350$$
$$X_{23} \leq 500$$
$$X_{ij} \geq 0 \quad i = 1,2,3; \ j = 1,2,3$$
$$Y_j \geq 0 \quad j = 1,2,3,4$$

Solution: $Y_1 = 7650$, $Y_2 = 9350$, $Y_3 = 3000$, $Y_4 = 1000$
$X_{11} = 361.875$, $X_{12} = 116.25$
$X_{21} = 116.875$, $X_{22} = 233.75$, $X_{23} = 233.75$
$X_{31} = 1187.5$; Total daily profit = \$1,712.25

16) X_1 = number of bulldozers purchased for the year
X_2 = number of bulldozers leased for the year
annual cost = (purchasing) + (leasing) - (salvage) - (interest)
= $(40,000X_1) + (8000X_2) - (20,000X_1) - 0.08(1,000,000 - 40,000X_1 - 8,000X_2)$
= $23,200X_1 + 8,640X_2 - 80,000$. Thus,
MIN $23,200X_1 + 8,640X_2$
s.t. $4,000X_1 + 8,000X_2 \leq 1,000,000$
$8X_1 + 5X_2 \geq 240$
$X_1, X_2 \geq 0$
Solution: Buy 0 bulldozers, lease 48; Annual cost = \$334,720

17) X_j = \$ invested in investment j; where j = 1(Uni Eq.), 2(Col. Must.), 3(1st Gen REIT), 4(Met. Elec.),
5(Uni Debt), 6(Lem. Trans.), 7(Fair. Apt.), 8(T-Bill),
9(Money Market), 10(All Saver's)
MAX $.15X_1 + .17X_2 + .175X_3 + .118X_4 + .122X_5 + .12X_6 + .22X_7 + .096X_8 + .105X_9 + .126X_{10}$

CHAPTER 4 | continued

17) continued

S.T. $\quad X_1 + X_2 + X_3 + X_4 + X_5 + X_6 + X_7 + X_8 + X_9 + X_{10} = 400,000$

$\quad 100X_1 + 100X_2 + 100X_3 + 95X_4 + 92X_5 + 79X_6 + 80X_8 + 100X_9 \geq$
$$65(X_1 + X_2 + X_3 + X_4 + X_5 + X_6 + X_7 + X_8 + X_9 + X_{10})$$

$\quad 60X_1 + 70X_2 + 75X_3 + 20X_4 + 30X_5 + 22X_6 + 50X_7 + 10X_9 \leq$
$$55(X_1 + X_2 + X_3 + X_4 + X_5 + X_6 + X_7 + X_8 + X_9 + X_{10})$$

$X_1 + X_5$	$\leq 60,000$
$X_1 + X_2 + X_3$	$\leq 160,000$
$X_4 + X_5 + X_6$	$\leq 160,000$
$X_3 + X_7$	$\leq 160,000$
X_1	$\leq 80,000$
X_2	$\leq 80,000$
X_3	$\leq 80,000$
X_4	$\leq 80,000$
X_5	$\leq 80,000$
X_6	$\leq 80,000$
X_7	$\leq 80,000$
X_8	$\leq 80,000$
X_9	$\geq 1,000$
X_{10}	$\leq 15,000$
$X_4 + X_5 + X_6$	$\geq 90,000$
X_8	$\geq 10,000$

$$X_j \geq 0 \quad j = 1,\dots,10$$

Solution: $X_1 = 0$; $X_2 = 80,000$; $X_3 = 80,000$; $X_4 = 0$; $X_5 = 60,000$; $X_6 = 74,000$;
$X_7 = 80,000$; $X_8 = 10,000$; $X_9 = 1,000$; $X_{10} = 15,000$; Total return = $64,355.

18) X_1 = amount invested in new soda advertising
X_2 = amount invested in traditional soda advertising
MAX $\quad X_1 + \quad 4X_2 \quad <==== 02(50X_1) + .04(100X_2)$
S.T. $\quad X_1 + \quad X_2 \leq 10,000,000$
$\quad X_1 \quad\quad\quad \geq 5,000,000$
$\quad\quad\quad X_2 \geq 2,000,000$
$\quad 50X_1 + 100X_2 \geq 750,000,000$
$\quad\quad\quad X_1, X_2 \geq 0$

Answer: spend $5,000,000 on new soda ad, spend $5,000,000 on traditional ad, profit = $25 mil

19) X_1-X_3 $\quad$ = number of students from NE to McHale,McCallum,McBride
$\quad X_4$-X_6 $\quad$ = number of students from SE to McHale,McCallum,McBride
$\quad X_7$-X_9 $\quad$ = number of students from SW to McHale,McCallum,McBride
$\quad X_{10}$-X_{12} $\quad$ = number of students from NW to McHale,McCallum,McBride
$\quad X_{13}$-X_{15} $\quad$ = number of students from Central to McHale,McCallum,McBride

MIN $1.5X_1 + 2.5X_2 + .5X_3 + 4X_4 + 1.5X_5 + 3X_6 + 2.5X_7 + 3X_8$
$\quad + 3.5X_9 + .5X_{10} + 4X_{11} + 1.5X_{12} + 1X_{13} + 2X_{14} + 1X_{15}$

CHAPTER 4 continued

19) continued

$$
\begin{aligned}
\text{S.T.} \quad & X_1 + X_2 + X_3 && = 700 \\
& X_4 + X_5 + X_6 && = 1100 \\
& X_7 + X_8 + X_9 && = 900 \\
& X_{10} + X_{11} + X_{12} && = 600 \\
& X_{13} + X_{14} + X_{15} && = 800 \\
& X_1 + X_4 + X_{10} + X_{13} && \le 1500 \\
& X_2 + X_5 + X_{11} + X_{14} && \le 1800 \\
& X_3 + X_6 + X_{12} + X_{15} && \le 1100 \\
& X_j \ge 0 \quad j = 1,2,\dots,15
\end{aligned}
$$

Solution: 700 students from NE to McBride, 1100 from SE to McCallum
500 from SW to McHale, 400 from SW to McCallum, 600 from NW to McHale,
400 from Central to McHale, and 400 from Central to McBride.

20) E = .968; Alabama store appears moderately inefficient

21) X_1-X_4 = number of full-time clerks starting at 8,9,10,11am
X_5-X_{11} = number of part-time clerks starting at 8,9,10,11am and 12,1,2pm

$$\text{MIN } 63X_1+63X_2+63X_3+63X_4+26X_5+26X_6+26X_7+26X_8+26X_9+26X_{10}+26X_{11}$$

$$
\begin{aligned}
\text{S.T.} \quad & X_1 && \ge 1 \\
& X_4 && \ge 1 \\
& X_1 + X_2 + X_3 + X_4 && \ge 4 \\
& X_1 + X_5 && \ge 5 \\
& X_1 + X_2 + X_5 + X_6 && \ge 4 \\
& X_1 + X_2 + X_3 + X_5 + X_6 + X_7 && \ge 6 \\
& X_2 + X_3 + X_4 + X_5 + X_6 + X_7 + X_8 && \ge 8 \\
& X_1 + X_3 + X_4 + X_6 + X_7 + X_8 + X_9 && \ge 10 \\
& X_1 + X_2 + X_4 + X_7 + X_8 + X_9 + X_{10} && \ge 9 \\
& X_1 + X_2 + X_3 + X_8 + X_9 + X_{10} + X_{11} && \ge 7 \\
& X_2 + X_3 + X_4 + X_9 + X_{10} + X_{11} && \ge 4 \\
& X_3 + X_4 + X_{10} + X_{11} && \ge 7 \\
& X_4 + X_{11} && \ge 5 \\
& X_j \ge 0 \quad j = 1,2,\dots,11
\end{aligned}
$$

Solution: $X_1 = 1$, $X_2 = 0$, $X_3 = 0$, $X_4 = 3$, $X_5 = 4$,
$X_6 = 3$, $X_7 = 0$, $X_8 = 3$, $X_9 = 0$, $X_{10} = 2$, $X_{11} = 2$, Total labor cost = \$616.

22) False	23) False	24) True	25) False	26) True
27) True	28)True	29) True	30) False	31) False
32) False	33) False	34) False	35) False	36) False

CHAPTER 5

8) a) MIN $Z = 2X_1 + 3X_2 + 8X_3$
   S.T. $4X_1 + 2X_2 + X_3 - S_1 = 15$
   $2X_1 + X_2 + 6X_3 - S_2 = 30$
   $X_j \geq 0 \quad j = 1,2,3$
   $S_j \geq 0 \quad j = 1,2$

   b) Cannot have negative numbers on RHS
   c) $X_1 = 15, X_2 = 0, X_3 = 0, S_1 = 45, S_2 = 0, Z = 30$

9) $X_1 = 5, X_2 = 3/2, X_3 = 0, S_1 = 0, S_2 = 19/2, Z = 8$

10) $X_1 = 3, X_2 = 0, X_3 = 4\ 2/3, S_1 = 0, S_2 = 2\ 1/3, S_3 = 2; Z = 13\ 2/3$

11) a) Tableau infeasible at this stage, but cannot yet state whether or not the problem is feasible:

Basis	C_B	X_1	X_2	X_3	S_1	S_2	S_3	A_2	
		10	8	6	0	0	0	-M	
S_1	0	0	1	0	1	0	-2	0	4
A_2	-M	-1	0	0	0	-1	-1	1	6
X_3	6	1/2	1/2	1	0	0	1/2	0	5
Z_j		M+3	3	6	0	M	M+3	-M	-6M+30
$C_j - Z_j$		-M+7	5	0	0	-M	-M-3	0	

b) Optimal: $X_1 = 0, X_2 = 14, X_3 = 0, S_1 = 18, S_2 = 0, Z = 84$
c) Problem Unbounded: X_3 column is non-positive
d) Problem Infeasible: A_2 positive in this "optimal" tableau
e) Tableau is feasible, but not yet optimal

Basis	C_B	X_1	X_2	X_3	S_1	S_2	
		4	5	7	0	0	
X_3	7	0	0	1	0	0	12
S_2	0	0	0	0	-2/3	1	2
X_2	5	0	1	0	1/3	0	6
X_1	4	1	0	0	1/3	0	26
Z_j		4	5	7	3	0	218
$C_j - Z_j$		0	0	0	-3	0	

CHAPTER 5	continued

12) a)

Basis	C_B	X_1	X_2	X_3	S_1	S_2	S_3	
		4	2	-1	0	0	0	
X_2	2	0	1	-1	6	0	1	10
S_2	0	0	0	4	2	1	1	20
X_1	4	1	0	0	-3	0	1	30
Z_j		4	2	-2	0	0	6	140
$C_j - Z_j$		0	0	1	0	0	-6	

b) $X_1 = 30$, $X_2 = 10$, $X_3 = 0$, $S_1 = 0$, $S_2 = 20$, $S_3 = 0$, $Z = 140$

c) increases by 1; increases by 3; unchanged; decreases by 12

d) X_3 enters; equations are:

$$X_2 - X_3 = 10 \qquad (1)$$
$$4X_3 + S_2 = 20 \qquad (2)$$
$$X_1 = 30 \qquad (3)$$

(1) shows X_2 increases as X_3 increases. (2) shows S_2 decreases as X_3 increases, and (3) shows that X_1 is unchanged as X_3 increases. Thus ratio test is applied only to positive numbers in the entering column.

e) S_2 would become -20. f) 5 g) New values: $Z = 145$; $X_2 = 15$; $S_2 = 0$; X_1 unchanged.

h)

Basis	C_B	X_1	X_2	X_3	S_1	S_2	S_3	
		4	2	-1	0	0	0	
X_2	2	0	1	0	13/2	1/4	5/4	15
X_3	-1	0	0	1	1/2	1/4	1/4	5
X_1	4	1	0	0	-3	0	1	30
Z_j		4	2	-1	1/2	1/4	25/4	145
$C_j - Z_j$		0	0	0	-1/2	-1/4	-25/4	

13) a)

Basis	C_B	X_1	X_2	X_3	S_1	S_2	S_3	
		5	2	1	0	0	0	
X_1	5	1	0	1/2	-3	1/2	0	4
X_2	2	0	1	-1/2	7	-1/2	0	0
S_3	0	0	0	-2	15	-5	1	4
Z_j		5	2	3/2	-1	3/2	0	20
$C_j - Z_j$		0	0	-1/2	1	-3/2	0	

Solution: $X_1 = 4$, $X_2 = 0$, $X_3 = 0$, $S_1 = 0$, $S_2 = 0$, $S_3 = 4$, $Z = 20$.
Not optimal (a positive number is in $C_j - Z_j$ row).

CHAPTER 5	continued

13) b)

Basis	C_B	X_1	X_2	X_3	S_1	S_2	S_3	
		5	2	1	0	0	0	
X_3	1	0	-2	1	-14	1	0	0
X_1	5	1	1	0	4	0	0	4
S_3	0	0	-4	0	-13	-3	1	4
Z_j		5	3	1	6	1	0	20
$C_j - Z_j$		0	-1	0	-6	-1	0	

Solution: Same as (a). This time, the $C_j - Z_j$ row indicates that this is an optimal solution.

c) When degeneracy occurs, an optimal solution may have been attained even though some $C_j - Z_j > 0$. Thus, the condition that $C_j - Z_j \leq 0$, is sufficient for optimality, but not necessary.

14) a) Produce 250 deluxe doors
b) There are many, including producing 200 standard and 100 deluxe doors

15) a) MAX $Z = 2X_1 + 5X_2 + 5X_3 + 3X_4$

S.T.
$$10X_1 + 12X_2 + 10X_3 + 9X_4 + S_1 = 150$$
$$X_1 + X_2 + X_3 - S_2 = 12$$
$$-X_1 + X_2 + X_3 - X_4 + S_3 = 0$$
$$X_j \geq 0 \quad j = 1,2,3,4$$
$$S_j \geq 0 \quad j = 1,2,3$$

b)

Basis	C_B	X_1	X_2	X_3	X_1	S_1	S_2	A_2	S_3	
		2	5	5	3	0	0	-M	0	
S_1	0	10	12	10	9	1	0	0	0	150
A_2	-M	1	1	1	0	0	-1	1	0	12
X_3	0	-1	1	1	-1	0	0	0	1	0
Z_j		-M	-M	-M	0	0	M	-M	0	-12M
$C_j - Z_j$		2+M	5+M	5+M	3	0	-M	0	0	

c) $X_1 = 4\ 1/3$, $X_2 = 0$, $X_3 = 7\ 2/3$, $X_4 = 3\ 1/3$, $S_1 = 0$, $S_2 = 0$, $S_3 = 0$; $Z = 57$

16) True   17) False   18) True   19) True   20) True
21) False   22) False   23) True   24) True   25) True
26) False   27) True   28) False   29) False   30) False

CHAPTER 6

7) a) shadow price is 4; $5 \leq b_1 \leq 8$ b) $3 \leq C_2 \leq 6$; when $C_2 = 4$, $Z = 28$

8) a) $X_1 = 10$, $X_2 = 0$, $X_3 = 0$, $S_1 = 0$, $S_2 = 4$; $Z = 50$
   Ranges of optimality: $C_1 \geq 3$, $C_2 \leq 5$, $C_3 \leq 5$, $C_{S2} \leq 5$, $-1 < C_{S2} \leq 5/2$
   b) Yes, since the shadow price is 5; Cannot tell as change falls outside the range of feasibility.

9) a) MAX $Z = 40X_1 + 60X_2 + 80X_3$
   S.T.
   $$X_1 + X_2 + 2X_3 \leq 500$$
   $$2X_1 + 2X_2 + 2X_3 \leq 600$$
   $$X_1 + 2X_2 + 3X_3 \leq 900$$
   $$X_1, X_2, X_3 \geq 0$$

   b) $40 \leq C_2 \leq 80$
   c) \$23,000
   d) Sunk cost – No, since shadow price = \$20
      Relevant cost – Yes; value = 20 + 16 = \$36

10) a) It can be increased without limit. b) $500 \leq b_2 \leq 800$; $b_3 \geq 800$
    c) Relevant costs if one need only purchase the amount required and these costs are reflected in the objective function coefficients – in this case the shadow price of \$20 for aluminum would be the premium above its current value for extra pounds of aluminum. Sunk costs if these costs are not reflected in objective function coefficients because they were considered fixed costs. In this case, the \$20 would simply be the value of extra pounds of aluminum. In either case, the value of extra steel is zero.
    d) 400

11) a) 20 X12's, 0 T7's, 40 V8's; Daily Profit = \$2,000
    b) Plastic package: (shadow price) x (quantity) is greatest.
    c) Yes; 33 1/3 x12's; 13 1/3 T7's; 0 V8's; Profit = \$2,066.67

12) a) MIN $Z = 15U_1 + 16U_2$
    S.T.
    $$U_1 + 4U_2 \geq 10$$
    $$3U_1 + U_2 \geq 8$$
    $$U_1, U_2 \geq 0$$

    b) Primal: $X_1 = 3$, $X_2 = 4$, $Z = 62$
       Dual: $U_1 = 2$, $U_2 = 2$, $Z = 62$

    c) The values for the dual variables are found in the Z_j row in the S_1 and S_2 columns.

13) a) MAX $Z = 3X_1 + 2X_2 - 3X_3$
    S.T.
    $$X_1 + 3X_2 + 8X_3 \leq 56$$
    $$2X_1 - X_2 - X_3 \leq 14$$
    $$-2X_1 + X_2 + X_3 \leq -14$$
    $$- X_2 \leq -5$$
    $$X_1, X_2, X_3 \geq 0$$

    b) MIN $Z = 56U_1 + 14U_2' - 14U_2'' - 5U_3$
    $$U_1 + 2U_2' - 2U_2'' \geq 3$$
    $$3U_1 - U_2' + U_2'' - U_3 \geq 2$$
    $$8U_1 - U_2' + U_2'' \geq -3$$
    $$U_1, U_2', U_2'', U_3 \geq 0$$

14) False	15) True	16) True	17) True	18) False
19) False	20) True	21) True	22) True	23) False
24) False	25) False	26) False	27) True	28) False

CHAPTER 7

8. a)

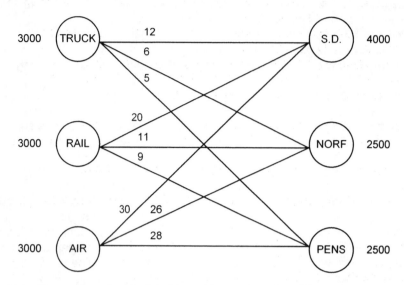

b) Let: P_{TS} , P_{TN} , P_{TP} = lbs. of material shipped by truck to San Diego, Norfolk, Pensacola
P_{RS} , P_{RN} , P_{RP} = lbs. of material shipped by railroad to San Diego, Norfolk, Pensacola
P_{AS} , P_{AN} , P_{AP} = lbs. of material shipped by airline to San Diego, Norfolk, Pensacola

Min $12P_{TS} + 6P_{TN} + 5P_{TP} + 20P_{RS} + 11P_{RN} + 9P_{RP} + 30P_{AS} + 26P_{AN} + 28P_{AP}$
s.t.
$$P_{TS} + P_{TN} + P_{TP} \leq 3000$$
$$P_{RS} + P_{RN} + P_{RP} \leq 3000$$
$$P_{AS} + P_{AN} + P_{AP} \leq 3000$$
$$P_{TS} + P_{RS} + P_{AS} = 4000$$
$$P_{TN} + P_{RN} + P_{AN} = 2500$$
$$P_{TP} + P_{RP} + P_{AP} = 2500$$
$$P_{TS} , P_{TN} , P_{TP} , P_{RS} , P_{RN} , P_{RP} , P_{AS} , P_{AN} , P_{AP} \geq 0$$

c) Truck – S.D. 1000; Truck – Norf. 2000; Rail – Norf. 500; Rail – Pens. 2500; Air – S.D. 3000

9) a) Let: A_{N1} , A_{N2} , A_{N3} , A_{N4} = number of newspaper ads by MR1, MR2, MR3, MR4
A_{T1} , A_{T2} , A_{T3} , A_{T4} = number of television ads by MR1, MR2, MR3, MR4
A_{R1} , A_{R2} , A_{R3} , A_{R4} = number of radio ads by MR1, MR2, MR3, MR4

Min $16A_{N1} + 10A_{N2} + 12A_{N3} + 12A_{N4} + 26A_{T1} + 20A_{T2} + 30A_{T3} + 21A_{T4} + 22A_{R1} + 15A_{R2} + 23A_{R3} + 14A_{R4}$

s.t. $A_{N1} + A_{T1} + A_{R1} \leq 15$
$A_{N2} + A_{T2} + A_{R2} \leq 25$
$A_{N3} + A_{T3} + A_{R3} \leq 10$
$A_{N4} + A_{T4} + A_{R4} \leq 20$
$A_{N1} + A_{N2} + A_{N3} + A_{N4} = 30$
$A_{T1} + A_{T2} + A_{T3} + A_{T4} = 15$
$A_{R1} + A_{R2} + A_{R3} + A_{R4} = 25$ and all A's ≥ 0

CHAPTER 7 | continued

9) b) Newspaper - MR1 15; Newspaper - MR2 5; Newspaper - MR3 10; TV - MR2 15;
      Radio - MR2 5; Radio - MR4 20; Total Cost = $1,065,000
   c) Newspaper - MR2 20; Newspaper - MR3 10; TV - MR1 15; Radio - MR2 5;
      Radio - MR4 20; Total cost = $1,065,000
   d) Many answers. One with TV-MR1 = 5 is: Newspaper - MR1 10;
      Newspaper - MR2 10; Newspaper - MR3 10; TV - MR1 5; TV - MR2 10;
      Radio - MR2 5; Radio - MR4 20; Total cost = $1,065,000

10) Ace: 25 Sanitation and 5 Police; Band: 25 Parks and 15 Administration;
    QM: 20 Police and 10 Administration; Cost $1,035,000

11) LA-Denver 25; LA-NY 10; CHI-NY 30; NY-ATL 35; Profit $2,165,000

12) Abbey-Cab3, Babbs-Cab4, Carla-Cab2, Diane-Cab5, Ellsa-Cab1; Performance rating total = 35

13) a) (diagram below)
    b) Computer Town - P5; Computer World - P4; Universal - P1;
       Local Computer - P2 and P3; Total Cost $71,000
    c) +M placed in matrix in row 2, column 5; no change in solution
    d) +M's placed in assignment matrix row 2 column 4, and in row 2 column 5;
       Computer Town - P5; Computer World - P2; Universal - P1;
       Local Computer - P3 and P4; Total cost = $77,000

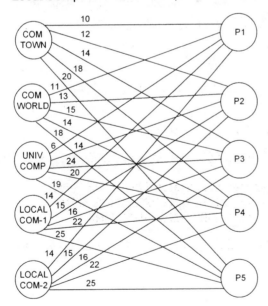

14) Division 1 - Bats; Division 2 - Golf Clubs;
    Division 3 - Racquetball Rackets; Division 4 - Tennis Rackets; Total 410

CHAPTER 7 | continued

15) a)

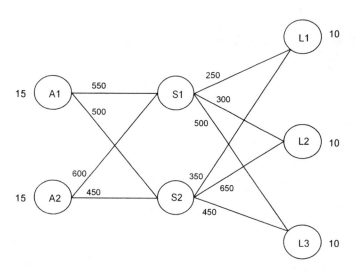

15) b) Denote A1 as node 1, A2 as node 2, S1 as node 3, S2 as node 4,
L1 as node 5, L2 as node 6, and L3 as node 7

$$\text{MIN } 550X_{13} + 500X_{14} + 600X_{23} + 450X_{24} + 250X_{35} + 300X_{36} + 500X_{37}$$
$$+ 350X_{45} + 650X_{46} + 450X_{47}$$

S.T.
$$
\begin{aligned}
X_{13} + X_{14} &\le 15 \\
X_{23} + X_{24} &\le 15 \\
X_{13} + X_{23} - X_{35} - X_{36} - X_{37} &= 0 \\
X_{14} + X_{24} - X_{45} - X_{46} - X_{47} &= 0 \\
X_{35} + X_{45} &= 10 \\
X_{36} + X_{46} &= 10 \\
X_{37} + X_{47} &= 10 \\
X_{ij} \ge 0 \text{ for all i,j}
\end{aligned}
$$

Solution: $X_{13} = 15$, $X_{14} = 0$, $X_{23} = 0$, $X_{24} = 15$,
$X_{35} = 5$, $X_{36} = 10$, $X_{37} = 0$, $X_{45} = 5$, $X_{46} = 0$, $X_{47} = 10$, Total cost = $25,500.

16) True	17) True	18) False	19) True	20) True
21) False	22) False	23) False	24) True	25) True
26) True	27) False	28) True	29) False	30) True

CHAPTER 8

6) a) $X_1 = 2.8$, $X_2 = 3.4$, $Z = 48.8$
   b) $X_1 = 3$, $X_2 = 3$ -- infeasible
   c) $X_1 = 2$, $X_2 = 3$ -- feasible but not optimal
   d) Optimal $X_1 = 2$, $X_2 = 9$, $Z = 48 < 48.8$
   e) Additional integer constraints restrict the feasible region further;
      optimal solution values: ILP $\le$ Mixed ILP $\le$ LP.

CHAPTER 8 | continued

7) a) $X_1 = 7/3$, $X_2 = 1/3$, $Z = 31/3$
   b) $X_1 = 2$, $X_2 = 0$, $Z = 6$
   c) L.P. -- optimal solution changes slightly; ILP -- infeasible

8) a) $X_1 = 1.5$, $X_2 = 2.5$, $Z = 17.5$; upper bound
   b) $X_1 = 1$, $X_2 = 3$, $Z = 17$
   c) $X_1 = 1$, $X_2 = 3$, $Z = 14$

9) MAX $Y_1 + 1.8Y_2 + 2Y_3 + 1.5Y_4 + 3.6Y_5 + 2.2Y_6$
   S.T. $20Y_1 + 55Y_2 + 47Y_3 + 38Y_4 + 90Y_5 + 63Y_6 \leq 175$
   $\qquad 15Y_1 + 45Y_2 + 50Y_3 + 40Y_4 + 70Y_5 + 70Y_6 \leq 150$
   $$Y_4 - Y_6 = 0$$
   $$Y_1 - Y_2 \geq 0$$
   $$Y_3 + Y_5 \leq 1$$
   $$Y_1 + Y_2 + Y_3 + Y_4 + Y_5 + Y_6 \leq 3$$
   $$Y_i = 0 \text{ or } 1$$

   Solution: $Y_1 = 1$, $Y_2 = 1$, $Y_3 = 0$, $Y_4 = 0$, $Y_5 = 1$, $Y_6 = 0$, Total profit = $6.4 million.

10) MAX $5.2X_1 + 3.6X_2 + 3.2X_3 + 2.8X_4$
    S.T. $.35X_1 + .50X_2 + .35X_3 + .50X_4 \leq 0.85$ (FIRST YEAR)
    $\qquad .55X_1 + .50X_2 + .40X_3 \leq 1.00$ (SECOND YEAR)
    $\qquad .75X_1 + .45X_3 \leq 1.20$ (THIRD YEAR)
    $\qquad X_1 + X_2 + X_3 + X_4 = 2$
    $\qquad - X_2 + X_3 \geq 0$
    $$X_i = 0 \text{ or } 1$$

    Solution: $X_1 = 1$, $X_2 = 0$, $X_3 = 1$, $X_4 = 0$, Total projected benefits = $8.4 million.

11) a) $X_1 = 3$, $X_2 = 4.25$, $Z = 49$ b) $X_1 = 4$, $X_2 = 4$, $Z = 52$

12) a) 4/5 container of Grain A, 2 containers of Grain B, $3960
    b) 2 containers of Grain A, 1 container of Grain B, $3900
    c) (1) (0,2) feasible, not optimal; (2-3) (1,2) infeasible

13) a) $X_1 = 3$, $X_2 = 3.2$, $Z = 34.4$
    b) $X_1 = 2$, $X_2 = 4$, $Z = 36$

14) False   15) True   16) False   17) False   18) True
19) False   20) True   21) True   22) True   23) False
24) False   25) True   26) True   27) False   28) True

CHAPTER 9

5)   Maximal flow is 4500 cubic feet.

x12 = 10	x23 = 10	x53 = 4
x13 = 10	x34 = 8	x56 = 14
x14 = 7	x36 = 16	x61 = 45
x15 = 18	x46 = 15	

6)   Total distance = 9,110 feet;   Ttoal cost = $455,500

7)   Total cost = $273;   Philadelphia – Chicago – San Francisco – Los Angelos – Las Vegas

8)   180 megawatts

9)   a) $3,750   b) $175

10)   At $6/hr, travel on C - J; cost = $85
      At $60/hr, travel on B - L; cost = $265

11)   (River-1),(1-4),(4-6),(4-5),(6-7),(4-3),(3-8),(3-2); or
      (River-1),(1-4),(4-6),(4-5),(6-7),(4-3),(3-8),(4-2); 2050 yards

12)   Path: 1-2-5-6-7-8; 50 minutes

13)   120,000 pounds of oranges

14) False	15) True	16) False	17) False	18) True
19) True	20) False	21) True	22) False	23) True
24) False	25) True	26) False	27) False	28) True

CHAPTER 10

6) a)

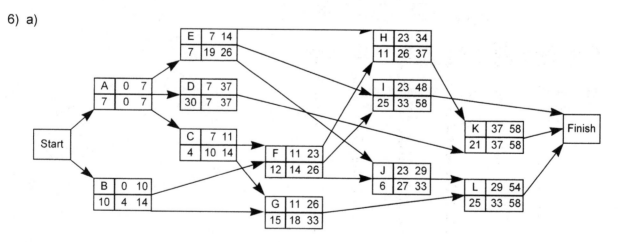

Expected Completion Time = 58; Critical Path = A - D - K

CHAPTER 10 | continued

6) b) Yes   c) Yes   d) Slack on G = 7 hours; Slack on L = 4 hours
   e) 4 hours; the slack times are not independent as G and L are on the same path.

7) a)

Activity	ES	EF	LS	LF	Slack
A	0:00	4:00	0:00	4:00	0
B	0:00	3:00	6:00	9:00	6
C	4:00	9:00	17:00	22:00	13
D	4:00	7:00	8:00	11:00	4
E	4:00	9:00	4:00	9:00	0
F	9:00	11:00	9:00	11:00	0
G	9:00	10:00	15:00	16:00	6
H	11:00	13:00	20:00	22:00	9
I	11:00	14:00	20:00	23:00	9
J	11:00	16:00	11:00	16:00	0
K	13:00	14:00	22:00	23:00	9
L	16:00	23:00	16:00	23:00	0

b) A - E - F - J - L; 23 hours

c) There are many; here is one. Note that for Man 2, activity D must precede activity C (D's LS is 8:00 and C's EF is 9:00).

Intern 1	Intern 2	
A 0:00 - 4:00	B 0:00 - 3:00	H 13:00 - 15:00
E 4:00 - 9:00	D 4:00 - 7:00	I 15:00 - 18:00
F 9:00 - 11:00	C 7:00 - 12:00	K 18:00 - 19:00
J 11:00 - 16:00	G 12:00 - 13:00	
L 16:00 - 23:00		

8) a)

b) 8 hrs.   c) .8264

9) a)

Activity	ES	EF	LS	LF	Slack
A	0	6	1	7	1
B	0	8	0	8	0
C	6	7	7	8	1
D	6	9	9	12	3
E	8	11	9	12	1
F	8	12	9	13	1
G	8	18	8	18	0
H	8	13	10	15	2
I	11	14	12	15	1
J	12	13	14	15	2
K	12	17	13	18	1
L	14	17	15	18	1

b) Critical Path: B - G; Expected completion time = 18 weeks   c) Train its own employees

CHAPTER 10 | continued

10) a) 16 weeks = Aug. 21 b) About Sept. 22 (20.66 weeks from May 1)   c) Do not accept the offer
$8457.50 > $7,716.00

11) a) Expected Project Completion Time = 32; Standard deviation = 3.16
    b) Do not spend the money
    c) Activities off the critical path may vary enough so that a new critical path could be formed.

12) a) For this problem label the activities as follows:
    A = Feasibility Study   D = Advert. Staff Selected   G = Prototype Manufactured
    B = Building Purchased   E = Materials Purchased   H = Production Run of 100
    C = Project Leader Hired   F = Manufacturing Staff Hired I = Advertising Campaign

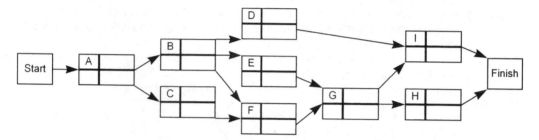

12) b) Define X_i = earliest finish time for activity i Y_i = the amount of time activity i is crashed
    MIN $20Y_A + 50Y_C + 50Y_D + 70Y_E + 60Y_F + 350Y_H + 75Y_I$ (in $000)
    S.T.
$$X_A \geq 0 + (6 - Y_A) \qquad X_I \geq X_D + (8 - Y_I)$$

$Y_A \leq 1$ $X_B \geq X_A + 4$ $X_I \geq X_G + (8 - Y_I)$
$Y_C \leq 1$ $X_C \geq X_A + (3 - Y_C)$
$Y_D \leq 3$ $X_D \geq X_B + (6 - Y_D)$ $X_H \leq 26$
$Y_E \leq 1$ $X_E \geq X_B + (3 - Y_E)$ $X_I \leq 26$
$Y_F \leq 3$ $X_F \geq X_B + (10 - Y_F)$
$Y_H \leq 1$ $X_F \geq X_C + (10 - Y_F)$ $X_i, Y_j \geq 0$ for all i
$Y_I \leq 4$ $X_G \geq X_E + 2$
       $X_G \geq X_F + 2$
       $X_H \geq X_G + (6 - Y_H)$

Solution: $X_A = 5$, $X_B = 9$, $X_C = 9$, $X_D = 18$, $X_E = 16$, $X_F = 16$, $X_G = 18$, $X_H = 24$, $X_I = 26$,
    $Y_A = 1$, $Y_C = 0$, $Y_D = 0$, $Y_E = 0$, $Y_F = 3$, $Y_H = 0$, $Y_I = 0$, Total crash cost = $200,000.

    c) The time reduction for each activity is proportional to the crashing money spent on that activity.
    d) Per-week reduction cost is shadow price for $X_H \leq 26$ or $X_I \leq 26$.

13) The PERT network for this problem is:

CHAPTER 10 | continued

13) continued

a) Define X_i = earliest finish time for activity i Y_i = the amount of time activity i is crashed

MIN $2000Y_A + 2000Y_C + 500Y_D + 500Y_E + 2000Y_F + 5000Y_G + 6000Y_H$

S.T.

$Y_A \leq 2$

$Y_C \leq 3$

$Y_D \leq 2$

$Y_E \leq 1$

$Y_F \leq 2$

$Y_G \leq 1$

$Y_H \leq 2$

$X_A \geq 0 + (6 - Y_A)$

$X_B \geq 0 + 3$

$X_C \geq X_A + (9 - Y_C)$

$X_D \geq X_A + (4 - Y_D)$

$X_E \geq X_B + (2 - Y_E)$

$X_F \geq X_B + (3 - Y_F)$

$X_G \geq X_C + (5 - Y_G)$

$X_G \geq X_E + (5 - Y_G)$

$X_H \geq X_D + (7 - Y_H)$

$X_H \geq X_F + (7 - Y_H)$

$X_G \leq 16$

$X_H \leq 16$

$X_i, Y_j \geq 0$ for all i

Solution: $X_A = 4$, $X_B = 6$, $X_C = 11$, $X_D = 9$, $X_E = 11$, $X_F = 9$, $X_G = 16$, $X_H = 16$, $Y_A = 2$, $Y_C = 2$, $Y_D = 0$, $Y_E = 0$, $Y_F = 0$, $Y_G = 0$, $Y_H = 0$, Total crash cost = $8,000.

b) Same formulation as (a) except: objective function is now MIN X_I with constraints $X_I \geq X_G$ and $X_I \geq X_H$ and $1250Y_A + 2000Y_C + 500Y_D + 500Y_E + 2000Y_F + 5000Y_G + 6000Y_H \leq 50,000$

14) [Activity, ES, EF, LS, LF, Slack]
[A, 0, 4, 0, 4, 0]; [B, 4, 7, 4, 7, 0]; [C, 4, 8, 6, 10, 2]; [D, 7, 9, 8, 10, 1]; [E, 7, 12, 7, 12, 0]
[F, 9, 11, 10, 12, 1]; [G, 12, 17, 12, 17, 0]; [H, 9, 15, 11, 17, 2]

15) True   16) True   17) False   18) False   19) True
20) True   21) False   22) False   23) False   24) True
25) True   26) True   27) False   28) True   29) True

CHAPTER 11

9) a) 75   b) Q* = 273.861, order 274   c) $164.32   d) Order every 4 mos. based on forecast

10) a) 1) Buy: Q* = 800; Tot. Annual Var. Cost = $1200;   Tot. Annual Cost = $76,200
      2) Make: Q* = 5345; Tot. Annual Var. Cost = $5,986.65; Tot. Annual Cost = $75,986.65.
   b) Harrison should manufacture displays; total cost is cheaper.

11) a) Q* = 109,544.5 or 109,545   b) 13.33   c) 115 days = 365 - (9.13)(13.33 + 14)

12) Order 2000 every week

13) a) (1) Q* = 16   (2) 20 or when inventory reaches 4 and one order is pending   (3) $47,840
   b) No; Yearly net profit under this policy is only $45,774

14) $Q^* = 233$, Total annual cost = $64,695.54

15) a) Order 648 every 3.08 weeks when supply reaches 42   b) 12 spark plugs   c) $6.60

16) 196

17) Z = 1.43 ==> Pr(Stockout) = .0764

CHAPTER 11 | continued

18) Yes; Annual manufacture = $38,600; annual purchase = $40,800

19) a) Machine I Profit = $40,000 (operating at full capacity with no inventory); Machine II = $41,520.
    b) For machine II, Q* = 92,582, resulting in 3.24 cycles/year each lasting 112.6 days. Production time is 33.8 days, so some of the meat sold will be as old as 78 days. Using Machine II, he would need more production runs per year thus incurring more setups and reducing his profit below the $40,000 from using machine I.

20) a) Order 32 when inventory reaches 7   b) Total annual variable cost = $1,301

21) a) .0951   b) 299

22) a) 71,600 loaves   b) 61,280 loaves

23) a) 46 pumpkins   b) .525

24) Order 1000 tubes of lipstick each time

25) Choose Option III

26) a) order 100 units when the supply on hand reaches 172   b) $24,024   c) 272 units

27) Order 555 bags; safety stock = 105 bags

28) True	29) False	30) False	31) False	32) True
33) False	34) True	35) True	36) False	37) False
38) True	39) False	40) False	41) True	42) True

CHAPTER 12

10) a) $P(X = 0) = .1353$
    b) $P(T < 45 \text{ min.}) = .6321$
    c) $W_q = 2\ 1/4$ hours
    d) $P_3 = 27/256 = .105$

11) a) Yes; Total Cost = $70/day for computer vs. $90/day without computer
    b) Better off with computer; Total Cost for second employee is $86.18/day

12) 30 percent

13) a) $\lambda = 40$ per hour
    b) $L_q = 4/3$
    c) $L = 2$
    d) $1 - P_0 = \lambda/\mu = 2/3$
    e) $\mu = 97.2$ per hour

14) Purchase digital router; total cost = $204/day ($255/day without router)

CHAPTER 12   continued

15) a) L_q = 1.04 at each desk; Consolidated L_q = .80
    b) P_0 = (3/8)(3/8) = .14; Consolidated P_0 = .23
    c) W = 1/3 hour = 20 minutes; Consolidated W = 12.31 minutes
    d) P(both busy) = $(1-P_0)(1-P_0)$ = (5/8)(5/8) = .39; Consolidated P_W = .48
    e) Yes if it will not result in a substantial loss in business. (Average wait time (part c)
       decreases by 38% when two servers are consolidated.)

16) No system: $49.20; System A: $50.00; System B: $47.20. Hence, install B.

17) a) George: W = 20 minutes; John: W = 3 1/3 minutes
    b) Total Cost: George -- $46.00; John -- $18.67. Hire John.

18) a) W = 6.22 minutes so total time in the store is 61.22 min.
    b) Yes; W = 6.01 minutes

19) a) .667
    b) .076 hrs = 4.56 mins.
    c) 1.43 vehicles
    d) .9772

20) a) no, 49.18%
    b) 18.03%

21) a) k = 4; P_W = .021
    b) P_0 = .331

22) a) L_q = .15
    b) W = .028 hr. = 1.7 minutes
    c) P_W = .417

23) a) L_q = .7094
    b) W_q = 4.96 days
    c) 1 - P_0 = .7151

24) True   25) False   26) False   27) False   28) True
29) True   30) False   31) False   32) False   33) False
34) True   35) True   36) False   37) False   38) True

CHAPTER 13

FOR ALL PROBLEMS IN THIS CHAPTER, IT IS ASSUMED THAT THE RANDOM NUMBERS ARE 00 - 99. THE COLUMN HEADINGS FOR THE EACH SIMULATION ARE GIVEN TOGETHER WITH THE FIRST ROW IN THE SIMULATION. THEN THE ANSWER BASED ON THE SIMULATION IS GIVEN.

7)

| | Routes 5 - 57 | | | Routes 55 - 91 | | |
RN	Time On 5	RN	Time On 57	RN	Time On 55	RN	Time On 91
63	7	59	6	71	8	51	4

Freeways 5-57 have 62 mins.; Freeways 55-91 have 61 mins.; Select 55-91.

CHAPTER 13 | continued

8)

Period	RN	Number of Arrivals	Service Free?	Number Waiting	RN	Service Time	Period When Service Completed
1	63	1	Yes	0	59	1	2

The average number of customers waiting in line for service is the average of the entries in the Number Waiting column. This average is 1.

9) a) Three critical paths with 17 weeks: B-C-F-G-H; B-D-G-H; A-F-G-H.
   b) Five complete PERT analyses must be done. The first is as follows:

Job	RN	Change	Completion Time
A	14	-1	6
B	41	0	4
C	35	0	3
D	38	0	6
E	91	+1	6
F	78	+1	4
G	90	+1	4
H	18	-1	3

Critical path is B-C-F-G-H completion time = 18. Repeating 4 more times:

Trial	Critical Path	Completion Time
2	B-D-G-H	17
3	B-C-F-G-H	17
4	A-F-G-H or B-C-F-G-H	17
5	A-E-H	17

The average completion time of the five trials is 17.2 weeks.

10) a) Order 8 when inventory level reaches 2 units

   b)

Day	Beg. Invent.	RN	Demand	End. Invent.	Order?	RN	Deliv. Time	Inv. Cost
1	6	59	2	4	No	--	--	$8

The average inventory cost per day is $13.00

11) a)

Week	Beg. Inv.	RN	Demand	End. Inv.	Avg. Inv.	Hold. Cost	Reord. Cost	RN	Lead Time	Stkout. Cost
1	5	51	3	2	3.5	$7	$40	80	2	--

The total cost for 8 weeks = $168.00

CHAPTER 13 | continued

11) b)

Week	Beg. Inv.	RN	Demand	End. Inv.	Avg. Inv.	Hold. Cost	Service Charge	Stockout Cost
1	5	51	3	2	3.5	$7	$12	--

The total cost for 8 weeks = $194.00; Since this is more than $168.00, the company should keep its current policy.

12) a)

Per.	RN	# of Cust.	Cust.	RN	Here/ ToGo?	RN	Serv. Time	Compl. in Per.	# Cust. Pres.	Profit
1	63	0	--	--	--	--	--	--	0	--
2	88	1	1	59	ToGo	71	4	6	1	$.90

b) $3.04   c) 64%   d) .84

13)

Day	RN	# of Cust.	Cust. Number	RN	Type Purch.	In Stock?	RN	Switch?	Remain. Invent. A L T
1	58	2	1	93	T	Yes	--	--	3 2 3
			2	63	L	Yes	--	--	3 1 3

Archie will sell out in 8 days in this simulation.

14) a)

Day	RN	Number Rented	Car Rented	RN	Day Returned	Cost of Unused Cars	Shortage Cost
1	63	3	1	59	3		
			2	09	2		
			3	57	3	$5	--

The 10-day profit of this simulation is $885.

b)

Day	RN	Number Rented	Car Rented	RN	Day Returned	Cost of Unused Cars	Shortage Cost
1	63	3	1	59	3		
			2	09	2		
			3	57	3	$10	--

The 10-day profit of this simulation is $970. Take the extra car.

CHAPTER 13 | continued

15)

Per.	RN	# of Arr.	Serv. Area Free?	RN	Type Purch.	Serv. Time	# of Lost Cust.	# of Cust. Wait.	Serv. Compl. This Per.?	Profit
1	63	1	Yes	59	Cone	30	0	0	Yes	$.12

a) Sum last column = $3.34
b) Divide total number of lost customers by total number of arrivals = 7/35 = 20%.
c) Divide the total # of customers waiting by 30 periods = 65/30 = 2.17.

16) a)

A Last	B Last	C Last
----------	----------	----------
A 00 - 49	A 00 - 29	A 00 - 09
Next B 50 - 79	Next B 30 - 74	Next B 10 - 44
C 80 - 99	C 75 - 99	C 45 - 99

b)

Flight	RN	Next Airline
1	71	C
2	95	C

20% of flights on Airline A
48% of flights on Airline B
32% of flights on Airline C

17) False   18) True   19) False   20) False   21) True
22) True   23) True   24) False   25) False   26) True
27) False   28) FALSE   29) True   30) False   31) False

CHAPTER 14

8) a) Stock C -- it dominates Stock B
   b) (1) Stock A; (2) Stock C; (3) Stock D
   c) Stock D

9) a)

		Rail Freight	
		Bid $470,000	Doesn't Bid
Transrail-	Bid $500,000	0	$100,000
	Bid $460,00	$60,000	$ 60,000

   b) Bid $460,000
   c) Bid $500,000
   d) $15,000

CHAPTER 14 continued

10) a)

	Sales (in 1,000,000's)		
	100	50	1
Introduce	$1,000,000	$200,000	-$2,000,000
Do Not Introduce	-$400,000	-$400,000	-$400,000

b)

	Sales (in 1,000,000's)		
	100	50	1
Introduce	$0	$0	$1,600,000
Do Not Introduce	$1,400,000	$600,000	$0

c) (1) do not introduce; (2) introduce; (3) do not introduce   d) Yes   e) No

11) a) Introduce root beer; $p \leq .483$
b) EVPI = $112,000
NOTE: The answers to (c)-(e) are very sensitive to roundoff error. Figures in parentheses are for two decimal places only.

c) Stanton: EVSI = $13,200 ($11,862)
Efficiency = .118 (.106)
New World: EVSI = $6,400 ($6,424)
Efficiency = .057 (.057)
d) hire Stanton (Stanton)
e) hire New World (Stanton)

12) a)

Plan	Number of Subscribers					
	10,000	20,000	30,000	40,000	50,000	60,000
I	-550	-400	-250	-100	50	200
II	-520	-340	-160	20	200	380
III	-500	-300	-100	100	300	500
IV	-460	-220	20	260	500	740

(table in $1000's)

b) (1) Plan IV; (2) Plan IV; (3) Plan IV   c) Plan II -- Expected Value = $11,000

13) a)

Number of Computers Manufactured	Number of Clients Purchasing a Computer				
	0	1	2	3	4
1	-40	50	30	10	-10
2	-70	20	110	90	70
3	-80	10	100	190	170
4	-70	20	110	200	290

(Payoffs are in $1,000's)

b) Build 4 computers
c) Nothing

14) a) Yes, Dollar should sell store   b) EVPI = $8,000   c) No; survey cost exceeds EVPI

CHAPTER 14 continued

15) a)

	Number of Copies (in 1,000's per month)					
Plan	12.6	14.4	16.2	18.0	19.8	21.6
I	341.6	370.4	399.2	428.0	456.8	485.6
II	351.2	372.8	394.4	416.0	437.6	459.2
III	317.2	356.8	396.4	436.0	475.6	515.2
IV	363.0	372.0	381.0	390.0	399.0	408.0

b) (1) Plan III; (2) Plan IV
c) Plan IV

16)

		Demand For Ovens			
		0	1	2	3
	0	0	-25	-50	-75
Ovens	1	-70	80	55	30
Ordered	2	-140	10	160	135
	3	-210	-60	90	240

a) Order one oven -- EV = $25.00
b) EVPI = $63
c) Favorable: order 2; Unfavorable: order 0; No opinion: order 1
d) EVSI = $9.10

17) a) $1075   b) $5000

18) Buy 3 leases

19) a) Risk averse   b) Produce root beer as long as $p \geq 60/105 = .571$ c) Choose Stanton

20) False	21) True	22) False	23) False	24) False
25) False	26) True	27) False	28) True	29) False
30) True	31) True	32) True	33) False	34) False

CHAPTER 15

9) a) Linear Programming constraints:
$$3X_1 + X_2 \leq 24 \text{ (total marketing employees)}$$
$$X_1 + X_2 \geq 6 \text{ (minimum required ads)}$$
$$50X_1 + 15X_2 \leq 250 \text{ (Goal 1: Budget in \$1000's)}$$
$$3X_1 + X_2 \leq 12 \text{ (Goal 2: 50\% of marketing employees)}$$
$$X_1 \geq 4 \text{ (Goal 3: TV ads)}$$
$$X_2 \geq 4 \text{ (Goal 4: Radio ads)}$$
$$X_1, X_2 \geq 0$$
There are no feasible points.

CHAPTER 15 continued

b) MIN $P_1(d_1^+) + P_2(d_2^+) + P_3(d_3^-) + P_4(d_4^-)$

$$
\begin{aligned}
\text{S.T. } 3X_1 + X_2 &\leq 24 \\
X_1 + X_2 &\geq 6 \\
50X_1 + 15X_2 + d_1^- - d_1^+ &= 250 \\
3X_1 + X_2 \qquad\qquad + d_2^- - d_2^+ &= 12 \\
X_1 \qquad\qquad\qquad\quad + d_3^- - d_3^+ &= 4 \\
X_2 \qquad\qquad\qquad\qquad\quad + d_4^- - d_4^+ &= 4 \\
X_1, X_2, d_j^-, d_j^+ &\geq 0 \text{ for all } j
\end{aligned}
$$

Optimal G.P. solution: 3 TV ads, 3 radio ads.
Priorities: $P_1(d_1^+) = 0$, $P_2(d_2^+) = 0$, $P_3(d_3^-) = 1$, $P_4(d_4^-) = 1$

c) The new objective function is:
MIN $P_1(d_1^+) + P_2(d_2^+) + P_3(2d_3^-) + P_3(d_4^-)$
Optimal G.P. solution: Produce 2.67 TV ads, 4 radio ads.
Goal 3 is missed by 1.33 TV ads
while the other goals are achieved.

10) MIN $P_1(d_1^-) + P_2(d_2^+) + P_3(d_3^-) + P_3(3d_4^-) + P_3(d_5^-)$

$$
\begin{aligned}
\text{S.T. } 3X_1 + 2.5X_2 + 2X_3 &\leq 200 \quad \text{(donation)} \\
X_1 &\geq 20 \quad \text{(athletic sch.)} \\
X_1 + X_2 + X_3 + d_1^- - d_1^+ &= 80 \quad \text{(P1, Goal 1: Total sch.)} \\
.75X_1 - .25X_2 - .25X_3 + d_2^- - d_2^+ &= 0 \quad \text{(P2, Goal 2: 25\% ath. sch.)} \\
X_1 \qquad\qquad\quad + d_3^- - d_3^+ &= 25 \quad \text{(P3, Goal 3: desired ath. sch.)} \\
X_2 \qquad\qquad\quad + d_4^- - d_4^+ &= 40 \quad \text{(P3, Goal 4: desired min. sch.)} \\
X_3 + d_5^- - d_5^+ &= 20 \quad \text{(P3, Goal 5: desired women sch.)} \\
X_j, d_j^-, d_j^+ &\geq 0 \quad \text{for all } j
\end{aligned}
$$

Optimal: Award 20 athletic, 40 minority, and 20 women's scholarships.
Goals 1, 2, and 4 are met. Goal 3 is underachieved by 5 athletic scholarships and
Goal 5 is underachieved by 10 women's scholarships.

11) X_1 = number of new non-minority hires
X_2 = number of new minority hires
X_3 = number of non-minority management promotions
X_4 = number of minority management promotions

$$
\begin{aligned}
\text{MIN } \quad & 3d_1^- + d_2^- + d_3^+ + d_4^+ \\
\text{S.T. } X_1 + X_2 &= 17{,}520 \\
X_3 + X_4 &= 598 \\
X_1 \qquad - d_1^+ + d_1^- &= 19{,}680 \\
X_3 \qquad - d_2^+ + d_2^- &= 472 \\
X_1 \qquad - d_3^+ + d_3^- &= 11{,}680 \\
X_3 \qquad - d_4^+ + d_4^- &= 399 \\
X_j, d_j^+, d_j^- &\geq 0 \quad j = 1,2,3,4
\end{aligned}
$$

Solution: $X_1 = 17520$, $X_2 = 0$, $X_3 = 472$, $X_4 = 126$,
d1minus = 2160, d3plus = 5840, d4plus = 73, all other d's = 0,
Obj. function = 12393.

12) SoftTrack = 135, <u>VersaSuite = 148</u>, N-Able = 141

13) Miss Northern State 18; Miss Central State 24; Miss Southern State 58.

CHAPTER 15 | continued

14) a) Location: BG - .360; B - .512; H - .128   b) GD - .255; B - .482; H - .264
   Price: BG - .589; B - .252; H - .159
   Cleanliness: BG - .123; B - .320; H - .557
   Parking: BG - .102; B - .612; H - .286
   Selection: BG - .100; B - .713; H - .187

c)

	LOC	PRI	CLE	PAR	SEL
LOC	1	1/7	1/7	1	1/3
PRI	7	1	3	7	3
CLE	7	1/3	1	5	3
PAR	1	1/7	1/5	1	1/7
SEL	3	1/3	1/3	7	1

d) CR = .073 -- good consistency   e) GD - .340; B - .380; H - .280

15) a) <u>Goal</u>: Choose the right candidate   <u>Criteria</u>: Party, Issue   <u>Alternatives</u>: Carter, Nixon, Anderson
   b)   Party   Issues

Party	C	N	A
C	1	1/7	1/3
N	7	1	5
A	3	1/5	1

Issues	C	N	A
C	1	6	5
N	1/6	1	1/3
A	1/5	3	1

c) Party: C - .083; N - .723; A - .193   Issues: C - .707; N - .092; A - .201
d) .082 -- good consistency   e) Party - .2; Issues - .8   f) C - .582; N - .218; A - .199

16) a) Goal: Choose the best database program
   Criteria: Price; Ease of Use
   Alternatives: BASE 8; DATA RECORD

b)   Price   Ease Of Use

Price	B8	DR
B8	1	8
DR	1/8	1

Ease Of Use	B8	DR
B8	1	1/6
DR	6	1

c) Price: B8 - 8/9; DR - 1/9   Ease of Use: B8 - 1/7; DR - 6/7
d) (1) B8 - .81; DR - .19   (2) B8 - .22; DR - .78   (3) B8 - .516; DR - .484
e) Ease of use is slightly preferred to price.

18) False   19) False   20) True   21) False   22) True
23) False   24) False   25) True   26) False   27) False
28) True   29) False   30) False   31) False   32) False

CHAPTER 16

6) a) 4 period weighted moving average; MSE = 408
    b) exponential smoothing   -- $298.48
        weighted moving average -- $294.27

7) a) σ = .6 is better MSE (9.12); σ = .2 has MSE = 10.82
    b) For σ = .6, F_9 = 22.86; for σ = .2, F_9 = 21.72

8) Year 6: Quarter 1 -- 56; Quarter 2 -- 48; Quarter 3 -- 79; Quarter 4 -- 40

9) a) The 3 week moving average gives the better forecast (MSE = 16,337)
        (compared to a MSE = 17,911 for the 4 week moving average)
    b) 3 week moving average forecast for week 11 = 1,200
        4 week moving average forecast for week 11 = 1,158

10) a) Yes; y = 11.93 + 1.0046x
    b) Week 17 -- 29.0; Week 18 -- 30.0; Week 19 -- 31.0; Week 20 -- 32.0

11) b) 141.44, 144.18, 119.44, 157.72, 111.93

12) a) F_t = 34.80 - 1.329t   b) 26 months
    c) After 27 months sales will be approximately -1 cars; this is clearly impossible;
        the assumption of a continued linear decline must be in error.

13) 42.15, 70.14, 52.17;   43.46, 72.30, 53.76

14) a) y = 80.8757 + 5.3605(x)
    b) y = 80.8757 + 5.3605(33.5) = 260.45245 hours for a 3350 sq. ft. house.

15) True	16) True	17) False	18) True	19) False
20) True	21) True	22) False	23) True	24) True
25) False	26) True	27) False	28) False	29) False

CHAPTER 17

5) P(buy) = .357   P(return) = .643

6) a) Network C   b) (p_A, p_C, p_N) = (.29, .41, .30)
    c) Network A: $14,300; Network C: $20,550; Network N: $15,200

7) a)

This Day		Next Day 1	2	3	4
Route A Not Congested	1	.600	.200	.120	.080
Route A Congested	2	.225	.075	.420	.280
Route B Not Congested	3	.075	.025	.540	.360
Route B Congested	4	.450	.150	.240	.160

CHAPTER 17 | continued

7) b) .36 + .12 = .48

8) a) .16   b) Austin: .199; San Antonio: .328; Houston: .473

9) B. Prince and F. Fowl's shares will drop by .196 and .054

10) a) .868   b) .281   c) .3 + .03 + .2 = .53

11) a) .6
    b) Making payments has higher probability (.4 versus .304)
    c) .06 + .03 + .10 = .19

12) a) $(p_A, p_B, p_C) = (.29, .37, .34)$
    b) (1) .15   (2) .09   (3) .14
    c) $42,333

13) a)

	Fail-F	Fail-M	Fail-P	New	Est.
Failure - Failure	1	0	0	0	0
Failure - Management	0	1	0	0	0
Failure - Product	0	0	1	0	0
New	.15	.20	.05	0	.60
Established	.10	.06	.03	0	.81

   b) .394
   c) (1) .47   (2) .39   (3) .14

14) True	15) False	16) True	17) False	18) True
19) True	20) True	21) False	22) True	23) False
24) False	25) False	26) False	27) True	28) False

CHAPTER 18

5) Produce one package of 16 ft. wire and purchase one package of 12 ft. wire.
   (2 feet of wire will be sold for scrap.) Total Profit = $1.66

6) Produce 3 batches in February, 1 batch in March, 3 batches in April, 2 batches in May.
   Total Cost = $125,000

7) a) 1-2-7-12-15; Distance = 36
   b) 1-4-9-13-14; Distance = 37

8) Total Profit = $245; Three solutions:
   (1) 2-A, 2-E, 1-B   (2) 1-A, 1-B, 3-D   (3) 1-A, 1-B, 1-C, 1-D, 1-E

9) Builder 1: 1 lot, Builder 3: 2 lots, Builder 5: 2 lots; Total Revenue = $442,000

CHAPTER 18 continued

10) Give $4,000,000 to Bolivia Telephone, $6,000,000 to Camden Insurance, and sell Host Baking

11) There are four alternative optimal solutions giving a total of $45,000:

Aug	6		6		6		6
Sep	2	or	3	or	4	or	5
Oct	4		4		4		4
Nov	3		2		1		0

12) Produce 4 boats in May, 3 boats in June, 0 boats in July, 3 boats in August;
Total Cost = $278,000

13) True	14) True	15) True	16) False	17) True
18) False	19) False	20) True	21) False	22) False
23) True	24) True	25) False	26) False	27) True

Appendices

APPENDIX A: AREAS FOR THE STANDARD NORMAL DISTRIBUTION

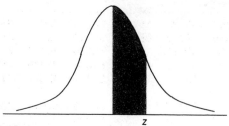

Entries in the table give the area under the curve between the mean and *z* standard deviations above the mean. For example, for *z* = 1.25 the area under the curve between the mean and *z* is 0.3944.

z	0.00	0.01	0.02	0.03	0.04	0.05	0.06	0.07	0.08	0.09
0.0	.0000	.0040	.0080	.0120	.0160	.0199	.0239	.0279	.0319	.0359
0.1	.0398	.0438	.0478	.0517	.0557	.0596	.0636	.0675	.0714	.0753
0.2	.0793	.0832	.0871	.0910	.0948	.0987	.1026	.1064	.1103	.1141
0.3	.1179	.1217	.1255	.1293	.1331	.1368	.1406	.1443	.1480	.1517
0.4	.1554	.1591	.1628	.1664	.1700	.1736	.1772	.1808	.1844	.1879
0.5	.1915	.1950	.1985	.2019	.2054	.2088	.2123	.2157	.2190	.2224
0.6	.2257	.2291	.2324	.2357	.2389	.2422	.2454	.2486	.2517	.2549
0.7	.2580	.2611	.2642	.2673	.2704	.2734	.2764	.2794	.2823	.2852
0.8	.2881	.2910	.2939	.2967	.2995	.3023	.3051	.3078	.3106	.3133
0.9	.3159	.3186	.3212	.3238	.3264	.3289	.3315	.3340	.3365	.3389
1.0	.3413	.3438	.3461	.3485	.3508	.3531	.3554	.3577	.3599	.3621
1.1	.3643	.3665	.3686	.3708	.3729	.3749	.3770	.3790	.3810	.3830
1.2	.3849	.3869	.3888	.3907	.3925	.3944	.3962	.3980	.3997	.4015
1.3	.4032	.4049	.4066	.4082	.4099	.4115	.4131	.4147	.4162	.4177
1.4	.4192	.4207	.4222	.4236	.4251	.4265	.4279	.4292	.4306	.4319
1.5	.4332	.4345	.4357	.4370	.4382	.4394	.4406	.4418	.4429	.4441
1.6	.4452	.4463	.4474	.4484	.4495	.4505	.4515	.4525	.4535	.4545
1.7	.4554	.4564	.4573	.4582	.4591	.4599	.4608	.4616	.4625	.4633
1.8	.4641	.4649	.4656	.4664	.4671	.4678	.4686	.4693	.4699	.4706
1.9	.4713	.4719	.4726	.4732	.4738	.4744	.4750	.4756	.4761	.4767
2.0	.4772	.4778	.4783	.4788	.4793	.4798	.4803	.4808	.4812	.4817
2.1	.4821	.4826	.4830	.4834	.4838	.4842	.4846	.4850	.4854	.4857
2.2	.4861	.4864	.4868	.4871	.4875	.4878	.4881	.4884	.4887	.4890
2.3	.4893	.4896	.4898	.4901	.4904	.4906	.4909	.4911	.4913	.4916
2.4	.4918	.4920	.4922	.4925	.4927	.4929	.4931	.4932	.4934	.4936
2.5	.4938	.4940	.4941	.4943	.4945	.4946	.4948	.4949	.4951	.4952
2.6	.4953	.4955	.4956	.4957	.4959	.4960	.4961	.4962	.4963	.4964
2.7	.4965	.4966	.4967	.4968	.4969	.4970	.4971	.4972	.4973	.4974
2.8	.4974	.4975	.4976	.4977	.4977	.4978	.4979	.4979	.4980	.4981
2.9	.4981	.4982	.4982	.4983	.4984	.4984	.4985	.4985	.4986	.4986
3.0	.4987	.4987	.4987	.4988	.4988	.4989	.4989	.4989	.4990	.4990

APPENDIX B: RANDOM DIGITS

63271	59986	71744	51102	15141	80714	58683	93108	13554	79945
88547	09896	95436	79115	08303	01041	20030	63754	08459	28364
55957	57243	83865	09911	19761	66535	40102	26646	60147	15702
46276	87453	44790	67122	45573	84358	21625	16999	13385	22782
55363	07449	34835	15290	76616	67191	12777	21861	68689	03263
69393	92785	49902	58447	42048	30378	87618	26933	40640	16281
13186	29431	88190	04588	38733	81290	89541	70290	40113	08243
17726	28652	56836	78351	47327	18518	92222	55201	27340	10493
36520	64465	05550	30157	82242	29520	69753	72602	23756	54935
81628	36100	39254	56835	37636	02421	98063	89641	64953	99337
84649	38968	75215	75498	49539	74240	03466	49292	36401	45525
63291	11618	12613	75055	43915	26499	41116	64531	56827	30825
70502	53225	03655	05915	37140	57051	48393	91322	25653	06543
06426	24771	59935	49801	11082	66762	94477	02494	88215	27191
20711	55609	29430	70165	45406	78484	31639	52009	18873	96927
41990	70538	77191	25860	55204	73417	83920	69468	74972	38712
72452	36618	76298	26678	89334	33938	95567	29380	75906	91807
37042	40318	57099	10528	09925	89773	41335	96244	29002	46453
53766	52875	15987	46962	67342	77592	57651	95508	80033	69828
90585	58955	53122	16025	84299	53310	67380	84249	25348	04332
32201	96293	37203	64516	51530	37069	40261	61374	05815	06714
62606	64324	46354	72157	67248	20135	49804	09226	64419	29457
10078	28073	85389	50324	14500	15562	64165	06125	71353	77669
91561	46145	24177	15294	10061	98124	75732	00815	83452	97355
13091	98112	53959	79607	52244	63303	10413	63839	74762	50289
73864	83014	72457	22682	03033	61714	88173	90835	00634	85169
66668	25467	48894	51043	02365	91726	09365	63167	95264	45643
84745	41042	29493	01836	09044	51926	43630	63470	76508	14194
48068	26805	94595	47907	13357	38412	33318	26098	82782	42851
54310	96175	97594	88616	42035	38093	36745	56702	40644	83514
14877	33095	100924	58013	61439	21882	42059	24177	58739	60170
78295	23179	02771	43464	59061	71411	05697	67194	30495	21157
67524	02865	39593	54278	04237	92441	26602	63835	38032	94770
58268	57219	68124	73455	83236	08710	04284	55005	84171	42596
97158	28672	50685	01181	24262	19427	52106	34308	73685	74246
04230	16831	69085	30802	65559	09205	71829	06489	85650	38707
94879	56606	30401	02602	57658	70091	54986	41394	60437	03195
71446	15232	66715	26385	91518	70566	02888	79941	39684	54315
32886	05644	79316	09819	00813	88407	17461	73925	53037	91904
62048	33711	25290	21526	02223	75947	66466	06232	10913	75336

This table is reproduced with permission from The Rand Corporation, *A Million Random Digits*, The Free Press, New York, 1955 and 1983.

APPENDIX C: VALUES OF $e^{-\lambda}$

λ	$e^{-\lambda}$	λ	$e^{-\lambda}$	λ	$e^{-\lambda}$
0.05	0.9512	2.05	0.1287	4.05	0.0174
0.10	0.9048	2.10	0.1225	4.10	0.0166
0.15	0.8607	2.15	0.1165	4.15	0.0158
0.20	0.8187	2.20	0.1108	4.20	0.0150
0.25	0.7788	2.25	0.1054	4.25	0.0143
0.30	0.7408	2.30	0.1003	4.30	0.0136
0.35	0.7047	2.35	0.0954	4.35	0.0129
0.40	0.6703	2.40	0.0907	4.40	0.0123
0.45	0.6376	2.45	0.0863	4.45	0.0117
0.50	0.6065	2.50	0.0821	4.50	0.0111
0.55	0.5769	2.55	0.0781	4.55	0.0106
0.60	0.5488	2.60	0.0743	4.60	0.0101
0.65	0.5220	2.65	0.0707	4.65	0.0096
0.70	0.4966	2.70	0.0672	4.70	0.0091
0.75	0.4724	2.75	0.0639	4.75	0.0087
0.80	0.4493	2.80	0.0608	4.80	0.0082
0.85	0.4274	2.85	0.0578	4.85	0.0078
0.90	0.4066	2.90	0.0550	4.90	0.0074
0.95	0.3867	2.95	0.0523	4.95	0.0071
1.00	0.3679	3.00	0.0498	5.00	0.0067
1.05	0.3499	3.05	0.0474	5.05	0.0064
1.10	0.3329	3.10	0.0450	5.10	0.0061
1.15	0.3166	3.15	0.0429	5.15	0.0058
1.20	0.3012	3.20	0.0408	5.20	0.0055
1.25	0.2865	3.25	0.0388	5.25	0.0052
1.30	0.2725	3.30	0.0369	5.30	0.0050
1.35	0.2592	3.35	0.0351	5.35	0.0047
1.40	0.2466	3.40	0.0334	5.40	0.0045
1.45	0.2346	3.45	0.0317	5.45	0.0043
1.50	0.2231	3.50	0.0302	5.50	0.0041
1.55	0.2122	3.55	0.0287	5.55	0.0039
1.60	0.2019	3.60	0.0273	5.60	0.0037
1.65	0.1920	3.65	0.0260	5.65	0.0035
1.70	0.1827	3.70	0.0247	5.70	0.0033
1.75	0.1738	3.75	0.0235	5.75	0.0032
1.80	0.1653	3.80	0.0224	5.80	0.0030
1.85	0.1572	3.85	0.0213	5.85	0.0029
1.90	0.1496	3.90	0.0202	5.90	0.0027
1.95	0.1423	3.95	0.0193	5.95	0.0026
2.00	0.1353	4.00	0.0183	6.00	0.0025
				7.00	0.0009
				8.00	0.000335
				9.00	0.000123
				10.00	0.000045